Let ALL the Children Come

A Handbook for Holistic Ministry to Children with Disabilities

Phyllis Kilbourn
Editor

PUBLICATIONS

Fort Washington, PA 19034

Let All the Children Come:
A Handbook for Holistic Ministry to Children with Disabilities

Developmental Editors: Christa Crawford Foster and Lianna Wlasiuk
Pre-publishing Copy Editor: Brad Koenig
Pre-publishing Editorial Manager: Lianna Wlasiuk

Published by CLC Publications, U.S.A.
PO Box 1449, Fort Washington, PA 19034
ISBN-13 (trade paper): 978-1-61958-067-1

CONTENTS

Contributing Authors...7

Introduction...11

Acknowledgments 15

Part I FROM DESPAIR TO HOPE

1. Disabilities: Context and Consequences 19
    Phyllis Kilbourn

2. Why, Lord?.. 35
    Marcia Mitchell

Part II DEVELOPMENTAL NEEDS: CONFRONTING THE HURDLES

3. Psychosocial Implications 43
    Wendy Middaugh Bovard

4. Educational Needs... 65
    Laura Sandidge

5. Physical Challenges.. 83
    Karyl Stanton

6. Roadblocks to Spiritual Development............................... 111
    Albert Blackston

PART III INTERVENTIONS: RESTORING HOPE

7. Training for Socialization... 121
    Phyllis Kilbourn

8. Helping Children Cope... 143
    Dietlinde Hoffman

9. Strategies for Training at Home, School and Work 163
    Laura Sandidge

10. The Building Blocks of Mobility....................................... 181
    Virginia Cruz

11. The Importance of Spiritual Nurture................................. 215
    Courtney L. Smith

PART IV   PROJECT DEVELOPMENT: PRINCIPLES AND PRACTICES

12. Recreational and Enrichment Activities.....................................237
    Phyllis Kilbourn

13. Developing Projects that Bring Healing and Hope....................251
    Debbie Childs

14. Making Christ Accessible 267
    Julie Bohn

Part V   COMPASSIONATE RESPONSES: GOD'S LOVE IN ACTION

15. Holistic Caregiving: Strengthening the Church's Response.....................289
    Wendy Middaugh Bovard

16. Advocacy: Give the Child a Mighty Voice.................................311
    Marjorie McDermid

17. Costs and Blessings of Advocacy: Tabi's Journey.......................323
    Tami Snowden

PART VI   CAREGIVER ISSUES: CHALLENGES AND SUPPORT FOR THOSE WHO CARE

18. Impact of Disabilities on Family Life 345
    H. Marie Murtha

19. Supporting the Caregiver 371
    Judy Raymo

PART VII   CONCLUDING REFLECTION

20. Be a Friend...379
    Joey Raymo

Appendix A: Disability Awareness Sunday Ideas 381

Appendix B: Architectural Accessibility Checklist.............................. 383

Appendix C: Sunday School Registration Form............................... 388

                Ability Skills Form... 391

Appendix D: Rapid Developmental Assessment 395

Appendix E: Disability Ministry Resources...................................... 400

Appendix F: Rights of Persons with Disabilities................................ 411

CONTRIBUTING AUTHORS

Albert Blackston, who grew up with cerebral palsy, was tormented by the taunting of his classmates and the "why" questions in his own heart. When he acknowledged that his handicap did not define his life, nor was he damaged goods, his experiences became the crucible for the refining of his personal relationship with Christ. He graduated from Columbia International University with a Master of Divinity and now serves as a prison chaplain with the Coastal Jail Ministries of Georgia.

Julie Bohn has a BA and MA from the University of Iowa in special education and elementary education. She was the international director of Disability Training Ministries with Handi*Vangelism and also an adjunct professor in teacher education at Philadelphia Biblical University, teaching the exceptionalities courses. Julie is currently a professionally certified educational therapist with the National Institute of Learning Development. She has a private practice devoted to children and adults with specific learning differences.

Wendy Middaugh Bovard has worked with children in crisis in five African countries and the Caribbean. Dr. Bovard's work has provided her with many opportunities to care for children with disabilities, including HIV/AIDS children in Kenya and former child soldiers in war-torn northern Uganda. Bovard also united children with their families in Rwanda after the genocide, developed the Outdoor Adventure therapy and most recently provided psychological support to Haitian children after the recent earthquake. Currently she lives and works in Haiti.

Debbie Childs has been in Southeast Asia for the past eight years training people in the villages how to work with children who are developmentally disadvantaged. Her objective is to duplicate her work by training nationals in organizing and developing projects. As local churches assume the tasks of taking ownership and leadership of the projects, more can be launched. Debbie also has worked with a seminary, educating students in hope that when they graduate they, too, will return to their villages and educate the people in their area.

Virginia (Ginny) Cruz is a board-certified pediatric clinical specialist in physical therapy. She has 28 years of experience in both clinical and educational settings. She has a heart for children and loves to assist families in finding useful and practical interventions to improve the function of children with special needs.

Sherry Gurney has worked for many years with children who are blind and deaf-blind at The Little Light House, a nonprofit Christian preschool for children with multiple disabilities in Tulsa, Oklahoma. She has also traveled with LLH teams to Pakistan, Kenya and China, helping to develop programs for children with disabilities. While serving as a missionary in Kenya, Sherry established the Bezalel Fund. Through the purchase of her drawings, the fund provides financial support to school programs in Kenya that are designed for children who are blind.

Dietlinde Hoffman was born to Wycliffe missionaries and raised in Papua New Guinea. Hoffman has a bachelor's degree in elementary education from Houghton College (New York) and a master's degree in special education from Binghamton University (New York). As a missionary, she has taught in Papua New Guinea, Indonesia and South Africa. Her teaching career spans from missionary kids to ESL, special education, orphans and curriculum writing. Her heart beats for the suffering and lost children in Africa.

Phyllis Kilbourn is founder of Rainbows of Hope and Crisis Care Training International, both global ministries of WEC International to children in crisis. She has worked with children having disabilities from war and street life. A child advocate, trauma trainer and author/editor of a number of handbooks focused on interventions for children in crisis, Phyllis also served in Liberia and Kenya with WEC International. She holds a PhD in education from Trinity International University (Illinois).

Marjorie McDermid, a missionary with WEC International to Equatorial Guinea, West Africa, has worked in various children's ministries. She also served in WEC USA's home office as editor of their mission magazine for twenty-five years. Since 1995 she has been a child advocate as well as a writer and editor for Rainbows of Hope and Crisis Care Training International. She is coeditor of *Sexually Exploited Children: Working to Protect and Heal*, a book in this series.

Marcia Mitchell took a dramatic turn in life when her daughter was born legally blind. Unable to find early intervention services for her child, Marcia ventured out in faith and founded a Christian developmental center called The Little Light House, which has served hundreds of children with special needs over the past four decades and today is internationally recognized as a model training center. Marcia chronicled her faith journey in her book, *Milestones and Miracles.*

H. Marie Murtha has a BA in Sociology from Kent State University (Ohio). She also attended Christ for the Nations Institute (Texas) where she majored in child evangelism, becoming a certified teacher. Marie has been an educator for thirty years in the U.S. and Thailand. She collaborated on a documentary, *Tiny Tears*, highlighting the plight of AIDS orphans in Thailand. She also had a personal view of family, observing and interacting with her nephew, a child with special needs. She dedicates her chapter to him.

Joey Raymo plans to begin a "Food Industries" course at a local technical college. He has always been interested in cooking and looks forward to working in that area. At church he is transitioning from his beloved high school youth group into the "Epic Grads" young adult group. He enjoys volunteering at the Salvation Army food shelf and continues to run with friends from his high school cross country team, participating in 5k races that support various charities.

Judy Raymo is a special mother. Along with raising her own three biological children, she also is mother to four adopted children with special needs. She and her husband, Jim, have served in various positions with Worldwide Evangelization for Christ (WEC International), including leaders of the WEC USA sending base.

Laura Sandidge has been in the field of special education for more than twenty years, where she has had a variety of experiences in teaching, administration and consulting both nationally and internationally. Currently Dr. Sandidge is an administrator for Advocates for Inclusion, a private developmental disabilities agency and Another Choice Virtual Charter School, a public school she originally founded. She has trained orphanage workers in China, Cambodia, Thailand, Africa and Myanmar in working with children with developmental and behavioral disabilities.

Courtney L. Smith, mother to several children with disabilities, understands the effects of disability firsthand. Courtney is a registered nurse and the founder of Links of Love Disability Ministry. Some key aspects of her work and experience with disability include community outreach and education, designing and implementing disability ministry models, designing and facilitating conferences, and supporting pastoral leadership and families.

Tami Snowden is an advocate for children at risk with Pioneers and the Evangelical Presbyterian Church's mission organization, World Outreach. She advocates for children at risk among the U.S. churches, raising awareness of children in crisis throughout the world. Tami coauthored the family curriculum *Red Card,* which engages children and their parents to respond to the needs of children at risk. Tami is also a resource and consultant for the many Pioneers and World Outreach teams throughout the world.

Karyl Stanton has an MD degree from the University of Texas Southwestern Medical School. Dr. Stanton is a diplomat in the specialty of neurology and is board certified by the American Board of Psychiatry and Neurology. She and her doctor husband, Paul, have four children, including two with developmental disabilities. They have extensive experience with medical missions, medical education and children's ministry. They started World Changer Kids, Inc., a nonprofit foundation dedicated to raising up the next generation of Christian missionaries through fun and exciting missions teaching and projects for kids worldwide.

INTRODUCTION

ALL throughout time mankind has had to deal with the limitations and frailties of humanity. In the Judeo-Christian traditions these difficulties have been attributed to the "fall of man." All of us are continually affected by these difficulties (both our own and those of other people).

It is frustrating for us to deal with these shortcomings and to understand fully both their cause and consequence. Our conflicts of mind are only enhanced as we consider those among us who face challenges above the normal limitations—those with what we sometimes define as disabilities. Compassionate people cannot dismiss these ones and their situations, whether the individuals are family, friends or strangers in a faraway place. We feel a responsibility and desire to assist them.

We often begin our study or contemplations with the question of cause or source of the disability—whether by birth or accident. However, God has not seen fit to reveal to us answers to all the mysteries of life. In our quest we still try to find an answer anyway. We share our theologies, which is man's best effort to define and explain what he believes. We even locate Scriptures to support our belief.

However, sincere and intelligent people do not always agree on aspects of life—such as, do our difficulties come because God allows or creates them, or is the source simply life? Scriptures can be found to seemingly support various and conflicting views. Thus, confusion can be the result as we confront these mysteries. Such conflicts of thought must not divide compassionate people in their desire to be of ministry and help to those in need. Nor should our beliefs (however sincere) be allowed to add to the confusion and hurt of both those suffering from disabilities, and their families and friends.

Therefore it is prudent that we to set aside the confusing issues of why and where God fits into the cause and creation of disabilities. Instead let us focus on two major themes that are clear—and certainly a source of comfort and guidance to those with disabilities, their loved ones and the people anxious to be of help to them.

Theme one: God is a *God* of *love* for all people.

He loves us equally without regard to our abilities and disabilities. His love is not determined or measured by our strengths or weaknesses. His plan for us, and He does have a plan for each and every one, can be fulfilled however inadequate we may appear to be.

Throughout both the Old and New Testaments, we see God working with and on behalf of people with limitations. Christ was an example of concern for the down and out, whether that was from a social, mental or physical inadequacy. Mary Magdalene was the first one to whom Jesus revealed Himself after the resurrection.

We must never forget that all of us are shackled with some inability and limitation(s). Some are more obvious than others. A few are defined as disabilities in a clinical sense, while most may be defined as the "normal" deficiencies of life. In either case we must come to the discussion with a realization that we are all in need. But we must also know that we are all blessed because of a God who loves us. Therefore, we have a responsibility to assist others through both our acceptance and action. We then hope for the same in return.

Theme two: God is a *God* of *redemptive power*.

Throughout Scripture we see God's promises to love and use people in spite of personal frailties. "My power is made perfect in (your) weakness" (2 Corinthians 12:9). Biblical examples abound. Moses was "slow of tongue," the Apostle Paul had his "thorn in the flesh"; consider even the youth and immaturity of people such as David and Samuel. But these were some of the "giants" used of God.

History (both spiritual and secular) only multiplies many times over these same truths. A Helen Keller. A sight-impaired Fanny Crosby became a prolific hymn writer. Joni Eareckson was a teenager when she had a diving accident and became paraplegic. But today she (now Joni Eareckson Tada) is an internationally renowned author, artist, singer and speaker. And there are many modern examples of those with physical impairments, even to the loss of limbs, who run marathons or compete in athletic activities.

Some such people may not be religious and, therefore, assume that their accomplishments have come solely through their own efforts. But certainly these achievements have come through not only their efforts, but also through God's power. This is true even if they did not recognize its presence. Others, such as a Joni Eareckson Tada, fully recognize the place of a divine, redemptive power and freely give acclaim to such.

Yes, God has the ability to overcome our frailties or to even use them in a way that is beneficial to us and for His glory. He is not in the business of hurting us. He is too holy to inflict evil upon us or to desire evil consequences to be in our lives. But He can take anything and re-create it for good. Never in that process does He lessen His love and compassion for the individual. What He does He does not only for His glory, but also for our good and the good of others.

Human example is a visual reminder of this redemptive power at work and on display. Through God's ability, human "disability" does not mean "without ability." "Disable" does not equate to "unable."

Aubrey D. Smith
Pastor
Fort Mill, South Carolina

ACKNOWLEDGMENTS

A FTER rounds of editing and helpful feedback from readers, one of our editors remarked, "It takes a village to raise a book!" This certainly has been true in preparing this special publication. If we were to take this thought further, we would name our village "Labor of Love," a name that would indeed be an apt description of how our village workers contributed to the book's development.

First on the list of acknowledgments are the villagers on the writing team. This dedicated group, composed of parents, doctors, social workers, educators, project leaders and psychologists, represents the largest team participating in a book in this series. They gave generously of their time and expertise to provide caregivers with healing strategies to restore hope and joy to children who, through their disabilities, have been wounded spiritually, physically and emotionally and also left with special needs including cognitive and social.

Other vital villagers are those who diligently served on the editorial team, without which this book would not have come together so flawlessly. Team members include Christa Crawford Foster and Lianna Wlasiuk (developmental editors) and Brad Koenig (copy editor). Lianna also guided the team in following the publisher's requirements for laying out the text. Our thanks go to the personnel at CLC Publications who completed the work of the village in raising this book to publication.

We appreciate the village artist, Sherry Gurney, for her deeply moving charcoal sketch, which so compassionately depicts Jesus' invitation to let *all* the children come to Him and the children eagerly accepting His offer of healing love and hope. In addition, our hearts are grateful for the village pastor, Aubrey Smith, who reminds us that although we may not have the same theological perspective on the whys of a disability, we can be anchored in the truth of God's sovereignty.

The life of every village largely depends on the "unseen" members who work tirelessly behind the scenes without recognition. These include the countless number of people who have supported our efforts through persevering prayer. When seeking the children's welfare, we can count on spiritual warfare. May the Lord bless you for your faithfulness.

Although each villager played a different role, together we share a common purpose: to inform, educate and encourage ministry for children with disabilities. Our hope and prayer is that through the training this book provides for the parents and caregivers, these children will have the joy of living immersed in inclusive communities where they know that they too are made in the image of God and are deeply loved and valued.

PART I

From Despair to Hope

People were bringing little children to Jesus for him to place his hands on them, but the disciples rebuked them. When Jesus saw this, he was indignant. He said to them, "Let the little children come to me, and do not hinder them, for the kingdom of God belongs to such as these. Truly I tell you, anyone who will not receive the kingdom of God like a little child will never enter it." And he took the children in his arms, placed his hands on them and blessed them.

(Mark 10:13–16)

CHAPTER ONE

DISABILITIES

Context and Consequences

* * *

Phyllis Kilbourn

She was only weeks old, so beautiful as I picked her up and held this little bundle of joy called Maria! Her story was one that was similar to so many I have heard. Found on the street, rejected, deserted by her mother, but there was a real significant difference. You see, little Maria was found in a cardboard box on a street in Guatemala City, left there not so much because the family was poor and destitute, although I am sure they were, but left there because she had Down Syndrome!

As you can imagine, as I held her and thought about this, my eyes filled and my heart ached! Yes, I knew that all over the world such children are often kept out of sight, hidden in back rooms and closets, and treated as if they are not human beings.[1]

* * *

MARIA is just one of the estimated one billion people in the world who have some form of disability, including physical, mental, nutritional or emotional. Of this population, UNICEF has estimated that around one quarter or 200 million are children.[2] Some studies, particularly in developing countries, indicate that the proportions and numbers may be significantly higher due to underreporting.

CHALLENGE FOR MINISTRY

As Peter Ustinov has said, "Our ability to deal with children with disabilities is a yardstick of our ability to deal with all children."[3] This also could be a valid measuring stick for the investment of the church and families into the lives of children with disabilities. Just as Jesus modeled compassionate and purposeful ministry to individuals with disabilities, taking time to be with them, to support and to fully accept them whether they were lame, blind, lepers or epileptic, so must we.

We face a big task. The situation of children with disabilities worldwide is often bleak:

- Eighty percent of all people with disabilities live in developing countries, places where there is a shortage of doctors, clinics and rehabilitation facilities.

- Children with disabilities frequently live in poverty, experiencing social exclusion and prejudice.

- Often children with disabilities are left to be cared for by others in orphanages.

- The presence of a child with a disability in an already poor family or community increases demands on limited resources and adds another dimension to the family's and community's ability to cope.

- Many children with disabilities end up living on danger-filled city streets with no provision of essential basic needs.

- Families of children with disabilities have significant needs as well.

A variety of opportunities for compassionate and holistic ministry can be gleaned from the situation and needs of children with disabilities; needs that, if met, help lay a solid foundation for their spiritual development. But in order to effectively meet those needs we must first understand the context surrounding children with disabilities and the consequences of disability on them.

THE CONTEXT OF DISABILITY

Understanding the true context of children with disabilities is not always easy or straightforward. Children with disabilities are often hidden, marginalized and misunderstood because of the ways in which we see—or fail to see—them and their realities, and because of the way in which we define and discuss disability.

"Invisible" Children

Children with disabilities are often "invisible" and underreported because some families hide children with physical or mental disabilities, excluding them from family and community activities. This is especially true in developing countries where the social stigma attached to a disability can be devastating, not only to the child but also to the family and community. Such stigma, coupled with chronic poverty, can result in families abandoning their children who are unable to mix with mainstream children. Those who, like Maria, are shunned, isolated and stigmatized by their communities are left out of census reports.

In addition, the belief that disability is caused by sin, voodoo or other curses, an incestuous relationship or black magic is deeply entrenched in some cultures, especially in the rural areas. "Without the most basic health awareness, misconceptions about the causes of disability can thrive. Such beliefs can ignite fear in a community and inflict terror on an already vulnerable child. In the worst cases, these beliefs can lead to neglect, abandonment or infanticide."[4]

Shame is another factor that keeps children with disabilities hidden. For example, many of China's 10 million children with disabilities are hidden away to avoid facing discrimination and are denied adequate access to social, medical and other vital basic services. In rural areas, parents who are ashamed of their child's disability may lock the child in their home. Girls who have disabilities often experience double discrimination because of their gender.[5]

Perceiving Disability

How we understand and perceive disability also influences our ability to recognize children with disabilities. How a society defines the term "disability" influences the count of how many people have a particular disability. It is therefore vital to have a culturally relevant definition to understand what one means when stating that a child has a disability. Ultimately the definition used will determine which conditions are considered disabilities and, therefore, who has one.

Furthermore, examining the various words used to describe disabilities and understanding the meaning of such terminology also helps us better understand the reality of the impact of limitations that a disability places on children physically, mentally, socially, spiritually and emotionally.

Definitions

There are many definitions given to the general descriptive word, "disability." The World Health Organization (WHO) defines disability as "an umbrella term for impairments, activity limitations and participation restrictions."[6]

According to the WHO, there has been a paradigm shift in approaches to disability. The move has been away from a medical understanding of disability towards a social understanding. The belief of the WHO is that disability proceeds from the interaction between people with a health condition and their environment (the circumstances, objects or conditions by which one is surrounded).[7] Similarly, the United Nations' Convention on the Rights of Persons with Disabilities acknowledges that the term "disability" is an evolving concept, but also stresses that "disability results from the interaction between persons with impairments and attitudinal and environmental barriers that hinder their full and effective participation in society on an equal basis with others."[8] Defining disability as an interaction means that disability is not an attribute of the person.

Disability is also understood to be a human rights issue. The Convention on the Rights of Persons with Disabilities reflects this emphasis on removing environmental barriers that prevent inclusion. Progress on improving social participation is made by addressing the barriers which hinder persons with disabilities in their day-to-day lives.

A balanced approach is needed in forming a definition for disability, giving appropriate weight to the different aspects of its meaning. This balance is observed in Save the Children's statement that a disability signifies a loss or limitation of opportunities to take part in the normal life of the community on an equal level with others due to physical and social barriers.[9]

Language

In addition, proper terminology must be used when talking about disability. The language one uses in referring to children with disabilities can either show respect for a child or reinforce common negative stereotypes. Terms like "the handicapped," "blind," "deaf," "retarded" and "dumb" tend to dehumanize and objectify people and should be avoided. More helpful is describing a child as "having a disability" (not a "disabled child") or a "child with an impairment" (not a "blind child" or "deaf child"). The importance of clarifying what the culturally appropriate terms are that show respect for persons with a disability or impairment cannot be overstated.

The terms "physically challenged" or "mentally challenged" are relatively new ways to describe someone with a disability. Previously society as a whole was less understanding of and sympathetic to physical or mental impairments. People with impairments were labeled "lame," "crippled," "retarded" and other negative terms, often in a belittling manner. Such terms implied that a person could do little or nothing to even participate in a routine, everyday activity. But no one, no matter their physical or mental condition, should feel limited or left out of mainstream everyday life. As such, the word "challenge," which is rightly defined as a stimulating or interesting task or problem, implying unlimited possibilities, is therefore a much more positive and optimistic term to use.

THE CONSEQUENCES OF DISABILITY

In addition to understanding the true context of children with disabilities, we must also understand the consequences that disability has on children, both in terms of risk of exploitation as well as in terms of barriers to rights.

Disability and Children at Risk

Many disabilities occur at birth or are directly attributable to deprivations of essential goods and services, especially in early childhood. Lack of prenatal care adds to the risk of disability, while malnutrition can result in stunting or poor resistance to disease. Some disabilities, such as those caused by polio, result from a lack of vaccines. Others occur because of natural disasters or various forms of exploitation.

For a large majority of the world's children, disabilities not associated with birth are acquired through crisis experiences that not only cause children not to function within the expected norms, but also make them vulnerable to abuse and exploitation. Children of war, street children and child laborers are prime examples of children who are vulnerable to disabilities resulting from dangerous occupations, accidents or harmful exploitation.

Children at risk are not only vulnerable to disability, but disability also increases risks to children. As confirmed through research, credible reports and statistics, children with disabilities are among the most stigmatized and marginalized of all the world's children. Negative societal attitudes expose children with disabilities to greater risk of violence, abuse and exploitation. While all children are at risk of being targeted victims of violence, children having a disability find themselves at significantly increased risk because of the stigma, negative traditional beliefs and ignorance associated with disabilities.

A child born with a disability or a child who becomes disabled may be directly subject to physical violence, or sexual, emotional or verbal abuse in the home, the community, institutional settings or in the workplace. Women and girls with disabilities are particularly vulnerable to abuse. A small 2004 survey in Orissa, India, found that virtually all of the women and girls with disabilities were beaten at home, twenty-five percent of women with intellectual disabilities had been raped and six percent of women with disabilities had been forcibly sterilized.[10]

The increased risk for violence reappears throughout the child's life span, compounding already existing social, educational and economic marginalization that limits the lives and opportunities of the children. For example, children with disabilities are far less likely than their nondisabled peers to be included in the social, economic and cultural life of their communities; only a small percentage of these children will ever attend school. Children living in remote and rural areas may be at increased risk. Lack of social support and limited opportunities for education or participation in the community further isolates these children and their families, leading to increased levels of stress and hardship. Children often are targeted by abusers who perceive them as easy victims.

Three contexts where children with disabilities are especially at risk are in situations of war, street life and child labor. Knowledge gained from examining these exploitive situations in the context of disability can be transferred to other forms of exploitation experienced by children.

Disabilities Caused by War

> At eight years old Nermina had been the joy of her family. She could make them laugh with just a smile, she could make them proud by the way she joined others doing the chores and the way she succeeded in her school work, and she always had friends with whom she played.
>
> But now that was over. The landmine had taken her foot. Now she was a burden. She could not smile; she had to be helped everywhere; and her friends were too busy running and jumping to just sit with her. Even her smile was lost somewhere in the past.
>
> It was Tuesday at the hospital. Nermina had been in this special hospital for two days. It seemed right that she was banished to this sterile place. Her friends probably no longer wanted to be with her; her family only cried when they looked at her; she knew that she could no longer walk the miles to school, pick berries for the market, or kick the ball when it rolled in her direction. She did not belong any more.[11]

Nermina's story so well describes the experiences of countless children caught up in violent civil wars. According to the WHO, "for every child killed in warfare, three are injured and acquire a permanent form of disability. In some countries, up to a quarter of all disabilities result from injuries and violence."[12]

Along with the disabilities children acquire through clearing fields of landmines is the difficult fact that, according to the United Nations, one of every four soldiers in the world is a child. Opportunities for disability-type injuries are rife for the child soldier, including mental and physical challenges from the drugs and alcohol given them for bravery in fighting during the day and forgetting what they have done when night falls.

Eleven years of civil war in Sierra Leone is another prime example of how war brings about an increase in disability. Thousands of young people were forced to suffer disabilities, "both as a result of forced amputations—the tragic hallmark of the rebel forces—and the collapse of the national health system including childhood immunizations. As vaccinations ceased, disabling diseases such as polio crept back into overcrowded slums, mainly affecting children under the age of five."[13]

Street Children with Disabilities

Children with disabilities are considered by many to be the most neglected children in our society. Perhaps nowhere is this more evident than in the lives of children who through poverty, neglect or abuse have been forced to live on danger-filled city streets. Living without parental support, protection and care, stigma and ignorance make life doubly hard for street children living with a disability.

According to UNICEF, thirty percent of the estimated 150–200 million street children and youth worldwide have disabilities.[14] Fengai, a street boy from Sierra Leone, knows all too well the realities of living on the streets with a disability. As a child, his legs were deformed by polio. Rejected by his family, Fengai had lived on the streets with other children with disabilities for ten years when the following was written:

> In an abandoned yard in central Freetown, a young man is making his way through the shadows of two burnt-out cars. His legs are buckled by polio into a knot beneath him and he pulls himself forward on his fists. His name is Fengai, he is 21, and this is his home: a neglected community of disabled street children in one of Sierra Leone's forgotten corners.
>
> "This," Fengai spits out, "is a bomeh, a dumping ground, for rubbish and for the crippled." He gestures around at a gathering of tiny broken huts. A crude tattoo on his arm spells out "Go Arsenal." "There are more than 50 of us here and we have nothing. No water, no food. They are sick, these boys, but who will help them? Go home," he shouts, "and tell them that we are living in misery!"
>
> Fengai is shaking with frustration and anger. But after ten years as a disabled street child in one of the world's poorest countries, he knows his voice is heard by few. The United Nations estimates as many as thirty percent of street children in Sierra Leone are disabled. Many have been

outcast because of their disability, chased into the shadows by social stigma and family shame. On the streets they are exposed to disease, abuse and hunger. Yet often the streets are safer than home.[15]

In many parts of the world, street children who were blind, deaf, crippled or disfigured often live as outcasts, reduced to a deplorable and dangerous lifestyle. Using these children as beggars is profitable because begging capitalizes on their disabilities, creates sympathy, attracts people's sentiment and results in financial profit for the ones controlling the children. Even more tragic is the situation where, for financial gain, children's parents or caregivers have purposefully maimed children so they could work as beggars.

Disabilities Induced by Child Labor

Light work that integrates the child into family and community life can be beneficial, building within a child a sense of confidence and responsibility. "Child labor" does not refer to those children. Rather it refers to the millions of children worldwide who are engaged, often forced, into assuming dangerous jobs and working far too many hours. According to the International Labour Organization (ILO), around 246 million children worldwide between ages five and seventeen work, many full-time. Of this number more than half are engaged in what is considered hazardous labor.[16] Working children usually do not go to school and have little or no time to play. Many do not receive proper nutrition or care. Being denied the chance to be children who enjoy healthy and happy childhoods, they experience developmental delays.

Reinaldo's story of his involvement as a child laborer in Brazil illustrates the hardships and dangers of children engaged in hazardous or exploitative labor:

> Unlike most boys his age, 9-year-old Reinaldo Silva Novais Pereira's most fervent dream is to spend the entire day in school. Instead, every morning Reinal, as he is called, wakes up before sunrise to trudge off to a quarry. For five long hours, he pounds hard, sharp rocks into gravel for road construction, and then, exhausted and weary, goes to school.
> For Reinal, getting an education is a real struggle. He loves learning, but because he only attends classes for half a day, he misses out on the arts and crafts courses that are part of elementary education in Brazil. He works because he has to. His mother who labors alongside him in the quarry needs the income he brings in to support them both. It is hard and dangerous work. The dry air in the Bahia region where Reinal lives, mingled with the dust from the rocks, makes breathing difficult. "It's strenuous and boring.

Stones can get into your face. The hammer can hurt you. We sweat a lot," he explains.

Working at the quarry is grueling for anyone, but especially so for a child. Sitting on the ground, Reinal breaks stones larger than his hands. The dust and sweat blind his eyes. He is acutely aware that he has no choice: "It's hazardous, but we have to do it to help our mother. It's necessary." Reinal's mother is very unhappy that her son has to work and desperately wants to give him more. But they barely survive on what they earn: the equivalent of $2.50 a day. "I myself worked as a child. The kind of life we have gives little hope," she says sadly. There is no break from the endless routine of hammering rocks, seven days a week, week after week.

The only time that Reinal is able to free his mind is when he is in class. But it is not easy to concentrate after a morning in the quarry. His back and arms ache. Nevertheless, he loves to read, write and sing, and dreams of a better future. He aspires to be a teacher some day. Reinal's only regret is that he cannot attend school full time because he does not have a Bolsa Escola—the scholarship program that replaces a child's income which poor families depend on to survive.[17]

Sadly, Reinaldo's story is repeated over and over again for children all around the world. For example, India has the largest number of working children in the world, with credible estimates ranging from 60 to 75 million. According to the United Nations, more than twenty percent of India's economy is dependent on child labor. Children under the age of fourteen are forced to work in dangerous situations such as glass-blowing, fireworks and, most commonly, carpet-making factories. The situation of the children at the factories is desperate. They work under harsh, hazardous, exploitative and often life-threatening conditions for extremely low wages. Most work around twelve hours a day, with only small breaks for meals. Undernourished, the children usually are fed only minimal staples such as rice. The vast majority of migrant child workers, who cannot return home at night, sleep alongside their looms, further inviting sickness and poor health.

Poverty is a key factor in children joining the workforce. Sometimes children's joining is a voluntary act, but more often it is forced upon them by their destitute families. Health effects of poverty increase the job risks for children. The International Labour Organization has found that "children who suffer from malnutrition, fatigue, anemia or other poverty-related health problems are at greater risk when exposed to work-related hazards. The combination of poor health and work hazards can lead to permanent disabilities and premature death."[18] But regardless of how children acquire a disability, they require special care and attention, or else they become at risk of being excluded from within their society, community and even family. Unfortunately for the vast majority of children, especially in developing countries, access to rehabilitative health care or support services is not available. Lack of care has resulted in hundreds of thousands of children with disabilities being destined to live their lives in institutions, often deprived not only of love and affection but also of the most basic physical requirements.

Barriers to Full Enjoyment of Rights

In addition to increased risk of exploitation, children with disabilities constantly face barriers that keep them from the full enjoyment of their rights. These rights include participation in community and family life; access to education, health services and rehabilitation; social and legal assistance; opportunities for play and cultural activities; and educational opportunities such as vocational and life-skills training. According to the World Health Organization:

> Across the world, people with disabilities have poorer health outcomes, lower education achievements, less economic participation and higher rates of poverty than people without disabilities. This is partly because people with disabilities experience barriers in accessing services that many of us have long taken for granted, including health, education, employment, and transport as well as information. These difficulties are exacerbated in less advantaged communities.[19]

The loss of a child's rights stems from root causes such as poverty, social issues (such as stigma and discrimination), lack of health care and rehabilitation services, inaccessible transport (especially for medical services), not enough "disability friendly" facilities, lack of helpful information and various forms of exploitation. These barriers hold children back from achieving their full potential. Often children's abilities are overlooked and their capacities underestimated. Consequentially, they are excluded from activities in their communities and families. Victor Pineda reminds us of the importance of helping children with disabilities achieve their full potential. He says:

> People with disabilities may have difficulty seeing, hearing, walking or remembering. But they also have dreams, hopes and ideas they want to share . . . Every person in the world looks different and has different ideas, experiences, traditions and abilities. I learned that these differences create new possibilities, new hopes, new dreams and new friendships.[20]

Space here does not allow us to deal with all the barriers children with disabilities confront. We will, however, briefly examine four that are at the top of the list as root causes for children being excluded from their "dreams, hopes and ideas they want to share." These barriers are poverty, social stigma, community values and attitudes, and education. Other barriers, along with their implications for the children, will be highlighted throughout the book.

Poverty

Poverty and disability go hand in hand. According to World Bank estimates, about two-thirds of all persons with severe to moderate disabilities live in poverty. They belong to the poorest of the poor of the world's population and are acutely affected by shortages in basic necessities such as water, food and housing, as well as bad or nonexistent public transportation, inadequate health care and the lack of income opportunities. In addition, persons with disabilities who live in poverty are more likely to be excluded from information, power, resources and access than any other group of society. As a result millions, particularly women and girls, have to live beneath any reasonable standard of living.

Disability is both a cause and a consequence of poverty. People living in poverty tend to become disabled because of aggravating factors such as malnutrition, squalid housing, hazardous occupations and heightened exposure to violence. Conversely, people with disabilities tend to be poorer or to become impoverished because they lack jobs or access to income, basic social and medical services and rehabilitation. In addition, the poor with disabilities are often exposed to the devastating effects of discrimination, exclusion, sheer prejudice or superstition, and the denial of participation and influence in society. Because children with disabilities are not educated or taught an income-generating skill, they simply perpetuate the cycle of poverty. Girls with disabilities suffer double discrimination due to their gender and have less opportunity to attend school than boys.

Equally troubling is the fact that for many people in poor countries their disabilities could have been avoided. People in developing countries are faced not only with the prospect of genetic disabilities and those caused by accidents, but also those disabilities which are a direct result of poverty, conflict and preventable diseases caused by malnutrition, poor health, unclean water, bad sanitation and lack of education.

Social Stigma

Words synonymous with "stigma" include "shame," "disgrace" and "dishonor." Almost all stigma stems from a person differing from social or cultural norms. Social stigma is defined as "a severe social disapproval of or personal discontent with a person on the grounds of their unique characteristics distinguishing them from others in society."[21] For children with disabilities, differences include such things as appearance, behavior, deformities and mental illness.

Stigma stands in sharp contrast to the desire of people with any disability in both developed and developing countries to be respected and to be integrated into their communities in ways that ensure their basic human rights are being met. Social stigma spawns prejudice, poverty, discrimination, government indifference and lack of resources that complicate this seemingly easy task of inclusion.

One strategy societies have typically used to avoid the embarrassment of social stigma has been the practice of placing their children with disabilities into institutions. Russia is an example of this practice. For decades vast numbers of Russian children with disabilities have been placed in institutions, and this practice has continued during the post-Soviet transition period. Such children usually face a bleak existence behind institutional walls, isolated from their families and communities and suffering from stigma and discrimination. Marta Santos Pais, director of UNICEF Innocenti Research Centre, observes that "although [Russian] children with disabilities have become more visible since the beginning of transition and attitudes toward them and their families are changing, many of them remain simply 'written off' from society."[22]

UNICEF advocates for a child's right to grow up in a family environment and in conditions that ensure respect for their dignity and promote self-reliance and active participation in social life. All children deserve quality of life, yet the socio-cultural dimension of disability—that which refers to status, dignity and self-respect—is seldom addressed.

Community Values and Attitudes

Another reality that forms a barrier focuses on community values and attitudes. Cultural values, traditional beliefs, educational environment and religion are factors affecting a community's attitudes towards those with disabilities. Research has confirmed that negative societal attitudes and values from both the family and community can inhibit and limit children's motivation to recover, adapt to and accept their disability.

The impact of community attitudes can be illustrated with the cultural beliefs and values presented in the Indian culture where the belief in karma, or payment for past deeds, attributes disability to the child's fate or destiny. While families go through the natural process of shock and grief when a child is born with a disability, the belief in karma causes them to have an attitude of resignation. This impacts how they treat the child. In a place where rehabilitation services are not easily available to the majority of the population, little help is sought for children with lifelong disabilities; instead, they are left to their fate. Economic hardship, poor transport facilities and a lack of education also make it harder for parents to access services for their child. In addition, karma means that the child's destiny—and potential—are sealed. Indians see their children as investments for the future. When a child is born with a disability, they do not see that child as a source of support or income in the future. For this reason, they would rather spend their income on the healthy children, especially those who are male.

By contrast, community values and beliefs lead to different treatment of children who are not born with a disability. When a person acquires a disability later in life, people in India are more sympathetic since they think of the person's level of function prior to the illness or injury. If there is hope that the person will be fully functional again, efforts are made to provide services. Empowerment of the individual, considered a Western construct, is deemed to be a selfish and undesirable goal. Altruism (unselfishness or self-sacrifice) for the sake of the family and the larger society is highly valued.

Educational Exclusion

Children with disabilities continually have to combat the barrier of educational exclusion. Not only physical, but also mental and social barriers prevent children with disabilities from enjoying their right to education. Some schools remain inaccessible to children who are physically disabled, while other schools are simply unwilling to accept them or unable to meet their special requirements.

Inclusion in school programs provides opportunities for socialization and friendships to develop. Inclusion also provides a sense of belonging and appropriate modeling of social, behavioral and academic skills. But, according to educational estimations for developing countries, ninety percent of children with disabilities do not go to school. According to the 2010 Education for All Global Monitoring Report, "children with disabilities remain one of the main groups being widely excluded from quality education."[23] The report states that disability is recognized as one of the least visible yet most potent factors in educational marginalization.

CONCLUSION

Barriers from poverty, stigma, community attitudes and educational exclusion: we must eliminate them all. As well, we must eliminate the exploitation and various violations of child's rights that often force people with disabilities to the margins of society. Because such barriers can hinder children from developing their God-given gifts and potential, the church also must join in advocacy and action for the elimination of these barriers, empowering children with disabilities to participate in all aspects of family, church and community life.

This book is designed to serve as a guide to equip the church (that is us!) to engage in holistic ministry that eliminates barriers and develops effective strategies that provide these children with opportunities to develop their God-given gifts and potential. Only then will they experience a hope-filled and meaningful "today and tomorrow."

Although working with children having disabilities is an arduous task, demanding much patience and endurance, this book is not about just entering into the children's world of barriers, limitations and sadness. No! On the contrary, it is about the mutual joy of opening doors that lead to hope, purpose and achievement.

As you journey through the pages of this book, may you be challenged and equipped to pass on the gift of hope to some exceptional children.

NOTES

1. Sam Martin, "Prayer Letter for the Arms of Jesus Children's Mission" (unpublished manuscript, n.d.).

2. UNICEF Innocenti Research Centre, "Promoting the Rights of Children with Disabilities," *Innocenti Digest* 13 (2007): iv, http://www.unicef-irc.org/publications/pdf/digest13-disability.pdf.

3. Christian Blind Mission, "Access for All: Marking the Coming into Force of the UN Convention on the Rights of Persons with Disabilities," http://www.slideshare.net/cbmuk/access-for-access-for-all-marking-the-coming-into-force-of-the-un-convention-on-the-rights-of-persons-with-disabilities-presentation, slide 18.

4. Libby Powell, "Beyond Beliefs," *The Guardian*, November 19, 2010, http://www.guardian.co.uk/journalismcompetition/sierra-leone-street-children?INTCMP=SRCH.

5. UNICEF, "China: Children with Disabilities," http://www.unicef.org/china/protection_community_485.html.

6. World Health Organization, "Disability and Health Fact Sheet No. 352," http://www.who.int/mediacentre/factsheets/fs352/en/index.html.

7. World Health Organization, "Disabilities," http://www.who.int/topics/disabilities/en.

8. UN General Assembly, "Convention on the Rights of Persons with Disabilities," January 24, 2007, http://www.un.org/disabilities/default.asp?id=259.

9. Hazel Jones, *Including Disabled People in Everyday Life: A Practical Approach* (London: Save the Children, 1999), 9.

10. United Nations, "Some Facts about Persons with Disabilities," http://www.un.org/disabilities/convention/facts.shtml.

11. Warren L. Dale, "Trauma and the Disabled Child: The Bosnian Project," in *Challenge and Hope: Disability, Disease and Trauma in the Developing World*, ed. Kerrie Engel and Jill Burn (Victoria, Australia: World Vision of Australia, 1999), 13.

12. Disabled World, "World Facts and Statistics on Disabilities and Disability Issues," http://www.disabled-world.com/disability/statistics.

13. Powell, "Beyond Beliefs."

14. UNICEF, *Global Survey of Adolescents with Disabilities: An Overview of Young People Living with Disabilities; Their Needs and Their Rights* (New York: UNICEF Inter-Divisional Working Group on Young People, Programme Division, 1999).

15. Powell, "Beyond Beliefs."

16. International Labour Organization, "World Day against Child Labour 2011: ILO Calls for Urgent Action against Hazardous Forms of Child Labour," news release, June 10, 2011, http://www.ilo.org/ilc/ILCSessions/100thSession/media-centre/press-releases/WCMS_156758/lang--en/index.htm.

17. UN Works Website, What's Going On? Child Labour in Brazil, "Between a Rock and a Hard Place," http://www.un.org/works/goingon/labor/reina_story.html.

18. Child Labor Publication Education Project, *Child Labor and Health Adult Education Workshop: Handouts* (Iowa City, IA: University of Iowa, 2004), 4, http://www.continuetolearn.uiowa.edu/laborctr/child_labor/materials/documents/clpephealthhandouts.pdf.

19. World Health Organization, *World Report on Disability* (Geneva: World Health Organization, 2011), http://whqlibdoc.who.int/publications/2011/9789240685215_eng.pdf, xi.

20. Victor Santiago Pineda, *It's about Ability: An Explanation of the Convention on the Rights of Persons with Disabilities* (New York: UNICEF, 2008), 3, 5.

21. *Wikipedia*, s.v. "Social Stigma," http://en.wikpedia.org/wiki/Social_stigma.

22. UNICEF, "Many Children with Disabilities Still 'Written Off,'" press release, October 5, 2005, http://www.unicef.org/media/media_28539.html.

23. UK AID Department for International Development, "Guidance Note: Education for Children with Disabilities – Improving Access and Quality," http://www.dfid.gov.uk/Documents/publications1/edu-chi-disabil-guid-note.pdf, 2.

*

CHAPTER TWO

WHY, LORD?

* * *

Marcia Mitchell

It was a beautiful spring Sunday evening. Our church was gathered for a special choir concert. With an air of anticipation, my husband and I slipped into the pew we normally occupy. We had been eagerly anticipating this concert, because our daughter Missy was in charge of it. She was serving as interim music administrator and choir director at our church and had been pouring her heart and soul into a concert featuring a collection of Brooklyn Tabernacle Choir songs. I glanced up to see her walking across the sanctuary platform at the front of the church. She took her place on the choir director's platform as the sanctuary became silent. She raised her arms in the air, and with a nod and a wave of her hand the orchestra began to play. Seconds later, our sixty-five-voice choir was filling the sanctuary with melodious sounds that echoed throughout the church.

As she directed, Missy's tiny 4-foot-10-inch frame moved ever so slightly to the beat of the music. Her degree in music and the countless concerts across the country had contributed much to preparing her for this moment.

Tears filled my eyes as I beheld her short blonde frame conducting under the stage lights. Joy and pride filled my heart, and my mind drifted back to the moment I first laid eyes on her.

* * *

MY husband Phil and I had been married for three years when I finally became pregnant. We were jubilant! From the start I had wanted a baby girl, and for the duration of the pregnancy I dreamed of nothing else. I could see her in my mind's eye, pretty and pink and covered from head to toe with ribbons and lace!

On August 11, 1970, at 11:59 p.m., the obstetrician finally announced, "It's a girl!" Unable to contain my exuberance, I laughed out loud with delight! When the nurse brought her closer for me to see, I was completely overcome with joy! Truly, she was beyond even my greatest fantasies! Her hair was the blondest I had ever seen; in fact, it was white! The nurses evidently agreed because they immediately nicknamed her "Little Snow White." She was extraordinarily fair from head to toe, almost Dresden-like. Phil and I had each been light-skinned and blond as children. My heart wanted to nestle into the comfort of my reasoning, but my mind was unsettled. Something stirred within me. Hesitantly, I asked the doctor, "Is she alright?"

The doctor's answer remains with me to this day: "She's as perfect as you would want her to be." His soothing words calmed my anxiety.

Finally, I was taken back to my room. Phil was there to greet me with a countenance that blended pride with exhaustion. We had a few wonderful moments together and finalized our decision to name our precious new baby Michelle Louise. With a grin Phil said, "But we'll call her Missy, okay?"

Shortly before he left, I gathered the courage to ask him if he felt anything might be wrong with her. He assured me she was fine and gently reminded me of my tendency to worry needlessly. He gave me a tender kiss and slipped quietly out the door, promising to be back bright and early the following morning.

He returned early the next morning, just as he had promised. He was in the best of spirits, still the epitome of a proud, new father! Moments later, the pediatrician arrived. Looking a bit too solemn, he spoke softly, "I guess you both know you have a very special baby."

"Of course she's special!" I quickly responded, bursting with pride. That a pediatrician, who saw so many children, would comment that our child was exceptional caused both Phil and me to spill over with delight, but the doctor's tone became more serious.

"I don't think you understand. You see, your baby is very special because babies *like* her are extremely rare—only one in 50,000 are born like her. She was born with a rare condition that affects her vision. It will be several years before you'll know the degree of vision she has. At best, she'll be legally blind. I'm afraid it's not correctable." His voice grew distant. Though he continued, I did not hear anything else he said. My heart and mind had locked in on one word—*blind!*

Phil saw the pediatrician to the door, and as he did so, tears began to sting my eyes. *No! It cannot be true! Surely the doctor must be wrong.* But other doctors only confirmed his diagnosis.

In the following days, Phil seemed pensive. As for me, I cried for hours as the same question echoed over and over in my head. *Why, Lord? Why have You done this to us? How could You do this to us?*

Several days passed. Then one particular day, Phil was late for his regular visit. When he finally arrived, I was anxious to know why he had been so delayed. His evasiveness heightened my curiosity all the more.

Stumbling over his words, he attempted to explain. "On the way to the hospital," he began, "I couldn't help wondering. What if things turn out for the worst? What if Missy can't see at all? Or what if she can see, but can't see well enough to . . . " He hesitated a moment as he stared out the window, " . . . to see a bird in flight, or the stars or clouds floating against the blue sky?"

I waited for him to collect his thoughts.

"I couldn't stop thinking about it, and so I just kept driving," he explained. "I studied the landscape and everything my eyes could absorb. I noticed how blue the sky was—clear, with only a few white, wispy clouds." He moved from the window back to my bedside. "I began to wonder how we might describe it all to her. I tried to think of words to capture it all. That's when I noticed the grass. Marcia, for the first time I realized that grass isn't simply a green mass. It's millions upon millions of tiny, individual blades! Even though I was looking at things I've seen every day of my life, it was as though, through Missy, I've been given a rare gift—a whole new look at our world!"

I took my eyes off him for a moment and looked at the roses by my bedside. As I studied them, they seemed to take on an added brilliance. In the days to come, we began to realize that we were seeing the way God had intended us to see for the first time in our lives. But the most important thing we began to see was that this was not something God had done to us. Rather, this was something God had done for us. For He had allowed us to give birth to a baby who had begun to teach us before she could even talk, and she had begun to lead us closer to our heavenly Father before she could even walk.

Indeed, our walk would grow even closer over the next few years as we leaned on the Lord for all our needs. As an educator I was extremely sensitive to the fact that we would need trained professionals who could teach us how to help Missy grow and develop. I knew that the first six years of life are the most important learning years we ever experience. We had heard of children who were blind who were placed in classes for the mentally challenged because they were so developmentally delayed by the age of six. I also knew that eighty-six percent of everything we learn takes place visually. We did not want to take any chances with Missy's development.

Finding no professional help available in Tulsa, we decided to trust God to show us how to begin our own center, and He did exactly that. In the fall of 1972 the doors to our dream center for children with special needs opened to five children: our own child, the cofounder's child and three other children with visual impairments.

Over the past four decades, The Little Light House has been transformed into a state-of-the-art developmental center which serves as an international model. Hundreds of children have received quality, individualized services through The Little Light House, and they have accomplished major milestones that medical authorities had considered impossible.

Missy, too, has grown up! After benefiting from the preschool she had helped inspire, she attended regular private schools in Tulsa and, though competing with sighted peers throughout her school days, she still graduated with a 3.95 grade average and continued on to graduate *cum laude* from Oklahoma Baptist University. Years later she received her master's degree in Christian Counseling: Marriage and Family Therapy. As always, she did not allow her vision to be an obstacle, even though this degree involved mountains of reading. She graduated with High Honors, a recognition given only to those who achieve a 4.0 for their entire degree program. Throughout her life she worked hard and did well, but life was not always easy for her. One particular part of her life represented great emotional pain and resulted in a significant, pivotal point in her life spiritually.

It was midway through her teen years, and it was a question I dreaded answering her whole life long. She came to me on one of those rare quiet evenings. Phil was attending a meeting, and I had decided to turn in early. I was sitting up in bed reading when Missy appeared at the bedroom door. I could tell immediately, something was terribly wrong. I patted the bed and beckoned her to come sit down. As she did so, tears began to stream down her face. "Mom," she cried, "I just need to know why! Why can't I see like everyone else? Why was I born this way? I didn't do anything to deserve this!"

I thought back over the last several months. All of Missy's friends were either preparing to get driver's licenses or already had them. They proudly swung their keys around at school as they chatted about what kind of cars they were driving or hoped to get! After school they rushed out to the parking lot to ooh and aah over each other's automobiles. I had not stopped to think how hard it had been for Missy when she had been forced to stand with the elementary children as she waited for her dad or me to pick her up from school.

Then there were all the other challenges. Reading with her magnifying glass required much more time for her to complete assignments than it did for her peers. We had constantly encouraged her to *not* allow her vision to stand in her way. Still her road had been steep! All the years of struggle, having to work so much harder at everything, and now the disappointment at not being able to get a driver's license was more than her young, teenage heart could bear!

My heart broke as I silently prayed for God to give me wisdom. I could not answer her question! I could not explain to her why she had been born legally blind.

She sobbed until there seemed to be no more tears left. She lay limp with her head in my lap as I pondered how to respond to her pain.

I silently prayed, *Lord, I need to give her an answer that will satisfy her soul. Please speak to me and through me.* Finally, the words came. "Darlin', I can't answer your question, but I can tell you this. You can ask 'Why?' for the rest of your life, and it will probably only lead you to misery and defeat. But if you will choose to turn that question around and instead of asking 'Why?'—ask God 'How?'—how He can use your circumstances for good, He will show you great and mighty things." As Romans 8:28 says, "In all things God works for the good of those who love him, who have been called according to his purpose."

"Sweetheart," I continued, "God has already used your life! Through you, God inspired the birth and the development of a ministry that has made a difference for hundreds of children. There is no telling what God has in store for you. Look to Him and trust Him to reveal and carry out His plan for your life."

Now a Christian concert artist, Missy has shared this moment of her life with countless audiences. She tells of how she went running back to God that evening and asked His forgiveness. She poignantly shares how God welcomed her with loving arms and forgave her for the bitterness she had been harboring in her heart. It was at that same time in her life that God began to unfold the music ministry He had planned for her, which would ultimately bring her great joy and fulfillment.

* * *

As I listened to the last sounds of the beautiful harmony coming from the magnificent voices of our choir, I marveled over how God was using Missy's life.

Indeed He was able to work all things together for good for those who are called according to His purpose. He still is!

PART II

Developmental Needs

Confronting the Hurdles

To a Special Teacher

When the sun rose
from under its misty veil,
you were there to watch,
like the birds over the sea.
When the wind came quietly
and rested in your ear,
you listened, as the earth would at dawn.
When the rain fell,
you reached out with your hands
and let it wash everything away,
like waves as they grasp the shore.
When the plain brown seed was planted,
you could already smell the fragrance of
the flower that was to come,
and you were proud
as a good gardener should be.
Thank you for believing
that there was a flower waiting inside
and for taking the time
to help
and watch it grow.
When the sun rose
from under its misty veil,
you were there to watch,
and I am thankful.

—Samantha Abeel

*

CHAPTER THREE

PSYCHOSOCIAL IMPLICATIONS

* * *

Wendy Middaugh Bovard

SEVERAL years ago, while we were building a home and school for street children in central Kenya, I met a young boy named Peter who changed my life.

It was a typical hot afternoon on the plain between the Aberdare Mountain Range and the Mount Kenya National Reserve. My husband had just left for yet another "safari" with the evangelism team, and I was left to hold down the fort and run our boys' home and school. As I sat down on our veranda for a cool drink, I spotted what appeared to be a very short young man coming across the field toward our house. I soon realized that this young man was not short, he was crippled. He was walking on his knees and balancing himself with his bent hands.

My mind immediately went back to the last time my husband had gone away and I had hired a blind man as a security guard. It had made perfect sense to me because Shangilia ("the joyful one") was the only one who, in the darkest night, could hear the elephants coming soon enough to raise an alarm and keep them from destroying our gardens. My husband did not appreciate my efforts in human-resource management and made it clear that I was not to hire anyone else in his absence. As this young man came closer and closer with a determined look on his face, my mind flooded with possible ways to tell him we had no employment opportunity here. But I was already in trouble.

The young man made his way through our gate and to the steps where I walked down to meet him. As I reached out to greet him, he took my hand in his crippled, twisted hand, looked me in the eyes and spoke in Swahili. He said, "Hello, my name is Peter. Can you teach me to read?" I was stunned and so ashamed of my former concerns. I invited him to sit on the veranda as I retreated into my house to wipe my eyes and repent. A few minutes later, I emerged from the front door with cool juice, and Peter and I began the journey of a lifetime.

He told me of his dream to study and how he was sure God had brought us to this spot, in answer to his prayers. I have never since doubted that statement. Within moments, my own children bounced from their home-school desks to meet this young man who had walked so far. Peter and my son, Jonathan, were the same age and quickly became friends. Jonathan suggested that Peter could share his room to avoid the long walk and dangerous river crossing—and it was done. We all piled into our 1979 Land Rover to take Peter home and talk to his parents about this great plan.

A BOY NAMED PETER

Peter is the fourth of eight children in a farming family with hardworking and caring parents. His was a difficult delivery, and the family was stunned that their firstborn son seemed to be different. As the years went by, visits to faraway hospitals confirmed that Peter was a victim of an irreversible, congenital condition. Dangerous operations could partially correct his bent hands, and the useless part of his legs could be amputated from the knees down. If he survived the surgeries, prosthetic legs could give him a chance to walk.

Such measures were too frightening for his parents to consider. They loved Peter and chose to accept what God had given them and to protect him from any possible danger or failure. When his brothers and sisters went to school, he stayed with his mother and watched as she milked cows, herded goats and knitted sweaters. His siblings walked several miles to school every day, which made education impossible for Peter, but did not stop him from dreaming and praying for a chance. At fifteen years of age, he heard about the *wazungu* (white people) who were building a school a few miles from his home, just on the other side of the river. Every night around the fire, he heard his family discussing the progress that the *wazungu* were making, and he was determined to know if these people who came to this bush were the answer to his years of prayer.

One day, while his mother grazed the cows, he slipped off. He could not cross the river near his home, so he struggled up the river to find safe crossing. By the time he arrived at my house in the late afternoon, he was visibly tired from walking more than six miles on his knees. Now, here he sat on my veranda, and we began to talk.

A year later, Peter was reading from his Swahili Bible and already developing a desire to preach. Our street boys' home was not equipped for young people with physical challenges like Peter's, but it was tremendous to see former street boys and orphans reach out to Peter and accept his limitations. I recall a time our boys' choir was to perform and our Land Rover got stuck on the way. Peter was to stay in the vehicle while the other boys walked several miles to the main road to find alternate transportation to the concert. Peter jumped from the vehicle and began walking on his knees across the field; he was not going to miss the performance! As I watched Peter's incredible determination, one of the older boys reached down, pulled Peter up over his shoulder and kept walking. The boys took turns carrying Peter, a strong young man by this time, until we reached the road. They were exhausted, but the concert was wonderful, and the boys had proven that their unconditional love for Peter would not let him be left behind.

HOLISTIC CHILD DEVELOPMENT AND CHILDREN WITH DISABILITIES

Psychosocial support is an important component of holistic development of children but, as the term implies, must be addressed in the context of the whole child. Holistic child development is a process that involves physical, cognitive, spiritual, social and psychological dimensions. We must, therefore, take great care to see that children progress well through each stage. In the case of children with disabilities, overprotection is common, which can limit a child's growth. With an understanding of the basic needs and development stages of children, parents and caregivers are better equipped to address the needs of children with disabilities.

Children cannot develop in a vacuum; it actually does "take a village to raise a child." Several factors, both internal and external, impact the development of every child. The significant relationships that children develop, for example, are crucial to their emotional stability and acceptance of their disability. Important relationships include those with the mother, father, siblings, extended family, church family, neighbors, schoolteachers, peers and friends.[1]

Children with disabilities are exactly that: they are *children* who have the same needs, desires and rights as other children. They may be more vulnerable in some cases and in special need of protection, but they are still children who want to love and laugh and play like all the others.

ACRWC: Protecting *All* Children

The *African Charter on the Rights and Welfare of the Child* (ACRWC) holds to the beliefs that all children have the same rights. There should be no discrimination against children because of their race, religion, color, sex, disability, language or ethnic group. Children have the same rights whether their families are rich or poor. Furthermore, the charter recognizes that *all* children have the right to such things as protection, nutrition, medical care, education and a nationality. It clearly states that children who are handicapped have the same rights as all children. Everybody should treat them with respect. They should be helped to live happily like all other children.[2]

In fact, the charter even gives children the right to a name.[3] That idea may sound a little extreme, but in many African languages and cultures, children with disabilities are called by the name of their particular disability rather than their given names. In Swahili, for example, children might be called Kiwete ("the crippled one"), Kipofu ("the blind one") or Kiziwi "the deaf one"). It is also worth noting that mothers who bear children with disabilities may be accused of being cursed or punished for some bad deed, financial debt or evil thought. Therefore, even the mothers themselves are targets of stigma when children are born with special needs.

A more recent problem in Africa is the number of children who have disabilities as a result of war and conflict. This situation is most difficult to understand, but these children make up a large percentage of all children with disabilities in war-torn countries such as Rwanda, the Democratic Republic of the Congo, Uganda, Liberia, Angola and Sierra Leone. Child soldiers are maimed on a daily basis, and even schoolchildren are brutally injured in conflicts that rage across the continent. The words of my own son through tears as we visited a hospital in the Rwanda border town of Ruhengeri still ring in my ears: "Mom, I've never seen so many children missing arms and legs."

The truth is that, in spite of the wonderful progress in reducing crippling diseases such as polio, we have more children with disabilities than ever due to constant war and conflict. Of late, efforts have been made by most governments and many nongovernmental organizations (NGOs) to bring attention to these issues and raise awareness through churches and communities that all children deserve loving care, especially when they have special needs. Awareness is one of the best ways to ensure that these young people get every opportunity possible for education, medical care and socialization.

To understand the impact of disability on a child, we first need to understand *normal child development*. The holistic development of a child takes place through personal and interpersonal relationships and usually expresses itself in the following stages:[4]

- Bonding

Every child is born with a natural need for bonding. One of the foundations for human relationship is the need for bonding through personal contact, breast-feeding, cuddling, talking, singing, playing and so on. These touches communicate a sense of security and help the child develop trust with the caregiver and later with family and community.

In Africa, as in many other places, bonding may be a potential problem for the child who is born physically different from other children. The extended family and community may shame the mother for having delivered a child with a physical disability. Even without realizing it, the mother may transfer feelings of fear, anger, resentment or guilt to the child. In Africa, the mother often has to work all day in the farming fields, and her child may be left unsupervised, alone or with another child. Therefore, the bonding stage may be interrupted and thus bring a host of attachment issues later in life.

- Developing healthy boundaries

Discipline with boundaries teaches children what is safe and acceptable. After children develop healthy bonds to their primary caregivers, they need discipline. The word "discipline" comes from the word "disciple"; hence, to discipline a child is to give the child guidance and boundaries. Discipline includes *correction* and *direction*, but if the proper relationship did not develop during the bonding stage, the child may lack the necessary trust and respect, making the stage of discipline difficult for both the child and the parent.

In the process of teaching, correcting and training, parents pass on moral standards and rules of conduct and tradition through reinforcement. The reinforcement may be negative or positive, but the entire experience is what now moves children into the next stage. Disciplining a child with disabilities is difficult for some parents because they may be experiencing guilt, or they may fear injuring the child. On the other hand, a parent may feel anger and resentment toward the child and be abusive. Therefore, the emotions of the parents or caregivers influence the child's understanding of healthy boundaries. Without the security that comes with boundaries, the child will not make the effort to begin exploration.

- Building self-worth

Parents provide a sense of security through bonding and boundaries, but they must also send their children positive messages of love and acceptance. This show of love may prove to be one of the most important stages for children with disabilities. Their ability to accept themselves and whatever disability they have may depend on their parents' ability to accept them unconditionally. Children need a sense of belonging, which, in turn, strengthens their sense of self-value and self-confidence. This feeling of self-worth is vital for the identity issues they may face in adolescence and is one of the pillars of resilience that will be addressed later in this chapter.

- Exploration

When children feel accepted and safe in their environment, they are more likely to explore their surroundings. Healthy children are curious, and when allowed to explore their surroundings in a safe environment, they grow and become more confident individuals. Exploration encourages autonomy and helps youngsters establish limits on their own. Children explore in different ways, but understanding their environment is vital to learning and gaining confidence for further growth and inquiry. Encouraging an investigative spirit can prove difficult for parents of children with disabilities. In an effort to lovingly protect their children from pain, the parents often keep them from attending social events and educational opportunities.

- Interacting with others

As children safely explore their surroundings, the need for interaction with peers and for interactive play becomes apparent. Children learn to share, to coexist and to respect others for who they are. This interaction not only builds the foundation for future socialization but also gives children the opportunity to fail and recover as they develop relationships. Building relationships is pivotal for the child with a disability, who needs the support of family and friends through every stage.

When we help children develop healthy relationships, we empower them to overcome the obstacles that may come their way. We also have the opportunity to introduce them to Jesus Christ and encourage them to engage in the most significant relationship available to humankind.

ENCOURAGING EMOTIONAL WELLNESS

Children with disabilities may often seem to resist relationship. They desire to be loved and accepted unconditionally, yet their behavior may seem antisocial. They use this coping mechanism to protect themselves from pain and rejection. Ironically, their behavior usually stems from an emotional need that can be met only by developing healthy, lifelong relationships. We should encourage children to take the risk of friendship so they may reap its wonderful rewards.

The Emotion Is the Motion

Emotions have been defined in many ways but, literally, they are "what *moves* [emphasis added] us to pursue our goals; they fuel our motivation, and our motives in turn drive our perceptions and shape our actions."[5] Hence, emotions shape our actions and behavior. Many believe that the physically strongest always wins, but history has given us many examples to the contrary. The battle does not always go to the strongest, but rather it is the "will to win" (emotional strength) that many times makes the difference.

Throughout my twenty-three years of working with children in Africa, I have seen children with disabilities that occurred at birth or by an illness, children traumatized and maimed by conflict and injustice, and children orphaned by disease or famine. I believe that emotional strength is crucial to a child being able to make sense of his world and to begin learning to adjust in it.

Emotional well-being is often measured by standards of "normal" behavior in children. As long as a child does not cry all the time or throw temper tantrums, we assume everything is fine. The truth is that by the time a child starts exhibiting behavior problems, the issue may be quite serious. By definition, the *emotion* produces the *motion*. For this reason, we should not be afraid of the emotions a child is expressing; rather, we should seek to understand their significance in light of the child's emotional needs.

Emotions affect the behavior and attitudes of children, with or without disabilities. My own daughter, who has a severe learning disability, expressed the following in a short composition for her ninth-grade English class.

If I Could Change Anything in My Life

By Reah Bovard

If I could change anything in my life, it would be to finish my schoolwork faster. If I finished earlier, I would not have to be so stressed out about it. I think it would be so cool if I could get all my homework done in two hours a day instead of four hours. If I had more free time, I would be in drama, basketball, soccer and field hockey. That would be so awesome to play all these games and be in drama instead of working on assignments 24 hours a day, seven days a week. I could have fun.

Another thing I would like to change would be to improve my concentration so I could improve my grades. If I have better grades, I could be able to some day reach my goal of being a pediatric doctor. I think it would be so cool if all my grades were As. One of these days . . . Just think with me for a minute about me being a doctor. I think it will be hard, but I will never give up. I think concentration is a big thing when it comes to schoolwork, so I am hoping that some day I will be able to improve my concentration.

Something I would want to change is how to understand people better. I think that would help so much, especially if I get to know somebody better and have friends.

It has been my observation that people generally think that a child with a physical handicap must have mental impairments as well. I have observed adults talking loudly to a child who is blind but whose hearing is acute, or talking down to a twenty-two-year-old man who happens not to have legs. While neither of these reactions seems appropriate, they are reality. Asking people with disabilities what they are feeling is uncomfortable for many of us. In the African context, people do little more than exchange greetings and inquire about the family's health or whether it rained. This lack of substantive conversation tends to leave these children lonely, full of questions and feeling quite misunderstood. Children may then become aggressive and seem angry, or withdraw and become passive.

Emotions, both negative and positive, are expressed in the lives of children with disabilities, so the best solution is not to try to suppress the emotion, but to try to help the child understand the origin of the emotions and express them in healthy ways.

Emotional Impact of a Disability

Several factors influence the impact a particular disability has on the child:

- The age or developmental stage at which the child became disabled.

For example, before age six, children tend to live in more of a fantasy world. Life is a cartoon, and they typically do not realize the extent of their disability or the consequences. The cartoon character who gets thrown down, beat up and run over by a train wakes up the next morning just fine. The children may not accept their situation as final, and they may, for example, expect a missing arm or leg to somehow come back at some point. They are also quick to blame themselves for the loss and for creating problems for Mom and Dad.

From six to eleven years of age, children's thinking becomes more concrete, and they are able to grasp the permanency of an injury. They ask specific questions, want factual answers and gain great strength from their playmates and friends who accept them and love them for who they are.

Youth think in abstract terms and may feel overwhelmed by the consequences of the disability. They tend to repress their emotions, avoid talking with adults and express their emotions behaviorally through conflicts with everyone around them. For them it is a "mad dash" to restore normalcy and control.

• The traumatic event that may have caused the disability.

If the child is the only one injured and the event was not shared by others, the child may be able to focus on her own injuries and issues, for the most part. However, if the injury is the result of a violent conflict that affected other family members as well, the child may be concerned for the others, and her own emotions may be delayed or repressed. It has been our experience, both in Rwanda and in Kenya, that children who have disabilities or who have experienced other losses due to conflict or war experience both primary and secondary trauma issues. As a result, they repress their feelings and eventually have symptoms of depression. For example, in Rwanda twenty-two percent of the orphans assessed showed symptoms of severe depression, and nearly sixty percent had symptoms of moderate depression. Only eighteen percent of the children had no symptoms of depression.[6]

This scenario sounds awful unless you know that, following the 1994 genocide, a UNICEF survey estimated that 99.9 percent of the children witnessed violence firsthand, 79.6 percent saw family members killed, 87.5 percent saw dead bodies or body parts, and 90.6 percent had experienced life-threatening events.[7] It therefore stands to reason that these children need more psychosocial support than others as they try to make sense of their world.

• The parents' reaction to the event and their emotional state.

Whether a child is born with a disability or the disability is the result of an accident or conflict, parental support is vital. This provision of care proves difficult because the parents are grieving and emotionally strained, while at the same time trying to "be strong" for their child. In addition, if the parents grow to resent their children because of the "bad luck" they have brought to the home, this attitude will negatively affect the children. When children have the support of their parents and family, they usually recover from the emotional impact much better. A five-year-old girl, whom I was counseling following the 1998 Nairobi bomb blast, told me plainly that during the explosion and chaos of that day she was not afraid at all. When I asked her why, she calmly reported, "My mommy was there with me." This revelation from a child who was blown from one office building into another and should have been terrified! The support of the parent is key.

- The reaction of siblings and extended family.

The response of parents and siblings is crucial to the emotional recovery and well-being of the child with a disability. The extended family provides critical support to the child and the parents of the child. If grandparents accept grandchildren with their disabilities and treat them the same as the other grandchildren, their affirmation helps these children develop self-esteem and self-confidence, which will encourage them to make greater attempts at socialization. Family acceptance is a way for children to "test the water"; if children feel accepted by their extended family, they may feel free to venture into the community and risk exposure to others.

- Attitudes of peers, friends and community.

The real test for children with disabilities comes when they meet the attitudes of peers and the community. Their parents and family may accept and love them because they "have to." They may tell children that they look great to make them feel better, but peers may not feel the same obligation or responsibility. They can find other friends. Acceptance among their peers is critical as children move into adolescence, when identity issues surface and become important. If friends and peers do not accept them, they may feel totally rejected, and their self-esteem and self-confidence are shattered. Failure to socialize at this point may produce wounds that take time to heal. At this juncture, parental acceptance and understanding is in order—and lots of prayer. The friends and peers also may need some information and some time to adjust to the changes.

- The family support system.

Another key impact factor is the support system that the family has within its community or church. If the family tends to stay away from functions and does not participate or have a strong church family or community care system, the parents may not receive the support they need to handle the situation.

The best illustration I have seen of a support system comes from our early days as missionaries in the Mbooni Hills in the Eastern Province of Kenya. If someone were sick and unable to reach the clinic, he would be put in a stretcher and carried by four men. When they reached the top of the mountain, sweating profusely, they would be happy to have made the journey in anticipation of the sick person being treated in the hospital. The four men carrying the sick person represent four pillars of support: the relatives, friends, church and community that may surround the family and provide comfort and encouragement in the time of need.

- The child's perception, personality and temperament.

The emotional impact of a disability is also affected by the perception children have of a traumatic event and the resulting injuries. How they view the event is related to their previous experiences, their personalities and their temperaments.

Perception is how children receive and understand the information, while their personalities and temperaments relate more to how they may deal with the information. *Personality* tends to determine how children think and act as they adjust to life. *Temperament* is related more to their natural disposition or the way they regulate themselves.[8]

These important internal dimensions affect the emotional impact of the trauma, the subsequent recovery, and the lifestyle the child will lead. All three dimensions are contributing factors in how the emotion translates into behavior when faced with the crisis of disability.

- Personal acceptance of the disability.

An additional internal factor affects the emotional impact: the character of a child. This dimension is one of the most powerful in that it can determine the life paths that children take as they adjust to having a disability and accept their purpose in life. This is when children make choices and "marks" along the way that influence others.[9] One of the most incredible things I have seen in children with disabilities is how, as they adjust to their situation, they become the most energetic in serving others. Esther, who is blind, leads our girls' choir and does her duties flawlessly. Peter, who still walks on his knees, is a tremendous caregiver for children living with AIDS and has been a great chaplain at the Bethany Crippled Children's Center in Kijabe, Kenya. These young people have overcome the greatest of difficulties to influence other children in a positive way.

Esther's Story

By Esther Sarah Wangui

My name is Esther, and I am 16 years old. I am glad because I am saved, and I love the Lord as my personal Savior. When I was not saved, I was getting mad and beating my fellow pupils in my school, but the Lord has changed me completely. My mother's name is Rose Nyambura. I do not know my father, even though I am told that he lives in Nanyuki town and that he is a policeman. They tell me his name is King'ori, but I do not know what he looks like. I was named after my grandmother, who is still living. My mother's parents were staying in Lamu, Coast Province, Kenya, where my grandfather died of malaria. I have three brothers, and I am the only girl in the family. Before I joined the Karundas Girls' Home, my mom used to lack school fees for me. She used to earn 70 shillings per day (US$1) and would take me to school later than other students. The family was under strain because of school fees, but these days it is a bit better because primary education is free in our country.

I became blind when I was six years old. It started on the day I was sent by my aunt to her friend's house to take her money for the "merry-go-round." (The members of the group make monetary contributions, and each one takes turns to receive the full amount given by the group.) Because her contribution was late, she was to pay a fine of 10 shillings. My aunt did not have the money, so I went back to inform her friend. When I got back to my aunt's house, I started feeling as if something was all over my body. I did not go to school the next day and had a headache and stomachache for the next three days. Over the next week, I had weakness in my legs and was unable to walk. Then my eyes began to be affected, and each time I told my teacher that I could not see, she told me I was pretending. She later realized there was a problem when I started writing in big letters, and I was sent back home.

When my mother realized that there was a problem, I was taken to the General Hospital in Nyeri town and was scheduled to go there every month for eye appointments. But my mother could not afford the treatments, so I became totally blind. My mother felt bad because of my blindness, but there was nothing she could do. She believed that the lady is the one who caused my blindness by casting some kind of spell over me. But the neighbors came to comfort her and told her not to seek revenge because the Lord knows about this. I was at a public primary school before I lost my sight, and then I went to Thika School for the Blind. I felt happy at school because I could do things like study and clean, and we sometimes went for trips in Nairobi. At school, I learned many different subjects like science, math, English and others in the normal school curriculum.

I dropped out of school again in the year 2000 because my mom could not afford school fees. Then I was sexually assaulted by a man, so my grandmother took me to a nearby clinic. I feel so bad when I think about that incident, that if I found him, I would like him to be killed because I feel shame.

I am fine, I am cared for and well protected, but I still have difficulty moving from place to place since I have to be directed so that I do not lose my way. I step on our dog sometimes. I am also happy because even the small children at the center love me, and many of the girls are my friends. I am also happy for the three special-needs teachers at the home and the staff who help me when I get depressed and worried.

I am not angry with my mother because, though she could not get everything I needed, she was trying. I like reading, singing and helping others. I also love myself the way I am because the Bible tells us to love ourselves and also to love others. I feel happy since other people also love me. I feel I am capable of doing something good for God and for others. I feel I must be beautiful, and I know I am bright in my schoolwork, and I can sing. I would like to be a teacher and a singer when I finish school.

Although depression may be associated with the emotional impact of a disabling injury, it should be regarded as part of the natural healing process.

Understanding the Emotional Impact of Loss

Loss is observed when people are deprived of, or go without, something they valued. When children have disabilities, whatever the cause—since birth or by accident or by war—they experience great loss. The loss may be of a limb or physical function, a developmental and educational opportunity, or independence and control of their environment.

The emotional impact of loss is evident in children. Self-blame is a typical reaction to a traumatic event that results in loss. Children may experience guilty feelings and believe that their loss is a punishment from God for bad words, thoughts or deeds. They may begin to blame themselves for problems that arise in the family, especially when they see their parents struggling to accept the situation.

David's Story

By David Peter Maina

My name is David Peter Maina, and I am almost 18 years old. I was born in a crowded town, and my mom always had trouble finding food and other things we needed. I guess I was not very good when I was young, and I did not like to stay in school. I was always running away from something. Well, one of the days I was running away, I happened to be on a bus in the city center of Nairobi. It was August 7, 1998, at about 10:30 in the morning when a bomb ripped through the American Embassy and decimated the surrounding buildings. Our bus was blown off the road, and most of the people on board were killed. They were in pieces all around me, and I did not know whether I was dead or alive. I felt so numb, and I could not think. When people discovered that I was still alive, they put me in a vehicle and rushed me to Kenyatta National Hospital in Nairobi. There the doctors found that my jaw was ripped off my face and I had multiple lacerations.

That event was only the beginning of my suffering. I woke up in the hospital terrified and in so much pain I thought I would go crazy. I tried to scream, but only strange noises came out of my mouth. I was given spoonfuls of water. I could hear the screams of agony from the hundreds of others being treated. Some of the doctors and nurses tried to calm me down, but others scared me. I did not know what had happened, and I did not want to know. I did not want to talk about anything; not that I could talk at that point. I did not even have a mouth. After much work, the doctors successfully built a temporary jaw from some bone in my leg. It was months before I could eat any food, and when I was released from the hospital, I had nowhere to go.

Lots of people tried to talk to me, but I just ran away from them. Until I met "Mom." She listened to me and did not mind that I could not get the words out right. I found it easy to talk to her. I even told her how stupid I thought those little yellow bomb-blast counseling books were and that I would tear them all up. I did not know she was the author, until one day she asked me if I would like to go home with her. She invited me to join her children's home because I was not coping well in Nairobi. Every little thing set me off, and I was not ready to go to school and have everyone looking at me. She thought I might do a bit better away from the city and with other boys with problems similar to mine.

Many boys who were trying to get over their problems lived at the Mount Kenya Children's Home. Many of us had been living on the street before we came here. I found out that "Mom" was Dr. Wendy Bovard, the one who wrote the little yellow book! I began to read it, and it made me desire to talk about everything I had experienced. Days turned into weeks and weeks turned into months, and before I knew it, my anger was melting away and I did not mind mixing with the other guys. I know I was not easy to live with; I could startle easily and get so upset over every little thing. I still had trouble eating and sleeping, but opening up to "Mom" and the staff and even other boys helped. The problem was that I had to keep having more operations, and every time I had to go back to the hospital, I got all upset again. Also, when I went to the anniversary events, I remembered those dead people and everything, and I felt sick for days. But one time I got to meet the U.S. secretary of state. She had seen me in the hospital once and remembered me. That was special.

Then I had to go to the United States for another operation. The surgery was terrible, but everything else was great. I liked it there and want to go back for school one day. I have been going to computer school since I finished my Standard 8 exam. It was hard to get the things I needed for school because I was having so many things fixed on my face. A few months ago I got new teeth, but the scars are still bad on my face. I wish they could make my face look like nothing ever happened, but for now I just want them to finish fixing my face and let me get on with my education. I would like to be a doctor some day and help kids that get hurt like I did.

David taught me so much about the natural emotional stages of the trauma-recovery process and illustrated much of what I had known intellectually, but had not experienced firsthand.

Assisting Children in the Trauma-Recovery Process

Wright makes the following observations about the normal stages of recovery in children:[10]

- *Stage 1*–Denial

The first stage, denial, is how children absorb the loss on their terms, so avoid arguing at this point.

The first time David saw the children's book I wrote, *Questions Kids Are Asking About the Bomb Blast*, he tore it to pieces! He was not ready to come face to face with what had happened. Later, when he finally was able to accept the situation he was in, the book became such a comfort to him, especially when he found out I was the one who wrote it.

- *Stage 2*–Frustration

Frustration leads to emotional outbursts, aggression and fits of anger. Encourage children to safely vent their anger and frustration.

I was asked to work with David because he had become so aggressive and so difficult to handle in the hospital that even his family could not take him home.

We slowly established a relationship, and when he did finally leave the hospital, he came home with me, and we walked through much of the recovery together.

- *Stage 3*–Guilt and self-blame

In the third stage, children feel guilty and begin to blame themselves.

David was not supposed to be on that bus that was passing the embassy at 10:35 that morning when the bomb ripped through the city center. He had jumped on without permission and had not even paid the fare. He was running from his own life and was one of the few survivors that were on that bus. His family did not know where he was for weeks.

- *Stage 4*–Distress

Distress and feelings of being overwhelmed may occur as a result of repressed emotion. Caregivers need to encourage continued communication and to help children find their own solutions.

- *Stage 5*–Depression and loneliness

These emotions may result when young people manage to push everyone away, although that was not what they wanted.

- *Stage 6*–Panic

Panic occurs because children may feel great anxiety about themselves and their future.

- *Stage 7*–Hostility and resentment

These are natural emotions, and children need to be helped to find positive ways of expressing these strong feelings.

- *Stage 8*–Hopeless to hopeful

Hopeless and helpless, children feel unable to return to their routine or usual activities. Hope gradually returns to children who receive support from those around them. They begin to think about the future in a more positive way and begin to appreciate it. It is a struggle to affirm their new reality but, little by little, a new identity emerges, and they eventually embrace it. They will never be the same, but they will be stronger individuals who understand themselves and are better able to accept their own and others' limitations.

That many of these children in crisis even survive their circumstances is a wonder; indeed, it is in these settings that we discover the true meaning of a word most difficult to define: "resilience."

THE CHARACTERISTICS OF RESILIENCE

Whether skipping rope in Zambia with orphans with AIDS, swimming in Rwanda with children who may have one arm but who survived genocide, or hiking through the Mount Kenya Forest with children who live on the streets or who are victims of tribal clashes, the faces are the same, the smiles are incredible and the stories even more penetrating. Children in the African continent have endured some of the most unbelievable situations known to humanity. Yet these precious children have shown great resilience in the midst of disheartening life conditions.

Why do some vulnerable children who have experienced such trauma find their way back to normalcy, while others live in fear and are never able to function again? Resilience is not easily understood or explained. Like the wind, you cannot see resilience, but you know it is there and you see its effects. Some have compared resilience to a ball that bounces back when thrown to the ground. When the ball is filled with enough air, it rebounds easily, but when the ball is flat, it cannot rebound well, if even at all.

Even though children have little control over some factors of resilience, others can be taught or built upon. Some of these factors are external in nature while others are internal. Some years ago, Stefan Vanistendael of the International Catholic Child Bureau illustrated resilience with a drawing of a house that included a foundation, walls and roof.[11]

- The *foundation* of the house, commonly accepted as the most important element, represents *unconditional acceptance* from family and significant adults.
- The *walls* represent the capacity to discover *meaning and purpose* in life and to develop *healthy self-esteem*.
- The *roof* represents life skills and a sense of humor.

Children who bounce back from the hard knocks of life seem to share these five characteristics and strengths.

Building the Foundation

The foundation of a building determines its strength and sets the standard for its structural soundness. The foundation of resilience is the unconditional acceptance of parents or significant adults. In my experience, this foundation most likely includes extended family, which is vital in the life of a child struggling with disability. Peter refers to the time he spent with his mother and his grandfather. He did not realize he was different until he began watching other siblings go off to school. His parents and grandparents had accepted him unconditionally, and that acceptance gave him the foundation he needed to move on with his life and accept himself and God's purpose for his life.

In Peter's Words

By Peter Gitonga

At first I did not know that I was not created like the other children in my family. My parents were kind. My mom would take me to the clinic once a year, but I did not think much of those trips. In fact, I enjoyed them so much because I got to visit and receive special gifts from other relatives that met us along the way. I came to think of my disability when my sisters and brother went to school. I felt lonely when they left me at home during the day and my mother went to work in the farm or to fetch firewood from the forest. I started thinking about myself and came to realize I could not walk to school, about six miles away, like they did. I used to comfort myself by sharing stories with my grandfather about the Kikuyu people of old. He even gave me a cow, and I was happy about it. But in 1996 my grandfather passed away. This loss was followed by a drought, and my cow died. I began to lose hope in life. Because of the drought, my mom went to work in an irrigated farm to provide food for the family. Life became even more difficult as my elder sisters had finished form four (grade 12) and they needed jobs. My mother used to pray and ask God to help her because of my condition.

In mid-1996 we saw *wazungu* coming in a Nissan vehicle and sometimes a lady and young children on bicycles. They used to pass by our house. One day I heard people talking about the *wazungu* who were building a school for children who had never been to school. The people who were working on that project started to come to the community and were kind to us. They encouraged my mother, who had to cultivate and farm for the family's food. I thought that was a good opportunity for her to go and seek a place for school for me, but she seemed hesitant; I think she was losing hope of finding help for me. One day when she was working, I walked all the way to that school. I came back a blessed child because of the way they welcomed me, even though I could not understand them because I never knew English. I told my family about the warm welcome I had received from the *wazungu* and some gifts that they had given me, which surprised my family. After meeting those *wazungu*, I came to find that they were friendly. Their son Jonathan loved me, and he could give me anything I needed.

I got to stay in Jonathan's room for about a year while I studied. He graduated from form four and went to college in America, so I moved into the boys' home. They all welcomed me and gathered around me and started asking me questions, like what happened to my hands and feet. It was difficult to explain to them, but they told me they had seen some people with legs like mine. Some of them became my friends, while others feared and did not come close to me. After some months, they became used to me and we became friends. Sometimes in the afternoon we used to go to the field and play football, and I used to be the goalkeeper. It was fun to jump and catch the ball.

Difficulties

One of the most difficult things for me was that I was used to only my parents and other members of my family. When I came to the boys' home, I met new people such as the staff and children whom I was not used to. It was difficult to socialize with them, and I found myself spending most of my time alone. I got lonely and missed my family. My mom used to wash my clothes for me, and now I had to do it for myself. It was difficult at the beginning, but I got used to it, and now I feel happy for being able to do such things for myself.

Dreams

I had dreams just like any other child. I dreamed that one day I would go to school and get a higher education, and after finishing school I would get a job and have my own money. I dream of becoming rich one day, building a house and having a family of my own.

Feelings

Most of the time I do not feel like I have a disability. I feel like I am as normal as anybody else in the community. What makes me feel bad is times when I cannot do some things I wish to do. Then I feel like I have done something to God, for which He could not forgive me. Sometimes I feel like this is a punishment. At such times I get quiet and stay alone for a while until I feel better.

Encouragement

After I joined the home, I started school and realized that there was still hope for me. I became interested in the Bible and would preach in the prayer meetings sometimes. Preaching helped me feel that I can do something that leaves people blessed. I also sang in church choirs and became interested in music. The verse in the Bible that blesses me is Philippians 4:13, which says, "I can do all things through Christ who strengthens me" (NKJV).

Just as the walls of a building protect its interior, the capacity to discover meaning and purpose in life and to develop self-esteem serves to protect children through the recovery and to strengthen their resilience for the long haul.

Establishing Strong Walls

Discovery is a pivotal point for children with disabilities. Discovering purpose in their lives gives them strength to focus on one thing that they can do to contribute. When Reah discovered that her purpose in life was to be a doctor, she began to focus on the steps that would make that goal possible. The first step she took was getting admitted into a school that did not admit children with learning disabilities. She then stunned the teachers with her two hundred and fifty-percent effort. Everyone needs to feel significant in some way, and we have seen that the capacity of children to discover their significance gives them emotional strength to take risks and try things that seem impossible. At that point, they decide it is better to risk and fail than to never have tried. When children discover meaning and purpose in life, they strengthen their resilience.

Healthy self-esteem is another "wall" that transforms the impossible into reality. Self-worth affects the way children perceive themselves in the circumstances and situations they face. For example, Esther is blind and yet convinced that she is beautiful. That belief motivates her to get up every morning, feel her way around her bed, bathe and dress herself, go to class and read in Braille, so that when she finishes school she can be a teacher and singer. More than self-esteem, that motivation is confidence and faith in her abilities and in the God of this universe, who "is not slack concerning his promise"(2 Pet. 3:9 KJV).

Without a roof, a house cannot offer much security. In the broken world in which they live, various life skills as well as a sense of humor give children a layer of competence and confidence that they need.

The Roof of Resilience

The Nairobi bomb blast left David scarred in many ways. His education was disrupted and, by the time the doctors pronounced him well, he was emotionally bankrupt. Only a few months later, his reconstructed jaw was broken. He was again unable to eat and faced another series of surgical operations. David joined our informal school and was able to study from a Christian home-school curriculum that my own children used. This plan enabled him to continue with education even with many visits to the hospital. In addition, he learned to use a computer and worked in the mechanic shop when he was up to it. This experience enabled him to continue developing additional life skills to build on for the rest of his life. Both informal education and vocational training have made the difference in his life.

Humor is always helpful to children as a way of processing life's difficulties. When children can laugh at their mistakes and see the lighter side of life, they are better able to face the harsh realities. Rehabilitation, transition and painstaking comeback all have lighter moments. Treasure those moments and hold on to them for the tougher days.

Wangechi, a ten-year-old street girl, had survived every kind of abuse you can imagine. When she was nine, she spent months recovering in the hospital after a car hit her. The doctors put metal plates in her hips, which enabled her to walk again. But we forgot about the metal plates when we gave her a part in the Christmas play that required her to bend in adoration of the newborn King. At our first rehearsal, when it came time to bow, she just smiled broadly and lay right down on the floor. It was all or nothing! We all laughed together with Wangechi as we do on many occasions. Her decision to laugh—and laugh loudly—has helped her integrate with the other girls and become friends with them. Laughter truly is a great medicine! When children are able to see some humor in their situations, they gain strength to "hang in there" on the tough days and keep putting one foot in front of the other, literally.

Children with special needs are indeed God's special people; no matter what the context, their lights shine bright. They bring much joy to the world, and their lives gain such meaning when we recognize their abilities to see as we have never seen, walk as we have never walked and teach what we could never have learned, had they not been such willing partners on the journey of life.

NOTES

The epigraph to part II is from Samantha Abeel, *Reach for the Moon* (New York: Orchard, 2001). Poet and writer Samantha Abeel was diagnosed at the age of thirteen with a learning disability called dyscalculia. Her gift for words not only gives her a way to share her feelings but also to shine. *Reach for the Moon* was published when she was fifteen years old.

1. Brigid Daniel, Sally Wassell, and Robbie Gilligan, *Child Development for Child Care and Protection Workers* (London: Jessica Kingsley, 1999), 31.

2. African Charter on the Rights and Welfare of the Child, OAU Doc. CAB/LEG/24.9/49 (1990), *entered into force* Nov. 29, 1999, Pt. 1.

3. Ibid., Art. 6.

4. *A Generation at Risk: Hope for the Future*, Report (Nairobi: AEA, 1996).

5. Daniel Goleman, *Working with Emotional Intelligence* (New York: Bantam Books, 1998), 126.

6. Adventist Development and Relief Agency (ADRA) Rwanda, *Outdoor Adventure Therapy Pre-Pilot Program*, Assessment Report, June 2001, 3.

7. United Nations Children's Fund (UNICEF) / United Nations Development Programme (UNDP), Report, 1999.

8. Archibald D. Hart, *Stress and Your Child: Know the Signs and Prevent the Harm* (Dallas: Word Publishing, 1992), 73.

9. Ibid., 74.

10. H. Norman Wright, *A Practical Guide for Pastors, Counselors and Friends: Crisis Counseling*, rev. ed. (Ventura, CA: Regal Books / Gospel Light, 1993), 157–58.

11. Stefan Vanistendael, *Growth in the Muddle of Life: Resilience; Building on People's Strengths* (Geneva: International Catholic Child Bureau, 1995).

CHAPTER FOUR

EDUCATIONAL NEEDS

* * *

Laura Sandidge

LOVING children is more than an emotion. It is a responsibility and a requirement. Loving children is not a passive endeavor; in contrast, it requires an intense amount of activity. One of the ways that activity manifests itself is by meeting the educational needs of the child. An educational need is something that needs to be taught. In most cases an educator or caregiver is the person who is doing the teaching. Educational needs are broad and encompass foundational needs, which would include social-emotional needs and behavioral needs, as well as academic needs.

The focus of this book is children with disabilities, or special needs. Children with special needs have in many ways the same needs that other children their age have. They need love, acceptance, belonging, security and a safe environment to grow in. All children have a certain level of academic needs; however, the formal education process is relatively a small part of life. In some countries, for some children, there is no formal education process at all. The goal of this chapter is to help you, the reader, to think of a variety of educational needs that a child may have so that your specific programming may better address those needs, formally or informally. An additional goal of this chapter is to help you be aware of what a huge responsibility it is for you to be a part of a child's education. If God has placed you in such a position, for whatever amount of time and for whatever reason, you are an important part of that child's overall development. This is the Lord's work, so it is not useless. We must face this task with enthusiasm, diligence and energy.

THE BASIC NEEDS

So what are the foundational, or basic, needs for a child? There are many, depending on the researcher that an individual studies. Glasser[1] states that children have five basic needs that must be met before we can address academic issues. Those are the need for survival, love, power, freedom and fun. This theory, called "Control Theory of Motivation," states that behavior is never caused by a response to outside things. Instead, behavior is inspired by what a person wants most at any given time: survival, love, power, freedom or any other basic human need, such as the need for fun. Glasser feels that all living creatures "control" their behavior to maximize their need for satisfaction. According to Glasser, if students are not motivated to do their work, it is because they view that work as irrelevant to their basic human needs. Many times as educators, we negate one or more of these needs. It is common sense to understand that a child needs to be able to survive and to have love. However, we often negate children's need for power, freedom and fun. We cannot if we want sound and happy children that are able to live life to their fullest.

There are other needs that young people have that need to be addressed. Brazelton and Greenspan mention several of them in their combined work.[2] These well-respected researchers state that there are six essential needs that all children have: (1) ongoing, nurturing relationships; (2) physical protection, safety and regulation; (3) experiences tailored to individual differences; (4) developmentally appropriate experiences; (5) limit setting, structure and expectations; and (6) stable, supportive communities and cultural continuity. To fully comprehend these needs, further study would be required. However, we will briefly discuss each of the above-stated needs.

The need for ongoing, nurturing relationships is becoming more and more understood as individuals comprehend the issues surrounding attachment. Children who attach to their caregivers in a healthy manner have a greater capacity to benefit socially and educationally than children who are unattached. Basically, they start life and often finish life in a better place than unattached children. Sadly, many children do not have the benefit of having a healthy attachment or an ongoing nurturing relationship. However, that does not mean that we cannot make every opportunity to create that situation for the child. An important concept to keep in mind when thinking about attachment is a concept called resiliency. Letourneau says,

> Resiliency refers to individuals' competence and successful adaptation in the face of significant adversity, such as biological risk factors or stressful life events. In this context, resiliency represents a state or characteristic within the individual. Protective factors, such as high-quality parent-infant interaction, mediate

the effects of adversity to promote resilient outcomes in the in-
dividual.[3]

A significant component of developing resiliency in a child is to have
a consistent and caring relationship with an adult. The adult could be a
parent, teacher or friend.[4] Higher cognitive, language and social-emotional
development has been correlated to positive interactions between a parent or
caregiver and the child.[5] This would indicate that an individual with special
needs, whether he is at-risk or significantly impaired, would benefit strongly
by the concept and facilitation of resiliency. We can do this by being caring,
trustworthy and stable individuals in the lives of children.

The second essential need that Brazelton and Greenspan said children
required was the need for physical protection, safety and regulation. The
terms "physical protection" and "safety" are globally understood. It should
be evident that all children, no matter what their circumstances, should
experience physical protection and safety. Unfortunately, that is not the
case for many children. Domestic violence, substance abuse, war and exploitation all too often prevent children from experiencing these basic concepts. The term "regulation" is not as easy to understand. Brazelton and
Greenspan state that central nervous system regulation involves "reactivity
to sensations (sound, touch, movement, pain), the capacity to process and
comprehend those sensations (e.g. language, visual-spatial thinking), and
the capacity to plan and sequence actions (e.g., problem solving, executive
functions)."[6]

There are many definitions of the term "regulation," or "self-regulation."
The term has been connected to concepts such as emotion regulation, impulse control and self-control. Bronson[7] does an excellent job of explaining
the application of the term by stating that it is often rooted in the parent-
infant attachment, and is manifested in the child's language, thought and
behavior.

Brazelton and Greenspan's third need is for experiences tailored to individual differences, which means that we acknowledge that children and
adults are unique. Everyone is born with their own temperament and physi-
ology. Every child has innate strengths and weaknesses, and children respond
to life's circumstances in a variety of ways. That is one of the great beauties
of God's creation. Having the expectation that all children will respond to
situations in the same way is irrational thinking on our part. We have certain expectations for children, given our culture and society, but we need
to understand that how a child responds to those expectations significantly
depends on her temperament, physiological makeup and life experiences.

The fourth need is for developmentally appropriate experiences. This essential need takes into consideration the child with special needs. There is a continuum of human development that we expect an individual to accomplish. It is typical for a child to complete certain developmental milestones in an age-appropriate manner. For example, we expect a child to begin talking, walking and interacting with others at certain ages in his life. Those milestones help us to gauge if he is age-appropriate. If he does not reach developmental milestones in a typical fashion, we can measure the developmental delay based on the time it takes him to reach those milestones. As parents, caregivers and educators, we need to ensure that children are given many opportunities to have developmentally appropriate experiences in an age-appropriate manner. This does not mean that all these experiences should be couched in work. It is important to remember that children learn through play. Remember Glasser's basic need of having fun? Children do that through play. Play is the work of children, and too many children do not have enough opportunities for play. Play can provide exploration, experimentation and manipulation opportunities that children can use to construct knowledge. During play, children experiment and refine their learning through feedback from the environment, peers and adults. Through play, children develop their imaginations and creativity. They practice and refine their skills. Never let it be said that play is unimportant for children. It is vital!

The fifth need Brazelton and Greenspan discussed was the need for limit setting, structure and expectations. This means that children need to know what they are allowed to do and what they are not allowed to do. They need to know when things are appropriate and when they are not. They need to know how far they can go physically and behaviorally. There are a variety of ways to do that. Depending on the life experiences of the child, one could approach setting limits, developing structure and determining expectations for her in a flexible way or in a structured way. Realistically, however, the life experiences of the adult caregiver often determine whether limit setting, structure and expectations for the child will be delivered in a firm or flexible way. Setting limits and having certain expectations for a child implies that there are outcomes for her if that set criteria is, or is not, met. When people hear the word "consequence," they often think of the word "punishment." That is not how the word is being used in this context. In this context the word "consequence" is being used behaviorally within the sequence of learning called "Antecedent-Behavior-Consequence," or ABC. For example, when a child is learning something, there is an *antecedent*, or something that happens prior, such as the caregiver saying, "Do not leave the yard," or an expectation has been set, such as the child should not steal. This sets up the choice for the individual. She can either meet the expectation and stay within the set limits, or not. There is an element of internal conflict that surrounds this choice. What happens next in the ABC sequence is the *behavior* of the child. For example, she does or does not do what you told her to do; or she does or does not comply with the expectation that was set. The pivotal component is that the behavior happens. What happens next in the consequence phase determines whether that behavior will or will not happen again. The *consequence* is the final component of the ABC sequence of learning. This consequence could be reinforcing or punishing. If a consequence is reinforcing, the behavior will maintain or increase. In other words, it will happen again. It does not matter if the behavior was desired or not.[8,9] If the consequence is punishing to the individual, the behavior will most likely diminish. This is a simple discussion of a complicated topic. However, it is foundational in setting limits, determining structure and setting expectations.

To further explain the ABC sequence of learning, imagine a scenario in which the antecedent is that a child sees some candy in the hands of another child. The behavior is that he takes the candy out of the other child's hand and eats it. In this particular scenario the antecedent and the behavior are fairly straightforward. The consequence is what happens next. He eats the candy. He wanted the candy, and he ate the candy. It would be logical to assume that the behavior that the child exhibited was reinforced. That means that it will happen again. Let us change the consequence in this next scenario. Let us say that the child begins to eat the candy, but it is not good; in fact, it is bitter, he gets sick to his stomach and his parent gives him a strong, stern warning about his behavior. All of these things are not pleasant to the child. He does not like what happened at all. Therefore, that behavior was punished; there was no physical outcome such as spanking, but the behavior was punished just the same. Consequently, the behavior will not increase; it will either stay the same or diminish over time. As a word of caution, remember that the expectations of a child's behavior must be age-appropriate. For instance, it is an unrealistic expectation to think that a two-year-old child will be able to sit still for an hour. That is not age-appropriate. Children who are two years old have a limited attention span and like to move from task to task. A more acceptable age-appropriate expectation would be to try to have the child sit still for three minutes.

Finally, Brazelton and Greenspan state that the sixth essential need for children is the need for stable, supportive communities and cultural continuity. Meeting the needs of a child is not a Western thought. It is a universal requirement and a global need. One culture is not better than another culture. It is a wonderful thing if we personally love and have pride in our own culture and country. However, that does not mean that our country or culture is the best. Children need to function within their society, no matter where that is. They need to understand an element of written and spoken language for that society. For some children it is simple. There is one culture and one society, and one language. For others it is not as clear. Their personal culture is different from the larger society, or one parent is from one cultural background while the other parent is from a different culture. Cultural diversity is a global phenomenon. In those situations, the process of learning often enhances the child's education rather than specific facts. Children need the support and activities that are offered through involvement in their neighborhood, school, church and other groups. Through participation in various groups, children learn to do things for the good of the community and the country as a whole.

Another foundational need that all children require is social and emotional competence. Welsh and Bierman say, "Social competence refers to the social, emotional, and cognitive skills and behaviors that children need for successful social adaptation."[10] "Social competence" is an umbrella term that includes social skills, peer relations, self-concept and adult relations. There is a significant amount of overlap between the terms "social competence" and "emotional competence." Consequently, we often combined the two into one term, "social-emotional competence." The research over the past several years has overwhelmingly suggested that children need a certain level of social competence or their adult life will be significantly at risk for any level of success.[11]

This world is relational. Schools, communities and the workforce all connect to people and the relationships with those people. In order to successfully function in our world, an individual has to have an element of social-emotional competence. In fact, more and more research is suggesting that a child's social-emotional competence is more at the root of a child's quality of life than academic intelligence.[12,13] Goleman goes so far as to say that social and emotional competence, or what he terms "intelligence," is a main factor in how well a person does in life. He feels that intellectual functioning only contributes to approximately twenty percent of an individual's success, while eighty percent comes from an individual's social and emotional competence. Children's current and long-term social-emotional development as well as cognitive and academic development is clearly affected by the child's social experiences with peers and adults.[14] Hartup states:

The single best childhood predictor of adult adaptation is not school grades, and not classroom behavior, but rather, the adequacy with which the child gets along with other children. Children who are generally disliked, who are aggressive and disruptive, who are unable to sustain close relationships with other children, and who cannot establish a place for themselves in the peer culture are seriously at risk.[15]

A child's long-term social and emotional adaptation, academic and cognitive development, and ability to connect successfully with the community are enhanced by frequent opportunities to strengthen social competence during childhood.[16] Therefore, if we want to help our children be successful in a variety of areas, we have to develop their social competence. The best way to do that is through the experience of developing friendships.

Peer interaction and friendships are how children learn a majority of their social and emotional competence. The ability to make and keep friends, or the development of social competence, is acquired through play and social interactions with other children. Sharing, exchanging play ideas, negotiating play roles, and responding to aggression are a few of the skills that children learn through social interactions with their peers.[17] Friendships are one of the most important parts of a child's life. It does not matter if that child has special needs or is age-appropriate. Friendships make up a major part of a child's day, and often it is the reason why a child goes to school.[18] Staub states, "Friendships with peers are often the key to a child's sense of self-identity and emotional security."[19] Friendships promote social development and social communication, and influence reasoning ability. They give the child experience with a wide array of emotions and reactions.

Children with special needs often have deficits in the area of social-emotional competence. In a study on preschool children with disabilities, they interacted less frequently with peers when compared to typically developing children.[20] In other studies, children with disabilities were less successful in their social connections with their peers and did not make the initial interactions with their peers, consequently developing fewer friendships.[21] Therefore, there is no question that if we want children to have a quality life we must help them learn to have social-emotional competence.

It would be negligent, when discussing foundational educational needs of children, if we did not mention Abraham Maslow's "Hierarchy of Needs."[22] Maslow determined a hierarchy of five levels of needs. These needs are consistent with Glasser's basic needs. In Maslow's research on the levels of the basic needs, he felt the individual, no matter what the age, could not move on to the second need until the demands of the first had been satisfied, or the third until the second level of needs had been satisfied, and so on. A diagram of Maslow's hierarchy is shown in figure 4.1.

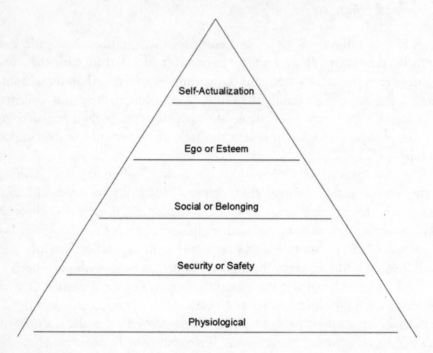

Figure 4.1 Maslow's Hierarchy of Needs

The first and most basic level is physiological needs. These are biological needs. They consist of the need for food, water, oxygen and a relatively constant body temperature. Naturally these are the strongest and most demanding of all the needs, because if a person were deprived of any of these primary needs, she could not survive.

The second level is the need for security or personal safety. When all physiological needs are satisfied and are no longer controlling thoughts and behaviors, the need for security becomes activated.

The third level is social needs, which means that the individual feels a need to belong and to feel love, affection and a sense of connectedness. At this point, people seek to overcome feelings of loneliness and alienation so they reach outward. This involves both giving and receiving love, affection and the sense of belonging.

At the fourth level, the individual looks inward and seeks to satisfy his ego needs or self-esteem and the esteem of others. When the other needs are met, the need for esteem can become dominant. These involve needs for both self-esteem and for the esteem a person gets from others. Maslow feels that humans naturally have a need for self-respect and respect from others. When these needs are satisfied, the person feels self-confident and valuable as a person in the world. When these needs are frustrated, the person feels inferior, weak, helpless and worthless.

The fifth and final level of Maslow's hierarchy is self-actualization. This means that the person experiences a sense of self-fulfillment. Maslow describes self-actualization as the point at which a person's need to be and do what she feels she was born to do is actually achieved. Because personal desires and needs are continually changing, an individual may go in and out of this final level many times within her lifetime.

There are many other foundational needs for children. Erikson felt that the concept of identity development was imperative for children and a central task in human development.[23] When thinking about identity development, he stated that there were three words that were significant—identity, impact and importance—or the three I's. Identity development entails a lifelong process for an individual to be able to understand who he is and why he is living in this place and time, or his identity. The individual needs to understand how he impacts his world. Finally, the child needs to understand his importance within his world. This process is facilitated by those vitally important caregivers in the child's life.

The three C's—capable, connected and contributing—are foundational needs and pertinent concepts that provide caregivers vital tools to make this world a better place for children.[24] All individuals, especially children, need to feel *capable* of completing the tasks given to them in a manner that meets an expected standard. All individuals, especially children, need to feel *connected* with both their peers and other adults. Finally, all individuals, especially children, need to feel that they are *contributing* in a significant way to some aspect of their life. If children are able to feel they are capable, connected and contributing in their environment, they will achieve success.

Summary of Foundational Needs of Children

The Three I's

1. Identity: Who am I?
2. Impact: What is my place in life?
3. Importance: Do I matter?

The Three C's

1. Capable
2. Connected
3. Contributing

Figure 4.2 shows the connections between these concepts.

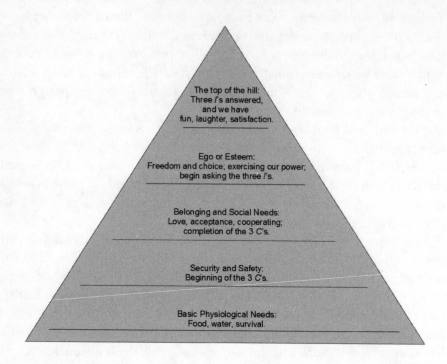

Figure 4.2 The three *I*'s and the three *C*'s develop in conjunction with Maslow's hierarchy.

As you can see, a child has many foundational educational needs, which cannot be neglected. They are vital for the well-being of our children. Caregivers have the important task of educating children in these foundational needs. They typically do that in an informal manner. This does not mean that it is not extremely important, however. Children are better able to benefit from formal academic education programs if these foundational educational needs are addressed.

ACADEMIC NEEDS

Teaching foundational educational needs to children is an ongoing process that begins before birth and is often never completed. Conversely, academic needs are addressed in a manner that is socially acceptable and valued within a culture. In many Western countries, formal academic education begins at age five and is completed after thirteen years of school or at the attainment of a certain level of expertise. In other countries, formal academics begin at the age of three and continue as long as the child shows she is able to benefit from such a program. The way a child is provided an academic education is dependent upon the culture that she lives in. Furthermore, the content and the presentation style are dependent upon the cultural mores of the country. In all actuality, even the decision to provide the child with a formal education depends on the culture. There is no question that the academic lives of children are connected to the values of their culture.

There are several global topics that are considered formal academic topics; these are typically Language Arts, Mathematics, Geography, the Sciences and History. It would spark quite a debate as to which of these topics were more important, as they all connect to each other at some level. Other courses that students learn in school are typically called "electives" in the Western culture, and there is a selection process as to who will take those courses. All of the formal academic topics are taught within the premise of a scope and a sequence. The scope consists of the topic's span, and the sequence relates to the timing that the topic components are presented. Typically the same broad topics are covered year after year. However, each year the learning is developed and expanded. In this way the premise of building upon prior knowledge is continually utilized until the individual has presumably learned all he can about a subject.

The learning process for many of the academic topics mentioned—particularly Language Arts, Mathematics and some components of the Sciences—actually begin prior to formal school. We begin the process of learning and understanding Language Arts sooner than any other academic topic through listening and speaking. Mathematic concepts such as addition and subtraction are often taught at home, before formal school begins. In most cases, children understand elementary concepts about weather and other scientific concepts prior to formal schooling. True, formal academics are taught, developed and solidified in school settings. However, many components of those topics become functional, or demonstrated within everyday life, based on experiences prior to and following formal schooling.

Language Arts typically consists of the four phases, or prongs, of listening, speaking, reading and writing. It is understood that these skills are typically learned in that order as well. Informally, children begin the learning of Language Arts literally in the womb. It has been documented that children can hear within the womb, and that they actually begin at that point of their lives to understand how to make the sounds that are typical for their culture.[25] Once they are out of the womb, they continually develop their listening, speaking, reading and writing skills. In fact, the skills of listening, speaking, reading and writing are used in every academic topic. Language Arts encompasses more than the outcomes of reading and writing. It expands to critical thought and the expression of those thoughts. It encompasses the research process, debate, and skills in reading and writing for a variety of informational texts.

There are a variety of facets that assist an individual in fully comprehending the block of learning called Language Arts. Research supports that children typically need to use oral language continually and to have a variety of informational materials read aloud to them daily. Children need to learn, understand and manipulate the building blocks of their spoken language. They also need to write and relate writing to their specific prior knowledge. They need to read and comprehend a wide assortment of books and various types of texts. They need to write and relate writing to new knowledge. Children need to develop and comprehend new vocabulary through reading and direct instruction, as well as to learn and apply comprehension strategies as materials are studied. Children utilize their critical thinking skills about what has been read and use that as their base to create new knowledge.[26] The Language Arts area requires formalized educational interventions to teach individuals skills, and it also requires informal practice of those skills to make an individual proficient. Additionally, there is no question that this area is vital to a certain measure of a quality of life for every culture and language group. It is true that an individual could learn many skills in this area without ever having formal education on the topic. However, formal educational processes enable children to have a much higher level of ability in the Language Arts area.

It has been said that math is a universal language. Math concepts are globally understood and consistent between countries, religions and genders. Math connects to music, art, science, geography and even alphabetization. Math is often thought of as conceptual thinking, or thinking that makes efficient use of the human capacity for abstraction. Math helps us learn how to organize information and to do so in a logical and analytical manner. Mathematics is the study of logical, symbolic, conceptual and quantitative relationships. Typically it is applied to physical systems. Math is taught prior to school and continues throughout life. Math has been around since the beginning of time and most likely will be around until the end of time. We use math skills every day of our lives. If we use any form of a barter system or money, read a thermometer, buy and sell items, or even cook, we are using our math skills. Math begins with the basics of adding, subtracting, multiplying and dividing. It goes on to include more demanding mathematic principles, such as algebra, geometry, calculus, trigonometry and even the formal course called "Logic." We have all benefited from a mathematician. Mathematics allows for the calculations necessary to build anything. If you are reading this in a house, math was involved. Mathematics is fundamental in its application to reality. New discoveries in math often lead to new discoveries in science, and vice versa. Math has to be presented in a systematic way. We have to present the information in such a way that the concepts build upon prior knowledge. Additionally, comprehension of this topic can be facilitated when it is presented in an active or hands-on manner.

Science and Mathematics are interconnected. Math is the foundation and structure that science rests on. Science is the study of natural, realistic, physical, qualitative relationships, generally applicable to reality.[27] Science combines information in a rational and systematic way. It uses the methods of observation, objectivity, experimentation and organization to understand and explain the patterns and structure of the universe. Science is an imperative topic; if we do not understand our physical world, we jeopardize it and our quality of life. Science connects to geology, ecology, technology and curiosity. Curiosity is at the root of understanding why. Science is a wonderful vehicle to help explain the "whys" of this world. I have often felt that God has explained many of His mysteries through science. He tells us how old a tree is through science. He helps us to understand the importance of a clean world through science. There is no question in my mind that science and religion connect and that both topics are imperative to our understanding.

Social Studies and History are the study of communities, societies and cultures. This topic may include geography as well. Perspective is imperative when teaching this subject. How we view history has everything to do with our perspective; for instance, Japanese and Americans view World War II differently. One culture is not right or wrong; however, how an individual presents a topic does depend on her worldview. History and understanding cultures, our own and others, allows us to develop pride about our community and culture. History gives us all a sense of continuance and interconnectedness. It helps us develop our sense of identity. In learning about history we fully understand where we started as a group and where we are going in our present. Amazingly profound concepts can be taught through the study of history. We learn about discrimination, the use and misuse of power, political and religious systems, and even why a culture no longer exists. Exciting presentations of historical facts can make a topic become real to a child. For a topic that is seemingly impossible to understand, presenting it in concrete terms helps him to visualize and imagine the concepts and events.

In teaching any of these subjects we need to utilize good teaching techniques. We need to remember to establish the relevance of the topic in order to assist the individual to create meaning about the topic. Individuals need to understand why a topic is important and how it has relevance to them. We need to help individuals connect their learning to prior knowledge in order to increase their comprehension. Teaching is not a sedentary or solitary activity; it involves participation, collaboration, facilitation and action. It is vital that we do not always expect individuals to understand a topic if it is presented in a passive way. Lao Tze, the Chinese philosopher, once said, "Tell me and I forget, show me and I understand, involve me and I remember."

There are several theories about how we learn. One of those is learning styles. People typically have a preferred learning style. Learning styles are sensory learning modalities. Usually, learning styles typically fall into either a visual, auditory or kinesthetic/tactile modality. Visual learners learn through seeing. These types of learners need to see a presenter or read a book. They prefer visual teaching aids. Visual learners learn by seeing and writing. Using visuals in your teaching is highly advised because children with special needs in particular are often able to learn faster with the use of visuals. Auditory learners learn through hearing, or listening. These learners pick up on the nuances of speech, such as the pitch or lilt of a voice or the fluency or speed of the speaker, and so on. These types of learners utilize anything they can to make sure that they hear the presentation. Kinesthetic/tactile learners learn through moving, doing and touching. They need to have movement or to activate their sense of touch to learn. You might notice kinesthetic learners by all the gestures they use when they speak. It is difficult for learners with this preference to sit for long periods of time. Kinesthetic learners use the large motor muscles and activate whole body learning. They learn by doing. Tactile learners utilize their small motor muscles to activate their learning. They typically learn by touching. A vast majority of children are kinesthetic and tactile up to the age of six because we expect, and encourage, children to touch and explore. Expectations typically change for children after the age of six; consequently many children then become more auditory and visual in their learning. This is likely due to the fact that teachers structure their teaching environments for auditory and visual styles after a child reaches school age, which is approximately around six.

Learning is an active process. Within that process, the more experiences we provide the better. Let children use all their senses. Help them to expand their learning capabilities by letting them build upon their knowledge. Children are curious by nature; they want to explore and study their topics of interest. They are discoverers. Let them have fun learning, and the natural motivation that occurs will make them never want to stop. Mihaly Csik-szentmihalyi feels that the joy of discovery, or learning, and consequently creativity, is realized by getting into a state of what he calls "flow." [28] Flow is an optimal experience for an individual; it is a point at which she gets so involved in a task that the discovery or the unfolding of the learning is all the motivation that she needs. When an individual is in the state of "flow," she often loses all sense of time. She becomes absorbed in the activity and has a difficult time pulling herself away from the task, even when it involves learn-ing something difficult! She is having too much fun to break away! We can help children, and even adults, get to this point. We all want our children to be responsible and achievement-oriented. By thinking through what we want for our children and then letting them get involved in their learning, we can facilitate this for our children. Doing our best to meet the needs of children is in fact glorifying God and His wonderful creation.

We could write many books on the needs of children. In fact there are many books. This chapter has only dealt with a small part of the needs that are classified into two different camps—the foundational educational needs and the academic educational needs. In closing, I would like to remind you that there is a final need that all children have. It is safe to say that this final need is in fact the most important need a child has. It is never outgrown. It is a need for consistent, heartfelt and loving prayers for the child's benefit. Ephesians 6:11–12 in the *Amplified Bible* says:

> *Put on God's whole armor [the armor of a heavy-armed soldier which God sup-plies], that you may be able successfully to stand up against [all] the strategies and the deceits of the devil.*

> *For we are not wrestling with flesh and blood [contending only with physical opponents], but against the despotisms, against the powers, against [the master spirits who are] the world rulers of this present darkness, against the spirit forces of wickedness in the heavenly (supernatural) sphere.*

We equip children by meeting their foundational and academic needs. However, we help children put on their armor by praying for them and teaching them to pray for themselves. Pray for children in the morning and pray for them at night. Pray without ceasing for our children! There is no greater need that a child has, and there is no other way we could glorify God more!

Notes

1. W. Glasser, *Control Theory in the Classroom* (New York: Harper & Row, 1986).

2. T.B. Brazelton and S. I. Greenspan, *The Irreducible Needs of Children: What Every Child Must Have to Grow, Learn, and Flourish* (Cambridge, MA: Perseus, 2000).

3. N. Letourneau, "Fostering Resiliency in Infants and Young Children through Parent-Infant Interaction," *Infants and Young Children* 9, no. 3 (1997): 36.

4. B. Benard, "Fostering Resiliency in Kids: Protective Factors in the Family, School, and Community" (Portland, OR: Northwest Regional Educational Laboratory, 1991).

5. Letourneau, "Fostering Resiliency," 36–45.

6. Brazelton and Greenspan, *Irreducible Needs*, 58.

7. M. B. Bronson, *Self-Regulation in Early Childhood: Nature and Nurture* (New York: Guilford, 2001).

8. J. Artesani, *Understanding the Purpose of Challenging Behavior: A Guide to Conducting Functional Assessments* (Upper Saddle River, NJ: Merrill Prentice Hall, 2001).

9. A. Donnellan, G. W. LaVinga, N. Negri-Shoultz, and L. L. Fassbender, *Progress without Punishment: Effective Approaches for Learners with Behavior Problems* (New York: Teachers College Press, 1988).

10. *Gale Encyclopedia of Childhood and Adolescence*, s.v. "Social Competence" (by J. A.Welsh and K. L. Bierman), Pennsylvania State University, http://www.findarticles.com/cf_0/g2602/0004/2602000487/p1/article.

11. G. W. Ladd, "The Fourth R: Relationships as Risks and Resources Following Children's Transition to School," *American Educational Research Association Division E-newsletter* 19, no. 1 (2000): 7–11.

12. D. Goleman, *Emotional Intelligence: Why It Can Matter More than IQ* (New York: Bantam Books, 1995).

13. S. Greenspan and J. Salmon, *The Challenging Child: Understanding, Raising, and Enjoying the Five "Difficult" Types of Children* (Boston: Addison-Wesley, 1995).

14. S. J. Kinsey, "The relationship between prosocial behaviors and academic achievement in the primary multiage classroom" (PhD diss., Loyola University of Chicago, 2000).

15. W. W. Hartup, *Having Friends, Making Friends, and Keeping Friends: Relationships as Educational Contexts*, ERIC Digest (Champaign, IL: ERIC Clearinghouse on Elementary and Early Childhood Education, 1992), 1.

16. Hartup, *Having Friends*.

17. K. H. Rubin, W. Bukowski, and J. G. Parker, "Peer Interactions, Relationships, and Groups," in *Handbook of Child Psychology*, ed. W. Damon and N. Eisenberg, 5th ed., vol. 3 (New York: Wiley, 1998), 619–700.

18. D. Staub, *Delicate Threads: Friendships between Children With and Without Special Needs in Inclusive Settings* (Bethesda, MD: Woodbine House, 1998).

19. Ibid., 18.

20. M. J. Guralnick and E. M. Weinhouse, "Peer-Related Social Interactions of Developmentally Delayed Young Children: Development and Characteristics," *Developmental Psychology* 20 (1984): 815–27.

21. M. J. Guralnick, R. T. Connor, M. A. Hammond, J. M. Gottman, and K. Kinnish, "Immediate Effects of Mainstreamed Settings on the Social Interactions and Social Integration of Preschool Children," *American Journal on Mental Retardation* 100 (1996): 359–77.

22. A. H. Maslow, *Motivation and Personality* (New York: Harper & Row, 1954).

23. E. Erikson, *Identity and the Life Cycle* (New York: Norton, 1980).

24. L. Albert, *A Teacher's Guide to Cooperative Discipline*, rev. ed. (Circle Pines, MN: American Guidance Services, 1996). First published 1989.

25. N. Chomsky, *Knowledge of Language: Its Nature, Origin, and Use* (New York: Prager, 1986).

26. Texas Education Agency, *Beginning Reading Instruction: Components and Features of a Research-Based Reading Program*, rev. ed. (Austin, TX: Texas Education Agency, 2000).

27. J. B. Wilson, "Science + Math = The Greatest Discovery/Invention," 2003, http://members.aol.com/SciRealm/ScienceMath.html.

28. M. Csikszentmihalyi, *Creativity, Flow and the Psychology of Discovery and Invention* (New York: HarperCollins, 1996).

*

CHAPTER FIVE

PHYSICAL CHALLENGES

* * *

Karyl Stanton

BECAUSE Jesus Himself placed value on children and gave them His attention, we also should embrace the heart of God concerning compassionate care for *all* His children, including those with disabilities. The World Health Organization's *World Report on Disability* reveals that about 15 percent of the world's population—more than one billion individuals—live with some level of disability.[1] But delivery of health care to children with disabilities is a frequently neglected task worldwide. Often, even simple interventions are overlooked by those who cannot see their worth and potential in God's eyes. This chapter seeks to change that by addressing the question: What are the special medical and physical needs of children with disabilities worldwide and how can they be met?

This chapter examines five key areas that must be addressed in providing health care to children with disabilities:

1. Improving health care delivery

2. Addressing special health care needs

3. Promoting a healthy environment

4. Supplying supportive nutrition

5. Making a difference with immunizations

Each one of these areas is essential to the provision of health care to all children regardless of disability. We will look at the key considerations for each area, with an emphasis on their application to children with disabilities.

IMPROVING HEALTH CARE DELIVERY

The first area to address is the delivery of health care to children with disabilities. This section discusses challenges that must be overcome in achieving this goal. Then it looks at two examples of effective strategies for health care delivery and sets forth some essential elements for improving health care delivery.

Challenges to Health Care Delivery

Health is a basic right of all children worldwide, regardless of disability. Article 6 of the United Nations Convention on the Rights of the Child (CRC) specifically recognizes every child's right to life, survival and development. Article 24 of the CRC provides that children have the right to the "enjoyment of the highest attainable standard of health," including medical care, nutrition, sanitation, clean water and environmental safety.[2]

Health care is also a specific right of children with disabilities. Article 25 of the United Nations Convention on the Rights of People with Disabilities (CRPD)[3] provides that individuals who are disabled have the right to the same amount and quality of free or affordable health care as people who are not disabled. In addition, Article 26 of the CRPD and Article 23 of the CRC provide that children with disabilities also have a right to special care and support, including health care and rehabilitation services.

Although it is clear that health care for children with disabilities is both an internationally recognized right and a God-given duty, it is often far from clear how best to deliver health care to them. Meeting the basic health care needs of children with disabilities is a goal for which we must strive. But nearly eighty percent of all people with disabilities live in developing countries,[4] usually in poor rural areas, characterized by transportation problems, poverty, accidents and isolation. Enabling such children to have access to health care poses an overabundance of logistical, social, cultural and economic problems. Yet we must be willing to overcome such obstacles through developing and implementing effective strategies.

Examples of Effective Health Care Delivery Strategies

Two strategies that have been effective in overcoming the challenges to health care delivery are Community-Based Rehabilitation and Community Health Evangelism.

Community-Based Rehabilitation

Community-Based Rehabilitation (CBR) is one effective strategy for recognizing and addressing the health care needs of children with disabilities.

Advocated internationally for over twenty-five years as the core strategy to help people with disabilities, CBR is a diverse and broad-based group of locally provided services (such as social counseling, training in mobility and daily living skills, financial assistance, vocational training, development of self-help groups and support groups, and facilitating school enrollment) that help improve the quality of life for people with disabilities in their local communities. Strategies such as CBR have had a positive impact on the self-esteem, empowerment, self-reliance and social inclusion of people with disabilities.

CBR is effective in identifying children who are in need of assistance. As one CBR participant observed, "CBR is good in the sense that it brought out so many other persons that had children with disabilities to understand that they had a place in society and that they should not be locked away and kept indoors."[5] Sherry Gurney, RN, who worked with children with disabilities and visual impairment in the Kibera slum on the outskirts of Nairobi, Kenya, discovered that many such children were considered a "curse" to the family and were hidden away in the darkness of the village huts. This belief is also the case in many other places around the world. But Gurney found that when families began to genuinely see the offer of assistance with health care and education, many children with disabilities began to "emerge" for evaluation and treatment. In effect, this health care strategy of searching for the disabled and taking health care to them is a reflection of the love and compassion of our Lord and Savior, Jesus Christ, when He taught about searching for the one lost sheep (Luke 15:4). When we consider the social isolation, fear and lack of understanding that surround children with disabilities in many poor rural villages worldwide, it becomes obvious that we must bring health care to them at both the village level and the home level, enabling the family, caregivers and children to participate in building a life of meaningful social inclusion and accomplishment.

Community Health Evangelism

Community Health Evangelism (CHE)[6] is another effective community-based strategy for delivery of health care to children with disabilities in developing countries. CHE is a unique strategy that seeks to transform lives physically, emotionally, socially and spiritually in local communities by meeting people at their point of need. Workers are trained in village health, water protection and agricultural development as well as in evangelism and discipleship. As the workers teach in villages, they also share the gospel as the opportunity arises and encourage their pupils to share information with friends and neighbors.

Both health care information and the good news of Jesus Christ are disseminated as people eagerly share what they have learned. The prototype of CHE challenges us to find a way to combine both compassionate medical care for children with disabilities and the gospel message for delivery of "abundant life" teaching (John 10:10) on the village level worldwide.

Essential Elements for Improving Health Care Delivery

How can we best deliver health care services to children with disabilities in our own settings? The study of health services delivery to parents who are disadvantaged and their children has shown that the following elements are essential.[7]

Choose a Competent Staff

Bring together doctors, therapists, educators, nurses, orthotics specialists and other professionals who understand the needs of children with disabilities and know how to work with them.

Use a Team Approach, If Possible

Clinicians, educators, child-care providers, professionals and paraprofessionals can all contribute something important to the care of each child. In situations where one person, such as a village health care worker, provides all the care for his community, that person should learn as much as possible about medical needs of children with disabilities. *Disabled Village Children* is a wonderful resource manual.[8]

Provide Services to Both Parents and Children

Addressing both parents and children is more effective than providing services to children alone with minimal parent participation. Involving parents in planned treatment or therapies ensures a greater degree of success in terms of short-term goals and planning. For long-term goals to be met, the *parents'* ability to adapt to and cope with their child's disability must be improved so as to assist them in skills for parenting a child with a disability.

Make Time for Communication

Make time for parents to voice their concerns and to hear your concerns regarding their child. Make time for the child to experience love and compassionate care. And make time for the staff to communicate with each other in a coordinated effort to help each child.

Individualize Medical Care and Delivery

Individualize medical care and delivery of health services to each child and her family. This requires flexibility and resourcefulness on the part of staff and health care programs.

Offer Support to the Health Care Delivery Staff

Working intensively with families who are disadvantaged and children with disabilities is rewarding, but can also be emotionally draining. Provide necessary care and support for the staff. Continuing education seminars may be helpful and intellectually stimulating as they provide for the ongoing development of the health care delivery team. In addition, concerns of staff should be taken seriously and problems resolved promptly to keep good morale among co-workers. Positive interactions among the health care staff should be encouraged.

Focus on Family-Centered Care

Finally, delivery of health care to children with disabilities must enable their families "to function as primary decision makers, caregivers, teachers and advocates for their children."[9] Parents are the ones who should implement the therapy that the professionals teach them. Care of a child who is disabled must, therefore, be balanced with the priorities of the family so that family needs and goals are met. Where possible, children with disabilities can be taught skills to help their families with daily living tasks such as cooking, cleaning, washing clothes and tending to the family garden or livestock. This integrates them into the family life while also teaching helpful developmental skills.

Maricela's story is a wonderful example of the benefit of family-centered care. Maricela's family was able to modify her therapy for cerebral palsy to village life through adapting household chores to enable her to participate with the family while also doing her therapy. For example, to straighten her legs and strengthen her muscles, Maricela needed to sit with an object between her legs. When she was shelling corn she used a large basket, and when she helped her mother wash clothes at the river she used a big rock. Her father also made special tools from simple materials that not only provided therapy, but also allowed her to perform household tasks such as shelling corn. He also made her a homemade rocking horse with stirrups, which helped improve her leg strength, foot position and balance. Eventually, she became able to ride the family mule and carry pails of water. All these activities were just the "therapy" she needed! She was also able to gain confidence by learning useful life skills while helping her family.

The Impact of Improved Health Care Delivery

Integrating these elements into the delivery of meaningful health care services to children with disabilities and their families may create the right environment of perceived concern, results and trust needed to make a long-term impact on the worldwide population of children who have disabilities and are disadvantaged.

Help is available! Many charities and organizations are willing to send teams of experts, adaptive equipment, medical supplies and educators to help "get the ball rolling" for care of the children with disabilities in your part of the world. (See appendix E for a list of charitable organizations that provide medical assistance and humanitarian aid to children with disabilities.)

ADDRESSING SPECIAL HEALTH CARE NEEDS

The second area to consider in providing health care to children with disabilities is addressing their special health care needs. All children have basic health care needs, but children with disabilities have special additional needs. This section looks at some common types of medical care and other assistance available to address those needs.

Children with Special Health Care Needs

Children with disabilities have special, and often multiple, health care needs. According to the Maternal and Child Health Bureau of the U.S. Department of Health and Human Services, children with special health care needs are those children "who have or are at increased risk for a chronic physical, developmental, behavioral, or emotional condition and who also require health and related services of a type or amount beyond that required by children generally."[10] A recent survey in the United States indicated that over nine million (12.8 percent) of American children currently have a special health care need.[11] Children with special health care needs can be found in one out of every five American households. With these alarming statistics occurring in a single country, one can only imagine the extent of special health care needs worldwide.

How can the special health care needs of children with disabilities be addressed? This question must be answered from both a social as well as a medical perspective. According to the World Health Organization, "disability" is an umbrella term covering physical impairments (problems in body function or structure), activity limitations (difficulties in executing a task or action) and participation restrictions (problems experienced in involvement in life situations).[12] Therefore the WHO concludes, "Disability is a complex phenomenon, reflecting an interaction between features of a person's body and features of the society in which he or she lives."[13]

The implication of this medical and social model means that when we seek to address the special health care needs of children with disabilities we must deal with social and political issues (involving human rights, inclusion and integration of the individual with a disability into society) in addition to medical considerations (including access to and delivery of health care services). Other chapters in this book discuss ways to address the needs of children with disabilities from a social perspective. From the medical perspective, although full coverage of specific interventions for the various types of disability is beyond the scope of this chapter, we briefly describe a few common types of interventions.

Using a Variety of Means

There are many ways to address the special health care needs of children with disabilities, including corrective surgery, assistive devices and adaptive equipment, and therapy and education.

Corrective Surgeries

Many children with disabilities benefit from corrective surgery for congenital deformities and acute or chronic conditions that affect body structure and function. A wide variety of surgeries are available that are helpful for different disabilities, including orthopedic surgery (to treat musculoskeletal problems such as club foot), plastic or reconstructive surgery (to restore function and appearance in conditions like burns or cleft palates) and neurosurgery (to repair disorders of the nervous system such as spina bifida and cerebral palsy). Some disabilities can be fully correctible with surgery, whereas for others surgery is able to significantly improve function and quality of life. In some places, medical missionaries and other nongovernmental organizations provide corrective surgery at a price that is affordable for the poor.

Assistive Devices and Adaptive Equipment

Assistive devices and adaptive equipment can help some children with disabilities manage better with their activities of daily living. Simple interventions—such as providing prescription glasses, hearing aids, seating and standing supports, walkers, wheelchairs, canes or crutches—can be life-changing for children with disabilities. Children with absent or deformed limbs, or limbs that have functional impairment due to abnormal muscle tone or weakness, may benefit from prosthetic devices, bracing, casting or splinting. Some assistive devices and adaptive equipment can be made from local materials by a local craftsperson working with a plan and a knowledgeable health care provider.[14] For information about making simple adaptive and assistive devices for mobility, see chapter 10.

Therapeutic and Educational Interventions

Many different kinds of therapies and educational techniques can be used to improve the functioning of children with disabilities. For instance, children with mobility issues, weakness and/or abnormal muscle tone may benefit from physical therapy (which involves specific exercises to improve gross motor skills, strength, muscle tone and balance) or occupational therapy (which involves specific exercises and activities to help improve fine motor control and hand muscle function). Children with communication disorders or swallowing difficulties may benefit from speech therapy and oral motor exercises. Cognitive and/or behavioral issues in children with learning and intellectual disabilities may be addressed with special education and behavior modification techniques.

Therapy is best taught by individuals who have been specifically trained in a particular discipline (for example, physical, occupational or speech therapy). Parents, family members and caregivers should be taught therapy techniques as they are usually the best ones to consistently deliver the therapy to the child with a disability through regular practice. Some basic physical therapy exercises to improve mobility are explained in chapter 10.

Children Are Children!

Despite the diversity of special health care needs, children with disabilities are still children! They have many physical and emotional needs that are shared by all children, whether disabled or nondisabled, worldwide: "Regardless of [disabling] conditions, our children have the same needs as able-bodied children. Handicaps and mental challenges do not cripple their innate desire to grow, to develop, to be accepted, to belong, to be loved and to love."[15]

PROMOTING A HEALTHY ENVIRONMENT

The third area that must be addressed in providing health care to children with disabilities is that of promoting a healthy environment. This section discusses the need for a healthy environment and introduces some basic strategies that can be taken to promote it.

The Need for a Healthy Environment

All children everywhere have the same basic physical needs, such as for food, water, shelter and safety. For children to develop to their highest potential, they must have a healthy environment that enables those basic needs to be met. Clean water, nutritious food, good sanitation practices, safe living conditions, adequate shelter and a loving family all go a long way to promoting healthy growth and development for children who are disabled and those who are not. On the other hand, when a healthy environment is not present, it can have detrimental effects on children, especially children with disabilities.

It is vital to promote healthy environments for children with disabilities. First, unhealthy environments can themselves cause disability. Low birth weight, malnutrition, lack of clean water, poor sanitation and unsafe living conditions are all factors that increase a child's risk for disability. For instance, the infectious diseases that thrive in unhealthy environments (particularly tuberculosis, elephantiasis, and HIV/AIDS and other sexually transmitted diseases) account in part for the prevalence of disability in low- and middle-income countries.[16] Prevention of these and other infectious diseases is crucial.

Second, unhealthy environments can exacerbate disability. Children with disabilities and chronic medical problems may already have weakened immune systems due to poor nutrition, chronic or recurrent infections, neglect or exposure to the elements. Unclean and unsanitary conditions breed disease and infection. Therefore, cleanliness and sanitation are even more important for these children to protect them from infections that could further compromise their health.

Strategies for Promoting a Healthy Environment

Four simple, yet effective, low-cost strategies for promotion of healthy environments have benefit for all children, whether disabled or not:

- Protect water sources
- Employ water purification
- Adopt cleanliness and sanitation guidelines
- Adopt safe food handling and preparation guidelines

These strategies can prevent most of the disease, disability and death caused by unhealthy environments, as well as improve the lives and functioning of children with disabilities.

Good Practices for Protecting Water Sources

To promote cleanliness and prevent many contagious diseases, people in the community should be made aware of the need for protection of water sources. Water can be protected through the use of fences and latrines.

Fencing. Protect village water sources, such as wells or springs, from dirt and animals by putting a fence or wall around the water source.

Latrines. Teach community members to eliminate human waste in a latrine or outhouse and not on the ground, in a water source or in the immediate area surrounding their home. Construct a simple latrine by digging a hole approximately one meter square and one to two meters deep. The latrine can be surrounded by a simple structure to provide privacy and to prevent animals from reaching the human waste and spreading disease. Latrines should be located at least 20 meters from all houses, rivers, wells or springs, and should be downstream from any nearby water source. The latrine may be covered between use. Lime, dirt or ashes may be thrown in the hole after each use to reduce odor and keep flies away.

Techniques for Water Purification.

If the cleanliness of the water source is at all questionable, then one or more of the following water purification techniques should be used. (Using two methods of water purification offers greater protection against diseases transmitted by contaminated water than just using one.) Purification of water is important for small children and in areas where many cases of diarrhea, typhoid, hepatitis or cholera exist.

- **Boiling.** To purify and disinfect water by boiling, the water should be boiled for one full minute, then covered and kept hot for several minutes. Boiling kills any cysts, parasites, bacteria or viruses in the water. The water can be kept pure by covering it until cool, then storing it in clean containers that have been washed with soap and water (or washed and boiled for extra safety). Water stored for longer periods of time should be chlorinated with two to four drops of household bleach (5 percent sodium hypochlorite) per liter or quart to prevent contamination from regrowth of microorganisms.

Filtration. Filtration alone does not remove viruses, which can pass through filter pores because of their microscopic size. In water that may be contaminated with human waste, viruses are a major concern in the transmission of diarrheal illness and hepatitis. Therefore, effective purification of water must combine both filtration and boiling. In most developing countries, surface water is assumed to be contaminated even if the water is visually clear. Cloudy water should be cleared first by sedimentation (allowing particles to settle by gravity over one to two hours), then filtered (if a standard water filter is available) and boiled for at least one minute or up to 20 minutes.

- **Chlorine or Iodine.** If boiling is not possible, water may be treated with chlorine or iodine drops after filtration. But drops do not kill everything. This makes disinfecting water with chlorine and iodine impractical if used alone in most village settings. Instead, always use drops in addition to another purification method.

- **Sunlight.** If no other method is practical or available, water can be purified by putting it in a clean, clear container (such as a closed plastic bag or a covered or capped bottle) and leaving it in direct sunlight for a few hours. This technique kills most of the microorganisms in the water.

Guidelines for Cleanliness and Sanitation

The following simple cleanliness and sanitation guidelines can also help prevent many deadly and disabling diseases among children.

- Wash hands with soap and water (before food preparation, before meals and after defecating).
- Use latrines for eliminating human waste products.
- Bathe often.
- Wear shoes to prevent hookworm infection (these worms enter the body through the skin on the soles of bare feet).
- Keep homes clean and well swept.
- Fill in cracks in walls or floors where roaches and other bugs may hide.
- Keep bedding clean by washing and/or hanging sheets and blankets in the sun.

- Keep animals in pens to prevent them from coming into the house or other places where children play.

- Keep children's fingernails clean and cut short to prevent dirt, germs and parasite eggs from "hiding" under dirty fingernails.

- Promptly treat children with infections and care for them separately from well children and babies.

- Cover one's mouth when coughing or sneezing.

- Never spit on the floor.

- Properly burn garbage or dispose of it in a pit far away from homes and drinking water sources.

Careful observance of these guidelines can substantially reduce the risk of transmitting or contracting infectious diseases, including diarrhea, which is the second most common cause of death in children, killing 1.3 million children each year.[17]

Guidelines for Safe Food Handling and Preparation

The following basic guidelines for the safe and sanitary handling and preparation of food can also help prevent infectious diseases.

- Wash hands with soap and water before preparing food.

- Wash food with clean water that has been purified.

- Soak fruits and vegetables that are to be eaten raw.

  Soak in a solution of one teaspoon of bleach (5 percent sodium hypochlorite) per liter of clean water for 30 minutes, then rinsed with purified drinking water. A solution of iodine instead of chlorine may be more effective in eliminating giardia.

- Prepare raw foods separately from cooked food.

- Cook food thoroughly.

- Keep foods at a safe temperature.

  Bacteria multiply rapidly in foods at temperatures of 40 to 140 degrees Fahrenheit. Foods are safest when cooked to an internal temperature of 160 to 212 degrees Fahrenheit.

- Use safe and clean cooking fuel.

- Ensure proper food storage and refrigeration.

  Foods should not be left unrefrigerated for over two hours; if the outside temperature is above 90 degrees Fahrenheit, food should not be left out for more than one hour.

Healthier Environments, Healthier Children

All children benefit from these strategies, but children with disabilities and their families have an even greater need for healthy, supportive environments. Such children and their families already have many challenges. Even basic living activities can be draining and demanding. Then, on top of life's regular demands, they often add therapy, exercises, trips to the local doctor or health care worker, special education programs and other activities that make for relentless "busyness" and tax the children's (and parents') stamina even further. Help from siblings, extended family, neighbors and friends can make healthy environments possible despite the stressful demands of caring for children with disabilities. In particular, carefully following each of these four strategies can help successfully prevent the conditions that cause and exacerbate disability in children, as well as promote the healthy environments that support their overall health.

SUPPLYING SUPPORTIVE NUTRITION

The fourth area that is needed to provide health care to children with disabilities is that of supplying supportive nutrition. This section examines the main threats to adequate nutrition in children with disabilities and introduces strategies to supply it.

The Need for Supportive Nutrition

Just as healthy children without disabilities need good nutrition, children with disabilities also depend on nutritious food and adequate calories for optimal growth and development. In addition, they rely on good nutrition to survive and thrive despite the challenges imposed by their disability. The lack of adequate supportive nutrition poses a serious threat to the health of children with disabilities.

There are three main causes of problems with nutrition: feeding difficulties, malnutrition, and deficiencies in vitamins and micronutrients. Some aspects of these problems are common to all children, but they are exacerbated in children with disabilities. We now turn to strategies to supply supportive nutrition for each of these problem areas.

Strategies to Address Feeding Difficulties

Many children with disabilities have feeding difficulties. In fact, according to experts, approximately "one-third of all children with a developmental disability will develop a feeding problem significant enough to interfere with their nutrition, medical well-being, or social integration."[18] Feeding problems may be caused by various factors, including structural problems affecting the nose, mouth, respiratory system or digestive system; neurological disorders affecting the strength, tone and coordination of the muscles of the mouth and throat; chronic medical disorders; and developmental delay that affects feeding. Furthermore, physical conditions that affect the muscles of the mouth and throat also make chewing and swallowing difficult for the child. These conditions include head injury or other causes of brain damage, cerebral palsy, epilepsy, Down syndrome, muscular dystrophy or other neuromuscular diseases. Finally, chronic illness such as congenital heart disease and kidney disease may also lead to poor feeding in children.

General Feeding Strategies

In general, children with swallowing difficulties usually need a diet of strained or soft, cooked, mashed foods. Children with feeding issues should be fed in an upright position with a spoon to work with gravity. Bottle feeding is discouraged because bottles and nipples are hard to keep clean and may contribute to infectious disease.

Children with disabilities may need practice and encouragement to learn proper chewing and manipulation of food in the mouth. Placing food in the side of the mouth between the upper and lower back teeth helps encourage chewing. Many baby teething toys offer good textures to practice chewing. Where available, a Nuk oral hygiene tool for babies (which has a handle like a toothbrush and soft bumps instead of bristles) can be dipped in a child's favorite foods and placed between his back teeth to offer chewing practice. Alternatively, a soft clean cotton cord can be used. The cord should be braided and soaked in tasty juice or food, then placed between the child's back teeth for him to practice chewing while the caregiver holds one end of the cord.

Many other helpful adaptive aids can be made from simple materials to help with feeding issues.[19] For instance, a nonslip plate or bowl with a built-up higher side for scooping and a spoon or fork with a thick, built-up curved handle for easy gripping can help a child with a disability learn eating skills. Special seating can help a child who is disabled have proper posture and positioning. Aids to help hold a cup or a spoon can assist a child with missing arms or hands. And modified cups (such as a two-handled cup, a cup with a piece cut out of the back rim allowing the cup to be easily tilted up to the nose, or a nonspill cup and cup-holder) can help a child with disabilities to better learn independent drinking skills.

Babies born with a cleft lip and palate (but not cleft lip alone) usually require help with feeding because the cleft palate prevents them from having the suction needed to suck milk from the breast or bottle effectively. Where available, a Mead Johnson Cleft Lip and Palate Nurser (a soft, plastic compressible bottle fitted with a longer, cross-cut nipple) allows the caregiver to squeeze milk onto the intact part of the baby's palate, coordinating with the baby's swallowing. An orthodontic-shaped nipple may be helpful for large clefts. If a feeder is not available, the child may be able to breast-feed if the breast is put deeper into the mouth, or the mother can express breast milk by hand into a clean cup and feed the baby in an upright position with a spoon. Surgical reconstruction is recommended for the best chance of social acceptance and development of speech and feeding ability. If possible, surgery should be done between 4 and 6 months for cleft lip and between 9 and 18 months for cleft palate. Nonprofit organizations, such as Operation Smile, provide reconstructive surgery of cleft lip and palate as well as other facial deformities to needy children in developing countries and the United States.

Problem-Specific Feeding Strategies

A number of specific feeding problems occur across a variety of disabilities. In addition to the general feeding strategies just discussed, there are also strategies to effectively address these specific feeding difficulties.

Oral-Motor Dysfunction. Poor lip closure or jaw instability from abnormal facial muscle tone can cause food to be lost from the mouth. "Tongue-thrusting" due to a persistent sucking reflex can also cause the tongue to push the food out of the mouth. A caregiver can provide jaw support to help improve oral-motor dysfunction by putting the caregiver's thumb underneath the child's lower lip and the caregiver's fingers under the child's chin and jaw. Additionally, tongue-thrusting may be prevented by using a flattened spoon with firm downward pressure on the middle of the tongue.

Prolonged Feeding Time.

 Weakness of the tongue and trouble transferring the food from the mouth to the throat for swallowing can lead to feeding times in excess of 30 minutes. Weakness or problems coordinating the throat muscles (pharynx) may slow swallowing further. A child with breathing difficulties may need to pause longer between bites to allow time to breathe. Medical evaluation may help for this frustrating problem. In addition, multiple family members or caregivers can help with feeding at mealtimes so the child can have ample time to eat and the main caregiver does not become exhausted.

Pocketing.

"Pocketing," or holding food in the cheeks or front of the mouth, may signify that the child is not able to manipulate food correctly with the tongue for transport into the back of the throat. Pocketing can also occur when a child's disability causes her to dislike certain textures of food, so she refuses to swallow it by pocketing. Being aware of the child's food preferences and placing the food in the side of the mouth may help.

Aspiration.

Aspiration refers to food or liquid entering the airway. Aspiration is a dangerous problem that can lead to pneumonia, bronchitis and even death. Symptoms of aspiration may include slowed or absent breathing and slowed heartbeat in babies or, in older children, coughing and nasal congestion or wheezing during meals. Prompt medical attention is required for diagnosis, treatment and prevention of aspiration. Children who have disabilities that cause feeding problems are at greater risk for recurrent aspiration. Weakness of their mouth and throat muscles causes difficulty in clearing food and secretions from their airway by coughing. Some ways that caregivers can help prevent aspiration are by feeding small, teaspoon-sized bites, reminding the child to chew thoroughly and ensuring that the child's mouth is clear after eating is finished.

Coughing, Gagging and Choking.

These occur when there are problems with swallowing, and are in fact defense mechanisms to prevent aspiration of food into the airway. Often children with disabilities have problems with a certain type or texture of food (liquids, solids or combination foods like soups that have chunks of solids in a liquid). To prevent coughing, gagging and choking, adjust the texture of the food by pureeing or mashing solids or thickening liquids with rice cereal, corn meal, instant pudding or other thickeners. Feed the child the texture that he tolerates best, and introduce any new food textures slowly. If coughing, choking or gagging with meals persists, seek medical evaluation as soon as possible to prevent aspiration.

Gastroesophageal Reflux Disease (GERD).

GERD refers to the backward flow of food and stomach contents into the esophagus. This can be caused by a weakened muscle in the lower esophagus that is not strong enough to close efficiently and prevent reflux of gastric contents. GERD can also be caused by increased abdominal pressure related to increased muscle tone, abnormal "posturing" in individuals with brain damage, constipation, delayed stomach emptying or delayed movement of food through the intestinal tract. GERD can cause serious and painful inflammation of the esophagus, nausea, vomiting and aspiration. GERD usually occurs after a meal and is more common when lying down. Small, frequent meals may help prevent GERD. Also, upright positioning after meals and thickened feedings use gravity to keep the stomach contents from refluxing into the esophagus. Medication may help to reduce stomach acid production and to help the stomach empty more efficiently. When GERD cannot be controlled by these therapies, surgery may be required for stomach reconstruction or insertion of a feeding tube.

Strategies to Address Malnutrition

Malnutrition also poses a problem for children with disabilities. Malnutrition is an imbalance between the supply and demand for nutrients and energy that the body needs to grow and function properly. An estimated 174 million children worldwide are malnourished. Children with a disability who have feeding problems are at increased risk for malnutrition.

Malnutrition is one of the five main causes of death among children in developing countries and contributes to over half of the 11 million childhood deaths per year worldwide. Malnutrition causes poor physical and mental development as well as lower resistance to infectious disease. Malnutrition can also lead to disability. According to the 2011 WHO World Report on Disability, the risk of disability increases as the severity of stunted growth and being underweight increases.[20]

Poor feeding practices combine with infections and limited access to food to produce malnutrition. General malnutrition in children has two forms. "Marasmus" is due to lack of calories and protein and causes an overall wasted appearance. "Kwashiorkor" is due to protein deficiency (and possibly also to toxins from moldy foods). Kwashiorkor causes swelling of the face, hands, feet and abdomen and has a higher death rate than marasmus. Cases of severe malnutrition can be complicated by dangerously low blood sugar, hypothermia, electrolyte imbalance, infection, dehydration (especially if the child has diarrhea) and septic shock.

Treatment of Malnutrition

Children at risk of malnutrition, including children with feeding problems, should have their caloric intake, growth (height and weight) and development closely monitored. Children can be screened for malnutrition by measuring mid-upper arm circumference (MUAC). Doctors Without Borders has a special "bracelet of life" to measure MUAC in children between six months and five years.

Children whose MUAC shows they are malnourished require supplemental feedings, perhaps at a special feeding center, if available. Severely malnourished children require hospitalization or full-time treatment at a therapeutic feeding center where they can receive frequent feedings of high-energy milk formula until they have gained enough weight to return to their family. If necessary, they should be rehydrated using an oral rehydration salts solution mixed with added sugar and minerals, and be given a refeeding diet consisting of special mixtures of milk, sugar, cereal flour, vegetable oil, mineral/vitamin mixes and water. Deficiencies of vitamins and minerals should also be corrected.

Prevention of Malnutrition

Malnutrition, with its complications and associated debilitation and disabilities, can be easily prevented with a diet sufficient in calories and rich in a variety of vitamins, minerals and nutrients. Children with disabilities need a nutritious diet to develop to their full potential. Some surveys have shown that children at risk for disability are less likely to have been breast-fed or received vitamin A supplementation, [21] both of which are helpful for preventing malnutrition.

Malnutrition in children occurs most commonly between six and twenty-four months of age, during the transition from exclusive breast-feeding to eating solid foods. Exclusive breast-feeding is the best diet for babies and is recommended for at least the first four to six months of life. Children older than four to six months should continue receiving breast milk as often as they want, up to age two or three, if possible. But mothers who are HIV/AIDS positive can transmit the virus to their babies through breast milk and should receive counseling on the best way to feed their babies.

Exclusive breast-feeding dramatically decreases episodes of diarrhea in infants by providing the best nutrition for the baby, boosting the baby's immunity with antibodies passively transferred to the baby through the mother's milk and giving milk that is naturally well-tolerated by the baby's digestive system. Breast-feeding mothers should feed their babies often, drink plenty of liquids and eat well.

After the child is four to six months old, solid foods should be started slowly to give the child's digestive system time to adjust to the new food. New food should be given for several days (preferably one week) before adding or trying another new food. New foods should be well cooked, mashed and mixed with a little breast milk to help the baby swallow easier. A porridge made from cereal or grains is a good starting food for a baby learning to eat solids. If the baby tolerates the cereal well, a little cooking oil can be added later to give the baby extra calories. Mashed, soft fruit can also be added to the cereal. Soft, cooked, mashed vegetables are also a good "first food." As the baby grows, her diet should be enriched with high-protein foods such as beans, peas, lentils (and other legumes), fish, cooked eggs, cheese, other milk products, meat and nuts. Beans or legumes can be cooked well and strained through a sieve (or the skin peeled off beans and mashed) to make high-protein baby food. Ideally, eggs and peanut products should not be introduced until after one year of age due to the high incidence of allergies to these foods.

Strategies to Address Micronutrient Deficiencies

Finally, children with disabilities can be deficient in certain micronutrients (vitamins and minerals) that are necessary for adequate supportive nutrition. In addition, the lack of these micronutrients can lead to a variety of childhood disabilities and irreversible damage to a child's development.

In general, to prevent deficiencies of micronutrients, children's diets should be varied and include plenty of fresh fruits and vegetables as well as other nutrients. If possible, children should take a multivitamin tablet every day; however, taking a multivitamin is not a substitute for a healthy, varied diet. The rest of this section discusses the nutrition, supplements and other measures that should be provided to children with disabilities to prevent and treat deficiencies in vitamin A, vitamin B1, niacin, vitamin C, vitamin D, iron, folate, vitamin B12 and iodine.

Vitamin A Deficiency

Vitamin A deficiency leads to xerophthalmia (dry eyes). The symptoms include night blindness, dry eyes, softening of the cornea and possible blindness from infection or scarring of the cornea. Vitamin A deficiency is the leading cause of preventable blindness in children, with an up to

500,000 children losing all or some of their vision due to vitamin A deficiency each year.[22] Because blindness is a disabling condition, this should
be prevented at all costs. Furthermore, Vitamin A deficiency also increases
the risk of death from severe infections. Half of the children who become
blind from Vitamin A deficiency die within 12 months after they lose
their sight.[23]

Vitamin A deficiency can be prevented by eating dark green, leafy vegetables, carrots, pumpkin, squash, papaya, mangoes, avocado, guava, enriched whole milk, liver, red palm oil and egg yolks. It can also be prevented
with Vitamin A supplements in capsule, liquid or injected form. Pregnant
and breast-feeding women can be given vitamin A supplements to prevent
the condition in their children. Children who have signs of developing xerophthalmia or who are particularly at risk for it (due to moderate or severe
malnutrition, measles (rubeola) infection or chronic diarrhea / intestinal
malabsorption) should receive oral vitamin A supplements every six months.
Children with developing blindness should be treated with vitamin A injections (or in oral form if injections are unavailable). Vitamin A is often given
along with polio immunizations, a measure that has prevented more than
1.2 million childhood deaths since 1988.[24]

Vitamin B1 (Thiamine) Deficiency

Vitamin B1 (thiamine) deficiency leads to "beriberi." The infant form of beriberi is most often seen in children between two and four months old who
are breast-fed by thiamine-deficient mothers. Vague symptoms of decreased
appetite, restlessness and vomiting may progress to heart failure and swelling
(edema). Older children can experience one or both forms of beriberi: "dry"
beriberi (which includes leg weakness and numbness and tingling in the feet)
and "wet" beriberi (which causes heart failure and swelling in the face and
feet).

Vitamin B1 deficiency can be prevented by eating whole grains, soy-
beans, legumes, peanuts, green vegetables and melon and also by avoiding
a diet of predominantly white rice. A medical missionary in Myanmar saw
several children in an orphanage who were so weak from beriberi that they
could barely stand. After one month of intensive vitamin replacement therapy, the children were strong and smiling again. The doctor remarked that
simple things like multivitamins could change a child's world there.

Niacin Deficiency

Niacin (nicotinic acid) deficiency leads to "pellagra," a syndrome classically associated with the three Ds: diarrhea, dermatitis and dementia. Niacin deficiency is seen more commonly in people who eat a diet high in maize. Adding beans, whole grains, nuts and other nutritious foods like meat, fish and eggs can prevent niacin deficiency. Daily supplements can also be used to treat pellagra.

Vitamin C Deficiency

Vitamin C deficiency causes, among other things, failure to thrive, irritability, bleeding around the gums and under the skin, anemia (low red blood cell count) and, in extreme cases, scurvy. Vitamin C deficiency is prevented by eating citrus fruits, berries, melons, mangoes, papayas, guavas, potatoes and sweet potatoes.

Vitamin D Deficiency

Vitamin D deficiency causes rickets in children. In infants, rickets leads to softening of the skull bones. In older children, it leads to deformities of the chest bones, bowing of the legs and prominence of the frontal bone of the skull. Vitamin D deficiency can be avoided by making sure children get plenty of sunlight on their skin and by eating eggs, fish, liver, and milk fortified with vitamin D, if available.

Iron Deficiency

Iron deficiency is the most prevalent nutritional disorder worldwide. According to the World Health Organization, two billion people worldwide are affected by anemia, many because of iron deficiency.[25] Common causes of iron deficiency anemia in children are hookworm infection, dysentery and chronic diarrhea. Toddlers nine to eighteen months old are at increased risk of iron deficiency anemia due to poor iron intake and increased iron needs in their bodies.

In addition, iron deficiency can lead to disability. Maternal iron deficiency during pregnancy can lead to low infant birth weight and increased premature births. Iron deficiency can also delay or impair normal motor and mental function in babies and small children.

Iron deficiency can be prevented by eating food cooked in iron pots as well as meats, fish, egg yolks, leaves (spinach), jackfruit, peanuts, red palm oil, legumes, dates, raisins, figs and iron-fortified cereals. The American Academy of Pediatrics Committee on Nutrition recommends that cow's milk not be given to children until one year of age and that toddlers be limited to twenty-four ounces per day because "cow's milk is low in iron, decreases children's appetite for iron-rich foods and can irritate the intestinal tract."[26]

Mild to moderate iron deficiency anemia can be treated with iron therapy of daily oral ferrous sulfate supplements. Severely malnourished children with very severe anemia should receive blood transfusions. Underlying conditions, such as parasitic infections, should also be treated.

Folate Deficiency

Folate deficiency in pregnant women can cause malformation of the unborn child's spine and nervous system called "spina bifida." Folate deficiency in children can cause anemia and poor growth. Children who are prone to folate deficiency include infants breast-fed by folate-deficient mothers, infants consuming goat's milk, children with conditions causing malabsorption or chronic diarrhea, and children with anemia due to thalassemia or sickle cell disease.

Folate deficiency is usually due to inadequate dietary intake. Folate deficiency can be prevented by eating foods that contain folic acid, such as liver and green, leafy vegetables. Anemia due to folate deficiency can be treated with supplements. Women who are pregnant or who may become pregnant should be sure to take daily folic acid supplements to prevent birth defects. Mothers who have already had a baby with spina bifida should take a higher dose to prevent recurrence.

Vitamin B12 Deficiency

Vitamin B12 deficiency is less common than folate deficiency. Vitamin B12 deficiency can affect the nerves in the legs and arms, causing loss of position and vibration sense, as well as damage to the part of the spinal cord that carries these sensory pathways. Severe vitamin B12 deficiency may lead to trouble walking and decline in mental function.

Vitamin B12 is found in meat, liver and animal products. Vitamin B12 deficiency is usually a result of malabsorption, or failure of the digestive tract to absorb the vitamin into the blood stream. Failure to absorb vitamin B12 results in a condition called "pernicious anemia," requiring lifetime treatment with injections of liquid vitamin B12.

Iodine Deficiency

Iodine deficiency is the leading cause of brain damage in the world and one of the major reasons for impaired cognitive development in children.[27] Iodine deficiency is caused by lack of iodine in the diet. Iodine deficiency disorders include goiter (enlarged thyroid) and hypothyroidism (underactive thyroid). Iodine deficiency in pregnant mothers and their developing babies before or immediately after birth can lead to cretinism, a developmental disorder causing mental retardation, deafness and severe growth delay resulting in short stature.

Yet iodine deficiency can be easily prevented through diet. Sources of iodine include seafood, foods grown near the sea and iodized salt. Iodine can be supplied with tablets, drops (Lugol's solution) or iodized oil, but the best way to prevent iodine deficiency is to use iodized salt on food. Ensuring that pregnant and breast-feeding mothers have adequate iodine in their diet is particularly important, especially in inland or isolated areas of the world where iodine is not naturally present in soil and food.

MAKING A WORLD OF DIFFERENCE WITH IMMUNIZATIONS

The final area to address in providing health care to children with disabilities is that of immunization. This section discusses the need for immunizations and looks at how immunization against polio has made a world of difference in preventing disability.

The Need for Immunizations

Each year infectious diseases cause the deaths of millions of children worldwide. Immunizations, or vaccinations, are an effective way to prevent serious infectious diseases in children both with and without disabilities. We have previously seen how sanitation and cleanliness can prevent infectious diseases. Immunization is another strategy that can be used. Immunizations are thought to prevent between two and three million deaths each year.

Immunizations are also a way to reduce the occurrence of disability in children by preventing the infectious diseases that cause disability (for instance, cataracts and vision loss in unborn children due to prenatal rubella, and paralysis from polio). Immunizations can also prevent the infectious diseases that lead to complications and even death in children with disabilities.

Table 5.1 lists the schedule for selected immunizations commonly recommended by health authorities for all infants worldwide. Other vaccines, such as typhoid, cholera, hepatitis A, influenza, meningococcal, pneumococcal (conjugate) and rotavirus, may also be recommended for children according to their risk and vaccine availability.

Table 5. 1 Recommended Schedule of Immunizations for Infants

Age	Immunization
At birth	▪ BCG (Tuberculosis) (in countries with high HIV prevalence, but should not be given if the child is HIV positive or suspected of having HIV) ▪ Oral polio (in areas endemic for polio or at high risk for imported polio transmission, with second and third doses at 4 and 8 weeks) ▪ Hepatitis B
At 4–6 weeks	▪ Oral polio (in lesser risk areas, first dose at 6 weeks) ▪ DTP (Diphtheria, Tetanus, Pertussis) ▪ Hepatitis B ▪ HIB (Haemophilus influenza, type b)
At 10 weeks	▪ Oral polio (second dose in lesser risk areas) ▪ DTP ▪ Hepatitis B (in countries where perinatal transmission is less frequent) ▪ HIB
At 14 weeks	▪ Oral polio (third dose in lesser risk areas) ▪ DTB ▪ Hepatitus B ▪ HIB
At 9-12 months	▪ Yellow Fever (in countries where children are a t risk for yellow Feveer) ▪ Measles* (a second dose of measles vaccine should be given at a later visit)

* In countries with a low incidence of measles, the vaccine for measles, mumps and rubella (MMR) can be given to the child when he is 12 months old or after, with a second dose between the child's fourth and sixth birthdays. Measles vaccination is 95 percent effective if given after 12 months of age, but only 60 percent effective when given at 6-9 months. In countries where measles is endemic, earlier vaccination is the standard of care.

See the WHO's Recommended Routine Immunizations for Children for a full, detailed schedule of recommended immunizations.28

The Success of Polio Immunization

Perhaps no other worldwide movement has impacted children with disabilities more than the global initiative to eradicate polio. Poliomyelitis is an infectious viral illness that invades the nervous system and can cause total paralysis in only a few hours. After entering the body through the mouth, the virus multiplies in the intestines and causes initial symptoms of fever, fatigue, headache, vomiting, neck stiffness and pain in the legs. "One in 200 infections leads to irreversible paralysis (usually in the legs). Among those paralysed, 5% to 10% die when their breathing muscles become immobilized."[29]

Children under five are the main population affected by polio. Polio cannot be cured, but it can be prevented with multiple doses of the vaccine. Due to vaccination programs, worldwide polio cases have decreased from an estimated 350,000 in 1988 to only a little over 1,300 cases reported in 2010, a 99 percent decline![30] Widely endemic on five continents and 125 countries in 1988, polio was endemic in only four countries in 2010: Afghanistan, India, Nigeria and Pakistan.[31] (In addition to these endemic areas, Angola, Chad, Democratic Republic of the Congo and possibly Sudan had reestablished transmission of polio following imported cases, and twenty-three other countries in Africa and central Asia had some cases and outbreaks due to imported poliovirus from 2009 to 2010.)

The Global Polio Eradication Initiative seeks to end all polio transmission in at least two of the four endemic countries by the end of 2011, and to end all wild poliovirus transmission by the end of 2012.[32] It seeks to accomplish this by interrupting transmission of the poliovirus as soon as possible through high infant immunization coverage (with 4 doses of oral polio vaccine in the first year of life), supplementary polio vaccine doses to children under five, aggressive reporting and testing of cases of polio symptoms in children under fifteen, and focused immunization campaigns in specific areas where cases of polio are reported. From the launch of the global initiative in 1988 through 2005 and beyond, more than "five million people—mainly in the developing world—who would otherwise have been paralyzed will be walking because they have been immunized against polio."[33] This fact underscores the vital importance of preventative medical programs, including immunization, combined with efforts that promote healthy environments in the battle to prevent and treat childhood disabilities.

Conclusion

Working together, we can meet the health care needs of children with disabilities worldwide. We have what it takes to make a world of difference by addressing these key health care areas:

- Overcoming challenges to improve health care delivery
- Providing medical and other interventions to address their special health care needs
- Following good practices, techniques and guidelines to promote healthy environment
- Implementing strategies to supply adequate nutrition
- Protecting children through immunizations

Notes

1. World Health Organization, World Report on Disability: Summary (Geneva: World Health Organization, 2011), 7, http://whqlibdoc.who.int/hq/2011/ WHO_NMH_VIP_11.01_eng.pdf.

2. UN General Assembly, "Convention on the Rights of the Child," 1989, http://www2.ohchr.org/english/law/crc.htm. See also: UNICEF, "Fact Sheet: A Summary of the Rights under the Convention on the Rights of the Child," http://www.unicef.org/crc/files/Rights_overview.pdf.

3. UN General Assembly, "Convention on the Rights of Persons with Disabilities," 2007. http://www.un.org/disabilities/default.asp?id=259.

4. UN Secretariat for the Convention on the Rights of Persons with Disabilities, "Fact Sheet on Persons with Disabilities," United Nations Enable, http:// www.un.org/disabilities/default.asp?id=18.

5. World Health Organization, Community-Based Rehabilitation as We Have Experienced It: Voices of Persons with Disabilities, pt. 1 (Geneva: World Health Organization, 2002), 25, http://whqlibdoc.who.int/publications/9241590432.pdf.

6. Medical Ambassadors International, "A Proven Strategy: Community Health Evangelism – CHE," http://www.lifewind.org/che.htm.

7. Terri L. Shelton, Elizabeth S. Jepson, and Beverly H. Johnson, Family-Centered Care for Children with Special Health Care Needs (Bethesda, MD: Association for the Care of Children's Health, 1987), 4.

8. David Werner, Disabled Village Children: A Guide for Community Health Workers, Rehabilitation Workers, and Families (Palo Alto, CA: Hesperian Foundation, 2009). Available at http://hesperian.org.

9. Shelton, Jepson, and Johnson, Family-Centered Care, 4.

10. U.S. Department of Health and Human Services, Health Resources and Services Administration, Maternal and Child Health Bureau, "The National Survey of Children with Special Health Care Needs Chartbook 2005–2006," http://mchb.hrsa.gov/cshcn05.

11. Family Voices, "Who Are Children with Special Health Care Needs?" http://www.familyvoices.org/work/caring?id=0007.

12. World Health Organization, "Disability and Health," Fact Sheet No. 352, 2011, http://www.who.int/mediacentre/factsheets/fs352/en/index.html.

13. World Health Organization, "Disabilities," http://www.who.int/topics/disabilities/en.

14. For illustrated instructions, see Werner, Disabled Village Children, 525–636.

15. Pat Downey, Let's Play with Our Children (Washington, DC: Association for the Care of Children's Health, 1986), 1.

16. World Health Organization, World Report on Disability (Geneva: World Health Organization, 2011), 32, http://whqlibdoc.who.int/publications/2011/9789240685215_eng.pdf.

17. Program for Appropriate Technology in Health, "Understanding the Crisis," DefeatDD.org, http://defeatdd.org/understanding-crisis.

18. Mark L. Batshaw, Children with Disabilities, 4th ed. (Baltimore: Brookes, 1997), 628.

19. For illustrated instructions for constructing feeding aids, see Werner, Disabled Village Children, 319–32.

20. World Health Organization, World Report on Disability, 36.

21. Ibid.

22. World Health Organization, "Micronutrient Deficiencies: Vitamin A Deficiency," http://www.who.int/nutrition/topics/vad/en.

23. Ibid.

24. World Health Organization, "Poliomyelitis," Fact Sheet No. 114, 2011, http://www.who.int/mediacentre/factsheets/fs114/en/index.html.

25. World Health Organization, "Micronutrient Deficiencies: Iron Deficiency Anaemia," http://www.who.int/nutrition/topics/ida/en/index.html.

26. Fredric D. Burg, Richard A. Polin, Julie R. Ingelfinger, and Anne A. Gershon, Gellis and Kagan's Current Pediatric Therapy (Philadelphia: Saunders, 2002), 634.

27. World Health Organization, "Micronutrient Deficiencies: Iodine Deficiency Disorders," http://www.who.int/nutrition/topics/idd/en/index.html.

28. World Health Organization, "Summary of WHO Position Papers: Recommended Routine Immunizations for Children," 2011, http://www.who.int/immunization/policy/Immunization_routine_table2.pdf.

29. World Health Organization, "Poliomyelitis."

30. Ibid.

31. World Health Organization, World Report on Disability, 33.

32. World Health Organization, Global Polio Eradication Initiative, "Strategy," http://www.polioeradication.org/Aboutus/Strategy.aspx.

33. World Health Organization, "Poliomyelitis."

CHAPTER SIX

ROADBLOCKS TO SPIRITUAL DEVELOPMENT

* * *

Albert Blackston

WITHOUT a doubt, my experience of having cerebral palsy has been the defining experience of my life. My story is filled with agonizing questions and the realization of answers achieved only over a period of time. But on the other hand, the fact of the disability itself has not defined my life. The handicap is only the crucible for the refining of my personal relationship with the Lord Jesus Christ. It is His love for me, His view of me and His use of me that has defined my life.

NOT DAMAGED GOODS

Prior to my becoming a Christian at age nine, my life was dominated by several realities that are essential for understanding the things that came later. The first of these things I call external realities.

External Realities

I received seemingly endless questions from people who did not know me personally, such as "Why do you walk like that?" or "Did you get in an automobile accident?" I honestly believe these queries came not from an overwhelming intention to be cruel but from a sincere desire to understand. But they produced hatred in my heart. I felt that people were not concerned about *me* at all but only about my disability. This hatred was couched in a smile and several stock answers that were designed not to say anything but the essentials.

III

Other external realities that I could not escape included the various braces, weekly rehabilitations, two major operations and several stints in a wheelchair that I have endured at various points in my life. These things stuck out in my daily interactions (not to mention the noticeable way in which I walk), bringing dozens of questions from others and creating in me such anxiety, anger and tremendous insecurity that I did not feel comfortable being around people or looking them in the eye. I fought a constant battle inside myself just to go about my day, even though the struggle was invisible to the majority of those with whom I interacted daily.

Internal Realities

Other realities I call internal realities. These surround the issues of the heart, and they can be summarized in the single word "Why?" I did not understand why God would do this to me. Had I done something so terrible that He hated me so much that He would do this to me? I believed that He hated me and whatever I had done was bad and He wanted to punish me.

This question was hidden from all but a few people, but thankfully I had a godly family and several close friends who were a huge support and encouragement to me in my dealing with these internal realities.

Countless times each afternoon after school, I would pour out my heart to my mother, asking her "Why?" No matter what we started to talk about, the conversation always came back to the single word "Why?" My mother would tell me, "Jesus loves you, and He has a plan for your life." But I did not want to hear that answer. I thought, *Yeah right! He loves me. I don't think so! Look where I am and the stuff that I have to go through that others do not understand; and worse still, they do not want to understand— not really. He loves me? Well, if He loves me like this, I don't want any part of Him at all.*

The Reality of a Divine Change

These two sets of realities combined to overwhelm me. I had many questions and no answers. I felt like I had been hit by a tidal wave that swept through my daily experience, and it did so without warning. I lived and died daily based on the looks I received and the questions I was asked. It is my firm conviction that I would not have made it to my twentieth birthday if not for Jesus and His coming into my life. This event and the resulting shift comprise the rest of my experience with cerebral palsy, even up to the present.

The day that Jesus came into my life was like dozens of others. I was sitting on the bed in my parents' bedroom talking with mom, going back over the all-too-familiar ground of "why" that always resulted in many tears and many other questions. Mother answered my "why" as she always did, saying in many different ways that God loved me and that He had a plan for my life.

This day was different in one fundamental aspect. I understood two key issues: I needed help, and I could not do this anymore on my own—it was too hard. This realization seemed like no big deal, but I remember a peace in my heart and a boldness in conversation the next day that had been previously missing. After accepting Christ as Savior, my situation did *not* miraculously change. If anything it stayed the same . . . the same challenges, issues and insecurities still were huge, but *I* changed in the midst of my situation.

The Reality of God's Truth

The essential verses for this period in my life were Psalm 139:13–16:

For you created my inmost being;
you knit me together in my mother's womb.
I praise you because I am fearfully and wonderfully made;
your works are wonderful,
I know that full well.
My frame was not hidden from you
when I was made in the secret place,
when I was woven together in the depths of the earth.
Your eyes saw my unformed body;
all the days ordained for me were written in your book
before one of them came to be.

This passage answered my nagging questions with comforting answers: God did not make a mistake with me. He had put a great deal of thought into me and planned all the days of my life. He takes an extreme interest in my life.

These truths were enormous for me and had an immediate impact. God's Word was where I went to find out who I was and how to act. I was no longer a prisoner to the ever-changing opinions, constant looks and questions of other people. The Word of God was the exact opposite: it did not change no matter what. To this place alone I went with my questions and to pour out my heart. Now, instead of leaning on my mother, I began to lean on the One to whom she had pointed me on so many afternoons after school.

My relationships with others also dramatically changed. I became vocal and was blessed with a wide variety of friends from many circles of influence. Conversations that were at best vague and a struggle prior to my relationship with Christ now became frequent and a joy. A burden to pray following many of these conversations became the foundation for ministry in later years. It was as if Psalm 139:13–16 was evident to people, like a neon sign in my life. They could see that I knew Jesus, and they knew that I was who He said I was. That truth was attractive to them, because these were the same issues with which they also dealt. The questions they had were equally important as my own questions had been, and these were the universal issues to which they also had no answers and for which they were searching desperately.

This work of Christ in my heart led to many deep relationships with people, although there were periods when I still dealt with the "why" question. The full answer to that question was not given to me until I was twenty-four years old, shortly after I had rededicated my life to Christ. The answer to this question would shape the direction my life was to take.

At that time I began attending a church through some Christian friends from college days. During this initial period, as I began to serve with the youth group, God began to deal with me about sin in my life, and I finally got the answer to the "why" question! The answer came on a Wednesday night while helping with the youth group. The youth pastor's text that night was John 9:3–4 in which Jesus said of a man who had been born blind: "This happened so that the works of God might be displayed in him." These verses told me clearly and exactly why things had played out the way that they had for me. These words from John 9 were as powerful as the words of Psalm 139 had been previously for me. In a sense they harkened back to my mother's words during so many of those difficult conversations early on: "God loves you and He has a plan for your life."

That was it! Just as the blind man knew, so now did I: things happened in my life so that God's work might be manifested in my life. I finally did not have to wonder anymore. This statement provided not just something that someone said to me, but something that God Himself said to me. It was His words alone that ministered to my heart and met that longstanding need for answers.

PERFECTLY SUITED FOR HIS USE

Then I had another question to answer: "What exactly are His works that are to be manifested in my life?" These works, I learned, are profound changes that far outweigh physical healing. They are His faithfulness in providing a support network of family and friends, recognizing the importance of living as the body of Christ. They are His refuge described in Psalm 71:1–3, where I can always come and pour out my thoughts, feelings and needs, no matter if they are in rage, confusion or even apathy.

Most of all, His works manifested in my life are the profound work in my own heart. This work allows me to come not only to a place of acceptance but also to a place of rejoicing over all the grace that I have been shown. Given that thousands of individuals the world over do not arrive at these realizations of God's power and provision and spend years—in many cases an entire lifetime—believing things about God and His plans and purposes that are totally false, how blessed I am!

But my acceptance of and rejoicing in God's truth did not mean an absence of further difficult times. Yet in the midst of those difficulties I have experienced incredible opportunities to minister to individuals in similar circumstances and also to their family members. The depth of God's wisdom and foresight not only to provide for me a firm place to stand in Christ but also a chance to help others get the same firm footing continually amazes me. These opportunities provide the occasion to minister in the realm of our shared experiences, but more importantly they put Christ on display.

HELPING OTHERS FIND THEIR WAY

Learning that I was not damaged goods and understanding that I was instead perfectly suited for God's use allowed me to successfully navigate the roadblocks that stood in the way of my spiritual development. The question of what to tell those who are dramatically affected by a physical disability is one to which I have given a great deal of thought. How can others like me find their way, and how can those around them help and not hinder their path? Here are a few recommendations.

Helping the Family

For the immediate family I would cover several relevant topics. First, be honest with yourself about how you feel. Your fears, anxieties and expectations are valid, and they have bearing on the situation of your family member with the disability.

Also, you are not responsible to be everything to everyone, to have all the answers or to be a person with super strength. Trying to "do it all" will be your first reaction, because you feel badly about how the one you love feels and what he is going through. But remember that your job is to be a place of love and acceptance. It is crucial that your loved one with these challenges knows that you are there, that your love is constant and that no matter what happens you are in his corner one hundred percent.

Your role involves prayer and some difficult decisions. You must be willing to let your loved one go through hard things and fail, to have to work hard to accomplish goals in life. You will bring confidence, pride and self-assurance by allowing your loved one to hit the ground and have to get up by herself, but be encouraged! Jesus hears your prayers for your loved one, and He knows your heart and desires for her, and He is in control! Trust Him, and be consistently there.

How Friends Can Share

For those who are close friends of the individual with physical disabilities, I would offer these suggestions. I would advise you, first of all, to be up front and candid with your questions and to ask them so that they can be addressed. For example, "How do you feel when friends reject you because of your disability?" Such questions, however, should be asked only within the context of willingness on your part to open yourself, to share and to be transparent. A real and meaningful relationship can only develop if based on mutual trust, respect and transparency.

Secondly, I would suggest to be yourself! Individuals with a disability are not defined by their condition. They happen to have a disability; they are not the disability. They have goals, dreams, likes, dislikes and interests. Be bold to share your interests and ask about theirs as well. Above all—*have fun*! That is what friends are for, right?

Pointers for the Casual Acquaintance

To those individuals who have what most would call "casual" contact among those with disabilities, I would offer these observations. Most importantly, you need to realize that even if you cannot identify with the person, careless words and actions can cause tremendous pain for those who have physical disabilities. Fearful and anxious looks, along with the never-ending questions, without a genuine desire to know and understand a person has the potential to do damage that will continue in the life of that individual for years after. So please be thoughtful, straightforward and real.

Second, it is important that you realize that this person desires to be as independent as possible. If you desire to give assistance in any way, please ask what is needed, and if the individual tells you, "No, thank you," then please respect those wishes.

A third pointer: if you have questions, address those issues directly and allow time for discussion. Questions that go unanswered create awkward tension.

Thoughts for the Individual with a Disability

If you are the person with a disability, the tough times will continue to be there, and days will occur when you may wish your situation to be different. These days continue to be present in my life and take varying degrees of strength. Determine in your heart that you can do all things through the One who loves you supremely. He is there to help you. Trust His strength and enabling.

CONCLUSION

There is one strategy for coping that is always effective. This strategy is relevant for the individuals themselves, for family members, for friends and for casual contacts. That tactic is the truth that we must continually return to the source of truth and the One who is in control—the Lord Jesus Christ.

It is essential to remember that the Lord is a faithful God who has promised never to leave us or forsake us (Hebrews 13:5–6). He is our refuge and strength and the source of safety in tough times (Psalm 46:1–2). He is the One who provides proper perspective and allows us to focus on what is important, regardless of our circumstances (Psalm 73:21–28). He is the One who can change hearts and cause us who have a disability, as well as those who are indirectly affected by a disability, to no longer spend our lives asking "Why?" Instead we can spend our lives in humble dependence on Jesus, thankful for His Word and His promises. We can rejoice in the opportunity that He gives us to be used by Him to minister to those around us from a platform that He alone can build and take the credit.

This shift will result in the furtherance of His kingdom in the hearts of men and women and will allow people with disabilities to remain humble, thankful and usable in His hands for His glory.

PART III

Interventions

Restoring Hope

If I regarded my life from the point of view of the pessimist,
I should be undone.
I should seek in vain for the light that does not visit my eyes
and the music that does not ring in my ears.
I should beg night and day and never be satisfied.
I should sit apart in awful solitude, a prey to fear and despair.
But since I consider it a duty to myself and to others to be happy,
I escape a misery worse than any physical deprivation.

—Helen Keller

Chapter Seven

Training for Socialization

* * *

Phyllis Kilbourn

ALL CHILDREN, including children with disabilities, belong in community. People living together harmoniously as one community where mutual respect and understanding contribute to an inclusive society is the ideal, at least by God's standards. An integral part of this ideal is inclusion of children with disabilities.

Inclusion involves more than merely the presence of children with disabilities in a community. Inclusion refers to the full and active participation of children with disabilities alongside of children who have typical development. Research findings recognize and public policies have promoted inclusion as an important element in producing positive outcomes for young children with disabilities and their families. Therefore a prime concern for such children is their right to community inclusion—the opportunity to live in the community and to be a full participant in all aspects of community life: education, holiday celebrations, recreational activities, church and daily activities. Such children also want and need to assume meaningful social roles in community life. The extent to which community inclusion is realized for individual children reflects the capacity of their social environments to support and sustain them physically, socially, spiritually and psychologically.

Disability Presents Barriers to Community

But not all communities are inclusive. Societies tend to classify themselves either by excluding a group of people or by associating with a particular group of people. In many societies people with disabilities are excluded. Why is this?

A society's value system and cultural beliefs determine what is acceptable in society and what is not. Those who adhere to what is acceptable are included in the society, whereas those who fail to adhere are excluded. Disability often causes people to lack acceptable behavior and social skills, resulting in their exclusion.

Children with disabilities face many barriers to inclusion in community. Social competence and emotional well-being are issues that children with disabilities struggle to obtain. If they are not successful in obtaining them, they are at risk of being left out of participating in family and community events. For various reasons, some children do not develop social skills as easily as others. They may earnestly seek peer relationships and then, having endured criticism and rejection (and sometimes downright meanness), retreat to the safety of home, family and their own company.

Additionally, the limitations of physical, mental and other disabilities present barriers. Children like to be active! Children with physical disabilities who cannot run or play like others may have a difficult time making friends. Where disability is mental or emotional, communication with others may be a problem. Some children have cognitive challenges that make it hard for them to read the social cues in the environment that typically develop a child's understanding. Reactions to these situations can lead children to behaviors that are extreme.

Finally, caregivers can play a part in creating barriers. Being liked, feeling accepted and having self-confidence are all related to a child's social skills. If caregivers do not understand the child and his abilities, they may place limitations that further isolate the child. This isolation and lack of social skills soon become root causes for barriers being raised that prevent children from becoming members of an inclusive society.

One must remember that, more than anything else, these children would like their situations to be different. Children want to be part of community. How can we help them to be included?

TRAINING FOR SOCIALIZATION IS THE PATHWAY FOR INCLUSION IN COMMUNITY

How does one become a part of community? Through socialization. Socialization involves the process of learning what is acceptable in a society and adhering to it. Socialization has been described as "the process of inheriting and disseminating norms, customs and ideologies. It may provide the individual with the skills and habits necessary for participating within their own society."[1] Children with disabilities must be properly socialized to be included in community. The Merriam-Webster Online Dictionary defines *socialize* in this way: "to make social; *especially*: to fit or train for a social environment."[2] This definition aptly describes the task we have as caregivers of children whose disabilities present barriers that prevent healthy socialization. We must train them to fit in their social environment through identifying and removing those barriers. This chapter will look at some common barriers in detail and then explain ways to use training in socialization to remove these barriers.

But it is not only individual children who must change. For them to become participants in an inclusive society, communities must also become inclusive of children with disabilities. Societies develop culture "through a plurality of shared norms, customs, values, traditions, social roles, symbols and languages. Socialization is thus 'the means by which social and cultural continuity are attained.'"[3] When a community's culture excludes children with disabilities, then it is necessary for the community's norms, customs, values and so on to change. We as caregivers must find ways to build relationships between the community as a whole and children with disabilities in order to unify the community.

BARRIERS TO SOCIALIZATION

A barrier is an obstacle or hindrance that prevents someone from making progress. Here the barriers are to socialization of children with disabilities. Although physical or mental barriers are considered significant impediments to full participation in the home or community, attitudes are in fact the most frequently reported barriers to their activity and participation. Often the barriers are related to the children's behavior. Children with disabilities sometimes engage in behaviors that hinder socialization. These behaviors are usually not fully understood and do not match up to society's cultural norms, preventing children with disabilities from being fully embraced in an inclusive society. Therefore it is vital to improve community understanding of disability and its impact on behavior and to confront negative perceptions of children with disabilities. It is also essential to address the behaviors themselves.

The following paragraphs highlight some of the main barriers that hinder socialization. Following this review, we will look deeper at ways to understand and address the behavioral barriers that prevent socialization. Removal of these barriers is a major part of intervention.

Stigmatization

For children with disabilities, stigmatization (being labeled socially undesirable) is a common, painful experience. Due to stigmatization, the children experience stereotyping (preconceptions based on popular beliefs about people with disabilities), prejudice (being viewed negatively because of disability) and discrimination (being treated negatively based on disability) that affect all areas of their lives, creating physical and social isolation, and limiting opportunities to live fully integrated lives in the community. Family members also face "stigmatization by association" in many areas of their lives, especially those where their children are involved, such as social settings, mental health systems and schools. Family members have often reported being subjected to discrimination and exclusion due to their association with the child having a disability.

Limited Language Skills

Limited language skills can make it difficult for children to positively express intents, needs or emotions. Such limitations can be frustrating. The need for food or a sweater to keep warm or even a drink of water are sometimes difficult to communicate, especially to those outside the home. Often a child's attempts to communicate are either ignored by the listener or the listener gives up trying to communicate with the child. For some children a language disability makes it difficult for them to process instructions, and their wrong responses are taken to be an act of rebellion or unwillingness to comply. These limitations in communication are frustrating to a child and can lead to temper tantrums. The child, instead of being understood, is rebuked and left with needs not met.

Social Rejection

Social rejection occurs when an individual is deliberately excluded from a social relationship or social interaction. Peer rejection, whether actively expressed by being made fun of, or expressed passively by being ignored by others, is difficult for children. Children with disabilities or children who have unusual characteristics or behavior may face greater risk of rejection by their peers. Children who experience rejection are likely to have lower self-esteem and to be at greater risk for internalizing problems like depression. Some children express rejection with external behavior and show aggression rather than depression.

When children see other children playing, they want to join in and participate. However, usually there are no special games or sporting events that allow children with disabilities to participate with their friends. The best they can do is sit and watch others having fun. This results in experiencing social rejection as well as isolation—a hurtful combination. When this happens, the majority of children respond by "acting out" verbally or physically. This can happen at home or in a public place such as a restaurant or store, and it can happen without warning. Such an outburst causes stress, not only for the child but also for the adult accompanying the child.

Family Isolation

Families may also face serious barriers to community inclusion, even experiencing exclusion from community-based activities due to their children's disabilities. When their children are refused entrance to (or are asked to leave) community-based activities such as child care, sports clubs or church gatherings, parents are also excluded from the adult social networks that support these opportunities for community inclusion. This clearly affects the families' quality of life.

Parents of children with severe disabilities and/or challenging behavior may also become isolated from family and social networks because of the all-pervasive caring role required. As the children grow older, their isolation may be even greater. A study of parents caring for young adults with severe intellectual disabilities and challenging behaviors at home revealed that very few had frequent or close contact with friends or family outside the household. Few families were even part of an active social network that provided moral support. Such isolation, especially of mothers, can result not only from the fact that they are tied to the house, but also because people tend not to want to visit such a household. Furthermore, as their children grow up, the parents have less and less in common with friends and relatives who have children the same age.

Lack of Positive Self-Identity and Low Self-Esteem

Self-identity is an awareness of and identification with oneself as a separate, unique individual. It is a foundational stone in the structure of a person's self-esteem. In turn, "whether a child suffers from emotional, physical, cognitive or behavioral disability, self-esteem is critical to a child's success."[4] However, positive self-identity and self-esteem can be fragile in children with disabilities.

Children can get stuck in a self-perpetuating cycle of poor self-identity and low self-esteem. According to child psychologist Steven Richfield:

> One of the most troubling dilemmas for parents [and caregivers] is when children show signs of low self-esteem. Despite our

best efforts to help them feel good about themselves, we watch with dismay as they resist social opportunities, narrow choices to [nonthreatening] activities, verbally punish themselves, or display a variety of other self-deprecating behaviors. Unfortunately, these signs serve to confirm their negative self-view, setting in motion a self-defeating cycle that can lead to even more disturbing consequences.[5]

From an early age, children compare themselves with others in areas such as academics, the ability to make and keep friends, and athletic ability. This can be deadly to the self-esteem of children with disabilities who

regardless of . . . age or cognitive ability [are] keenly aware of the differences between [their] abilities and those of other children or siblings, and the expectations of parents. Because a child may require extra help or modifications to their environment, the presence of these aids is a constant reminder of their difficulties.[6]

For younger children, the comparisons and subsequent self-judgment can be rather simplistic or "black and white." For example, children with learning disabilities may judge themselves as "stupid," "slow" or "dumb," based on academic comparisons with other children. These self-judgments are often comprehensive in nature such that children who are having difficulty at school may perceive themselves negatively in all areas of their development.

Furthermore, children who lack positive self-identity and self-esteem will be reluctant to try to progress if they believe they are incapable, unimportant or a failure; instead limiting themselves to activities that assure them of success:

Many children with disabilities are unwilling to participate in activities that would benefit them because they are insecure, embarrassed, or lack confidence in their skills, perceived or real. This takes away opportunities to realize and develop the skills they need to be successful, which stunts their overall growth and development even further.[7]

Particularly vulnerable to this devastating cycle are children who have been in the foster care system. Having been cared for by multiple families, they have experienced—at least in their minds—multiple rejections. These children feel unwanted and worse than useless. Often they have never been taught how to be helpful. These children come to their new families feeling that they bring virtually nothing; they are miserable, feeling like nonchildren with no positive feelings about who they are.

Excessive Environmental Stimulation

Disabilities can result in children's brains being able to process only a limited amount of sensory input at a time. When information comes in faster than they can sort it out, they get confused. Quite often there is a lot more stimulation going on in the environment than caregivers realize. For example, imagine an autistic child and her parents going to the home of family friends for dinner. Stepping from the quietness of the car they enter a room where a football game is playing on television, several people watching the game are talking excitedly, the doorbell rings announcing more visitors, the dog barks and the child is hungry.

All this noise and activity are too much sensory input for the child. To those watching, it seems like the child is sitting quietly, unaffected. But in her head she is on overload, with more information going into her brain than she can handle. When it becomes overwhelming, she tries to stop it in the quickest and most reliable way she knows: she throws a tantrum. If parents or caregivers are not aware of what is going on in a situation like this, they can feel embarrassed and irritated by their child's behavior.

Short Attention Span

Children with short attention spans are likely to display negative behaviors such as becoming impatient while listening or waiting for their turn to speak. They also have a hard time returning to an unfinished task once they are interrupted. Disruptive children, children who do not mind adults, and aggressive children are sometimes included under the broad category of short attention span.

Having a short attention span is a significant characteristic of children with Attention Deficit Disorder (ADD) and Attention Deficit Hyperactivity Disorder (ADHD). ADD and ADHD are syndromes characterized by serious and persistent difficulties in the following three specific areas: attention span, impulse control and sometimes hyperactivity. Children with ADD/ADHD often have problems with sitting still, staying focused, following instructions, staying organized, completing a task or doing homework. Many children who do not have emotional disturbances may also display some of these same behaviors at various times during their development. However, when children have an ability-related emotional disturbance, these behaviors continue over long periods of time. Their behavior signals that they are not coping with their environment or with their peers.

Lack of Adequate Structure

All children need the protection and predictability that structure provides. Without structure, life becomes chaotic and unpredictable. Sometimes parents' busy schedule of caring for other siblings along with the child with disabilities leaves little time for planning structured activities. The often-resulting chaos, especially when rushing to keep scheduled activity or appointment times, leaves the child frustrated and confused. With a structured day, limitations are placed on a child's behavior, helping the child learn internal control. This natural form of discipline provides children with a sense of security and well-being. But when structures are lacking, children fail to learn and experience these important things.

THE BARRIER OF CHALLENGING BEHAVIOR

As we have seen, many of the barriers to socialization are either caused by or result in challenging behaviors. We need to understand and address these behaviors to fully remove barriers to socialization.

Impact of Challenging Behavior

Challenging behaviors can prevent children with disabilities from learning important social skills and concepts. Their unacceptable behaviors often impede the development of friendships and a sense of belonging in a group. The behaviors also can cause children to be denied access to settings and experiences that would enrich their lives and provide them with the joy of community. Instead, these children frequently find themselves rejected by their peers. They become isolated and are denied opportunities to practice and develop the social skills they so desperately need. Such behaviors also make it difficult to give them a sense of belonging.

Children with disabilities have varied and unique issues from which their behavioral problems arise. For example, it is common for children with developmental disabilities to have problems with behavior because of their cognitive deficits or deficiencies. If a child has deficits in language and social skills, those deficits can significantly impact the child's ability to live in a social environment. It is important that caregivers understand children's ways of learning, not only for a child's education but also for managing their behavior.

Reasons for Challenging Behavior

It is important for caregivers to understand that there are reasons for a child's negative behavior. When children persist in a certain behavior, it is because that behavior is serving some purpose for them. We must be able to recognize and respond to the reasons behind the behavior, and not just to the behavior itself. Knowing why a behavior is occurring makes it easier to come up with solutions that promote socialization. There are two basic purposes for children's negative behavior.

First, children use behavior to communicate. If children have a difficult time stating their needs or wants using language, they are likely to find another means to express themselves. For children who have developmental disabilities, that expression can often be in the form of tantrums, aggression, self-injury or other problematic behaviors. But what they are trying to communicate are messages such as:

- "You are asking me to do something I cannot do."
- "I do not understand what you want me to do."
- "I want something and I want it now."
- "I am bored."
- "I need some attention."
- "I am feeling embarrassed."
- "I am tired."
- "I am experiencing more stimulation that I can handle."
- "I am feeling threatened."
- "I am hungry."

It is crucial to understand what children are saying through their behavior so that we can teach them new ways to communicate their wants and needs. We must know the child! Only by understanding why the problem behavior is occurring can we assist a child in developing more appropriate ways to express desires, needs and emotions.

Second, children use behavior to express their feelings. Children with disabilities often lack control over their emotions, which can result in behavioral problems. Angry defiance is common. When rejection, isolation, ridicule and a host of other negative expressions of disapproval are heaped on children—especially on those who look or act differently—they feel hurt, confused and angry. But often they do not know how to identify or handle these feelings except through aggressive or defiant behavior such as hitting, kicking, screaming or breaking things. Experts give several explanations for anger:

Anger may be a defense to avoid painful feelings; it may be associated with failure, low self-esteem, and feelings of isolation; or it may be related to anxiety about situations over which the child has no control.

Angry defiance may also be associated with feelings of dependency, and anger may be associated with sadness and depression. In childhood, anger and sadness are very close to one another and it is important to remember that much of what an adult experiences as sadness is expressed by a child as anger.[8]

To make things worse, children with disabilities not only find it difficult to identify their own feelings but they also often miss visual cues that should let them know how others are feeling. Their inability to "read" others' feelings may cause them to respond to a situation with inappropriate behavior.

Responding to Challenging Behavior

How then should we respond to negative behavior? First, we must address the effects of the behavior on the child, rather than just the effects that behavior has on us as caregivers, such as frustration or embarrassment. Although the child's behavior usually does affect the caregiver, focusing on the impacts on the caregiver prevents us from recognizing the effects on the child. These effects could include interference with the child's learning, development and success at play; harm to the child, other children or adults; or being at high risk for later social problems or failure. Therefore it is important that we recognize and address these effects.

Second, caregivers understandably find it easy to let their frustration take hold as they care for children who exhibit challenging behaviors. They must, however, avoid letting their own negative emotions determine how they will respond. Instead, caregivers must look at these situations of challenging behavior as opportunities to teach and assist children in becoming accepted members of the family and the community. In the next section we will look at how to use training to address negative behavior as well as to pave the way to healthy socialization.

Training for Healthy Socialization

Now that we understand the behavioral and other barriers to socialization, what can we as caregivers do about them? Caregivers need to provide training that allows children to remove the barriers that keep them from establishing meaningful relationships in their homes and in their communities.

Removing these barriers will diminish children's behavior problems and make healthy socialization possible.

Basic Principles of Training

Before we look at specifics of what training should entail, we must understand a few basics about what effective training is.

First, disciplining children with disabilities must first and foremost be thought of in terms of training, not punishment. Caregivers must keep focused on the goal of empowering children to engage in healthy socialization in the home, school and community:

> *In dealing with angry children, our actions should be motivated by the need to protect and to teach, not by a desire to punish. Parents and teachers should show a child that they accept his or her feelings, while suggesting other ways to express the feelings. An adult might say, for example, "Let me tell you what some children would do in a situation like this . . ." It is not enough to tell children what behaviors we find unacceptable. We must teach them acceptable ways of coping.[9]*

Second, training must be geared to the child's individual level of social development. This will impact, for example, the way caregivers correct the behavior of children with disabilities. Poorly developed social skills mean that the natural social consequences that shape typical children's behavior may not be effective. Children deficient in social skills may not be as likely to feel embarrassed or remorseful as other children might, because they do not fully understand the social situation. Therefore it may be ineffective to use the same type of correction that would be used for a child with typically developing social skills. For example, to ask children with poorly developed skills to apologize or to ask them how other children felt when they took their favorite toy might not result in the child wanting to change the way they behave in the future.

Third, training must be consistent with how children learn. Children, like all people, learn through interacting with their environment. They often learn by observing others and doing what others do. This is why modeling good behavior is vital in helping children not to pick up wrong behaviors. Children also learn through trial and error. Children soon learn that when they engage in a particular behavior a consequence always follows that behavior. Consequences are important in helping children decide whether they should act that way again in the future. Consequences that are pleasing lead them to engage in that behavior again. Consequences that feel punishing cause them to avoid that behavior again in a similar situation. Consequences can also be more neutral, not motivating them either way. Therefore, training should include consequences that encourage desired behavior and discourage unwanted behavior.

Finally, training should create the conditions for correct behavior to occur. We have seen that children use challenging behavior to meet needs that are not otherwise being met. Therefore the first step in helping children learn appropriate behavior is to establish safe environments that make it less likely that the children will feel the need to use inappropriate behavior. If inappropriate behavior is no longer needed, it is less likely to occur. Furthermore, reducing the occurrence of negative behavior also leads to a lesser amount of negative behavior in the future. When a child repeatedly engages in negative behaviors, these behavior patterns become more strongly embedded in the brain, making it even more difficult for the child to stop the problem behaviors. Consistency, therefore, is extremely important, especially in the beginning stages of dealing with behaviors.

With these important principles in mind, we will now look at specific training components to provide caregivers with insight into how they can help children achieve success in socialization. You will doubtless become aware of other components to include that will also enhance their socialization skills.

Have Reasonable Expectations

Having reasonable expectations for a child with special needs includes ensuring that expectations are neither too high nor too low. When expectations are too low, children can become "spoiled" by having others do everything for them. If the goals, however, are set higher than a child can reasonably attain, the children can lose hope and give up.

Children must be assessed as individuals, taking into account their developmental stage. If children have mental challenges, autism or other severe cognitive disabilities, caregivers must not expect them to be at the same level as typical children of the same age. This can be difficult to remember, especially if a child does not look any different from other children.

Expectations must be communicated at a level the child can understand. Some children, for example, may find it hard to follow complex instructions. In that case we should not say things like, "Mary, that was a very bad thing you did, and it hurt your brother's feelings. You should not do that, and I do not want you ever to do it again. You are too big of a girl to be hitting your little brother." Instead, we should say, "Mary! Do not hit! That is bad!" This same caution applies to assigning tasks, especially those that require several steps to complete.

Teach Problem-Solving and Conflict-Resolution Skills

Good social skills such as problem-solving skills and conflict-resolution skills are critical to successful functioning in life. Problem-solving skills include knowing how to ask for help, accepting consequences and being able to decide the best thing to do or the best way to respond to a problem. Conflict-resolution skills include knowing how to deal with teasing, losing, accusations, apologizing, being left out and peer pressure. Knowing how to use these skills enhances interpersonal relationships and is a key factor in acceptance on a social level. Therefore it is essential that we train children with special needs in the social skills that they are lacking.

It is important to teach children how to act appropriately before problems happen. Research has shown that children who have received problem-solving training show more positive social behavior than children who have not received training. Younger children need to learn how to resolve common childhood problems such as sharing and taking turns. In the case of older children, they need to learn to problem solve for themselves and to come up with strategies to manage and cope with difficulties. This builds their independence and mastery of coming up with options, finding solutions, or finding other ways to comfort themselves.

Give Positive Feedback

Children need help to see and understand the positive things about themselves and to believe that they are worthwhile persons. Experiences of stress and tension can serve to defeat children's confidence in themselves. Rejection is a major cause of stress in children with disabilities and an assault on their sense of self-worth, but it is a difficult concept for them to grasp, because "they are starved for positive feedback and approval to fuel their self-esteem and self-worth" and yet they "often respond to and remember negative comments more easily than positive ones."[10]

Positive feedback can rebuild their self-esteem and self-worth as well as encourage positive behavior. Children thrive on approval, acceptance and love. No child or adult ever wants to feel unloved. Caregivers can encourage a positive environment for children by praising them for the acceptable things they do. The more attention kids get for the good things they do, the more they want to repeat the positive behavior. There can be amazing results in the positive effect of such encouragement on children's actions and behavior when caregivers use phrases such as: "I am impressed"; "Wonderful job!"; "Your smile lights up the room"; "I knew you could do it!"; "I thank God for you each day"; "I am so proud of you"; and "I love you." Be specific about what the child did to deserve the positive feedback, and give appropriate praise. Create your own special expressions and use them often.

Children need to know that they have something special and unique to contribute in all spheres of their lives. Imagine the years ahead and the effect such encouraging words can have on a child, your relationship with the child, the child's relationships with other people and the child's feelings about his own self-worth.

Plan for Achievement

Achievement, whether in school work or in completing a task, is a desire of every child. Sadly, children with disabilities often fail to experience the joy and satisfaction of accomplishment that comes with achievement. According to occupational therapist Joel Desotelle, "One of the reasons we tend to take away responsibility is because a child may not have the skills to complete the entire task on their own, so we do it for them."[11] He suggests that to prevent this from happening, we should instead "grade the task" to enable the child to achieve success in a given portion of a task or project.

The basis of this strategy is the fact that success or achievement involves giving children some measure of responsibility at a level that is doable for them. This key is finding the part of a task that the child can do or is able to learn to do, no matter how small, such as helping Daddy build a shelf by opening the toolbox or helping Mommy make pancakes by cracking open the eggs. Such participation "gives a child the opportunity to use and develop important skills, and to work or play with [caregivers] on a social level."[12] Having a part in accomplishing a task also reinforces the child's feelings of value, acceptance and self-esteem. Desotelle warns:

> Learning how to grade a task is not always easy. You need to first understand what skill level they are functioning at and find the "just right challenge." In other words, you need to change how easy or hard a task is so that the child can be successful at a level he or she is capable of. You have to gauge this "just right" level as you work or play with them, being sure to challenge, but not frustrate them.[13]

Provide Structure: Rules and Routines

Determining how much structure is helpful for children with disabilities and how much unstructured time they need can be a challenge. Children need structure in order to know what is expected of them, to give them a sense of order and security, and to help them learn to follow a routine. Structure also can make children's lives feel safer and more dependable. On the other hand, children also need time that is not scheduled or highly planned. Unstructured time is developmentally important because it gives children time to be free—to think, dream or relax. Finding the balance that works for each child in light of her particular disability is a key part of the strategy.

For young children, structure is normally provided by interactions with parents or significant adults, as well as the rituals, routines or schedules of family and community. Older children get much of their structure from the school context. Because children with disabilities have difficulty understanding and interacting with the world, they find that a predictable routine gives them a sense of security. If everything happens in the same way and in the same order each day, they will not have to remember exactly what they were supposed to be doing or where they were supposed to go next. They find that a routine is less frustrating and increases their level of comfort in interactions.

Set boundaries and rules are part of the structure children need to give order and predictability to their world. Caregivers should be careful to make as few rules as possible, because children cannot remember long lists of instructions. Be sure to explain the rules to the child in simple terms along with the consequence for breaking them. The focus should be on rules that keep the child safe and happy. Safety always should be a first concern (road safety, safety in the home, fire safety, people coming into the home, and so on). Repeat instructions about safety issues frequently, and be sure that the child knows what he is allowed to do independently. If a child breaks a rule that compromises his safety, tell him immediately in a firm voice that you are displeased. Explain the reason for your concern using simple terms. Be prepared to revise some of these rules as the child gets older and is capable of living more independently.

Maintain Low Levels of Environmental Stimulation

Excessive sensory input can cause triggers (words, images, sounds and so on) that set off behavior problems in children with disabilities. Common triggers are too much noise, crowds and too many distractions. Some children's brains can only process a limited amount of sensory input at one time. As stated earlier, when information comes in faster than children can sort it out, they get confused and frustrated. It is important to reduce the level of environmental stimulation where possible.

Quite often there is a lot more stimulation going on in the environment than we realize. When a child who is negatively affected by sensory stimuli experiences a "meltdown," it is helpful to keep track of how many sensory inputs were happening at the time. This will help establish the child's tolerance level so that in the future you can find ways to decrease the sensory input the child experiences.

Be Sensitive to Short Attention Spans

Caregivers need to be sensitive to the fact that children with disabilities usually have some measure of physical or emotional difficulties that causes them to have short attention spans. Such children need lots of patience, understanding and praise for every good effort they make to overcome this deficiency. Affirmation helps build children's confidence and trust, not only in themselves but also in others. Praise children often for extending their attention span, even if by only a short time. On the other hand, avoid giving them negative comments when they are not achieving. Children need and feed on any type of attention and should learn that they will get it for achievement but not for failure.

Where possible, train children how to lengthen their attention spans. Be alert to discover what a child is interested in—where she has demonstrated a longer attention span. Use this interest to help the child develop new and challenging skills that are achieved through being involved in the activity for longer periods of time. It may be helpful to consider setting up a reward system to encourage her to pay attention longer. Make sure that the system includes short-term, achievable goals that are rewarded almost instantly in the beginning. Success should inspire children to try to break their own records.

Build Healthy Self-Esteem

It is essential to help build self-esteem in the children in our care. "Recognizing and understanding the importance of a child's self-esteem is necessary to optimize overall physical, social and emotional development."[14] One of the best ways to build self-esteem is to make children feel needed; for instance, by asking them to do a task that they can succeed at. Children who are shown affirmation and appreciation for a job well done not only feel good about themselves but they will also feel more competent to participate in activities and tasks in the future. Along with giving children tasks, we must also give the time needed to complete them. Desotelle reminds us:

> *Giving a child time to participate and complete an activity is an investment in her self-esteem and overall function. This also has a snowball effect on the child's growth and development: more opportunity, more skills, more self-esteem, greater compliance and motivation, and more opportunities!*[15]

Another way to build healthy self-esteem in children is through empathy. According to Richfield, empathy can help "pierce the isolation" that stems from a child's low self-esteem. "Correcting the problem begins with parents demonstrating love and acknowledging the child's painful feelings. Before healing can begin children must know that they can lean on us for understanding and guidance."[16] In addition, we must also help them change their negative self-thoughts to positive ones.

Help the Child Express Feelings

Sometimes a primary focus is placed on eliminating the negative behaviors that occur when children with special needs become emotionally upset and out of control, with little or no time spent on helping them learn to identify, understand and regulate their emotions in a healthy way.

Children need help to feel comfortable in expressing their feelings through means other than behavior. First they need to be able to identify what they are feeling. We can teach children the names, colors or other words to use in describing their feelings (for example, pink for happy and blue for sad). We also need to teach them appropriate ways to express their feelings. Let children know that it is all right to feel angry, alone, scared or lonely. Show more interest in what feelings they are experiencing than in the behavior that results. We must also correct any misconceptions that the children may have about themselves or their feelings.

An effective way of helping children identify and express their feelings is through reflective listening as you encourage them to express and share their feelings with you. Reflective listening is briefly summarizing and restating to children both their feelings and the situation that seems to have caused those feelings.

Another activity caregivers can use to help children understand and express feelings is to place photos of children who are displaying emotions (for example: anger, fear, love, hate, loneliness) around the walls for the children to carefully observe. Then make a game of having the children copy the expressions in the photos on their own faces. Talk about what they might be seeing, feeling or thinking. Plan lots of similar activities that allow them to think through and label their feelings; for example, identifying with characters in books, art activities, puppetry or play. If needed, assist them in clarifying what they are feeling.

Provide Family Support

Families of children with disabilities function more successfully with effective family support. Family support services are based on the belief that families are the greatest resource available to children and that all children need and have the right to a stable family relationship in the community. Like children with typical development, children with disabilities need enduring relationships in nurturing homes. However, the extraordinary care needs related to a developmental disability may stretch family resources, strength and energy. Family support services are proactive and are intended to help prevent families from going into crisis. These services provide families with the assistance they need to remain healthy, independent and safe.

Family support can include a wide array of formal and informal services and material goods that are defined and determined by the needs of a particular family. The family support needs will vary, but the important thing is to help parents and caregivers know how to access needed community resources. Family support requires those providing support to be willing to do "whatever it takes" to help the family care for and live with a child who has emotional, behavioral, mental or other forms of disability. Ultimately, family support keeps families together while enhancing their capacity, independence and quality of life.

Empower the Child

I like the analogy that child development expert Maureen Healy uses when talking about parents empowering their children:

> Similar to the acorn that holds the latent potential of the oak tree within, each child holds his or her greatness. It is "believing in" this greatness, nurturing it and empowering your child to become his or her best self that marks this new age of positive parenting. Gone are the days where parents solely want their kids to get "good jobs," but now we want them to have rewarding lives! It is a shift of epic proportions.[17]

Empowering children entails "helping them gain a sense of inner confidence, courage and strength to successfully surmount whatever life presents,"[18] in spite of whatever disability they may have. Empowering children also includes encouraging them to persevere against obstacles such as rejection, failed grades, mistakes or disappointments.[19] Empowerment gives children the self-assurance to try new things, and the patience to work through more difficult tasks.

Empowered children are more in control of their actions because they are able to think for themselves and understand the long-term consequences of their actions. Empowering children also means telling them, "I trust you. I trust your skills." This increases their self-esteem immeasurably and makes them feel like an accepted contributor to the family or community.

Celebrate Successes

Instead of focusing on the failures or shortcomings of children with disabilities, caregivers need to focus on celebrating every success whether small or large. Celebrations have the benefit of providing opportunities for children to experience social interactions with friends and family. Social interactions celebrating achievement also increase children's self-esteem. In turn, "greater self-esteem produces more opportunities to perform beneficial tasks, which allows a child to witness first-hand what they are capable of accomplishing."[20] These added accomplishments result in more occasions for celebration! This is a cycle we are happy to see continue. Celebrations not only increase children's self-esteem, they also give children the courage and belief in themselves required to strive for higher goals and the encouragement needed to believe in the fulfillment of their dreams.

CONCLUSION

All children are healthiest when they feel safe, supported and connected to others in their families, neighborhoods and communities. Children with disabilities face real barriers to community, but true inclusion is possible through training for socialization. A caregiver's task is not to "cure" a child's disability, but rather to train the child in the social and emotional tools necessary to work through the behavioral and other challenges that confront him. In the long run, confronting and overcoming these challenges can help a child grow stronger and more resilient. Training for socialization is an effective pathway around the barriers that stand in the way of true community inclusion.

We must not only help children with disabilities overcome their own barriers to socialization, we must also help society overcome the attitudinal and other barriers that exclude people with disabilities. Fear or perceived negative attitudes, or practical obstacles such as lack of basic needs or lack of encouragement in the community, all contribute to decreased community connectedness for children with disabilities. Measures must be taken that eliminate the barriers that keep these children from participating fully within the life of their community, and that enable healthy socialization to occur.

It may seem that children with disabilities are living in a different world. We wonder, "Why take on the difficult task of bridging such different worlds?" Joni Eareckson Tada, however, does not see the worlds as different as we might imagine. She assures us:

> *Oh, yes, my life is different because of my disability and things like pressure sores, catheters, and corsets that wear wounds on my hips. Then there are the obvious emotions involving deep and permanent loss. But the basic issues of life are the same with me as they are with you. I need love and a sense of security. I wonder about my place in the world. I have tastes and opinions. I battle the flesh and sometimes wish that I was better, faster, kinder, smarter, prettier, and younger. And I want heaven to be here now.[21]*

If we follow Jesus' example in ministering to and establishing friendships with children and adults who have disabilities, we can give them the mutual joy of an inclusive society in the community, at home and with friends. And we might even be able to find a little bit of that ideal of heaven here.

NOTES

1. *Wikipedia*, s.v. "Socialization," http://en.wikipedia.org/wiki/socialization.

2. *Merriam-Webster Online Dictionary*, s.v. "Socialize," http://www.merriam-webster.com/dictionary/socialization.

3. John A. Clausen, ed., *Socialization and Society* (Boston: Little, Brown and Company, 1968), 5, quoted in *Wikipedia*, s.v. "Socialization."

4. Joel Desotelle, "Self-Esteem Is Crucial for Children with Disabilities," *Frederick's Child Magazine*, February/March 2008, 1, http://www.amberhillpt.com/news_articles/self_esteem.pdf.

5. Steven Richfield, "Strategies to Bolster Self-Esteem," Children's Disabilities Information, http://www.childrensdisabilities.info/parenting/self-esteem.html#richfield.

6. Desotelle, "Self-Esteem," 1.

7. Ibid.

8. National Institute of Mental Health, *Plain Talk about . . . Dealing with the Angry Child* (Rockville, MD: US Department of Health and Human Services; Public Health Service; Alcohol, Drug Abuse, and Mental Health Administration; 1981), http://www.kidsource.com/kidsource/content2/angry.children.html.

9. Ibid.

10. Desotelle, "Self-Esteem," 2.

11. Ibid., 3.

12. Ibid.

13. Ibid.

14. Ibid., 1.

15. Ibid., 4.

16. Richfield, "Strategies."

17. Maureen Healy, "Empowering Kids," *Creative Development: Growing a Child's Unique Gifts* (blog), Psychology Today, June 15, 2009, http://www.psychologytoday.com/blog/creative-development/200906/empowering-kids.

18. Ibid.

19. Ibid.

20. Desotelle, "Self-Esteem," 2.

21. MaLesa Breeding, Dana Hood, and Jerry Whitworth, *Let All the Children Come to Me: A Practical Guide to Including Children with Disabilities in Your Church Ministries* (Colorado Springs, CO: Cook Communications Ministries, 2006), 107.

CHAPTER EIGHT

HELPING CHILDREN COPE

* * *

Dietlinde Hoffman

"A DISASTER!" That is what was written on Victor's report card. Although not written on Tim's report card, his teacher used the same words at Tim's parent-teacher conference.

Neither one sat still or paid attention in class. Both in fourth grade, Victor and Tim were still reading and doing math at a first-grade level. Finally their school psychologists evaluated them and concluded that both boys had a learning disability and Attention Deficit Hyperactivity Disorder. The good news? Their IQ scores were in the bright range.

Tim's scenario: Despite his evaluation, Tim was placed in a regular fifth-grade program the following school year. By sixth grade, he was impossible to direct. Every time he struggled hopelessly with a math problem, every time he stumbled over a sentence in his first-grade reader, he grew a little more hostile, a little more withdrawn, a little more convinced of his worthlessness. He developed intense anger toward himself and the world. His disruptive classroom behavior included throwing everything in his sight. His barking and hiding made him the class clown and banished him from the learning environment that he needed. In high school, his counselor never saw the test results, and his teachers never knew what to do to reach him. His parents tried to get the school to help him but gave up in frustration. He quit school at age sixteen. He moved from job to job while spending more time riding his motorcycles and getting into trouble with the police. It almost seems like the inevitable end of the story to hear that Tim is now in prison for killing two policemen while trying to rob a bank.

Victor's scenario: Victor joked and broke items in the psychiatrist's office as he took part in his testing, but because of the team of people who were involved with Victor, he was placed in a full-time special education program, received therapy and started medication. He was congratulated for getting as far as he did, even though he struggled with learning. He was told that he was not the "retard" that he felt like he was. His family members worked together to improve their own responses to him. Although he spent the first year in his new classroom still blaming others, he took baby steps of progress and headed in the right direction. By his second year, he realized that he would need to do the work to get back to the regular classroom and reach the potential of his IQ. Victor would still get frustrated, but instead of throwing a desk, he talked about his feelings with his teacher. He made up two years of academic work in that one year. He and his father healed their relationship. Victor returned to his local school in the seventh grade still receiving support, and went on to college. Today Victor is a special-education teacher.

Tim and Victor were the same age when they found out about their IQ scores and the label for their disability. How is it that they are turning out so differently? What if Tim had received help earlier? Without access to a psychiatrist, what coping strategies might have helped him? What if a good counselor had been available to help Tim talk through his strong emotions? What if Tim's teachers, parents and testing psychologist had all communicated clearly and designed a plan?

This chapter is about those strategies that you can implement yourself and for the child in your life to help both of you cope, preserve your dignity and rekindle hope. Good coping strategies strengthen the bonds of your family, or the family you are working with, and fortify the child. Your challenges may be the same as Tim's and Victor's or may be quite different. You may have a label for your child, or you may be struggling through without definition. The ideas in this chapter can help any child to cope, no matter the disability.

As I interviewed people I knew who have handled their own disabilities and as I thought about how I have overcome challenges in my life, I realized that successfully overcoming our circumstances never happens overnight and the same plan does not work for every person. It is an ongoing, individualized battle.

Ongoing: The ongoing part of the battle can be compared to getting a wheel to turn. In his book, *Good to Great*, Jim Collins named it the "flywheel effect."[1] You push the wheel with great force at first, fighting against inertia and friction. A wheel needs many small pushes to begin turning. When it gets going, no single push can be identified as the "one" big push. It takes a significant amount of sustained effort. With continued pushing, your momentum alone turns it faster and faster. Choose a direction and put all your weight behind it.

We heat our food in a microwave instantly. Online we find, in seconds, the meaning of the Indonesian phrase *terima kasih*. Although we prefer to swallow a little red pill to take away our pain, that impulse takes away from the appreciation for the process of growth and the success that comes with baby steps of progress over time.

Individualized: The individualized part of the battle is recognizing that all children are unique. Their battles with their own disabilities are going to look, sound and feel distinct. One child's struggle will be different from another child's struggle with the same diagnosis. In fact, a child's struggle will be different from his own battle from the year or even month before.

The ideas described in this chapter may work one day and not another; they may work for one child but not another. The good news is that there is no one right answer, so let that take away your fear of failure. The bad news is that there is no one right answer, so you need to do the hard work of finding the answers. This chapter is less like a recipe book and more like an open-air market where you are going to browse and follow your instincts and your own tastes to find what works for you and the child you need to help.

AFFECTS OF DISABILITIES

According to the article "The Causes of Disabilities in Children," published on the Exploring Developmental Disabilities website, "most of the disabilities that occur in human beings occur in children."[2] To understand disabilities, we need to understand how a child's world is affected by her disability.

How a Family Is Affected by Having a Child with Disabilities

Families go through life's pressures and joys in stages together, but the transitions between stages lead the way as the most difficult times. Normal stages that families everywhere typically experience are identified through the children's milestones: first steps, first words spoken, beginning school, onset of puberty and the twenty-first birthday.[3]

Transitions are even more difficult when a family includes a member with special needs. Each transition is anticipated with trepidation. For parents, the transition marks one more milestone passing in which attention is drawn to every discrepancy as they compare their child to others.

The stages of a family have different characteristics when a child has a disability:

- *Birth and early childhood*—"Parents spend much of their child's early life learning to accept that the child they have is not the child they wanted."[4] The relationship with the parents is not the same, either because the child is not responsive, which is hard for the parents, or the parents are not responsive because of their own adjustment, which is hard for the child.[5]
- *Childhood*—Here the child is exposed to more children and their parents, who are used as a comparison tool. More people are available to share control with and make decisions with because of the school setting. Usually a diagnosis happens at this stage, and the child's parents need time to adjust to an official label.[6]
- *Adolescence*—This difficult stage comes with the child's competing needs: personal autonomy on one hand, and continued dependence on the family on the other hand, at a time when other children have more personal autonomy.[7]
- *Young adulthood*—When children enter this stage, family members may experience sadness. There may be no decreasing dependency on parents, with no relief in sight. The child is larger and harder to care for physically. Parents are older and find that the increasing demands lead to diminishing resources. Often less professional help is available as well.

Another five stages can occur for the whole family of a child with disabilities. These can happen at any age, so they are not as chronological as the first five stages. These turning points in families should be given extra care by family members and their communities:

- When handicap is identified
- When school placement occurs
- When a younger sibling surpasses the skills of the older child
- At the time of an unusual health crisis or behavior
- When guardianship and long-term care are decided[8]

How a Child Is Affected by Having a Disability

Although a child's disability does not define him as a person, it affects him in these major ways:

- *Stress*—Increased stress from daily threats to his well-being, his body, his independence and his future.
- *Crisis*—While a crisis is time limited, the psychological effects are long lasting.
- *Loss and grief*—The grief one feels following the loss of a body part or a function is "in a manner parallel to that evidenced following the loss

of a loved one, the individual exhibits feelings of grief, bereavement and despair."

- *Body image*—Because a disability can affect the physical appearance and functional capabilities, and cause pain, a person with disabilities has an altered and even distorted body image.

- *Self-concept*—Losing who you are to the "disabled" person whom most people see and focus on.

- *Stigma*—After regularly dealing with people who are prejudiced against them, people with disabilities may internalize that stigma and withdraw from social encounters, including treatment and rehabilitation.

- *Unpredictability*—Some disabilities are more unpredictable than others (epilepsy, diabetes, Tourette's syndrome and so on). The greater the unpredictability, the lower the chance of psychological adaptation.

- *Quality of life*—Quality of life is negatively affected by all the stressors listed above. While one extra stress is hard enough, when we combine all the stressors that a family and individual have to deal with, the quality of life can be greatly diminished.[9]

Disengagement versus Engagement

When facing a tough situation, it feels natural to get lost in our emotions, but choosing to be engaged instead of disengaged will bring positive results.

Disengagement

Disengagement occurs when a family copes with the stressful disability by seeking to avoid reality. By acting passively, indirectly, denying, blaming self, blaming others, abusing drugs or avoidance, a family is choosing poor strategies.[10] Another way to think about it is to call it "emotion-focused."[11] The following phrases are based in negative thinking:

- *Deny*—"It is just a matter of time before she grows out of it."
- *Hide*—"I know, but I am so embarrassed . . ."
- *Overwhelmed*—"I feel hopeless because . . ."
- *Blame yourself*—"If only I had . . ."
- *Blame others*—"If only his teacher had . . ."
- *Panic*—"We need to change everything right now."
- *Worry*—"I keep thinking about . . ."[12]

Engagement

When family members choose to be engaged in the disability, they can work out ways to defuse the stress. What does engagement look like? Add these words to your vocabulary: active, direct, goal, seek information, problem-solve, plan, seek support.[13] Another term that describes engagement is "problem-focused coping."[14] The following phrases are based in positive thinking:

- *Listen*—"Tell me more about . . ."
- *Clarify*—"Are you telling me that . . . ?"
- *Take notes*—"When we last spoke, we agreed that . . ."
- *Seek information*—"What I need to know is . . ."
- *Focus on one problem*—"My specific concern is . . ."
- *Seek social support*—"Who can I turn to when I need to talk about . . . ?"
- *Become a self-advocate*—"What I need you to provide for my child is . . ."
- *Reduce tension*—"Let's think about what is best for . . ."
- *Focus on positive*—"One good thing is that . . ."
- *Seek and acknowledge professional guidance*—"With her help, I realized . . ."
- *Share your wisdom*—"What I now know is . . ."[15]

COPING STRATEGIES

Let us get into the practical skills that you can start putting into practice today.

A Firm Foundation

To help the children in our lives, we need to start with building a firm foundation to provide stability for future growth.

Treat with Dignity and Love

This is the most important thing you can do for a child with a disability. LeComer says it better than I can:

> It is too easy—and unfortunately, very common—to begin to distance yourself from your child as the little person who needs you, while instead focusing on your child as the one who must be "fixed" and who happens to have an open day on Tuesday and could maybe use more therapy. Remember that your child is a person with feelings and not a "project in motion" to be managed.[16]

This is the area in which you can have the biggest impact in terms of pushing your flywheel and gaining momentum. Lena Maria Klingvall writes about living without arms and with only one fully formed leg. The core message I found in her book is how her parents treated her with dignity. She says, "Mum and Dad had never tried to hide either my handicap or me. So I was used to people looking and asking. And I had learned early in life that my worth was intrinsic and not in my looks. There was nothing of which I had to be ashamed."[17]

Teach about God

Klingvall grew up with parents who shared their faith with her, and she drew on that faith throughout the challenges of her life. "Having faith in God gave me a tremendous security."[18] What a powerful message to provide for your child to help her understand at a heart level that she was knit together in her mother's womb (Ps. 139:13). Relying on God's messages from His Word have provided comfort for generations, and sharing those messages will help children feel secure. Tell your child: God has "plans to prosper you and not to harm you, plans to give you hope and a future" (Jeremiah 29:11).

Develop a Christ-like love to model for your children how to love others and handle teasing and rejection. Pray together often. Read the Bible when you are in waiting rooms. Memorize Scripture together.

Teach Independence

Doing things for children makes their life easier for the moment, but teaching them independence has long-term benefits. Klingvall describes how her mother encouraged independence and self-reliance:

> *Suddenly I fell and cried out for Mummy. I wanted her to come and lift me up. She said, "If you crawl over to the fence and lean against it you can get up." And this I did. My mum was particularly keen on my being enabled to help myself, from her work as a physical therapist she had seen quite a few examples of how terrible it can go when parents are over-protective of their children.[19]*

To resist helping might be a challenge for any mother, but this mother was the mother of a girl with no arms and only one normally formed leg. The long-term benefit of her parents teaching her independence is that she is now a gold-medal swimmer in the Paralympics, an artist, a singer, a piano player, a writer and speaker, and a car driver. Independently, Lena completes the thousand day-to-day tasks that we might think would be impossible for her.

Make Family a Priority

Create positive family experiences. Stick together. The child needs at least one consistent parent or adult to show him that his life is not falling apart. Share dinners together and have each person share a high and low from his day. Siblings need attention as well. Strengthen your family by finding support groups.

Discipline Your Child

Children with disabilities need boundaries and attitude adjustments like other children, even if they seem more fragile. Be patient but firm.[20] Spend time on productive activities and not on punishments.

Consistency is the key for discipline and behavior change. Use tools like rewards charts when your child meets daily, weekly or special goals. Chart behavior on an *ABC* chart. When you record *A* (Antecedent = cause of the behavior), *B* (Behavior = negative or positive behavior) and *C* (Consequence = negative or positive follow-up), you can track both the child's behavior and your own behavior. Track for patterns of whining, physical reactions, verbal outbursts, or noncompliance. Take note of when the incident occurred, whether consequences are consistent, what the emotional level was, and so on. Identifying themes can lead to positive interventions.[21]

Have Hope and Expectations for Your Child

One mother's advice to other parents with children with disabilities was to have hope. Do not get so discouraged that you stop having any dreams for your kids. Keep a journal so you can see for yourself the baby steps of progress. Rework your dreams and create a "new normal" so your children know that someone believes in them.

Be Your Child's Advocate

Your child needs a defender from bullies, a champion at school, a cheerleader through difficult situations, a promoter of every success, and an educator for friends and community.

Early Identification

The earlier the delay or disability is treated, the better. Children can make dramatic progress when their difficulties are addressed early, especially before school age.[22]

Encourage Inclusion

Inclusion involves supporting children while they learn and play side-by-side with children who do not have disabilities. Look for opportunities at school, parks, libraries and church. Look for inclusive environments when choosing family activities and recreational activities. Providing the least restrictive environment depends on the individual's needs. There is a continuum between the two extremes of living independently with no adjustments made and living in an intermediate care facility, which provides 24-hour care. The goal is to find the right place for children—in the home, at school and on the job—in which they are most included, least restricted, most integrated, most normalized and least intensive.[23]

> I was in special class for ten years. I was very angry. I used to look out the door and see the kids. I want to be with them. Now I have a locker and take government, journalism, marketing and economics. The kids I used to look at are my friends now. I learn better in the regular class. I watch my friends and do what they do. My Special Eductions [sic] teacher, my speech teacher and my OT [occupational therapist] help me, too. If someone said that I could go back to the special class I would say "no" I will never go back! Please change the laws to help kids like me be in Regular classes with their friends.[24]

This is a testimony from a girl named Maureen who was asked to speak to the education committee of her state assembly on the topic of least restrictive environment. From age five to fifteen Maureen was in a small, self-contained classroom, and at age fifteen she moved to an inclusive setting in which she continued her therapies and her class work was adjusted. In the general-education setting, her inappropriate behaviors stopped. Her speech showed the biggest improvement, and friends even noticed her walking without a slouch. At age five, IQ testing showed Maureen to be moderately retarded; after inclusion, her IQ test indicated that she was mildly retarded.[25]

Learn Laws

Knowing your school's policies and your state and federal laws enables you to help your child if she does not get the help and education she deserves. In the United States, Public Law 94-142 or IDEA ensures specific services to children with disabilities. The law promises (1) a free and appropriate education for all children, (2) nondiscriminatory evaluation, (3) an individualized education plan, (4) that children will be placed in their least restrictive environment, (5) due process when checking for fairness and accountability, and (6) parental participation in decision-making.[26]

Gain Knowledge

Research relevant medical information. Gain knowledge and share it. "Knowledge is not quite power; it is at least the equipment you must have to fight for the best attention and treatment you can get for your child."[27] This chapter provides general advice for a broad audience, but you still need to learn about what will help for your own specific needs.

Find Support and Stay Involved

All children need support to grow in all the areas that make them whole: emotional, spiritual, mental, educational, social and physical. If one area is not strong enough (as is often the case with children with disabilities), the wheel will not turn properly. Find support for your child and get all involved specialists talking to each other: psychiatrist, social worker, psychologist, counselor, teacher, physical therapist, play therapist, music therapist, family therapist, principal, special education teacher, occupational therapist and so on. "Children with parents who are involved in their children's education experience more success in school than students whose parents are not as involved."[28] What a great way to support your child when other issues weigh him down.

Emotional Health

Mental health problems develop when people are unable, or not allowed, to put into words what they are feeling.

Feel the Emotions

Talking to a counselor, friend or parent about the struggles that come with a disability is necessary for all those emotions not to boil over and gain control. Robert Murphy, whose slowly progressing physical disability came to him as an adult, said:

> From the time my tumor was first diagnosed through my entry
> into wheelchair life, I had an increasing apprehension that I
> had lost much more than the full use of my legs. I had also lost
> a part of myself. It was not just that people acted differently to-

ward me, which they did, but rather that I felt different towards myself. It left me feeling alone and isolated.[29]

An emotionally healthy person finds it difficult to be honest with her emotions at the best of times. When experiencing difficulties, we all need help finding that safe place to talk. When walking through difficult emotions, you might feel as though your flywheel is not turning, but talking through them will wipe away whatever is holding the movement back.

Shame is a frequent emotion, even when your disability is not your fault. Others, especially bullies, like to use shame as a means of social control. The desire to withdraw may be strong at a time when you need support.

Grief might be the most common emotion, and allowing yourself to cry is cleansing. "The term 'chronic-sorrow' has often been used to depict the grief experience by people with chronic disabilities because of the constant physical reminder of their disability."[30] For the parents, there is the mourning of the loss of the "perfect" family or maybe even grieving for losing a job or career that is no longer possible.

Picture Talks

In her book *Dancing with Max*, Emily Colson wrote about her discovery that she could use her gift of artwork to draw out her then-seven-year-old autistic son's emotions.

> *Every day I would pull out paper and pen and ask Max what he wanted to talk about. His language would pour out onto the page as I took dictation and drew the images he was describing. He trusted me with his most intimate thoughts, fears, hopes, dreams, likes, dislikes—all the things I longed to know but until now had been hidden from view.[31]*

She calls these her "picture talks" with her son. She still uses these with her son now at 14 years of age.

Refocus Anger

Your child's anger about his situation is a valid emotion. Unfortunately, staying stuck in emotion can keep you and your child from finding remedies. Marc Lerner (the Life Skills Guy) writes on his blog, "All of that energy that goes into this anger must be rerouted toward educated action—patient, unremitting, effective action."[32] Here are some example phrases that help children feel their anger and then move on:

- "I guess it's easier to get mad at the desk than to get mad at yourself because you can't do the math. How about picking up the desk so we can sit down and I can help you?"[33]

- You are angry that it is taking you so long to complete your homework. How about taking a four-minute break?

- You are turning our dinner conversation into a joke. I think hearing your brother talk about camp is hard because you feel angry that you could not go.

- You have been teasing your sister by saying she has cooties whenever you are upset at her, and I wonder if it is hard to want to be around your sister when you want to look grown-up in front of your friends.

Read Children's Books Together

A child who reads a book about a character who is going through a similar difficulty may feel less alone and may gain mastery over her challenge, like the child in the book. Joan Fassler's book *Helping Children Cope: Mastering Stress through Books and Stories* suggests which books to start with and what questions to ask. For example, after reading *Curious George Goes to the Hospital*, Fassler recommends asking the following questions:

- "How do you think George felt when he had to go to the hospital? Was he frightened? How did you first feel when you went to the hospital?"

- "Do you want to bring something special from home like George did?"

- "George cried when the nurse gave him a shot. Do you ever feel like crying? Does it help you feel better? Do you think that it makes you bad to cry?"

- "Why did Curious George have to go to the hospital? Why do you have to go?"[34]

Using favorite children's book characters such as Madeline, Peter Rabbit, Little Bear and Harry the Dirty Dog can help you initiate and encourage conversations on topics such as hospitalization, independence, difficult feelings, building courage, illness, pain and death.[35]

Create Homemade Books

A great idea for helping kids cope comes from Robert Ziegler in his book *Homemade Books to Help Kids Cope*. Ziegler noticed that when children hear something new, they often get confused or forget the important details. By turning the new event/lesson into a story that you write and illustrate with your child, he sees and hears the story multiple times. Ziegler found this technique could work with all ages and in varied settings. "Stories about events reduce their size and shape to fit a child's understanding."[36] Use these homemade books to help your child describe a situation, define feelings or make an empathic statement.

Ziegler's son Jeffrey had chronic ear infections and got used to extra attention to help him get to sleep. After Jeffery had tubes inserted in his ears, he needed to get back to a regular bedtime routine, which meant he would need to sleep in his own bed. Here is a simple example of a book to help Jeffrey.[37]

Jeffrey's New-Bedtime Story

Page 1: When Jeffrey was sick, it was very hard for him to get to sleep because his ears hurt. He would cry so his Mommy and Daddy took turns walking with him. Sometimes he would even get to sleep in Mommy's bed and get his back rubbed.

Page 2: Now Jeffrey is well. Jeffrey finds his teddy. He get hugs and kisses from Mommy and Daddy. He waves "nite, nite."

Page 3: Sometimes Jeffrey still cries when he goes to bed. He gets an extra pat, but because his ear is better, he can hug his teddy and go to sleep. Nite, nite everyone!

Recreation = Re-Creating

Just as it is important to be there for your child, it is also important to take time to re-create yourself and your family. Too much focus on one child and his needs leads to an out-of-balance family or classroom.

Make Recreation a Priority

Take time as a family to relax and re-create. "Studies have shown that psychologically healthy families have less-than-perfect housekeeping."[38] Taking a few hours off to go for a hike, play a game together or swim in a pool will do more to help your child than another ten minutes of flashcard practice. All family members need a hobby they can enjoy and be good at that does not feel like work.

Take Care of Yourself

"Your happiness will give you a positive outlook that will no doubt help your child and family have a positive outlook too."[39] Find a place of retreat to go and cool off. Maybe this means reading a book in the bathroom or getting a weekly babysitter for an evening out. Use relaxation tapes and exercise to calm down.

Celebrate Your Child

Maybe your days are not what you imagined. Maybe your family is not what you imagined. Even so, look for ways to celebrate your child's *being*. Watch for growth and celebrate milestones using something like a "How I've Grown" book including pictures and autographs. Reserve a large, special, bright dinner plate for the family member who reaches a big goal. Track memories in a scrapbook. Take a trip for a special treat when a milestone is reached.

DEVELOPING HABITS THAT PROMOTE COPING

Teaching healthy coping skills is best done when children are young and their brains are still developing, and it will become a skill they can carry through their life.

Adopting a Glass-Is-Half-Full Attitude

In my research on the influences that affect the level of success people attain in coping with their disability, seeing things as possibilities rather than difficulties emerged as the most common theme. Noted journalist John Hockenberry said of the sudden accident that left him in a wheelchair for the rest of his life, "To them, I was standing on a ledge and not jumping off. To me, I was climbing up to get a better view . . . Far from being a blank wall of misery; my body now presented an intriguing puzzle of great depth and texture."[40]

Livestock-handling equipment designer Temple Grandin, who is the subject of the eponymous HBO movie *Temple Grandin*, said, "If I could snap my fingers and be nonautistic, I would not, because then I wouldn't be me. Autism is part of who I am." She is dismayed when scientists speak of eliminating the genes that cause autism.[41]

In his blog about perception, Marc Lerner gives as an example a lion that escapes from its cage. An old woman might scream and run away, but the animal trainer walks onto the scene purposefully with authority and confidence. Lerner writes of his own disabilities, "My symptoms stayed the same, but I perceived them with a perspective that eliminated being a victim."[42] He continues:

> *How you perceive your handicap may become one of your most significant treatments and that is totally in your control . . . There is a healthy way to be sick and the quality of your life as*

you heal has significant influence on how your immune system deals with your challenge . . . Our body responds to medical treatments better from a high quality of life.[43]

Thought Stoppage Techniques

When negative thoughts pop up, and they often will, do not dwell on them. Use "thought stoppage" techniques to turn those thoughts away:

- Snap a rubber band on your wrist every time you have a negative thought.
- Tap your leg and count to ten.
- Tell yourself, "I use only gentle and loving words for myself and others."
- Call it an ANT (Automatic Negative Thought) and tell it to go away.
- Take slow, deep breaths, inhaling positive thoughts or promises from the Bible and exhaling the negative thoughts.

Keeping a Gratitude Journal

"People who made simple lists of what they're thankful for are twenty-five percent happier, sleep half an hour more per night and exercise thirty-three percent more each week than those who don't."[44] Writing in a gratitude journal every day will keep your thoughts on what you have instead of what you do not have. Keep a special book for yourself or keep a list for the family at dinner every evening, and on days when it is hard to be thankful, look back over the previous days.

Finding Personal Meaning

Assist your child in exploring personal meaning in the situation. For example:

- By keeping up with my peers in my school work, even though I have to work harder, shows that I am an overcomer.
- By learning how to use a wheelchair I will be able to help others who need to learn.
- I have this special opportunity to see life differently than most people and relate to people who feel left out.
- I never would have known I was good at ___ if I did not have to overcome this disability.

Finding Heroes

Did you know that Leonardo da Vinci often wrote backward? Woodrow Wilson, 28th president of the United States, did not learn to read until he was eleven and was labeled as "dull." In school Auguste Rodin was described as "an idiot" but became a famous artist and sculptor. Winston Churchill had learning disabilities. Albert Einstein did not talk until age four, did not read until age nine and went to a special school. The famous author Ernest Hemingway was a poor speller. Examples that are more recent include Tom Cruise with dyslexia. Bruce Willis, Rowan Atkinson and Julia Roberts all struggled with stuttering as children. Those who use wheelchairs include Joni Eareckson Tada, Itzhak Perlman, and the late Christopher Reeves. Famous people with epilepsy are Hugo Weaving, Neil Young, Napoleon Bonaparte, Agatha Christie and Charles Dickens.

Encourage your child to learn about someone who has overcome a challenge similar to her own. Maybe her hero is someone in your church or circle of friends, or a famous person. Follow an inspiring blog authored by a writer with disabilities.

Practical Tools You Can Build

When he became deaf, Beethoven carried a "conversation book" with him for his friends to write in. Figure out what will help you and your child in practical ways. After you identify what is causing the difficulty for you or your child, you can focus on building a practical coping tool that will lead to less frustration. Do you need to use Velcro instead of buttons? Can you sew a loop onto the top of each sock so that they can be pulled up easier? Buy double-stitched clothing to prevent holes from tough wear and tear. To play card games, make a simple cardholder by cutting a groove into a 12-inch piece of 2 x 4 wood.[45]

CONCLUSION

Why did Tim and Victor turn out so differently? Look back at the wheel analogy and take note of momentum's role.

> Pushing with great effort, you get the wheel to inch forward moving almost imperceptibly at first. You keep pushing, and after two or three hours of persistent effort, you get the wheel to complete an entire turn. You keep pushing . . . nine . . . ten . . . it builds momentum . . . eleven . . . twelve . . . moving faster with each turn. Then at some point—breakthrough! The momentum

*of the thing kicks in, in your favor, hurling the wheel forward
. . . its own heavy weight working for you. You're pushing no
harder, but the wheel is going faster.[46]*

Unfortunately, if you do not maintain consistent pushing, you will feel
the opposite of the turning-wheel effect, which is known as the doom loop.[47]
The doom loop starts when you find yourself reacting without understanding.
Or running after another new fad, another new director or another new
therapist and then, before anything shows results, jumping ship and chasing
another program. Caught in the doom loop, the wheel never gains accumulated
momentum. Everyone around feels the awkwardness of the constant
start-stop syndrome: starting, stopping to go in a new direction and then
starting again.

Worse yet is facing the challenge of pushing the wheel but giving in to
the inertia that results from feeling overwhelmed by the task ahead. This
seems to be where Tim and his family got stuck. They probably got stuck in
the doom loop by focusing on a single person, such as a teacher, or a single
event, such as a test result. Without everyone working together and pushing,
the momentum slowly fizzled out, the task felt too much like pushing
a brick wall, and inertia seemed the easiest alternative. Choosing the easiest
alternative in the moment can have long-term negative consequences.

Are you inspired to build your own momentum? This is exactly what
happened to Victor. With a team supporting him, he got his anger under
control, received consistent discipline and started to find his own firm footing.
He started pushing the wheel instead of giving in to inertia, and then
the wheel began turning. It took years before the momentum started for Victor,
but he graduated high school and college and became a teacher himself.

I hope you can see that with combinations of these ideas, you can make
a difference for a child you know who struggles with disabilities. Now is
the time to start pushing the wheel by teaching your child coping strategies.
When your child sees how much you care and watches you pushing
the wheel, he will be encouraged enough to push for himself. Choose your
direction, learn about it and *go*!

NOTES

1. Jim Collins, "The Flywheel and the Doom Loop," in *Good to Great* (New York: HarperCollins, 2001), 165–87.

2. Exploring Developmental Disabilities, "The Causes of Disabilities in Children," http://www.naddc.org/the-causes-of-disabilities-in-children.htm.

3. Norris G. Haring and Linda McCormick, eds., *Exceptional Children and Youth* (Columbus, OH: Merrill, 1990), 479.

4. Robin Simons, *After the Tears: Parents Talk about Raising a Child with a Disability* (San Diego: Mariner Books, 1987), 5.

5. Fred P. Orelove and Dick Sobsey, eds., *Educating Children with Multiple Disabilities: A Transdisciplinary Approach*, 3rd ed. (Baltimore: Brookes, 1996), 460.

6. Ibid., 464–65.

7. Ibid., 468–72.

8. Haring and McCormick, *Exceptional Children and Youth*, 498.

9. Hanoch Livneh and Richard F. Antonak, "Psychosocial Adaptation to Chronic Illness and Disability: A Primer for Counselors," *Journal of Counseling and Development* 83 (2005): 12–13.

10. Ibid., 14.

11. Sharon L. Judge, "Parental Coping Strategies and Strengths in Families of Young Children with Disabilities," *Family Relations* 47, no. 3 (1998): 263.

12. Sheldon H. Horowitz, "Coping: Parents of Children with Learning Disabilities," National Center for Learning Disabilities, 2009, http://www.ncld.org/in-the-home/parenting-issues/coping-with-ld/coping-parents-of-children-with-learning-disabilities.

13. Livneh and Antonak, "Psychosocial Adaptation," 14.

14. Judge, "Parental Coping Strategies," 263.

15. Horowitz, "Coping."

16. Laurie F. LeComer, *A Parent's Guide to Developmental Delay* (New York: Penguin, 2006), 241.

17. Lena M. Klingvall, *Footnotes: A Life without Limits* (Deerfield Beach, FL: Health Communications, 2001), 53.

18. Ibid., 53.

19. Ibid., 30.

20. William C. Kroen, *Helping Children Cope with the Loss of a Loved One* (Minneapolis: Free Spirit, 1996), 86–89.

21. Larry B. Silver, *The Misunderstood Child* (New York: Random House, 2006), 16.

22. LeComer, *A Parent's Guide*, 12.

23. Haring and McCormick, *Exceptional Children and Youth*, 31.

24. Diane L. Ryndak, "Portrait of Maureen Before and After Inclusion," in *Curriculum Content for Students with Moderate and Severe Disabilities in Inclusive Settings*, ed. Diane L. Ryndak and Sandra K. Alper (Boston: Allyn and Bacon, 1996), 351–52.

25. Ibid., 335.

26. *Education for All Handicapped Children Act*, Public Law 94-142, 94th Cong., 1st sess. (November 29, 1975). See also the Families and Advocates Partnership for Education (FAPE) project website http://www.fape.org/idea/idea2004.htm.

27. Silver, *The Misunderstood Child*, 295.

28. Beverly Rainforth and Jennifer York-Barr, *Collaborative Teams for Students with Severe Disabilities* (Baltimore: Brookes, 1997), 59.

29. Robert F. Murphy, *The Body Silent* (New York: Norton, 1990), 85–89.

30. Livneh and Antonak, "Psychosocial Adaptation," 13.

31. Emily Colson, *Dancing with Max* (Grand Rapids: Zondervan, 2010), 71.

32. Marc Lerner, "How to Perceive a Handicap," *The Life Skills Approach* (blog), January 26, 2008, http://www.lifeskillsapproach.com/2008/01/how-to-perceive.html.

33. Silver, *The Misunderstood Child*, 10–15.

34. Joan Fassler, *Helping Children Cope: Mastering Stress through Books and Stories* (New York: Free Press, 1978), 53.

35. Fassler, *Helping Children Cope*.

36. Robert G. Ziegler, *Homemade Books to Help Kids Cope* (Washington, DC: Magination, 1992), 3.

37. Ibid, 7.

38. "Coping with Stress for Parents of Children with Disabilities," Family-Friendly-Fun.com, http://www.family-friendly-fun.com/disabilities/coping-stress.htm.

39. LeComer, *A Parent's Guide*, 242.

40. Deborah Kent and Kathryn A. Quinlan, *Extraordinary People with Disabilities* (Danbury, CT: Children's Press, 1996), 209–12.

41. Ibid., 181–85.

42. Lerner, "How to Perceive a Handicap."

43. Ibid.

44. Robert A. Emmons, *Thanks!* (New York: Houghton Mifflin, 2007), 17.

45. Orelove and Sobsey, *Educating Children*, 140–42.

46. Collins, "Flywheel," 164.

47. Ibid., 178.

*

CHAPTER NINE

STRATEGIES FOR TRAINING AT HOME, SCHOOL AND WORK

* * *

Laura Sandidge

A T TIMES it may appear that we are not making any headway in educating children with disabilities. Their situations can appear to-tally futile and impossible to improve. Trainers can be prone to dwell on the negatives such as feeling that there will never be enough money, time or energy to provide a child with the education he deserves. The words of l Corinthians 15:58 are important to keep in mind when you are planning training for individuals with special needs, some with significant needs that seem impossible to address:

> *Therefore, my beloved brethren, be firm (steadfast), immovable, always abound-ing in the work of the Lord [always being superior, excelling, doing more than enough in the service of the Lord], knowing and being continually aware that your labor in the Lord is not futile [it is never wasted or to no purpose]. (1 Cor. 15:58 AMP)*

It is true that cognitive growth is minimal for some children. There are elements of truth in statements such as, "If I could have started working with them sooner, we could have done so much more," or "If the situation were different, we could make some wonderful advances." I am sure that all of us have been in positions in which we felt that if we could remove the child from the current environment we could make a difference. But even in the best situations we have limited control. At these times we must remem-ber that we are workers for God. He is working through us in the current

163

situations confronting us. The children we are working with are where they are right now. This is the starting point. Knowing this, we have to be armed with strategies and techniques to assist us in making the most out of the situation we are engaged in.

PHILOSOPHICAL UNDERPINNINGS

Philosophical underpinnings are theoretical philosophies or viewpoints that give a base or a foundation to all of the strategies and techniques an individual chooses to use, no matter what the environment. They permeate your approach to different situations and your interpretation of the outcomes. They act like a filter. For example, if one of your philosophical underpinnings is that you believe people are basically good, then your interactions with people will reflect that philosophy. It is important to consider and reflect on your personal philosophical underpinnings.

Do you believe that people with disabilities can have a quality life? Do you believe that people with disabilities have emotions and dreams and desires? It is important to think about these things, because whether one likes it or not, your attitudes are reflected in your behaviors. Your behavior is directly affected by your philosophical underpinnings. Needless to say, there are several possible philosophical underpinnings when it comes to working with individuals with special needs. This section highlights those that could be, and should be, incorporated across all environments.

Respect and Dignity

The first philosophical underpinning that must be firmly rooted in all of us is the belief that people with disabilities are human beings who have many of the same desires and dreams that individuals without disabilities have. All human beings deserve respect and dignity to be afforded to them. They should never be belittled and demeaned in any way. What is the Golden Rule? Do unto others as you would have them do unto you. Every one of us can, and most likely will, experience a disability at some point in our lifetime. "Disability is a natural part of the human experience."[1]

One way to show respect and dignity to individuals with disabilities is to use people-first language. Kathie Snow—writer, speaker and trainer—has brought the concept of people-first language to the public eye.[2] People-first language refers to the person first and the disability second. Rather than saying "the significantly delayed child," we say "the child with significant delays." It is a simple thing, but it does help us to look at the person first and the disability second. Although some individuals in the world of disabilities disagree with people-first language,[3] the vast majority use it to show dignity toward individuals with a disability.

Inclusion

A basic yet vital underpinning in working with individuals with disabilities and in structuring programs for those individuals is the concept of inclusion in all environments. Inclusion, according to *Webster's College Dictionary*, is the act of making sure that one part of the whole is considered part of the whole.[4] In the special education field, inclusion means much the same thing. Jorgensen states it succinctly:

> *Inclusion is defined as all students being educated where they would be educated if they did not have a disability (i.e., in age-appropriate general education classes in their neighborhood school), with necessary supports provided to students, educators, and families so that all can be successful.*[5]

This definition can be expanded to apply in all environments. Incorporating inclusion as a concept is a foundational priority for your program. Incorporating inclusion in the school, home and community is one important way you can show that you value and respect the individuals with whom you are working.

Tested Educational Principles

Another foundational base, or philosophical underpinning, in developing appropriate programs for individuals with disabilities is the use of solid and time-tested educational principles to maximize learning in any environment. These principles may include establishing relevance, utilizing consistency, incorporating choice, generalization and maintenance.

For example, we can maximize learning by taking a teachable moment and making sure that there is enough impact and relevance for the individual so that he can remember what was taught and use it in that environment. We maximize learning by being consistent in our approaches and endeavors. If we believe that individuals with disabilities should be treated with dignity and respect, it follows that we should incorporate choice in our programs. All individuals deserve an element of choice in their lives. We also increase learning by making sure that our programs incorporate generalization and maintenance. Generalization takes a skill that was taught in one environment and uses it in a variety of other environments. Maintenance ensures that the skill is maintained and able to be replicated over time.

Recognizing Diversity

Another underpinning is the acknowledgment that just as individuals are different, individuals with disabilities are different too. The words "individual with a disability" have a wide range of meaning. Having a disability can have a huge impact on both the individual and her learning environment. A disability may range from a learning disability, which may be a language dysfunction that could be as simple as a slower rate of language processing, to a more involved dysfunction in learning in all areas, which could be considered a severe developmental delay. Some individuals with disabilities require minimal help to be successful, but others have needs so complicated that they require a full-time nurse or assistant to derive educational or social benefit from the environment. All people are different, and people with the same disability are different.

For example, a child with spina bifida often cannot walk. We can try to make him walk, but if he does not have the physical capacity, we are wasting critical time and causing him considerable despair. However, depending on the child and his condition, it is possible that he could have the capacity to walk. We do an individual with a disability a disservice when we globally classify all disabilities with the same name as the same disability and fail to take the time to teach him a particular task. That is the complexity of working with individuals with disabilities. Not everyone with the same disability is the same. Variation is the rule, not the exception. This is the same for all disabilities, both visible and hidden. With physical impairments we are more readily able to (visually) see the abilities and the disabilities. Hidden disabilities, such as a learning disability, are a different matter.

Integrity

Programs for children or adults with disabilities must be based on integrity and ethics and have accountability measures in place. Individuals who have integrity do what they say they are going to do. They are honest. You can depend on them. Ethics entails doing the right and moral thing because it is the right and moral thing to do. A program based on integrity demands an uncompromising insistence on acting ethically and morally. Accountability ensures that everyone involved with the program has integrity and is ethical. All three concepts interconnect. They flow into one another. They are vital to any program—and even more so when a program involves working with individuals with disabilities. By nature children are vulnerable. Children and adults with disabilities are even more vulnerable. Any program that does not highly value integrity, an ethical base and accountability measures is unacceptable.

STRATEGIES AND TECHNIQUES

The philosophical underpinnings of treating individuals with respect and dignity, including them in all aspects of our communities, maximizing learning, understanding that disabilities vary, being developmentally and age appropriate in our programming, implementing sound behavioral principles, and being accountable and ethical are the foundation of all of the strategies we use. These strategies can and should be used in all environments. No one concept or strategy is more important than another; all have importance in their own right, although some are more complicated than others.

In this section we look at the three main environments in which children spend a considerable amount of time: home, school and, when age appropriate, the community work environment. Specific strategies pertinent to each environment will be given. All the foundational philosophical underpinnings are applicable in these environments.

In training programs we talk about strategies and techniques. But what are strategies and techniques? *Webster's College Dictionary* states that a strategy is a plan or method to achieve a goal.[6] Techniques are ways to accomplish goals. The goal of this chapter is to equip you with a variety of strategies that will enable you to help individuals with special needs in various environments, particularly the home, school and work environments. There is no question that this source is not all encompassing. Many other sources can and should be used to supplement your skills and training programs.

Training at Home

The old saying, "Home is where the heart is," is true in many ways. Hopefully, home is the family's safety zone, where family members can get away from all the hazards in the world, relax and be themselves with loving family members close-by. In the best-case scenario this is true; people are successful in their homes. For individuals with disabilities this also may be true. But there is another aspect that must be considered. For individuals with disabilities, the home is often the place where they spend the most time. Home is a place where children need to learn to navigate, to be functional in, and to have routines set up that allow for independence. Often the home is a place where most individuals with disabilities need support to be successful living there. Though most of us likely never even question being successful living at home, for individuals with disabilities, especially individuals with significant disabilities, this is a huge question. How do we optimize the home to be a successful environment for an individual with a disability? Three strategies can make this environment highly successful.

Functional Living Activities

The first strategy is to have daily living activities in place that are functional. Functional activities have a purpose behind them; these activities have meaning to the individual in his daily life. If he does not know how to do a task, someone else has to do it for him. For example, an academic goal is the ability to add and subtract. If we make that goal functional for an individual, we would most likely look for ways that he could use money in a store when purchasing items.

Functional skills are typical skills that an individual is required to do often in the home, community and vocational setting. Home-, community- and vocational-based programming should be functional. It should be authentic, meaning that it uses real settings and real materials. It should have immediate usefulness to the individual to allow her to be more independent in her environment. Functional activities are activities that are done often within the day. They always promote independence and competence in the individual. Functional programs are important because they are designed and developed with the ultimate outcome of life independence in mind.

Assistive technology is a wonderful complement to functional programming. An assistive technology device can be any item, piece of equipment or product system that could be purchased off the shelf, modified or customized, and used to increase, maintain or improve functional capabilities of a child with a disability. Often we think of assistive technology as something expensive. Granted, glasses, leg braces and wheelchairs are more expensive assistive technology devices. But pencil grips, rubber mats, shower chairs and lever-style door handles are inexpensive assistive technology devices. If our goal is to be functional and facilitate independence, then the creative use of assistive technology can assist us.

Routine-Based Intervention

Another wonderful strategy to incorporate in home-based programming is called routine-based intervention. Every home has routines that are typical to that environment. For example, one routine occurs at bath time, another at dinnertime, another at cleaning time. All of these routines are completed in a home setting in the manner that the family has established. A routine is something that has a beginning and an end, it has an outcome, it is meaningful and predictable, it is sequential or systematic, and it is repetitious.

With routine-based intervention the caregiver uses naturally occurring routines as opportunities to teach and learn. It is another way to maximize learning. The caregiver starts with established routines as the familiar framework or the base and then builds, or embeds, more sophisticated skills into the routines for the individual. Therefore, this systematic approach accommodates the skills, preferences and strengths of the individual while also providing opportunities to embed learning new skills within the established routine. This teaching tool, when used appropriately, is effective, family friendly and efficient.

Supported Living

Our goal is to promote independence and a satisfying quality of life for individuals with developmental disabilities. Unfortunately, there are times when these concepts do not overlap. In those situations we have to think of different ways to develop a satisfying quality of life. One way is to incorporate the supported living concept. Supported living preserves individual choice and allows an individual with disabilities to live in his own home with personalized assistance.

Many issues can go along with this choice; poverty, loneliness and isolation, relationship issues, supervision issues, emergencies and family issues are some of them. But there are also several benefits that go along with this choice, such as increased independence and overall life satisfaction. Analyzing supported-living options forces us to be creative. The options are varied, such as living in the family home, or in a group-home situation, or in an apartment alone or with peers.

Typically, incorporating supported living requires careful planning. Live-in support services in which a person assists with personal care and supervision on a live-in basis may be needed; or possibly a therapist or trainer who comes into the home on occasion to teach and enhance skills such as laundry, cooking, cleaning, budgeting, meal planning, shopping and so on. The services of an attendant or personal care companion might also be needed. That is a person who comes into the home to assist with feeding, bathing, dressing, transferring, turning, repositioning, activities of daily living, ambulation, emergency procedures, fitness or other daily appointments. Home, vehicle and/or accessibility modifications often have to be made, which can include architectural changes, ramps, widened doorways or adaptations to bathrooms. Those are some of the issues that need to be considered before moving into a supported living situation. Funding, quality of life and many other issues are areas of concern. This is not an option taken lightly. However, for many people, supported living is the only option that provides them with independence, dignity and the quality of life that they choose.

Being successful in the home environment is important. Home is where many people realize their dreams. The decision to stay in the family home or move out to their own home is an emotional decision for individuals with disabilities and for those without disabilities. Decisions related to our living environment are not simple; factors such as money and level of support are paramount and cannot be ignored. Determining the quality of life once we are in the home also involves major decisions. What is functional and needed? How are we going to ensure the individual learns the tasks? All of these things take time, thoughtful consideration and considerable prayer to ensure a quality home life for individuals with disabilities.

Training at School

For many individuals, school-based learning is a major activity for many years. A variety of schools or learning environments are available. Our focus is more in the area of a formalized school setting. Many wonderful strategies can be incorporated in an environment that focuses on learning for groups of individuals of similar ages. In this section three strategies will be defined: the technique called positive behavioral support, curriculum revision and development, and visual strategies. All three strategies can be administered to groups or individuals and also can be used outside of the formal school setting.

Positive Behavioral Support

The concept of understanding student behavior, and the motivation behind it, is part of a larger undertaking called positive behavioral support.[7] A positive behavioral support, or PBS, is a comprehensive strategy that addresses behavioral challenges through a variety of dimensions. PBS is an individualized, ongoing process with three key components: preventing, teaching and reacting. Preventing means that we change circumstances that tend to lead to challenging behaviors. Teaching means that we replace challenging behaviors with new skills. Reacting or responding means that we plan consistent, proactive responses to challenging behaviors.

PBS includes completing a functional behavioral assessment to determine the motivation, or why a person is engaged in the behavior or behaviors. We then analyze the underlying reasons the behavior is being reinforced, and therefore continuing. Ultimately, a plan of action is developed to address the behavioral issues, to prevent the behavior from occurring, to teach appropriate replacement behaviors and to respond to the appropriate behaviors as well as the inappropriate behaviors. Vaughn and others state:

Positive Behavioral Support (PBS) is the application of a comprehensive set of procedures and strategies aimed at providing the individual with problem behavior with an improved lifestyle that includes a reduction of problem behavior, changes in social relationships, an expansion of skills, and an increase in community inclusion.[8]

Another integral component of PBS is to look at the existing supports that are possible in the school system and build on them. Overall, the method looks at the behavioral cycle of the child, or the group of children, and helps the teacher, parent and administrator make the necessary interventions that could change the cycle from something that has been negative to something positive.[9]

Another component of PBS is making the necessary adaptations or accommodations to the environment or to the curriculum to diminish the unwanted behaviors and increase desired behaviors. Consequently, curricular revision is also a part of positive behavioral support.

Curriculum

According to Dunlap and Kern:

A child's curriculum defines both the content and mode of instructional delivery . . . specific curricular variables can influence the occurrence or nonoccurrence of problem behavior. By identifying these variables through functional assessment, features of a child's curriculum can be modified to reduce or eliminate problem behaviors. The host of instructional and curricular variables can be broadly grouped as setting or ecological factors, instructional and curricular content, instructional delivery, and social variables.[10]

The term "curricular revision," or "curriculum adaptation," refers to modifying or supplementing one or more curricular elements to meet the needs of the individual student.[11] Lipsky and Gartner elaborated further on the definition of curriculum adaptation. They state: "Classroom practices that have been reported as supporting inclusive education include cooperative learning, multilevel instruction, activity-based learning, mastery learning, use of instructional technology, peer support, and tutoring programs."[12]

The curriculum can be adapted on many levels. A simple accommodation may be to provide physical assistance to help the student complete the assignment; another adaptation may require revising the curriculum to meet the needs of the student. An adaptation could also entail using an overlapping, parallel or functional skills curriculum.

An *overlapping* curriculum is a curriculum that meets the needs of a student who requires repetition by presenting the same material in a variety of ways, settings and formats. The overlapping of the curriculum allows the child to have an opportunity to comprehend the material. This is used when age-appropriate curriculum is presented so quickly that the child with special needs cannot understand the concept or achieve mastery over it.

A *parallel* curriculum is used when the child that you are working with is unable to do the same activities that the other children in the class are able to do. She can be included in the classroom, enjoying and learning many important skills such as socialization or on-task behavior, but he works on a parallel curriculum. For example, all students work on spelling. One child may work with five words, whereas another has twenty. One child may have words at a first-grade level, while another has words at a higher grade level.

A *functional skills* curriculum is based on teaching individuals domestic, vocational, independent living and leisure skills in the environments where they would exhibit those skills.[13]

Visual Supports

Visual supports or strategies are interventions that enhance communication.[14] Many individuals with disabilities are unable to pick up social or verbal cues that are provided to them. Therefore they could benefit from visual strategies to assist them in accessing communication and in facilitating understanding of a variety of concepts. Several tools, and variations of tools, are used. Visual communication tools include

- visual schedules that use pictures rather than words to show what is happening throughout the day,

- visual calendars that use the same concept as schedules but for a longer period of time,

- choice boards that allow an individual to choose which task he would like to do, and

- communication boards for individuals that cannot communicate verbally but can do so by pointing to a picture.

A visual strategy facilitates understanding and provides a level of independence for the individual. For example, if we are going out to eat, it is typical that individuals will order for themselves. By using visuals, an individual could point to the menu items she wants to get her needs met.

Visual supports can be used for individuals with a high level of cognitive ability as well as those with a lower level of cognitive ability. They can be used in a class to remind the group about particular rules or skills, or the schedule of the day. If you use shopping lists, you are benefiting from a visual cue or reminder.

The three strategies described—positive behavioral supports, curriculum revision and development, and visual strategies—are only a few of the many strategies that can be used in a school setting. Thousands of techniques and strategies can be used in this environment to maximize learning. When determining which strategy to use, it is best to use time-tested and proven interventions that are efficient for both the child and the individual providing the intervention. Positive behavioral supports, curriculum revision and development, and visual strategies are time tested and efficient for individuals with and without disabilities. They can be delivered in any culture and in a variety of settings, allowing individuals to be more successful in a school or group environment.

Training at Work

The average individual spends a majority of his life working. It is possible for him to spend forty-five years in the workforce. That is a significant portion of his lifetime. People often evaluate their perceived self-worth based on what they do for a living. Our creativity, interests and abilities are often manifested in and throughout our work. Our social connections are often developed through work situations. Having a job indicates that we are experiencing some level of acceptance in the community and are considered contributing members; we are a part of our community. Sadly, in America the prevalence rate of employed adults with disabilities, ages sixteen and up, was 17.9 percent in 2011.[15] It does not have to be that way. Several strategies can be incorporated in the vocational setting. Three specific strategies are: facilitating self-determination, utilizing compensatory strategies and supported employment, and incorporating assistive technology in the work environment.

Facilitating Self-Determination

Self-determination is a broad strategy that encompasses many components. The term "self-determination" is used when describing an individual with disabilities who is able to make decisions independently. A self-determined individual knows what choices to make, as well as how to make her needs known. Wehmeyer, Agran and Hughes define self-determination as a com-bination of skills, knowledge, and beliefs that enable a person to engage in goal-directed, self-regulated, autonomous behavior. Wehmeyer goes on to state that there are four characteristics of a self-determined individual.[16]

First, the individual acts autonomously. This means that the individual feels he is independent and acts that way. He senses that he has a level of control over his own life.

Second, the individual's behaviors are self-regulated. Self-regulated be-haviors include self-management strategies, goal setting, and problem-solv-ing behaviors. A self-regulated individual can make personal decisions about how to act and follow through with those decisions, even if it means that she needs to revise her plans.

Third, the individual can initiate and respond in a psychologically em-powered way, meaning that he realizes he has some element of control over his circumstances. He either possesses or could possess the skills he needs, and if he decides to apply those skills, he will achieve his goals.

Finally, a self-determined individual acts in a self-realizing way. She knows her abilities, strengths and weaknesses and can capitalize on them.

When professionals talk about what young children with disabilities need, they use the terms "age appropriate" or "developmentally appropriate." When working with young adults with disabilities, we need to encourage and promote self-determination. It takes years for an individual to become self-determined. However, by making sure that we maximize learning and independence in the home and school environments, we can achieve our ultimate goal of individuals with disabilities living an independent and self-determined life.

Compensatory Strategies and Supported Employment

It is contradictory to think that an individual could live an independent life without having some connection to the workforce. Having a job in itself provides a level of independence by providing the individual with the funds that allow him to make decisions or choices about his life, living environ-ment and leisure activities. Supported employment is employment with sup-ports.

One way of providing supported employment is by establishing com-pensatory strategies in the work environment. These strategies are set up in vocational environments for both the employers and the employees. The term "compensation" means that individuals get or receive something for their services. Therefore a compensatory strategy for an employer could be a tax benefit for hiring an individual with a disability. A compensatory strategy for an employee could be providing reduced hours, or even setting up visual strategies in the work situation. Both the employer and employee benefit from the strategies and so does the community. If an individual with a disability earns more money for the work she does, it typically means that she will need less support from some other funding source, such as a government-supported program.

Supported employment could entail the provision of personalized job development, training or consultation. It could mean that the individual gets on-site support in an individual- or group-delivered format. A group work situation is typically called a "work enclave." No matter how supported employment is delivered, the practice ensures that there is an individual job or vocational assessment that determines the initial strengths and abilities an individual has. A vocational assessment would include the preferences of an individual so that, rather than just placing him in any position, he is placed in a job that will be enjoyable for him. Other components of supported employment are job development, on-the-job training and ongoing support.

Job development is used to make sure that there are appropriate jobs for individuals to work in. For example, if an individual has a particular strength, a job developer tries to develop or access a job focusing on that strength. Being in a job that an individual enjoys increases her motivation and her rate of success on the job. On-the-job training ensures that the individual knows how to do the job and the job is being completed in an appropriate and efficient manner. Ongoing support is vital for successful placement in the work environment.[17]

Assistive Technology

Louis Harris and Associates and the National Organization on Disability conducted a study of unemployed persons with disabilities and discovered that sixteen percent of the participants could have been successful in a job setting with the appropriate assistive technology.[18] I am sure that in our world this statistic could be much higher, particularly for individuals with a higher level of need. We have already defined an assistive technology device as any item, piece of equipment or product system that is purchased off the shelf, modified or customized, and used to increase, maintain or improve functional capabilities of an individual with a disability.

Because the vocational setting is such an important environment, we should utilize any assistance we can to make work a successful experience for the individual. We could do this by using low-tech or high-tech assistive technology. Low-tech devices include a trackball rather than a mouse for the computer, an enlarged keyboard, a headrest or armrest. Low-tech devices are typically inexpensive and often redesign creatively the use of objects that are already part of the environment. High-tech is not always more expensive, but typically incorporates more expensive materials. High-tech assistive technology devices include a talking calculator or communication device. High-tech equipment typically entails more computer or mechanical components. Assistive technology can assist in making the work environment successful.

In the workforce, it would begin with an assistive technology assessment to answer the question, "Which technologies and strategies can I use to improve the individual's functioning during a specific activity?"

The SETT Framework

Packaged vocational assessments are available that are based on an understanding of the value of assistive technology. The SETT Framework[19] is a cost- and time-efficient assessment strategy that was developed for schools. It could easily be adapted for use in a vocational setting.

The SETT Framework incorporates a series of questions to help analyze what supports need to be put in place to facilitate the optimum level of independence. SETT is an acronym that stands for Student, Environment, Tasks and Tools. It was set up for a student in the school environment but could be modified for an employee in a work environment.

These are some of the questions that could be answered during the assistive technology assessment process:

- What does the student or employee need to do?
- What are his special needs?
- What are her current abilities?
- What materials and equipment are currently available in the environment?
- What are the physical and instructional arrangements?
- Are there likely to be changes?
- What supports are available to him?
- What resources are available to the people supporting her?

- Are the attitudes and expectations aligned?
- What activities take place in the environment?
- What activities support his curriculum or program?
- What are the critical elements of the activities? Is it possible to accommodate the activities in light of her abilities?
- How might technology support his active participation in the activities? (The tools are anything needed to support the individual. It could be devices, services, strategies, training and so on.)
- What "no-tech," low-tech and/or high-tech options might be considered when developing a system for an individual with these needs and abilities doing these tasks in these environments?
- What features need to be added?
- What strategies might be used to invite increased performance?
- How might these tools be tried with the individual in the customary environments in which they will be used?
- What training will be required and for whom?
- How will success (or lack thereof) be measured and documented?
- Does the technology fit in the physical, social and cultural environment? Is the appearance and design of the technology acceptable to the individual?
- Will she use it?

We can use many possible solutions and strategies to assist an individual with disabilities in the work environment. The strategies of facilitating self-determination, using compensatory strategies and supported employment, and incorporating assistive technology in the work environment are a few. It is not easy to make work environments successful for an individual with disabilities. It takes time and commitment on the part of all involved. But the ultimate goal is worthwhile in every way.

CONCLUSION

There are many things that we need to know to help children and adults with special needs. This chapter has touched on a few considerations. With that in mind, I encourage you to gain as much information from as many sources as possible. The field of special education is eclectic. A variety of ideas, philosophies and techniques are useful, and likewise some are not as useful. In this field there are always new approaches and ideas. The ideas presented in this chapter have been proven sound over time and can be used in a variety of environments with a wide range of individuals who all have the same goals: to achieve as much independence as possible and to have a higher quality of life. It is my hope that these strategies and techniques will help you design and implement special education programs in a variety of settings.

Individuals with developmental disabilities can be capable and contributing members of society, but they may need your help to reach their full potential and to achieve their utmost in their quality of life. Matthew 25:34–40 sets the gold standard for us when working with any individual of any age who could be considered vulnerable:

> Then the King will say to those on his right, "Come, you who are blessed by my Father; take your inheritance, the kingdom prepared for you since the creation of the world. For I was hungry and you gave me something to eat, I was thirsty and you gave me something to drink, I was a stranger and you invited me in, I needed clothes and you clothed me, I was sick and you looked after me, I was in prison and you came to visit me."

> Then the righteous will answer him, "Lord, when did we see you hungry and feed you, or thirsty and give you something to drink? When did we see you a stranger and invite you in, or needing clothes and clothe you? When did we see you sick or in prison and go to visit you?"

> The King will reply, "Truly I tell you, whatever you did for one of the least of these brothers and sisters of mine, you did for me."

You may be asking, "Why do I need to go through all this work to make life better for an individual with disabilities?" My answer to you can be found in Ezra 10:4: "Rise up; this matter is in your hands. We will support you, so take courage and do it."

NOTES

1. *Developmental Disabilities Assistance and Bill of Rights Act of 2000*, Public Law 106–402, 106th Cong., 2nd sess. (October 30, 2000), Sec. 101.

2. Kathie Snow, "People First Language: Let's Put the Person First, Not the Disability!" Disability Is Natural, http://www.disabilityisnatural.com/explore/pfl.

3. C. E. Vaughan, *People-First Language: An Unholy Crusade* (n.p.: National Federation of the Blind, 1999).

4. *Webster's College Dictionary*, s.v. "Inclusion" (New York: Random House, 1996).

5. C. M. Jorgensen, *Restructuring High Schools for All Students: Taking Inclusion to the Next Level* (Baltimore: Brookes, 1998), 4.

6. *Webster's College Dictionary*, s.v. "Strategy."

7. G. Dunlap and L. Kern, "Modifying Instructional Activities to Promote Desirable Behavior: A Conceptual and Practical Framework," *School Psychology Quarterly* 11, no. 4 (1996): 297–312.

8. B. J. Vaughn, G. Dunlap, L. Fox, S. Clarke, and M. Bucy, "Parent-Professional Partnership in Behavioral Support: A Case Study of Community-Based Intervention," *Journal of the Association for Persons with Severe Handicaps* 22, no. 4 (1997): 198.

9. K. K. Cessna and R. J. Skiba, "Needs-Based Services: A Responsible Approach to Inclusion," *Preventing School Failure* 40, no. 3 (1996): 117–23.

10. G. Dunlap and L. Kern, "Assessment and Intervention for Children within the Instructional Curriculum," in *Communicative Alternatives to Challenging Behavior: Integrating Functional Assessment and Intervention Strategies*, ed. J. Reichle and D. Wacker (Baltimore: Brookes, 1993), 179–80.

11. J. J. Hoover and J. R. Patton, *Curriculum Adaptations for Students with Learning and Behavior Problems: Principles and Practices* (Austin, TX: Pro-ed, 1997).

12. D. K. Lipsky and A. Gartner, *Inclusion and School Reform* (Baltimore: Brookes, 1997), 102.

13. Jorgensen, *Restructuring High Schools*.

14. L. A. Hodgdon, *Visual Strategies for Improving Communication* (Troy, MI: Quirk Roberts, 1995).

15. Bureau of Labor Statistics, "Economic News Release," United States Department of Labor, 2012, http://www.bls.gov/news.release/empsit.t06.htm.

16. M. L. Wehmeyer, M. Agran, and C. Hughes, *Teaching Self-Determination to Students with Disabilities: Basic Skills for Successful Transition* (Baltimore: Brookes, 1998).

17. R. W. Flexer, T. J. Simmons, P. Luft, and R. M. Baer, *Transition Planning for Secondary Students with Disabilities* (Upper Saddle River, NJ: Prentice Hall, 2001).

18. Louis Harris and Associates and the National Organization on Disability, *The N.O.D./Harris Survey on Employment of People with Disabilities* (New York: International Center for the Disabled, 1994).

19. Joy Zabala, *The SETT Framework: An Assessment Process*, Assistive Technology Training Online Project, 2000–2005, http://atto.buffalo.edu/registered/ATBasics/Foundation/Assessment/sett.asp.

Chapter Ten

The Building Blocks of Mobility

* * *

Virginia Cruz

PICTURE a child. Chances are that the child in your image is running, skipping, jumping or otherwise moving around. This ability to move around in one's environment is called mobility. Children who can move all of their limbs enjoy unimpaired mobility and can move around in their environment through sitting, standing, crawling, walking, running and so on. But children with special needs often experience challenges with mobility. These mobility challenges encompass a great range of severity and impairment requiring different levels of mobility assistance. For example, a child who has a mild lack of function in her leg may need a cane to walk long distances, but a child who has complete paralysis or severe deformity needs a wheelchair in order to enjoy mobility.

Fortunately, whatever the level of challenges and impairments, lay people can perform simple actions to improve a child's mobility. For example, a child may lack sufficient mobility in his torso and limbs to feed himself. But something as simple as a properly placed small pillow can enable him to relax and swallow properly or even to have proper sitting posture to feed himself. That small pillow, placed in the correct position, can make a major change in his function, comfort and life. But to do so, the caregiver must first know that he needs the support of a pillow and must further know where to place it. This chapter introduces caregivers to the basic building blocks of mobility that once understood and safely applied can accomplish the ultimate goal of improving the child's mobility in his environment.

This chapter focuses on the basics that are required, regardless of whether the caregiver is an experienced professional or has only limited experience. Although novel information that is "advanced" and "modern" often seems

more desirable, it is more valuable and useful to first have a proper understanding of the basics (which are often overlooked, even by professionals).
For example, the mother of a child who lacks mobility may wish she had
a special fancy spoon to make it easier for the child to feed herself. Yet, if
the mother has not yet learned how to place the child in the proper sitting
position for eating (by using a small pillow for example) then the spoon
may not be helpful. Learning the simple, basic application of proper positioning is more effective than acquiring fancy equipment. Once the basic
foundation of proper posture has been established, then it can be determined whether the special spoon will be beneficial. And once the basic
building blocks of mobility are understood and safety precautions taken,
then anyone can develop ways to assist a child to improve her function,
in a manner that is fun, playful, colorful and creative—just like children
themselves are.

BASIC BUILDING BLOCKS OF MOBILITY

Most people have a basic understanding of the basic elements needed to
build a house: foundation, walls and roof. The foundation of the body consists of strong head and body control reflected in the posture of the child.
The head should be properly balanced and centered over the body and hips,
and the body (or trunk) should be equally balanced right to left. Next, the
walls are built upon this foundation of proper posture. The walls of the body
are the movements of the arms and legs. They should be properly aligned,
flexible and strong. Finally, the roof is placed on top of the walls. For the
body, the roof represents mobility and encompasses acts such as rolling,
crawling or walking.

The foundation of all mobility is built upon a solid foundation of proper
body posture, adequate joint and muscle range of motion and flexibility,
adequate strength to function against gravity, a desire to move and function (from both the child and the parents or caregiver), and proper assistive
equipment (if necessary). In summary, these are the four building blocks
needed to build mobility:

1. Posture and position of the trunk and limbs
2. Range of motion and flexibility of the trunk and limbs
3. Strength to move against gravity in the trunk and limbs
4. Encouragement of and assistance with mobility

Understanding how the building blocks work gives the caregiver insight into how to improve mobility. Just as the walls and roof of a building must be built on a solid and level foundation in order to stand, so must the human body be built on a strong and symmetrical foundation in order for a child to move optimally around his environment. When you see a crooked roof on a house, check the foundation. When you see a child who cannot lift a spoon to feed himself, check out his sitting posture. Once again, it is about the basics—nothing fancy or modern is required.

CHALLENGES TO MOBILITY

The human body is beautifully and wonderfully made. Although it is able to create and adapt to overcome obstacles, it works best when it rests on the foundation of proper posture. All of the bones, joints and muscles of the head and trunk must be aligned properly in order for the muscles to work within the normal arcs of motion. When those ranges of movement are not as they should be, disabilities and deformities arise. For example, a child whose range of movement is impaired by cerebral palsy may experience reduced mobility in her elbow. This happens because tightness makes the muscles that bend the elbow too short, reducing the "arc" in which bending movement can take place. This decreases the power of the muscles that bend the elbow, resulting in a tight elbow. Similarly, where a child has sat crookedly in a chair for many years the prolonged, improper positioning of his trunk leads to scoliosis, or a crooked back (see figure 10.1).

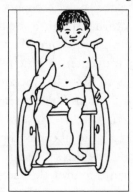

Figure 10.1 Not sitting in a straight, upright position can lead to scoliosis.

Primary and secondary disabilities can cause challenges to mobility. Primary disabilities are diseases or conditions that directly cause problems with the building blocks, including

- cerebral palsy,

- head or brain trauma resulting from blunt trauma, gunshot wounds, anoxia (lack of oxygen), birth defects, spinal cord injury, spina bifida, or tumors of the brain or spinal cord,

- arthrogryposis (also known as AMC, a congenital joint contracture disorder),

- muscular dystrophy, and

- polio.

Secondary disabilities also cause problems with the building blocks, but they arise not from an underlying condition but often as a consequence of that condition, such as lack of movement, disuse, pain or fear. For example, a child's hip can lack adequate extension because she spends most of her time in a seated position.

A true story may help illustrate the concepts of primary and secondary disabilities more clearly: Baby Mary was born with cerebral palsy. From her first weeks, she was irritable when she was not held and rocked. Her muscles were tight and she did not move her arms and legs much. Mary's mother did her best to keep her baby happy and comfortable and, not knowing any better, she did not try to challenge her to get used to different positions other than being held and rocked. By the time Mary was two years old she could not hold up her head and could not sit without someone holding her up. She continued to be irritable and fussy. Mary's mother was unable to place her anywhere where she was comfortable. This created a strain on Mary's mother because she had other duties around the house needing her attention. By the time Mary was two, her arms and legs had become restricted in movement, which limited the motions available to her. For example, her elbow had become so tight it could not be straightened and now Mary was unable to reach out to put her arm in a coat even if she had the strength.

Mary has the primary disability of cerebral palsy that causes her muscles to be too tight, but now she has the secondary disability of an elbow that does not straighten out (a contracture). At age two, it is not too late to try to remedy this situation, however, it may be more difficult because Mary's habits are more ingrained and retraining at age two will be more difficult. This situation illustrates why it is easier to prevent disabilities than to try to limit them once they have occurred. The building blocks discussed in this chapter give some ideas of what Mary's mother can do to improve mobility with regard to these primary and secondary disabilities.

USING THE BUILDING BLOCKS TO BUILD MOBILITY

The building blocks are helpful for building mobility in children with many different types of primary disabilities, including

- cerebral palsy, spina bifida, club feet or other congenital conditions that can lead to gradually increasing deformities;

- paralysis;

- progressive nerve or muscle diseases, including muscular dystrophy;

- loss of all or part of a limb (for example, from birth or amputation); and

- illnesses or injuries causing damage to the brain or spinal cord, including polio, infections of the brain (such as meningitis or encephalitis), spinal cord injuries, and stroke or brain trauma (for example, from gunshot or missile injuries, blunt trauma or falls).

In addition, the building blocks are also helpful for building mobility in children who are suffering from secondary disabilities, such as weakness or loss of flexibility that occur as a result of a primary disability (for example, muscular dystrophy).

Assessment

Before using the building blocks, a basic assessment should be done of the child with his family member or other caretaker present. The assessment should start with general observation (watching or looking at the child) and include the following questions:

- What is the family member/primary caretaker concerned about?

- How well does the child see, hear and feel/touch?

- How well does the child move or control her movements?

- How well formed, deformed or damaged are different parts of the body, such as joints, backbone and skin?

- How much does the child understand?

- How well do different parts of the body work together (for example, eye-hand coordination)?

- How well does the child do things compared to other local children of the same age?

Important assessment guidelines

- If possible, the child should be well rested, well fed and in a good mood.

- Try to avoid provoking pain, anger or fear in the child as much as possible. It is extremely important to establish trust and friendship with him. Once he is afraid, it is difficult to establish trust.

- Wear regular clothes instead of a white uniform because the child may remember and fear pain from a previous experience with a medical person.

- Talk to the child and engage in conversation with her. Touch her in gentle and reassuring ways.

- Approach the child at his height, not from above. Try to have your head at the same level as his head.

- Try to examine the child as she is being held by the family member/primary caretaker or with the family member/primary caretaker close by.

- Give the child lots of praise and have him do things he can do (such as touching his face) as well as things he cannot do (such as reaching behind his back). Start with a win and end with a win.

- If the child is too nervous or fearful, have the family member / primary caretaker move her as you direct her so you can observe what you need to observe.

Looking Ahead

The remainder of this chapter discusses each of the building blocks in detail and explains the ways in which activities, exercises and devices can be used to build mobility in each area. Illustrated instructions from David Werner's *Disabled Village Children*[1] demonstrate how.

BUILDING BLOCK 1: POSTURE AND POSITION

Whether a child has been recently injured, undergone surgery or has a long-term disability such as cerebral palsy, proper positioning of the body is vital to maximize function. Posturing activities can minimize pain and stiffness and, more importantly, prevent life-threatening problems such as blood clots and pneumonia.

What Are Positioning Activities?

Positioning activities refer to placing the child in specific beneficial positions. Whether the child is lying in the bed, sitting in a chair or sitting on the floor, it is important to make an effort to place the child or have him place himself in positions that prevent deformity and maximize function. For example, a child who sits on the floor with her legs positioned in the shape of the letter W should be encouraged to sit crisscross style to prevent the legs from becoming deformed.

Why Do Positioning Activities?

Proper positioning is done to prevent secondary disabilities such as weakness, tightness, pain, blood clots, pneumonia or skin breakdown from remaining in one position for too long (also known as bedsores). It is also done to promote proper alignment of the bones and muscles so that the muscles have a better chance of being used. For example, a child with spastic cerebral palsy cannot lift his head when lying on his back, so the muscles that lift the head do not get used. If the child is placed on his side and encouraged to roll to his tummy, then the muscles that lift the head may get used.

Goals and Expectations of Positioning Activities

For primary disabilities, the goals of positioning activities are to maintain or improve the child's current level of function and to prevent further, secondary disability, such as tightness, weakness from disuse, pain and/or skin problems. For primary disabilities, positioning problems may never completely go away. Positioning activities must be done daily for the remainder of the child's life.

For secondary disabilities, the goals of positioning activities are elimination of tightness, weakness, pain or fear of moving, and the need for positioning activities may be more short-term. Once mobility is restored, specific positioning activities are often no longer needed.

When Should Positioning Activities Be Started?

Early! It is best to start before secondary problems arise. It is much easier, on both the caregiver and the child, to prevent secondary problems than it is to get rid of them once they occur. For example, a child who develops skin breakdown on the buttocks because of prolonged sitting will be required to stay completely off the buttocks until the bedsores heal. This healing process can take months.

How to Do Basic Positioning Activities

The specific positioning activities required are dependent on the needs of the child. But the positions for lying, sitting or standing are similar for most conditions.

Frequency

Positioning should be incorporated into daily activities. Just as a person who is not disabled frequently changes position during the day, so should a person who is physically disabled frequently change position.

Precautions

When doing positioning activities, do not mobilize areas that need to remain immobilized due to fracture or wounds.

Instructions

Figures 10.2–10.5 give instructions for activities and aids for lying, sitting and standing positions.

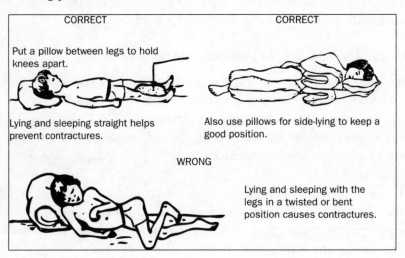

Figure 10.2 Lying positions

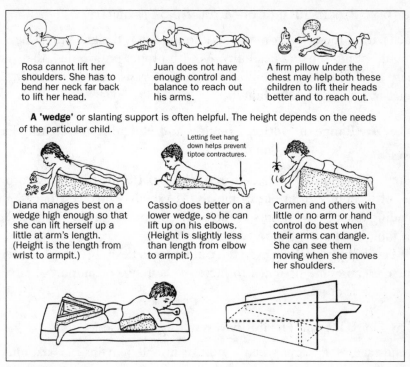

Rosa cannot lift her shoulders. She has to bend her neck far back to lift her head.

Juan does not have enough control and balance to reach out his arms.

A firm pillow under the chest may help both these children to lift their heads better and to reach out.

A 'wedge' or slanting support is often helpful. The height depends on the needs of the particular child.

Letting feet hang down helps prevent tiptoe contractures.

Diana manages best on a wedge high enough so that she can lift herself up a little at arm's length. (Height is the length from wrist to armpit.)

Cassio does better on a lower wedge, so he can lift up on his elbows. (Height is slightly less than length from elbow to armpit.)

Carmen and others with little or no arm or hand control do best when their arms can dangle. She can see them moving when she moves her shoulders.

Figure 10.3 Lying aids

Figure 10.4 Sitting positions

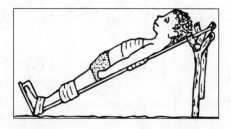

Figure 10.5 Standing position

BUILDING BLOCK 2: RANGE OF MOTION AND FLEXIBILITY

Each part of the body from the neck to the feet is designed to have a certain amount of motion and flexibility. As with proper positioning, there are primary and secondary disabilities that require assistance to maintain proper range of motion and flexibility.

What Are Range of Motion Exercises and Flexibility/Stretching Exercises?

Range of motion (ROM) exercises can be performed regularly to prevent loss of flexibility from occurring. ROM exercises involve straightening or bending one or more joints of the body and moving it in all the directions the joint is normally supposed to move.

Flexibility/stretching exercises can improve flexibility that has been lost. These exercises are designed to increase the range of motion of an already tight muscle or joint.

Why Do ROM and Flexibility/Stretching Exercises?

A contracture develops when a joint or muscle remains in a stationary position for a long time. Some of the muscles become shorter and the joint becomes stiff, preventing the limb from moving fully. The joint is then said to have a contracture. Once developed, a contracture often requires surgery to repair. But most contractures can be prevented through exercise and positioning. Daily ROM exercises are done to prevent joint contractures and other secondary disabilities such as stiffness and deformities.

Sometimes, even with twice-daily ROM exercises, flexibility and joint ROM are lost. Therefore, flexibility/stretching exercises need to be done. Flexibility/stretching exercises are performed to increase the arc of motion of a joint or a part of the body. The benefits are improved function, eased pain and prevention of skin problems.

Goals and Expectations of ROM Exercises and Flexibility/Stretching Exercises

For primary disabilities, the goals of ROM and flexibility/stretching exercises are to maintain or improve the child's current level of function and to prevent further, secondary disability, such as more tightness, weakness from disuse, pain and/or skin problems. For primary disabilities, tightness may never completely go away. ROM and flexibility/stretching exercises should be done daily for the rest of the child's life.

For secondary disabilities, the goal of ROM and flexibility/stretching exercises is elimination of tightness, weakness and pain, as well as fear of moving. For secondary disabilities, the need for such exercises may be more short-term. Once flexibility is restored or significantly improved, and the child gains mobility, the flexibility gains can be maintained through normal daily activities.

When Should ROM and Flexibility/Stretching Exercises Be Started?

Early! It is best to start ROM exercises before loss in range of motion begins. It is much easier, on both the caregiver and the child, to prevent tightness than it is to get rid of tightness once it has been established.

Start flexibility/stretching exercises as soon as tightness or loss of flexibility are noticed.

Common-Sense Precautions When Doing ROM and Flexibility/ Stretching Exercises

1. Do no harm.

    Always keep in mind that it is "better to be safe than sorry." In an effort to help, it is possible to do too much too fast and harm the child. Do a small amount, apply a small amount of pressure, and let her slowly gain confidence. Both you and she need to start slowly to get used to these new activities.

2. Protect the joint.

    Weak joints can easily be damaged by stretching exercises, unless care is taken. Hold the limb both above and below the joint you are exercising and support as much of the limb as you can.

3. Be *gentle* and move the joints *slowly*.

    This is especially important when the child has spasticity (muscle tightness caused by conditions or diseases such as cerebral palsy) or when joints are stiff or painful. Fast movements make spastic muscles tighter, so it is essential to move slowly and gently.

4. Never force the motion.

Stretching often causes discomfort but it should not be overly painful. If the child cannot tell you, or is not able to feel, be extra careful.

How to Do Basic ROM Exercises

All of the joints the child does not move through normal range of motion during his daily activities should be exercised. When these exercises are fun and incorporated into the daily routine, it is easier to continue them for life.

Frequency

ROM exercises should be done twice a day. Each exercise should be done for 10 repetitions each.

Precautions

In addition to the common-sense precautions discussed previously, it is important not to move recently broken bones or joints that are near broken bones. Wait until cleared by a doctor or at least four to six weeks.

Instructions

ROM exercises can be done passively by someone other than the child or they can be done actively by the child. It is best to have her to do as much as she can independently and assist only as needed. That way some strengthening can be accomplished along with the added bonus of improved her self-esteem!

Figures 10.6–10.9 give instructions for ROM exercises for the shoulder, elbow, forearm, wrist, fingers, thumb, knee, hip, ankle, foot, toes, neck, trunk, upper back, ribs and jaw.

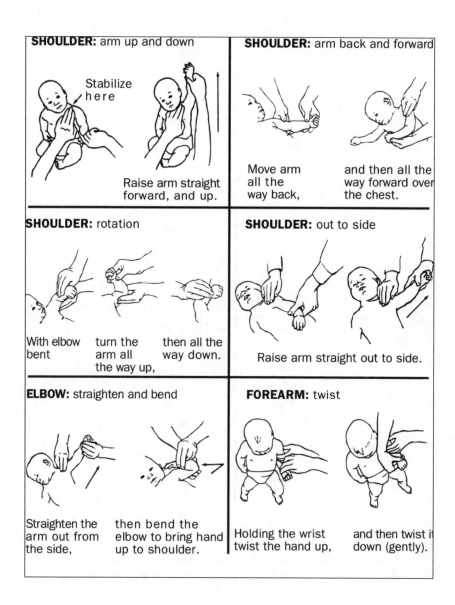

SHOULDER: arm up and down

Stabilize here

Raise arm straight forward, and up.

SHOULDER: arm back and forward

Move arm all the way back,

and then all the way forward over the chest.

SHOULDER: rotation

With elbow bent   turn the arm all the way up,   then all the way down.

SHOULDER: out to side

Raise arm straight out to side.

ELBOW: straighten and bend

Straighten the arm out from the side,   then bend the elbow to bring hand up to shoulder.

FOREARM: twist

Holding the wrist twist the hand up,   and then twist it down (gently).

Figure 10.6 Shoulder, elbow, forearm

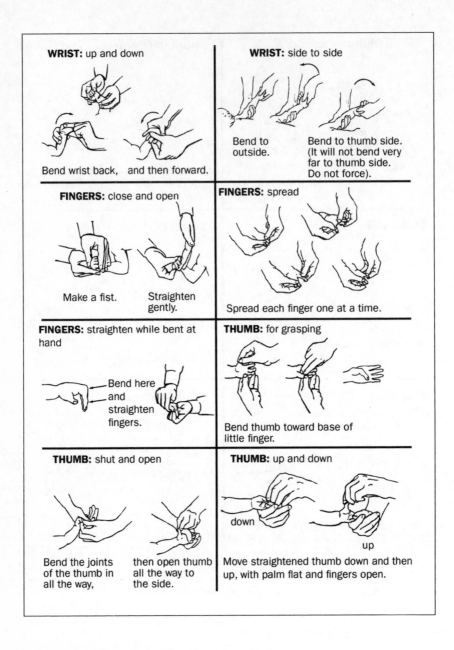

Figure 10.7 Wrist, fingers, thumb

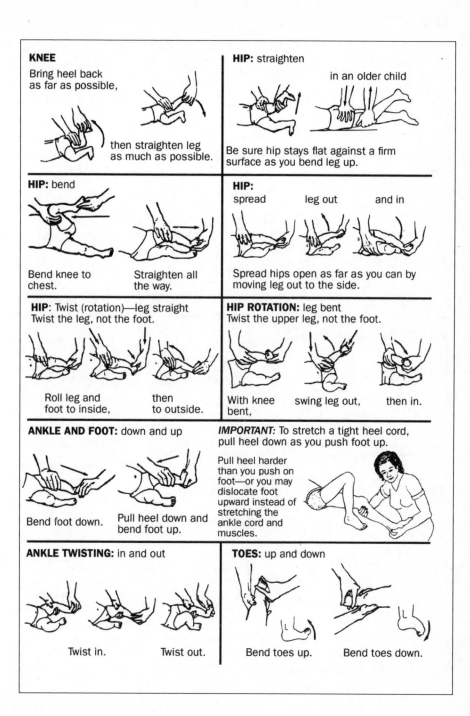

KNEE

Bring heel back as far as possible,

then straighten leg as much as possible.

HIP: straighten

in an older child

Be sure hip stays flat against a firm surface as you bend leg up.

HIP: bend

Bend knee to chest.

Straighten all the way.

HIP:

spread   leg out   and in

Spread hips open as far as you can by moving leg out to the side.

HIP: Twist (rotation)—leg straight
Twist the leg, not the foot.

Roll leg and foot to inside,

then to outside.

HIP ROTATION: leg bent
Twist the upper leg, not the foot.

With knee bent,   swing leg out,   then in.

ANKLE AND FOOT: down and up

Bend foot down.   Pull heel down and bend foot up.

IMPORTANT: To stretch a tight heel cord, pull heel down as you push foot up.

Pull heel harder than you push on foot—or you may dislocate foot upward instead of stretching the ankle cord and muscles.

ANKLE TWISTING: in and out

Twist in.   Twist out.

TOES: up and down

Bend toes up.   Bend toes down.

Figure 10.8 Knee, hip, ankle, foot, toes

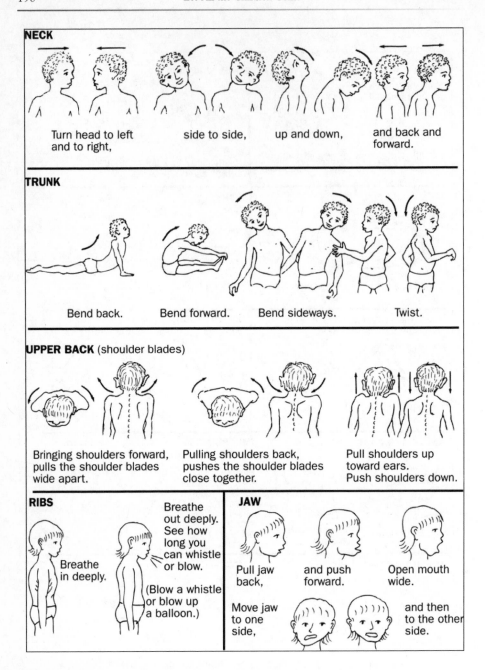

Figure 10.9 Neck, trunk, upper back, ribs, jaw

How to Do Basic Flexibility/Stretching Exercises

Use flexibility/stretching exercises to stretch the joints or muscles that are limited. It is best to do them along with ROM exercises. For example, the child moves his arm through a ROM exercise as far as he is able, then the caregiver moves the arm through the remaining range of motion. If the range of motion is limited, the caregiver can stretch the arm a bit to try to increase the flexibility so the arm will move through the expected range of motion.

Frequency

Flexibility/stretching exercises should be done at least twice daily.

Precautions

It is important to follow the common-sense precautions discussed previously.

Guidelines for Flexibility/Stretching Exercises

1. When performing flexibility/stretching exercises, consider the position of the child, not just the joint you are moving.

2. If the joint is stiff or painful, or the muscles are tight, it usually helps to apply heat to the joint and muscles for ten to fifteen minutes before beginning the exercises. Heat reduces pain and relaxes muscles and soft tissue around the joint. Heat can be applied with hot water soaks, a warm bath or warm compresses. Be extremely careful with this technique if the child lacks or has impaired sensation in the area being heated.

3. Move the joint slowly through its complete range of motion. If the range of motion is not complete, try to stretch it slowly and gently. Hold the limb in the stretched position twenty-five seconds. Try to gain a little more range of motion each time.

4. Have the child do as many of these activities as she can independently.

Instructions

Figures 10.10–10.13 give instructions for flexibility/stretching exercises for the heel, knee, hip and back.

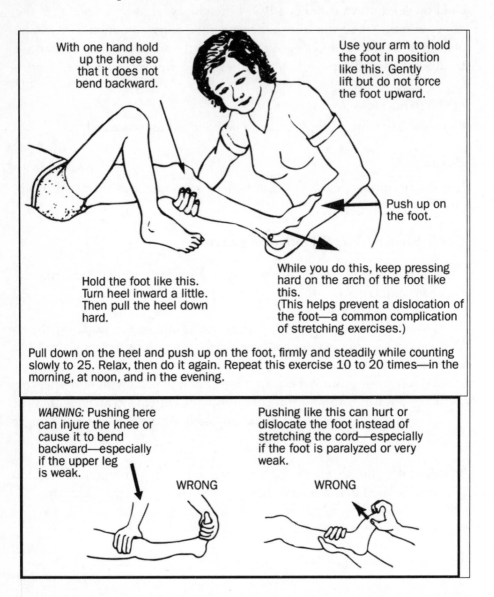

With one hand hold up the knee so that it does not bend backward.

Use your arm to hold the foot in position like this. Gently lift but do not force the foot upward.

Push up on the foot.

Hold the foot like this. Turn heel inward a little. Then pull the heel down hard.

While you do this, keep pressing hard on the arch of the foot like this.
(This helps prevent a dislocation of the foot—a common complication of stretching exercises.)

Pull down on the heel and push up on the foot, firmly and steadily while counting slowly to 25. Relax, then do it again. Repeat this exercise 10 to 20 times—in the morning, at noon, and in the evening.

WARNING: Pushing here can injure the knee or cause it to bend backward—especially if the upper leg is weak.

WRONG

Pushing like this can hurt or dislocate the foot instead of stretching the cord—especially if the foot is paralyzed or very weak.

WRONG

Figure 10.10 Heel

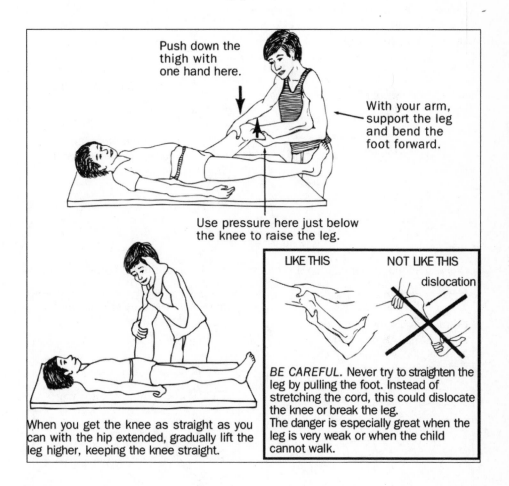

Figure 10.11 Knee

Push down on the butt. (If the hip dislocates easily, hold in the hip bone as you push down.)

Rest the thigh against your thigh, and support the leg with your arm.

With firm and steady force, pull the leg up while counting slowly to 25.

Hold the other leg bent to keep the hips from lifting.

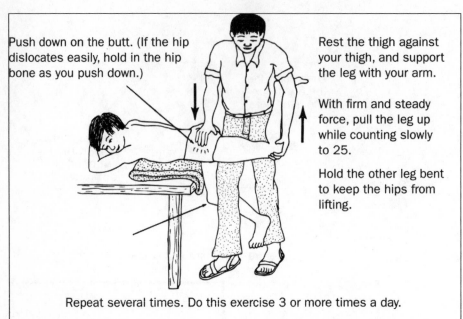

Repeat several times. Do this exercise 3 or more times a day.

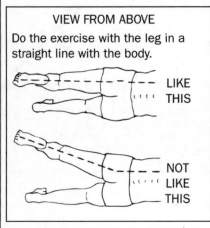

VIEW FROM ABOVE
Do the exercise with the leg in a straight line with the body.

LIKE THIS

NOT LIKE THIS

Make sure the hips are against the table and that they do not lift up as the leg is lifted.

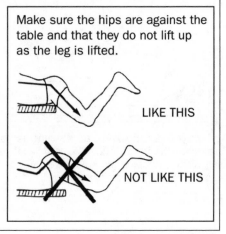

LIKE THIS

NOT LIKE THIS

Figure 10.12 Hip

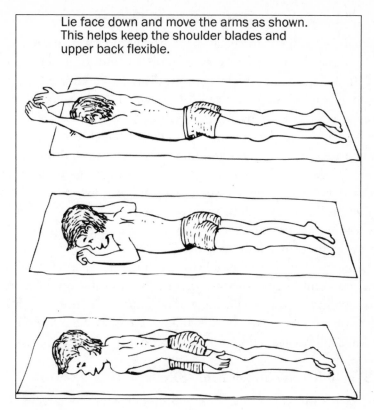

Lie face down and move the arms as shown. This helps keep the shoulder blades and upper back flexible.

Figure 10.13 Back

BUILDING BLOCK 3: STRENGTH TO MOVE AGAINST GRAVITY

When assisting a child with physical disabilities, the ultimate goal is to improve his mobility in the environment. General strengthening exercises are an integral building block in providing more mobility options for him. For example, a child with weak legs may be unable to stand; however, once he gains more strength by performing certain exercises, he may be able to stand with the assistance of a walker.

What Are Strengthening Exercises?

Strengthening exercises are regularly repeated exercises to improve strength in the muscles.

Why Do Strengthening Exercises?

Use daily strengthening exercises to eliminate or prevent weakness, pain or further disability.

Goals and Expectations of Strengthening Exercises

For primary disabilities, the goals of strengthening exercises are to maintain or improve the child's current level of mobility and to prevent further, secondary disability, such as weakness from disuse, pain and/or skin problems. For primary disabilities, the need for assistance with mobility may never completely go away. Strengthening exercises, assistive devices or caregiver assistance may be needed for the remainder of the child's life. Devices may need to be altered as he grows and improves or as the equipment wears out.

For secondary disabilities, the goal of strengthening exercises is elimination of weakness and pain, as well as the fear of moving, and the need for strengthening exercises may be more short-term. Once strength and mobility are restored or significantly improved, the strength gains can be maintained through normal daily activities.

Walking may not be achievable for all children. Walking is often encouraged before a child has learned to roll or crawl and this can be a bit dangerous. As a child learns to walk, she will fall during the learning process. We all do! But if a child has weak arms or a weak trunk, she is more likely to be injured in a fall because she cannot protect her head well.

Who Should Receive Strengthening Exercises?

Children with any of the types of disabilities listed in the section "Using the Building Blocks to Build Mobility" should receive strengthening exercises.

In addition, strengthening exercises are also helpful for building mobility in children who are suffering from weakness not associated with a disease or condition that causes progressive weakness (such as muscular dystrophy). Weaknesses of this type may be caused by disuse or immobility.

When Should Strengthening Exercises Be Started?

Early! It is best to start as soon as weakness is noticed. It is also helpful to start strengthening exercises to prevent weakness if the child will be inactive for a while. For example, a child who has surgery and will be sitting or lying down during the prolonged recuperation should do strengthening exercises for the arms and legs to keep them strong.

How to Do Basic Strengthening Exercises

All of the muscles that the child does not move through normal range of motion during his daily activities should be exercised. Increasing strength in certain muscle groups in the legs and arms can quickly increase the ability to stand and use an assistive device. When strengthening exercises are fun and incorporated into the daily routine, it is easier to continue them for life.

Frequency

Strengthening exercises should be done once or twice a day.

Precautions

It is important not to exercise muscles in the immediate area of a fracture or a recent wound, such as a large cut or a surgical incision, because movement could hinder healing of the fracture or wound.

Where weakness is caused by a condition of progressive muscle weakness, such as amytrophic lateral sclerosis (ALS or Lou Gehrig's disease), extreme care should be taken so the child does not perform strengthening exercises to the point of fatigue. Fatigue can potentially increase the progression of the weakness.

Instructions

Strengthening exercises must be done actively by the child. Assistance can be provided but she must do as much as she possibly can in order to improve strength. (Passively moving a weak limb of the child improves your strength, not hers.)

Figures 10.14–10.22 give instructions for strengthening exercises for the arms, thighs, hips, hands, head and trunk.

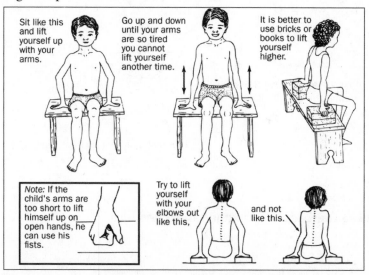

Figure 10.14 Exercise to strengthen arms to use crutches or walker.

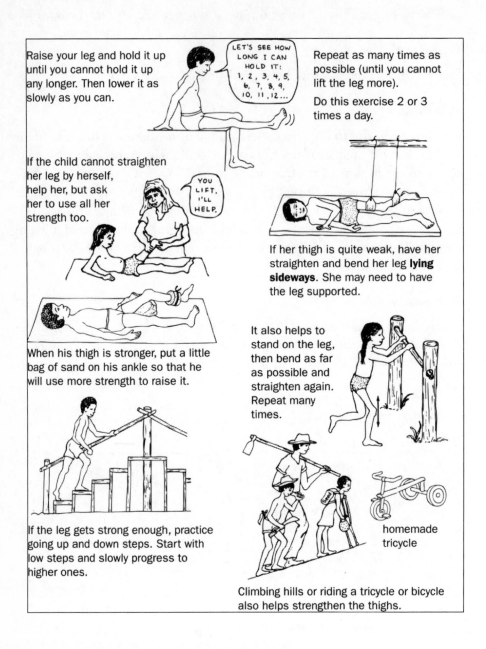

Figure 10.15 Exercises to strengthen knees and hips.

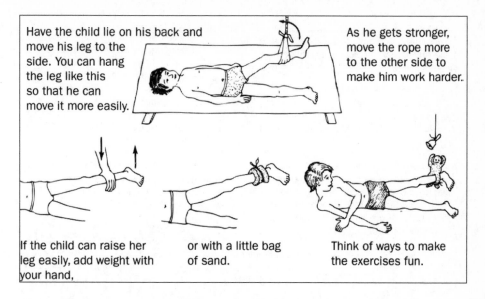

Figure 10.16 Exercise to strengthen knees and hips.

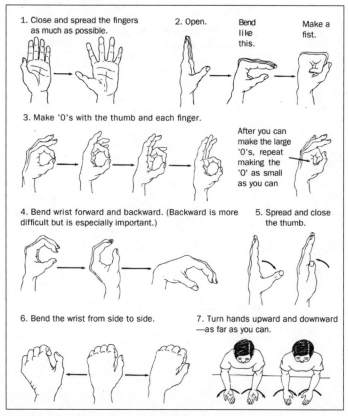

Figure 10.17 Exercises to strengthen the hands.

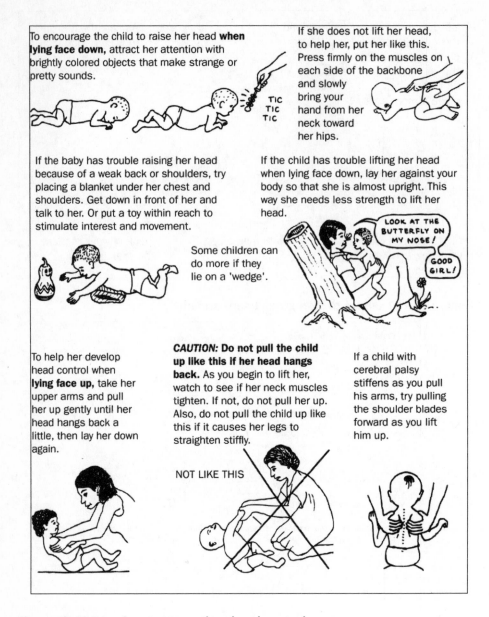

To encourage the child to raise her head **when lying face down,** attract her attention with brightly colored objects that make strange or pretty sounds.

If she does not lift her head, to help her, put her like this. Press firmly on the muscles on each side of the backbone and slowly bring your hand from her neck toward her hips.

If the baby has trouble raising her head because of a weak back or shoulders, try placing a blanket under her chest and shoulders. Get down in front of her and talk to her. Or put a toy within reach to stimulate interest and movement.

If the child has trouble lifting her head when lying face down, lay her against your body so that she is almost upright. This way she needs less strength to lift her head.

Some children can do more if they lie on a 'wedge'.

LOOK AT THE BUTTERFLY ON MY NOSE!

GOOD GIRL!

To help her develop head control when **lying face up,** take her upper arms and pull her up gently until her head hangs back a little, then lay her down again.

CAUTION: **Do not pull the child up like this if her head hangs back.** As you begin to lift her, watch to see if her neck muscles tighten. If not, do not pull her up. Also, do not pull the child up like this if it causes her legs to straighten stiffly.

NOT LIKE THIS

If a child with cerebral palsy stiffens as you pull his arms, try pulling the shoulder blades forward as you lift him up.

Figure 10.18 Exercises to strengthen head control.

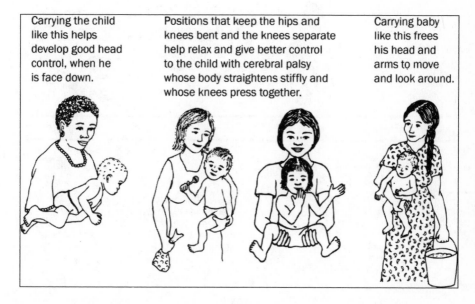

Carrying the child like this helps develop good head control, when he is face down.

Positions that keep the hips and knees bent and the knees separate help relax and give better control to the child with cerebral palsy whose body straightens stiffly and whose knees press together.

Carrying baby like this frees his head and arms to move and look around.

Figure 10.19 Carrying positions to promote good head and body control.

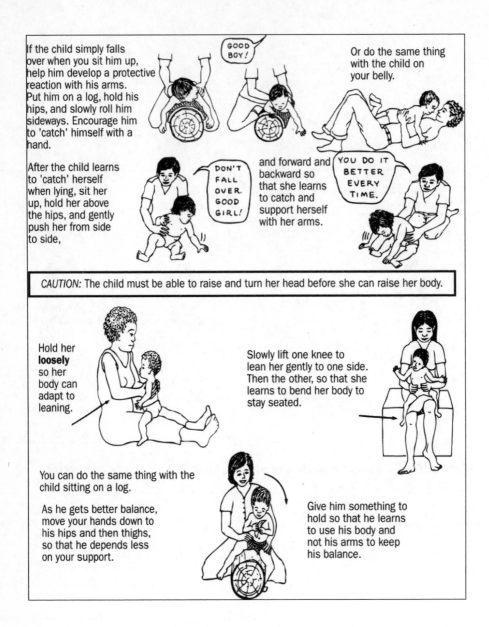

If the child simply falls over when you sit him up, help him develop a protective reaction with his arms. Put him on a log, hold his hips, and slowly roll him sideways. Encourage him to 'catch' himself with a hand.

GOOD BOY!

Or do the same thing with the child on your belly.

After the child learns to 'catch' herself when lying, sit her up, hold her above the hips, and gently push her from side to side,

DON'T FALL OVER. GOOD GIRL!

and forward and backward so that she learns to catch and support herself with her arms.

YOU DO IT BETTER EVERY TIME.

CAUTION: The child must be able to raise and turn her head before she can raise her body.

Hold her **loosely** so her body can adapt to leaning.

Slowly lift one knee to lean her gently to one side. Then the other, so that she learns to bend her body to stay seated.

You can do the same thing with the child sitting on a log.

As he gets better balance, move your hands down to his hips and then thighs, so that he depends less on your support.

Give him something to hold so that he learns to use his body and not his arms to keep his balance.

Figure 10.20 Exercises to strengthen sitting.

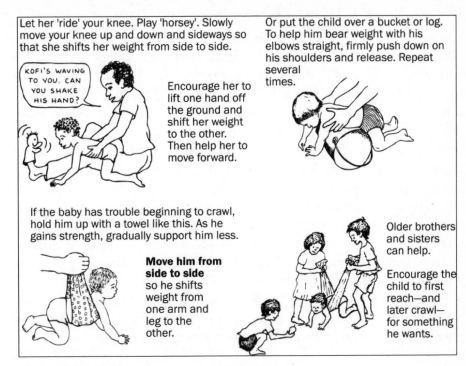

Let her 'ride' your knee. Play 'horsey'. Slowly move your knee up and down and sideways so that she shifts her weight from side to side.

Or put the child over a bucket or log. To help him bear weight with his elbows straight, firmly push down on his shoulders and release. Repeat several times.

KOFI'S WAVING TO YOU, CAN YOU SHAKE HIS HAND?

Encourage her to lift one hand off the ground and shift her weight to the other. Then help her to move forward.

If the baby has trouble beginning to crawl, hold him up with a towel like this. As he gains strength, gradually support him less.

Move him from side to side so he shifts weight from one arm and leg to the other.

Older brothers and sisters can help.

Encourage the child to first reach—and later crawl—for something he wants.

Figure 10.21 Exercises to strengthen the trunk.

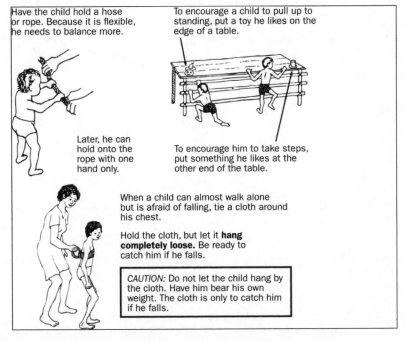

Have the child hold a hose or rope. Because it is flexible, he needs to balance more.

To encourage a child to pull up to standing, put a toy he likes on the edge of a table.

Later, he can hold onto the rope with one hand only.

To encourage him to take steps, put something he likes at the other end of the table.

When a child can almost walk alone but is afraid of falling, tie a cloth around his chest.

Hold the cloth, but let it **hang completely loose**. Be ready to catch him if he falls.

CAUTION: Do not let the child hang by the cloth. Have him bear his own weight. The cloth is only to catch him if he falls.

Figure 10.22 Exercise to strengthen standing and walking balance.

BUILDING BLOCK 4: MOBILITY ENCOURAGEMENT AND ASSISTANCE

Once a child has adequate strength, she should be encouraged to be as mobile as possible in the environment, whether the environment is a room, an entire house, a school or outside in a park. If the child can roll, then he can roll around a room or through the house. If the child is only able to crawl on her hands and knees, then she should crawl. If he can propel a wheelchair, then he should propel it as much as possible. If she can walk, even if she needs equipment and assistance, she should be encouraged to walk as much as possible. The child will gain self-esteem and confidence if he can manage some of his mobility needs independently.

In general, a child should be as mobile as possible with the least amount of assistance or equipment as necessary. Occasionally, however, more equipment (if available) can increase function and prevent secondary disabilities from arising. For example, a child whose knee hyperextends may prefer to walk without a knee brace; however, in the future, the knee will become more unstable, the muscles surrounding the knee will become weaker, and the knee will likely become painful. The proper use of a knee support could possibly prevent these secondary disabilities or at least prolong the time before they arise.

It is common for a child to need both a device to assist walking and wheeled mobility. Many children can walk short distances such as in a house, but they are unable to walk safely in more challenging situations. If possible, the child should be encouraged to walk where she is able and to use some type of wheeled mobility where she is unable. Short walks are better than none at all.

Devices to Assist Walking

Many types of devices to assist walking are available. The following are the major types, from least to most stable:

- Canes

Canes come in a variety of styles, including straight canes and canes with multiple points at the bottom. Tripod canes end in three short "legs," and quad canes end in four. Multipoint canes are more stable than straight canes, but they are less stable than crutches. Straight canes are the least stable form of assistive devices for walking.

- Crutches

Crutches also come in a variety of styles; two common styles are the forearm crutch and the auxiliary crutch. Forearm crutches attach to the arm between

the wrist and the elbow. Auxiliary crutches extend all the way up to the under-
arm. Auxiliary crutches are more stable than forearm crutches.

Usage of canes and crutches

Both canes and crutches can be used singly or as a pair; using one in each
hand provides greater support. When using only one cane or crutch, it
should be placed opposite the weak side, if possible. For example, if a child
has weakness of the left leg, the device should be used in the right hand. This
improves balance and lessens the physical energy needed to use the device.

- Walkers

Walkers are four-legged movable devices (see figure 10.23). Sometimes the legs
end in wheels or slides.

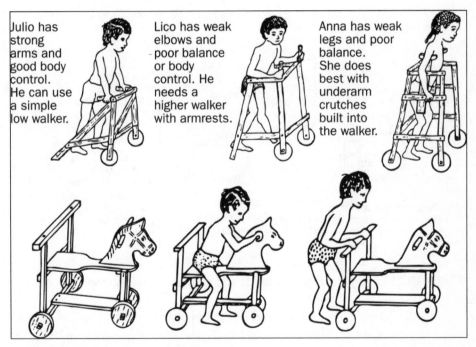

Figure 10.23 Examples of walkers

Walkers are the most stable devices to assist walking, but they are more
bulky than canes or crutches and they require two hands to use.

Wheeled Mobility

Wheelchairs, carts or various other creative ways are used to wheel a child around the environment. As shown in figure 10.24, it may be necessary to adjust a wheelchair to ensure a good sitting position for the child.

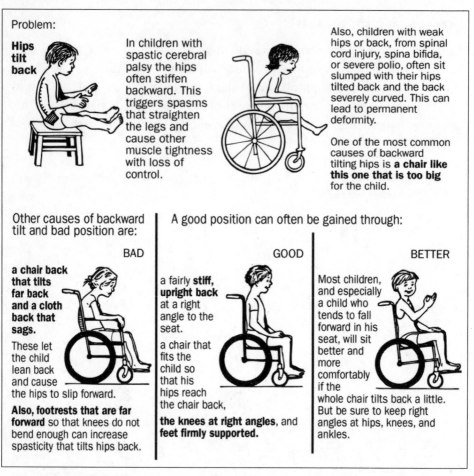

Problem:

Hips tilt back

In children with spastic cerebral palsy the hips often stiffen backward. This triggers spasms that straighten the legs and cause other muscle tightness with loss of control.

Also, children with weak hips or back, from spinal cord injury, spina bifida, or severe polio, often sit slumped with their hips tilted back and the back severely curved. This can lead to permanent deformity.

One of the most common causes of backward tilting hips is **a chair like this one that is too big** for the child.

Other causes of backward tilt and bad position are:

A good position can often be gained through:

BAD

a chair back that tilts far back and a cloth back that sags.

These let the child lean back and cause the hips to slip forward.

Also, footrests that are far forward so that knees do not bend enough can increase spasticity that tilts hips back.

GOOD

a fairly **stiff, upright back** at a right angle to the seat.

a chair that fits the child so that his hips reach the chair back,

the knees at right angles, and **feet firmly supported.**

BETTER

Most children, and especially a child who tends to fall forward in his seat, will sit better and more comfortably if the whole chair tilts back a little. But be sure to keep right angles at hips, knees, and ankles.

Figure 10.24 Examples of problematic and proper wheelchair seating.

Try to devise ways so the child can propel the device. Wheeled devices need not be expensive, but can be made from ordinary materials in developing contexts.

Conclusion

This chapter includes a lot of information that can potentially be overwhelming to caregivers who are new to mobility. Assisting a child with special needs is a complex undertaking, even for a trained professional. But with the information and training provided in this chapter, even lay people can help a child to build mobility.

Do not be afraid to use trial and error. Do your best to figure out why a child cannot do something, and begin to try ideas to assist. For instance, if a child walks on his toes, check to see if his ankle is tight. If it is, try to stretch it. As long as safety concerns are followed and you do not try to do too much too soon, the child should improve in function. When offering assistance the first thing to remember is "Do no harm." Proceed slowly, try small things, and know that a little can go a long way!

NOTE

1. David Werner, *Disabled Village Children: A Guide for Community Health Workers, Rehabilitation Workers, and Families* (Palo Alto, CA: Hesperian Foundation, 2009), http://hesperian.org.

*

CHAPTER ELEVEN

THE IMPORTANCE

OF SPIRITUAL NURTURE

* * *

Courtney L. Smith

But Jesus said, "Let the children come to me. Don't stop them!
For the Kingdom of Heaven belongs to those who are like these
children." —Matthew 19:14 (NLT)

SARA and Joe (not their real names) are a lovely Christian couple who
have been married for six years. They are also the parents of an adorable
boy named Max. Max is five years old; he has curly dark brown hair
and bright blue eyes with lashes a mile long. Max loves cars, he loves to draw
and he loves to laugh.

The moment Max hits open space, he makes a mad dash, without regard
for safety. He spins in circles and flaps his hands when he is excited. He cannot speak well and sometimes has trouble understanding when he is spoken
to. When something is not in the exact order he expected, he screams. It
takes Max's mom sometimes as long as a half hour to get his clothes on each
morning and each night because the texture of the clothing makes him feel
as though his skin is crawling.

Each Saturday Sara has to take Max grocery shopping with her because
Joe works a second job to keep up with the medical bills. At the store, Max
goes from laughter to major meltdown. He tries endlessly to get out of his
seat. He screams and kicks. Sara does her best to parent Max. She gives him
toys to distract him, she hugs him tightly, she speaks firmly to him when

needed and she gives him a visual schedule, but the bright signs, lights and colors of the market are just too much stimulation for Max to handle. At last she quickly grabs what she needs, making as little eye contact as possible with the staring shoppers. She tries desperately to ignore the frequent under-the-breath comments that come her way and zooms to the car with Max screaming in tow.

Sara typically spends most of her week at doctor and therapy appointments in hopes of hearing Max say a few more words. Every word spoken is an achievement, a reason to celebrate. Every word not spoken is a reminder of the battle he will face daily for his lifetime. Sara spends what is left of her time battling Max's school for services and keeping in contact with his teacher and the team of professionals that it takes to help Max through his day: speech therapist, occupational therapist, physical therapist and special-education teacher. Sara also picked up a job to help out financially, and she and Joe switch roles at three o'clock in the afternoon when she leaves for the evening shift. They say their hellos and good-byes in nearly one breath.

Although they are a married couple, they often feel like single parents. Frustration and fights between them seem to be erupting more and more. They are hanging on to their faith; just clinging to Jesus for answers, for the strength to get through what feels relentless. Every day they feel like they need a miracle; both are growing weary of the burdens carried. They long for belonging; a place where Max is accepted as God made him. They long for a place of worship where they can soak in the Lord's presence for an hour to renew.

They wonder if Max understands. They want him to know the Lord as they do. Sunday comes, and they decide to try (again) to find a church home. They were asked to leave the previous two because, they were told, Max was too difficult. They wonder how it will go. They wonder if they should bother.

You may be wondering why a chapter on the importance of spiritual nurture opens with a picture of spiritual hindrance. This snapshot is just one of many pictures of what commonly occurs in families affected by disability across the world today. According to a report by the Lausanne Movement, the majority of people with disabilities are in need of gospel outreach:

> *Only 5 to 10% of the world's disabled are effectively reached with the gospel, making the disability community one of the largest unreached—some say under-reached—or hidden groups in the world. Jesus, aware that this population would be overlooked, made people with disabilities a target group of the Great Commission (Luke 14:12–24).*[1]

In fact, two-thirds of Jesus' miracle ministry ministered to people who were affected by disability. Now, however, they are one of the most under-reached groups. The gap is wide, but it can be filled. Disability is on the rise worldwide, the economy is suffering even in the richest of nations, and eyes are turning to low-cost and no-cost solutions: the faith-based community. We must respond to Jesus' biblical mandate to "invite the poor, the crippled, the lame, the blind" (Luke 14:13).

In Rachel Held Evans' blog post, "Blessed Are the Un-cool," she posed a poignant question in response to Luke 14:13: "Jesus taught us that when we throw a banquet or a party, our invitation list should include 'the poor, the crippled, the lame, and the blind.' So why do our church marketing teams target the young, the hip, the healthy and the resourced?"[2]

What will our response be to Jesus should he ask us the same question? My hope for this chapter is that, with our eyes opened to our human error, we make a recommitment to Jesus' mission, way and image. Providing spiritual nurture to a child with a disability is a beautiful place to start.

The need for spiritual nurture, which is so important for us as adults and the children we raise, is no less significant because a child has a disability. Some may reason that because their behavior can be disruptive to the teaching and learning of the other children it is best to create a "special" room for those who fall under the "disabled" label. In a day and age of business and constant demands, we may be tempted to pass off the responsibility of caring for or ministering to those with disabilities. As churches, we can reason away this ministry responsibility due to its size and scope, or the lack of volunteers and/or available funds. However, no good reason in the world changes the truth and mandate of the Bible.

As brothers and sisters in Christ, we must uphold one another to our Father's work and ways. When we get off track, there is no condemnation in Christ, but merely some eye-opening reminders to stay on the road less traveled and to come together with one another, calling on the presence of the Lord to help with what we may view as the impossible. The moments in which we see the impossible being done are the moments we sit back and receive confirmation that Jesus is alive and well. And, yes, He still works best in the impossible.

In agreeing that our views are now checked and aligned with that of our Father's word, we are prepared to explore how to provide successful spiritual nurture to children affected by disability in our congregations.

A Snapshot of Spiritual Nurture

As the founder of Links of Love Disability Ministry, I have seen firsthand the positive impact of spiritual nurture. One family in particular illustrates how we can change the course of a young person's life by including them in the larger community and encouraging them to participate. (The names have been changed to protect the family's privacy.)

During one of my night shifts working as a nurse at the local hospital, I was assigned a patient who needed to be admitted for a cardiac arrhythmia. I was completing her assessment and asking questions about her stress level, when Lauren began to share with me about her daughter, Sandy. She was concerned about her well-being and shared her feelings of frustration. "She has Asperger's syndrome." Lauren described her different levels of stress in attempting not only to cope with her daughter's behaviors and struggles but also to help her daughter to cope. My heart went out to this single mom, a Christian woman who dedicated a majority of her time to homeschooling and working with her daughter. From the sound of it, she needed someone to come alongside her, help bear her burden and give her direction.

As nurses, we are often taught not to share too much personal information with our patients, but I could not resist God's pressing me to share. The look on Lauren's face reminded me of a time when I was in a very similar place, and my empathy level was full size. We talked for quite some time, probably too long according to the other nurses on the floor, but we were on God's time. Lauren requested information about our ministry, and I gave her my card.

Several months later, a woman with a familiar voice called Links of Love. Lauren, my sister in Christ whom I had cared for as my patient months earlier, was calling to talk about possibly getting her daughter involved with our congregation and joining in worship with the help of Links of Love. She explained that although Sandy was nervous and had experienced trouble in the past with any type of social situation, she wanted to give church a try. "Developing a relationship is the number-one key factor in making this work," I told Lauren. "If we get to know each other first, when Sandy comes to church she will recognize at least a few faces with whom she is comfortable, and she will not feel like she is swimming in a sea of strangers in a land of sensory overload." I asked if she would feel comfortable coming to my house with Sandy to have lunch and get to know each other.

Before Sandy and I met, I asked Lauren to tell me a little bit about her daughter, not her diagnoses. She told me about Sandy's Italian heritage, writing, art, and her love for science. Surprisingly, these were all things we happened to have in common. This common ground gave us an excellent starting point. I decided to make my grandmother's meatballs-and-sauce-from-scratch recipe to fill my house with a familiar smell for her. I laid out books and encyclopedias about animals and fish. On another table, I left colored pencils and paper. That is where our relationship began.

Since working with Links of Love, Lauren informed us that her knowledge and understanding of Asperger's syndrome have increased, as well as her understanding of their situation, from a biblical view. She shared that since we came alongside her daughter to nurture her spiritually in an individualized way, she has watched Sandy grow in maturity and understanding in her relationship with the Lord. She also shared that the communication between mother and daughter improved dramatically.

Our relationship as siblings in Christ has grown since our initial meeting several years ago. This mother and daughter sat in the front pew for my first full-length sermon as my biggest encouragers. Sandy showed up every Wednesday night to go to youth, even though she could not stand other teenagers. She worked through her social anxiety and discomfort because of her dedication and love for God. She prank-calls me for fun, a favorite pastime of my own that many people do not know about, so I get a good chuckle out of it. She shared with me her talent for writing, and she allowed me to read her stories, which, by the way, are the best stories I have ever read. Her writings give me a glimpse into her mind, which she cannot always express through conversation. The detail and depth of biblical understanding in her stories minister to me. I have helped Sandy understand biblical theology surrounding her Asperger's; she has helped me apply it.

LINKS OF LOVE: A SNAPSHOT OF A DISABILITY MINISTRY

In 2008, after two years of "prenatal" care, Links of Love Disability Ministry was born in Lansdale, Pennsylvania. It has since become one of the model ministries that is being implemented in congregations through Peaceful Living, a faith-based nonprofit company that provides services for individuals with intellectual and developmental disabilities.[3] Links of Love is a five-part ministry designed with a holistic and inclusive approach with the intent to support and serve *with* the individual with a disability, his family unit and the congregation. The ministry's five parts include the following:

- Link program
- Marital support group
- Prayer team

- Resource center
- Special Needs, Special Gifts program

Link Program

Having a disability may prevent the child/adult from fully enjoying service in the inclusive setting. A *link* is a volunteer trained to bridge the gap, should one exist as a barrier to inclusive worship. For instance, the link volunteer might serve on a one-to-one basis in Sunday school for a variety of reasons, or might volunteer to drive someone to church and help that individual through the door. The link concept is based on 1 Corinthians 12:18–20: "But in fact God has placed the parts in the body, every one of them, just as he wanted them to be. If they were all one part, where would the body be? As it is, there are many parts, but one body." A fundamental part of the ministry, the link is a representation of the interdependent relationships that God designed for us; one side cannot function properly without the other.

Marital Support Group

The marital support group offers support, prayer and community. Its objective is to protect the family unit and the sanctity of marriage. The group strives to equip couples with the tools to cope as well as offer a biblical understanding of how God may be working in their situations. This support group is vital; marriages affected by disability often are subject to additional related stressors, as described in the opening story about Sara and Joe and their son Max. It is no wonder that a much higher than average divorce rate occurs for these couples.

Prayer Team

To ensure specific and consistent prayer support, a group of prayer warriors is assigned to the families served through the Links of Love Disability Ministry and within the congregation. This team also sends cards of encouragement and may make personal visits to represent the physically present body during the week as well as on Sundays.

Resource Center

We created a center at the church to provide hearing impairment devices, Bibles for the blind, sensory baskets (a collection of sensory items that are used to extend a child's attention span) and information on community resources. Each Sunday, a volunteer at the resource center table is available to help connect people with resources, links, or other families in similar situations. The volunteer also assists people in navigating the church.

Special Needs, Special Gifts Program

A wise person once said, "Everyone is gifted, but some people never open their package." The Special Needs, Special Gifts part of the ministry is a program designed to identify, celebrate and incorporate the gifts of an individual with a disability. Volunteers are taught to encourage and celebrate gifts that they observe within individuals and, if they feel led, to pray about where these gifts might best be used in the congregation, if the individual is receptive to sharing. A link volunteer is provided, if needed, to assist in removing barriers that may prevent the individual from otherwise sharing her gifts.

Links of Love has had a one hundred percent success rate with full inclusion, from the most severe cases of physical and behavioral disability to the mild. The success-rate credit goes to the Lord and His blessing. When we follow His design, things work! Jesus taught us: get to know people, help them where they need it most, and encourage the gifts that are God-given. At Links of Love, we take to heart the following sentiment: "You have to get to know the person. You can research what the disability is and get informed, but you will never connect with the disability, you will connect with the person."

When training someone who has no experience working with children affected by disability, starting with the concept of getting to know a person is helpful. Putting this concept into practice is a good way to encourage people who may be considering volunteering. The idea is that you identify someone in the congregation with similar likes and interests and introduce him to a potential volunteer. "This is so-and-so, who likes soccer and the outdoors, I heard that you like the same." Having common interests helps to sidestep the awkwardness and feelings of hesitancy of both people. It helps build relationship, which in turn fosters belonging, which in turn helps all members to flourish and be blessed.

A Links of Love Success Story

A boy came to Links of Love when he was 10 years old. The parents informed us that he had been asked to leave several other churches. The previous church did not ask them to leave, but rather consistently pulled one of the parents out of service to come get the child or sit with him in service. The parents told me that as a result they had not worshiped together since their son was a toddler. At times the child would bang his head on the floor and carry on very loudly when he was frustrated. He might also wander around the room and interrupt the pastor while she was preaching by asking her a question. However, we wanted to give it a go. We promised the parents that we would not interrupt them unless it was an absolute emergency. We started out by praying. Then we found out what this child liked: gadgets! We prepared a visual schedule for him so he knew what to expect, and we gave him a bag of sensory items.

The first Sunday was hard, as we anticipated, but that was the day for setting our boundaries for expected behavior. He was having trouble with the concept of waiting until the end of service to look at the soundboard, which he loved. After taking him out of service for a short while to regroup, we decided to help him by letting him know we were not "waiting," we were "participating." We showed him what participating was, and as he began to grasp it, we reinforced his behavior with stickers and lots of praise.

When one of the children's pastors heard that he liked gadgets, he found and fixed a small handheld gauge that the boy could hold while sitting and "participating" in service. Before long, he was enjoying every moment of service from beginning to end. He was reciting Bible verses and even began to participate in the Royal Rangers group for boys, something his dad never thought he would be able to do.

We worked with him to learn another child's name every week. Sometimes it took two or three weeks, but he would get it down. Soon the children were inviting him to sit beside them. Over one year, this child needed to leave service to regroup two times, and neither of those times did we have to call in his parents. The mother once shared, "Everyone told me to just give up. Told me I would never find a church that would accept my child. I told them I would never give up, that for sure there must be one church. That one church is here. Thank you!" The blessing goes both ways.

Providing spiritual nurture to this child was critical for him and his quality of life. Spiritual nurture influenced how he viewed himself, how he viewed God and how he viewed his fellow believers. It also influenced his family in the same way.

In the body of Christ, it never stops at one. The blessing from serving is twofold. This may sound cliché, but the families bless us far more than we bless them. Through Links of Love, the Lord has granted us a snapshot of His greatness. He has taken us beyond the unexpected, had us in tears, had us on the floor with laughter, and has done what He does best: the impossible. Doing the impossible is His signature move. There are many who try, but no one else can replicate it.

PARENTAL CONCERNS AND EMOTIONS

Rarely is there a heart of heavier concern for the spiritual nurture of a child than that of a parent. When disability comes along, whether at birth or thereafter, this concern only deepens. So many questions may arise concerning your child's disability:

- Was this my fault?
- Am I being punished?
- Why her? Why us?
- Will my child ever know God as we do?
- What can my child understand about God?
- Does the Word still apply to my child if he cannot understand?
- Will other Christians understand or accept my child?
- What can I do to provide my child with the spiritual nurture she requires?

Disability affects not only your child but also every member of your household, which in turn affects the way you as a parent understand and provide spiritual nurture for your child who has a disability.

The effects of a disability can infiltrate all aspects of life and relationships. Siblings, careers, schedules, finances, marriage, in-laws, friendships, education, health, ongoing stress levels, mental health issues; there is barely an aspect of life that goes untouched. For parents, an array of emotions may accompany having a child with a disability. On one side of the emotional spectrum, you may experience grief over losing the child you envisioned (grief is a process that will and does reoccur at a variety of milestones from birth to adulthood), anger, exhaustion, bitterness, betrayal, loneliness, impatience, and feeling misunderstood and isolated. On the other side, you may experience positive emotions such as joy (especially when your child triumphs big or small) or feeling grace-filled, strong, blessed, refined, humbled, motivated, patient and loved.

Understanding and coping with your own emotions will help you heal from some of the painful aspects of a disability's affect. That emotional healing will help you move forward in your relationships and become the best source of spiritual nurture for your child. Consider also that when we work through our own emotions, we are better able to empathize with others.

> *All praise to God, the Father of our Lord Jesus Christ. God is our merciful Father and the source of all comfort. He comforts us in all our troubles so that we can comfort others. When they are troubled, we will be able to give them the same comfort God has given us.* (2 Cor. 1:3–4 NLT)

Understanding the biblical basis and motivation behind your struggles and trials will help you change your perspective and align your struggles with the perspective of the Word rather than the world's. This understanding helps bring to life the promise that the Lord will take our own struggles and suffering and use them for good.

A Perspective-Changing Story

Teresa Alderfer is an author and the creator and blogger at *Special Savings Special Needs*. The mother of four girls, two of whom have cerebral palsy, shares an incredible and thought-provoking look at perspective and "luck." The complete text of this story can be found on her website.[4]

Artichokes, Parades, and Matryoshka . . . or Being the Littlest Nesting Doll

It happened again. No surprise, really. When we go anywhere we arrive as our own parade. Six of us in a line, two driving power chairs. Not just any two, though. A matched set, a pair, identical twins. I understand it, really. Either one of those situations causes people to take another look so the combination adds up to an extra looong look to process it. And it can be interesting how people process our family. I don't generally take notice anymore as it is just a part of our comings and goings. But this time it was hard to overlook.

As we headed into the grocery store to hit up their hot and cold foods bar for lunch, we passed another mixed generational group chatting on their way out. The eldest gasped and directed the group to look at the twins exclaiming how lucky they all were. Not the twins, the rest of the people in her group. She was lucky, too, she acknowledged, and asked several to agree with her over their luckiness. In that moment, I was feeling that we were stamped "unlucky." If there is anything great about passing 40 years old, it is that I am older. Seems like an obvious statement, but it works for me. I am older and no longer feel like a quiet spectator on the side lines of the real world. I am in it, just not of it, so I spoke up. Apparently, I got my driver's license at 16 and my speaking up license at 40. Who knew. I simply said, "I feel lucky, too." It did startle her a moment. I am not sure what surprised her, that I could hear her conversation taking place next to my ear, or that I was declaring us members of her *lucky club*. She recovered and assured me it was good that I felt that way. I ended it there and continued our parade. OK, OK, I almost ended it. The rest of my thoughts were muttered into Brielle's ear. Sorry, dearest.

It took me a moment to shake it off, and I ended up with quite a combination of foods touching each other on my plate. Tuna salad, pickled red beet eggs, warm mac and cheese, fried chicken, and artichokes with olives. Did I mention they were *touching*? Yikes.

I wondered yet again why we all do that . . . look for someone who we decide is in a worse situation than us to make us feel better about ourselves or *lucky*. In fact, I hear people encourage the behavior as a part of their counsel. Admit it, we have all encouraged someone to look around and find someone who is worse off, saying "see, it could be worse." It makes me think of those Russian nesting dolls. Somehow we need to be sure there is a smaller doll that would stand below us. Doesn't change our journey and our struggles and doesn't really encourage the other party. (Have you ever wondered just *who* it is that ends up defined as that last little doll?) I suppose it is to spur us on to help someone else worse off. How about we just help one another? Whoever shows up in our *real world,* where ever we are on our journey, and where ever we fall in the line up of nested dolls!

Ironically Jesus had a whole upside down/backwards view of the nested doll theory. I have always heard of it described as the upside-down kingdom.

Unfortunately we are not a very patient people by nature. It would be better to us to be that middle doll, or even the second to last doll, right now than to wait to be at the top of the line later . . .

When Alyssa was in elementary school I became concerned that certain areas in school were disproportionately difficult for her. While she was filling up notebooks with stories she concocted that actually kept *me* reading to see how they turned out, she avoided reading books like they were torture. She misspelled certain words over and over again.

And the *mad minutes* for math facts, forget about it! I felt ridiculous pressing for extra help, she was getting all As while I had little ones at home with disabilities and yet undiagnosed learning disabilities who were sure to struggle through all aspects of education. Finally I called the reading specialist that I was connected to from my own days of teaching, and poured out my feelings. I was unsettled by my daughter's struggles. She did not feel *lucky* by comparing her struggles to others. It didn't really matter if she was at the middle of the line up of nested dolls. When she was frustrated, she felt awful and so did I. That woman was very wise. She assured me that she did need some extra time to work through her learning issues, eventually we gave her the label of *suspected dyslexia*, because your struggles on your journey are your very real frustrations. If the kid in the seat next to you is struggling, it doesn't negate the fact that you need help too. We parents of special needs kids should probably keep that in mind for the rest of our clan more often. Mrs. Horaho's help was a godsend and gave Alyssa the tools she needed to work through some of her difficulties, and the validation of her own frustrations.

So I once again go back to the fact that I cannot control many situations, but what I can control is my reactions to them. While I may not need to seek out people to label as worse off than myself at this temporary stage of my life's journey, others may indeed label me as being less fortunate. It reminds me of something Joni Eareckson Tada said at a ladies' group she held one afternoon at Family Retreat. She said something along the line that perhaps the truly disabled persons are those who do not even recognize their own shortcomings and struggles and their need to rely on God. Enough said.

I think from now on, when I find myself functioning as a parade for onlookers I will just utter the word *matryoshka*. Try it . . . it kinda rolls off with just the right attitude. It is another word for nesting dolls. Only I will picture my family all nested up, inside the one who can heal and love us all.

"I would like to be a guest in your tent forever and to take refuge under the protection of your wings. Selah" (Psalm 61:4, GOD'S WORD Translation).

What a beautiful story. Consider the refining that the Lord brought Teresa through. Only through His refining since the birth of her twin daughters was Teresa able to handle gracefully the situation at the grocery store.

Understanding the Process of Refining

The refined Teresa coped with and tolerated the stares of others and comforted her daughter who was present in the store. When she heard those women's comments, Teresa conveyed to her daughter that she feels "lucky too," and she modeled self-advocacy for her.

Through refining, Teresa also learned that even her "typical" daughter's struggles, which may have seemed less important in the hierarchy of disability, were just as important. She acknowledged how much it meant to her daughter to show her, as her parent, that whether the problem was big or small it matters to her, as it does to God. How those feelings of inadequacy and "unluckiness" as posed by the world had to be wrestled with . . . maybe even burned out in the flaming fires of refinement and then replaced with the Lord's pure and true view; the upside-down kingdom[5] view to be exact. The view echoed in Luke 14:13–14, which tells us that when we invite the poor, the crippled, the lame and the blind that we will be "blessed" and not unlucky. We have daily opportunities for the refining of faith when raising a child affected by disability. The refining does not always feel good; sometimes it even feels like punishment, but something so much more pure and precious than gold is rendered.

> These trials will show that your faith is genuine. It is being tested as fire tests and purifies gold—though your faith is far more precious than mere gold. So when your faith remains strong through many trials, it will bring you much praise and glory and honor on the day when Jesus Christ is revealed to the whole world. (1 Peter 1:7, NLT)

The process of refining gold is designed with the intent to purify an already beautiful metal. It may be helpful to think of yourself and your child as unrefined golden nuggets, and consider each of your trials as part of the refining known as the *smelting* process (a technique that uses high heat and chemicals to separate the gold from other metals and impurities in the nugget). The result rendered is purified gold; think of this purified gold as God's good outcome.

Consider that with Jesus as our cover and blueprint for life, we are made one hundred percent pure. Consider all the uses for gold—after it is rendered pure. Now consider how much more the Lord will use this refining process for His plan and purpose in our lives and our children's lives and just how much more precious than gold the results will be. I cannot help but wonder if the woman in Teresa's story went home and thought about what it meant to be lucky.

Considering Your Child's Spiritual Experience

Children who are affected by disability often have great burdens to deal with from early on in life. Possible issues include the following:

- Frequent medical and therapy appointments

- Struggles with learning

- Pain

- Overwhelming sensory sensations

- Nutritional issues

- Isolation

- Impaired social interactions

- Physical inability to go to or perform in typical activities

- Sleep issues

- Depression

- Impaired communication

- Hyperactivity

The list could go on. Depending on their functional level, children may also feel guilty for what they view as the "trouble" they are causing the family. They are likely to feel and experience many of the same emotions—negative and positive—as their parents (the emotional spectrum is discussed previously in this section). All of which they attempt to process with limited (with regard to the broad spectrum of disability) cognitive, developmental or physical abilities. Note also that children with disabilities experience the "typical" stages of development, even if the typical milestones are not reached or the stages occur at atypical times.

All children have their own inner struggles, but children with disabilities may be unable to verbalize them. Caregivers may not consider a child's spiritual growth because they are often overwhelmed by the disability itself and all that it involves. Managing medication and progress in therapy (or lack thereof) may take center stage, and caregivers may unintentionally demote the spiritual aspect. However, the spiritual component may be the area of greatest achievement for a child and the catalyst for the deepest level of healing and for the development of coping skills.

Jesus told us that He works best in our weakness; our children's weaknesses may become their greatest strength in Christ. This is not to say that they do not struggle with sin, too. Though the understanding may be on a different level, the flesh we live in is the same. If we ignore this fact or overemphasize it, we risk missing a great opportunity to instill spiritual nurture. To lay the foundation for successful spiritual nurture, address the following with your child:

- Help your child learn the biblical view on disability.

- Encourage your child to begin a relationship with Christ, even in its simplest form.

- Read the Bible to your child, and impart that the Holy Spirit is the one who brings understanding. The Holy Spirit speaks through the Bible—the Word is alive, not mere literature.

- Apply practical techniques (see the next section) to enhance your child's learning and spiritual experience.

- Be able to appropriately advocate for your child in your congregation to dispel misconceptions and break down barriers infiltrated into the Church by worldviews.

- Teach your child to self-advocate to the best of his ability.

- Know your child's personality (strengths, weaknesses, gifts) aside from the disability.

- Pay attention to how the disability may impact your child's personality so you can respond accordingly. For instance, a child who is wheelchair-bound may be a gifted athlete. The wheelchair is simply a barrier that must be dealt with accordingly, but only if the child shows a desire for such.

The story of the nationally recognized Hoyt family is a wonderful example of acknowledging and accepting each other, with or without a disability.[6] The father, Dick, now in his seventies, and his eldest son Ricky, who is quadriplegic and confined to a wheelchair, have competed together in thousands of races including the Ironman Triathlon competition in Hawaii. After their first race in 1977, Ricky was quoted by his father as saying, "Dad, when I am running it feels like my disability disappears." Dick is quoted as saying, "Rick is my motivator; he inspires me. To me he is the one out there competing, I am just loaning him my arms and my legs to compete."[7]

If the body of Christ were to look at people with a disability in just this way, think of how full, lively and blessed our congregations would be.

PRACTICAL TECHNIQUES

You can provide spiritual nurture and teaching to your child using practical techniques. In addition to customizing existing Bible lessons for your child's needs, you can augment the lessons using the techniques described in this section. Many of the techniques are equally effective with the "typical" child, and implementing and using these techniques works with siblings, too.

Visual Cues and Schedules

Visual cues are simple pictures of an item or action. Recent research from Baylor College of Medicine in Houston and the City College of New York "shows that the visual information you absorb when you see can improve your understanding of the spoken words by as much as six-fold."[8] This technique works well across the board, unless the child is affected by sight impairment.

You can purchase commercial visual support software programs, such as Boardmaker, but the price can be steep. You can download free images from online sources for free or low cost. If no access to technology is available, consider creating simple pictures yourself. For example, draw a stick figure sitting, a stick figure singing, and so on. The images do not need to be complex. In fact, the simpler the better. Most images, regardless of their source, have been used with equal success, but consistency in image use is key. You can also use these visual cues to create "visual schedules."

To create a visual schedule, post a picture of each scheduled activity and the time at which each occurs. If the order of activities varies, another option is to post the visual cues on a Velcro board, or laminate the cues and keep them on a ring. You can write them on a chalkboard, too. Review the visual cues at the beginning of a session and again before you transition to the next activity.

Visual cues and schedules increase comprehension, decrease anxiety and provide a way to communicate more effectively. Public school teachers often use them in their special education classes. Visual cues provide consistency across multiple settings, which helps with communication and learning retention. Visual cues can also be used in conjunction with Bible stories and verses.

Music

At a training on dementia and Alzheimer's disease, the staff of Penn Foundation mentioned a study of Alzheimer's patients in which scientists found that music is the last memory a person will lose.[9] The connection between music and memory is also featured in an article at the HelloLife website: "Researchers have found that music and memory are processed and retrieved in the same part of the brain, called the rostromedial prefrontal cortex, located just behind the forehead. Music is especially hard-wired into the brain, it seems, often being the last memories to go."[10] Based on these studies of the brain and our understanding of memory, we can learn new strategies to increase memory retention and recall in people who may have deficits in this area.

Use music as a tool not only to increase memory and enjoyment but also to teach concepts such as waiting, taking turns, stopping, going slower and faster, as well as, if not more importantly, Christ's message. This gives a whole new meaning to singing His praise!

Repetition

Repeat, repeat, repeat. A good idea is to find out from your children's pastor what verse they will be covering or learning on a certain week. Even if you are the one doing all the teaching, the same idea applies. Parents with crazy schedules and possible crises do not always have loads of time for sit-downs for children's activities. So when you are driving to appointments, consider saying the verse, maybe even singing it. When you are home, look at the verse together. If possible, find a picture that will remind the child of the words.

Depending on your access to technology, another option is to search online for videos or movies available on the topic or verse. When your child attends service or Bible study, the verse will be familiar. She may even have it memorized.

Sensory Baskets and Blankets

Many children with developmental special needs, and even many with physical special needs, have sensory systems that are different from ours. Their nervous systems tend to interpret the outward stimuli in a different manner than is typical. For instance, imagine you are outside talking to a friend, the wind blows, a car drives by and the birds are chirping. You probably tune in only to the person talking, unless a sound is overly obvious. A child with a very sensitive sensory system to sound will hear it all—and all at the same time. Perhaps he has a sensitivity to light, too. Try to imagine that along with having to learn and take in what is being taught. It would be difficult. However, there are small tricks that help in "regulating" the system, even if only temporarily. Each child will be a little different, so again, if you are teaching, it is important to know each child on an individual basis.

To regulate a child's "defensive" or "seeking" sensory system and enable her to learn more effectively, have sensory baskets and blankets available. To make a sensory basket, fill a bag with small sensory items such as brushes, putty or clay, balls with lots of texture, squish toys or weights. My own son Kevin, who has autism and a rare seizure disorder that affects him cognitively, is known as a seeker. He cannot stay still for more than a moment; a minute in literal terms. His system is almost always on go, and when it turns off it means he is asleep. But put some putty in his hand and give him a small figure to squish into the putty and you can get fifteen to twetny minutes out of him. For Bible lessons, we actually purchased small biblical characters that he held onto and squished quietly into the putty while listening. It even got him to ask for "Jesus and putty" to help him! We laugh with joy thinking about it.

Offering a child a heavy blanket or weighted vest to wrap up in while listening to a story can also be helpful. For children who are not overly sensitive to physical touch, brushing their skin just before or during a listening activity can have a calming effect. Swinging on a swing set before a lesson also helps. If you have an opportunity to talk with an occupational therapist who is trained in the science of sensory integration and who has an actual certification in this portion of the field, it can be tremendously helpful.

Once, we had a nonverbal child who was attending the older children's worship for the first time. He loved music, but the mix of the big crowd, noise and music was too overwhelming. We did not want to give up on inclusion, so we prepared a visual schedule for him, prayed for him, and gave him headphones to listen to his favorite worship music. The headphones made the sound feel closer and helped him drown out the rest of the noise until his system adjusted to it. Day one was hard, but in a matter of three weeks he had his schedule down, took off the headphones and was dancing to the music with the rest of his peers. Amazing and God glorifying for sure! He soon became the spiritual nurture for many of us!

CONCLUSION

As you consider the importance of spiritual nurture for your child who is affected by disability, take your child's world into account, through a sensory lens. Consider how it feels for her to move, feel, hear, see and taste. Try to enter her world for a day. If you can find ways to simulate what it might be like for her, do it for a couple of hours or a day. Perhaps you will find that certain negative or odd behaviors have root causes, and perhaps you will find ways to connect in a new way. You may develop a new appreciation for and view of how she gets through her day, and you may be able to nurture her more fully in mind, body and spirit despite the disability. Spiritual nurture gives your child the opportunity to belong and, ultimately, to flourish.

Strip away the barriers of worldly views on disability, and let the Word of our great Savior quench your thirsty soul and free you from any binding ways and thoughts—as only He can. Allow our Savior the room to come alongside you to touch you, touch your child, work in your weaknesses, and refine you and your child. He may or may not heal him from the disability, but He will surely heal you both from your true ailments. Understand that your child is important, not only to you but also to the body of believers. Remember that one part of the body cannot say to the other, "I don't need you" (1 Cor. 12:18–21). God does not make mistakes. God never designed us to go this long road alone. He designed us for interdependence. Having a disability does not negate or change His design, it merely enhances it. Give your child the gift of spiritual nurture, and let our great Savior Jesus Christ do the rest.

NOTES

1. Lausanne Committee for World Evangelization, "Hidden and Forgotten People: Ministry among People with Disabilities," Lausanne Occasional Paper No. 35 B, 2005, http://www.lausanne.org/docs/2004forum/LOP35B_IG6B.pdf.

2. Rachel Held Evans, "Blessed Are the Un-cool," *Rachel Held Evans* (blog), June 15, 2011, http://rachelheldevans.com/blessed-are-the-uncool.

3. Peaceful Living, http://www.peacefulliving.org/.

4. Teresa Alderfer, "Artichokes, Parades, and Matryoshka . . . or Being the Littlest Nesting Doll," *Special Savings Special Needs* (blog), May 17, 2011, http://www.specialsavingsspecialneeds.com/2011/05/artichokes-parades-and-matryoshkaor.html#more.

5. Donald B. Kraybill, *Upside-Down Kingdom*, rev. ed. (Harrisonburg, VA: Herald, 2011).

6. Team Hoyt, http://www.teamhoyt.com/.

7. *Ironman: The Dick and Rick Hoyt Story*, DVD (n.p.: World Triathlon Corporation, 2006), http://ironmanstore.com/accessories/dvds/reedemer-dick-and-rick-hoyt-dvd.html, excerpt accessed December 1, 2011, http://youtu.be/dDnrLv6z-mM.

8. Baylor College of Medicine, "Visual Cues Help People Understand Spoken Words," *ScienceDaily*, March 4, 2009, http://www.sciencedaily.com/releases/2009/03/090304091326.htm.

9. Penn Foundation Behavioral Health Services, https://www.pennfoundation.org/.

10. HelloLife, "Music and Memory: What's the Link?" HelloLife.Net, 2008,
     http://www.hellolife.net/health-interest/b/music-and-memory-whats-the-
     link.

PART IV

Project Development

Principles and Practices

A child needs both to be hugged and unhugged.
The hug lets her know she is valuable. The unhug lets her know that she is viable.
If you're always shoving your children away, they will cling to you for love.
If you're always holding them close they will cling to you for fear.

—Polly Berrien Berends

Chapter Twelve

Recreational and Enrichment Activities

* * *

Phyllis Kilbourn

I N PREVIOUS chapters we have discussed many church and community-based strategies and programs whereby children who have disabilities can be helped with their special needs such as social adjustments, educational achievement, medical care and spiritual nurture. This chapter focuses on enrichment and recreational activities that combine learning and fun. Most experts agree that regular recreational activities for children with disabilities, as for any child, are a crucial component of their growth and development. Although activities can be challenging to accomplish at times, the advantages for both child and caregiver are certainly worth the effort.

Because some children may not be able to communicate their specific wishes for the kind of recreational activities they would like, it is important to try a variety of activities and see how they respond. Try as much as possible to expose them to the things that you observe make them happy: the way they like to play, the things that make them laugh, or the things that make them clap their hands and smile or even cause them to dance around!

Another way to ensure that an activity will be fun and interesting, yet help children create a healthy lifestyle, is to evaluate the activity by asking questions such as: does the activity help your child achieve feelings of belonging/acceptance? success? accomplishment? growth? or competence?

The following describes several categories of helpful recreational activities for children with disabilities. Some can be done within the family, others will involve community or organization involvement. Be sure to research local newspapers, the internet, local churches and community-based organizations to learn of additional opportunities for your children to enjoy recreational opportunities. Remember, however, that you know best what your child enjoys. You will want to incorporate your ideas into the sampling provided below and even come up with totally new activities that uniquely provide for the special needs of children in your care. You also may want to talk with other caregivers, especially those caring for children with a disability similar to your child's, comparing and sharing ideas.

FAMILY-CENTERED ACTIVITIES

Home is the center of a child's world, so children will cherish fun family activities. Family activities promote the psychosocial foundation for a healthy environment for all children. Often children with sensory, physical or cognitive disabilities may need a greater emphasis on recreational activities that involve the family. Family activities require no instructors other than parents, and aside from materials, they are free.

Everyday Chores

Because time for extra activities may be limited due to the time-consuming task of caring for a child with special needs, you may want to start your program of activities by making everyday tasks, like food shopping or dog walking, into a family affair. Children will enjoy being given responsibilities commensurate to their abilities, like taking turns holding the dog's leash for a specified distance or helping choose or find items on the grocery shelf. Make these simple activities into fun games.

Family Night

Caregivers should also try to plan a special weekly (or biweekly) "Family Night" for activities that provide family togetherness. Children thrive on routines and will look forward to the dependability of a regular night just for the family. "Doing it together" activities on family nights could include baking special treats such as cookies or brownies, working puzzles or playing table games. Family night also is a good time to start special holiday traditions the children can participate in. Along with the usual holidays, such as Christmas or Easter, also plan special celebrations for important milestones in the child's or family's achievements. Children will enjoy being recognized for some special event in their lives and will want to help plan the celebration.

Extended Family "Togetherness" Time

Occasionally, extended family time activities such as going on picnics, cook-outs, camping or field trips are special treats children can look forward to; the activities also are great bonding times. Building things together is an example of a great extended family time activity. Not only does such provide an activity that allows families to work together as a team, it also makes children feel that they have accomplished something.

As a family team, start with planning your building project, including what you would like to build, who will do what and the materials you will need to construct it. Children's toys, puzzles or games may be a manageable starting place for projects. Try using bits of wood, mat board, cardboard or other materials the children can easily handle and glue together. Even children who are visually impaired can feel their creations as they evolve.

Family Pets

Having a family pet also can have a significantly positive impact on children with disabilities. As they assume responsibility for the pet and it becomes dependent on them for food, water and grooming (bathing and brushing), the pet will give children a sense of feeling needed or useful. If it is not possible to have a family pet, you can introduce animals into a child's world through recreational activities that involve animals, such as riding horses or a visit to a petting farm or zoo. Animals can play an important role with children because they are adept at communicating trust to people.

The children's response to private family time activities can be overwhelmingly positive, giving them confidence to stretch their environment to include community activities.

EXPLORING THE CREATIVE ARTS

No matter what one's disability, every child will be able to experience expressing themselves through some form of the creative arts. Whether it is painting, music, drama, dance or writing, the freedom of expression the arts provide makes for a memorable recreational activity for children with disabilities and gives them an enormous sense of accomplishment and self-esteem. Mentally challenged children, for example, can learn to express themselves through art mediums such as theater, painting and sculpture. Know what limitations a child's disability may cause and find a venue of art that will not be hindered by it. Venues can be researched by checking media publications and recreational sites that advertise such facilities as community play houses, dance studios, drama classes and musical programs that allow not only attendance but also participation.

Art Work

Art is a natural and age-appropriate means of communication for a child. Although working with paint, colors or other art mediums can be a fun-filled activity, it can also become more than play. Art can become a powerful form of therapy. When using paint, clay, collage materials, or any items that can be transformed into the child's own special work of art, children feel free to express their feelings—positively or negatively. Art offers children a safe and supportive vehicle to express their thoughts and feelings. The colors children use for their artistic pieces may vary according to their feelings or mood: bright colors signifying happiness and dark colors expressing sadness. The work is not interpreted or judged; rather the creation of the art work forms part of the relationship between the child and the observer.

Art teachers have found that children with special needs do well with clay. Children can create things (animals, houses and people) from the clay or enjoy painting the objects others have made. Children also enjoy blending the colors of clay to create new colors. Depending on their disability, some children may have fun pounding on the clay. The tactile feel of the clay also may be good for dexterity.

Some things to consider when planning art projects include:

- If your child is visually impaired, gather a variety of textures to experiment with—smooth papers, rough handmade papers and so on.
- Make available lots of modeling materials like clay or homemade play dough.
- Scented markers, if available, are always fun.
- Have lots of "big paper" for large movements of the hands and arms.
- Finger paint (bought or homemade) is a terrific tactile material.

Dance

Dance is a fun and effective activity for children with disabilities. Dance movements, along with the accompanying music, have many positive effects on children. Various studies suggest that dance can help children grow emotionally as they learn to express their emotions in positive, versus destructive, ways. Being able to express their feelings, a common goal for all art forms, allows children to come out of their protective, withdrawn shell, enabling them to enjoy socializing with others.

On the physical side, dance has been shown to help children with strength, posture and flexibility. Children with cerebral palsy have experienced increased muscle tone. Many kids with special needs have difficulty with motor skills. Whatever type of dance one chooses to participate in, dance movements emphasize all body parts and the way they move. Children learn through dance therapy to move their arms, legs and bodies smoothly and in a more coordinated way, improving motor skills. Because it is done to music, dance tends to be a more enjoyable way to practice motor skills than simply exercising. Also, the interaction during dance between the parent or caregiver and the child, and between a group and the child, improves social and communication skills.

Avery Rogers gives children in wheelchairs a hopeful reminder for their participation when she reports:

> *Just because you can't walk doesn't mean you can't dance. Believe it or not, wheelchair dancing is an up and coming sport pursued by people with disabilities in 40 countries around the world, including the United States. IPC Wheelchair Dance Sport is a great resource that links internet users to the major organizations around the world that promote wheelchair dancing on both the recreational and competitive levels.[1]*

Roger further claims that wheelchair users can pursue square dance, line dance, ballet and jazz.

Music and Rhythm

Music can be a motivating and fun way to teach children, particularly those who have special learning needs. Music and rhythm games can help children learn and retain information and skills and build motor skills. For those with cerebral palsy, music strategies may be an effective way to stimulate speech development, provide organization for cognitive and motor development, and create a meaningful environment for socialization and leisure pursuits. Ultimately, because musical experiences foster communication and social growth, all children benefit from group experiences with music.

From infancy, children are exposed to rhythms and songs by adults or through interaction with their physical surroundings. In a report sponsored by the U.S. Department of Education, Bruce O. Boston suggests that lullabies sung to infants "communicate adult love and the experiences of joy and delight; they teach children that the world is a pleasurable and exciting place to be."[2] What a delightful way to communicate such truths to children with disabilities—of all ages.

In addition to fostering communication from an early age, music and rhythm also support self-expression. Young children often discover the pleasure of making rhythms when they learn to tap on household objects with their hands and feet. As babies begin to use their voices, they quickly experiment with the sounds they can create. The fact that rhythm and music are beneficial during the earliest years of childhood development highlights the importance of children being given opportunities to learn through and about music in a variety of ways while young.

Rhythm and music experiences also support physical development. During early childhood, various motor skills are developing rapidly. Music and rhythm are often used (together or separately) to help children learn to skip, gallop, jump or increase fine motor coordination. Hearing music can often inspire children to dance or use their bodies in new ways, which enhances physical coordination.

Informal music education continues to occur throughout the child's life experiences, such as learning to sing songs or playing with musical toys. Adults can also foster an appreciation of music by modeling; as children see adults creating or listening to music, they will likely grow to appreciate it as well.

Michelle Lazar, director of **Coast Music Therapy**, explains some additional benefits of music:

> *Because singing and speech share many similarities, yet are accessed differently by the brain, music strategies can be used as a means to improve functional communication. Songs of varying lengths can increase the duration of a child's speech, while rhythm can be used as a timing cue to aid in speech pacing and intelligibility. Singing and wind instruments including whistles, recorders, and horns are also a fun way to increase breath support and oral motor strength. In the social environment, music activities are ideal for children who need more exposure or practice with peers in a motivating setting. Interactive strategies including music instruments and song games can promote social skills such as turn-taking, following directions in a group, eye contact, and cooperative play.[3]*

Rhythm instruments are ideal when working on fine motor skills due to the variety of grips and hand positions required to produce a sound. Rhythm instruments can be made with things that children can shake, beat or hit. Examples of rhythm instruments include plastic castanets, egg shakers, rain sticks, triangles, rhythm sticks and drums with mallets.

Some fun learning ideas to use with music and rhythm include the following:

- Sing a familiar song, but leave out a word at the end of a phrase or verse for the child to fill in. If the child is able to use full sentences, you can take turns singing verse by verse of a song.

- For children who have more limited language skills, try using pictures to accompany songs. For example, while singing "Old McDonald Had a Farm," the child can pick from a variety of animal photos to choose which animal should be used in the next verse. Be sure you use culturally relevant songs! You may want to help children make up some songs and let them illustrate them.

- Tapping or beating a drum to a steady, slow rhythm is a great way to elicit appropriate pacing and articulation of speech. Encourage the child to match his speech to the rate of your beat.

- Many children's song games involve partner interaction or group collaboration. Simple, local childhood songs such as "London Bridge Is Falling Down" or "The Farmer in the Dell" encourage teamwork and physical contact with peers.

Drama

Drama is a universal form of human expression found in cultures all over the world. This art form is an excellent art medium for children with disabilities because it allows them to try out many different roles in the process. Costume and set design, acting, directing and reading are all activities that children, including those who are mentally or intellectually challenged, can participate in. Drama can help create confidence and inspire creativity, enriching the lives of children and helping them build self-confidence. These qualities contribute to the emotional and educational development of children.

Children who have experienced emotional trauma from experiences such as bereavement or abuse also can benefit from drama. Children with other problems such as autism and developmental disorders also will find help through drama. Drama encourages children to think about and explore their painful circumstances in a safe and supportive space. By expressing themselves in this way, children are in effect externalizing some of their pain, and are able to look at it in more manageable pieces. The children must first find a voice through what their artworks communicate, and then, over time, they are able to begin sharing verbally.

PARTICIPATING IN SPORTS

Fitness is important for all children, and participating in sports is a great way to achieve it. One must not be tempted though to set the bar lower for a child with a disability, for either the child or the caregivers' sake. A child's participation in a sporting event can be frightening to parents or caregivers who usually do whatever can be done to shield their child from danger. Children, however, must have the fun of getting out there and winning or losing like any other able-bodied children.

Dr. William J. Schiller, associate director and technology coordinator for the National Center of Physical Activity and Disability (NCPAD) highlights the benefit of sports and exercise activities when he states, "The focus is trying to reduce secondary health problems: obesity, high blood pressure, diabetes, depression. (Exercise) promotes flexibility, motor control, social relationships, and reduces the need for medications. The body needs a certain amount of activity to function optimally."[4]

It is important that all sports activity begin with exercise. According to the NCPAD, there are three kinds of exercise, all equally important:

- Cardiovascular—primarily benefits the heart, circulatory system and lungs
- Strength and muscle endurance training
- Flexibility—promotes a greater range of motion and ease of movement[5]

The center asserts that people with disabilities need:

- separate exercise guidelines that are age- and functional limitation-sensitive, to help assess how "fit" they are, using appropriate standards and measures; and fitness facilities they can get to, enter and use, integrated and convenient, not special
- exercise facilities (YMCA and other community-based fitness centers and programs) that are aware of and comply with their legal obligations under local rules and legislation
- exercise equipment that incorporates universally designed features so the equipment can then be used by people with a broad spectrum of strength and abilities without reducing the equipment's usability or attractiveness for all exercisers[6]

Adapted/Adaptive Sports

Adapted sports—also called adaptive sports—are activities in which the equipment and rules have been modified just enough to allow people with disabilities to participate. For instance, in "sitting" volleyball, players sit on the floor and play on a smaller court with a lower net. In wheelchair tennis, the ball is allowed to bounce twice instead of once.

Sporting activities will depend on what equipment and opportunities are available for children to use. Adapted sports can include swimming, weight lifting, horseback riding, wheelchair basketball, throwing or "blowing" darts, or riding a bicycle with hand pedals, which is similar to a stationary bicycle but is pedaled with the hands. They can also include competitive dancing, rock wall climbing, fishing and even skydiving.

By removing the barriers to exercise that children and youth with disabilities usually face, they can choose to take actions that can significantly improve their health and quality of life. A good sports program also can work wonders for a child's self-esteem and mental and physical well-being.

Water Sports

Most of us have heard the expression that children take to water like ducks. This describes their natural love for water. Tapping into this interest, water can be used as a means of exercise and other types of enjoyable activities. Water has a special relaxing quality that promotes emotional health. Ball-throwing games are useful and easy ways to promote exercise and fun in the water that can be adapted for most children with special needs. Be sensitive to the fact that some children with special needs may fear water and need to gradually be introduced to the fun of water activities or, where possible, learning to swim. Some older teens may even be able to learn water skiing, canoeing or boating skills.

GOING TO CAMP

Attending camp gives children the opportunity to benefit by having fun and interaction with other children, by increasing their confidence and independence, and by finding positive role models from adults and counselors caring for them. Camping opportunities include all the exciting "traditional" activities associated with camp, but each activity is carefully planned and supervised so every individual can participate fully, in spite of any physical and/or mental limitation. Camp also gives parents and caregivers a much needed break. Christian camps usually include in their mission statement elements similar to that of SpringHill Camps: "To create life-impacting experiences that enable young people to know and to grow in their relationship with Jesus Christ."[7]

Choosing a Program

Some camp programs are inclusive, or those usually termed "community-based camps." These camps are open to those with or without disabilities. Although the environment of these camps is geared to the children's special needs, they can provide opportunities for children to interact with their peers who do not have a disability in low-pressure settings. These camps usually are close to home and inexpensive. This enables siblings to attend, too. Such a camp is an educational tool for the community, giving people in the community a chance to get to know the children who have special needs as children, not as a disability. Noninclusive camps are only for those having a disability. Noninclusive camp sessions tend to be shorter than those of an inclusive program. Both inclusive and noninclusive camps are fully geared to the children's special needs. Several camping options are available:

- Family camps (usually noninclusive but may be inclusive)
- Sleepaway for children (inclusive or noninclusive)
- Day camps (inclusive or noninclusive)
- Family camping trip

A huge plus for a noninclusive family camp is that its programs usually provide separate recreational and special events for parents who also are in need of a meaningful break. In chapter 18, one mother describes and gives testimony to the wonderful refreshing the "Jonicamps" (as her children called the Joni and Friends Family Retreats) held for her as a caregiver of a child with a severe disability.

The Family Retreats provide dynamic programs that refresh and strengthen families who live with disability. The camps are held at accessible camp and conference centers across the United States; the program is flexible and designed to provide the entire family with time together in a camp atmosphere.

The retreat offers a change of pace where caregivers and children have fun together in a safe and accepting environment. Together they enjoy God's creation, meet and fellowship with others who face similar concerns, build lasting memories together as a family and have a renewed hope in God. Several sites have amenities such as climbing walls, ropes courses, boating, hiking trails, mud pits and a host of other activities to energize the week.

Each day the youth and children enjoy exciting age-appropriate camp activities, crafts and recreational activities and, most importantly, they will have the freedom to be themselves. Moms and dads have the opportunity to enjoy Christ-centered worship, teaching and practical seminars that address family life and issues related to life with a disability. The afternoons are free to relax or participate in a variety of optional activities. Evenings are full of family-oriented activities such as talent shows, campfires, concerts, carnivals and more . . . all in a warm, accepting environment.[8]

Handi*Camp Camping Program

Another ministry that conducts noninclusive family camps is Handi*Vangelism. Julie Bohn (chapter 14), who has been involved in running camps for Handi*Vangelism for a number of years, describes a typical Handi*Camp camping program in the following section.

Kathy Cronkrite, a woman with cerebral palsy who attends one of the Young Adult Bible Conference weeks of Handi*Camp, wrote the following poem to share her feelings about what occurs at a typical camp:

> Every year God sees a group of people get together to worship and praise Him. They are ordinary people except for their wheelchairs, crutches, canes and communication systems.
>
> All year long they are alone in their Christian walk but when the last week of June comes along they get together to share what is on their hearts and minds. They get ministered to by someone who really knows where they are coming from.
>
> They lift their voice in whatever way they can and by the end of five days, God must be overflowing with joy at the afflicted.
> Praise God for this assembly. May it always be.

Kathy uses an electric wheelchair for mobility, a feeding tube for nourishment and a computerized communication system as well as a language board with some words and the letters on it to communicate. It requires a great deal of effort on her part to control the switch for the computer or to point to the words or letters on her language board, yet she has much she would like to say.

Many of the rest of the guests who come to that week of camp, along with the campers who come to the other weeks of camp, can relate to her comment, "All year long they are alone in their Christian walk." Kathy is a part of a church that is accessible. They are beginning a ministry to those who are deaf, and many are taking the time to learn sign language. Rarely, though, does anyone sit down with Kathy and wait patiently as she tries to communicate what is on her heart through her computer or language board. Are we afraid, or would it take too much of our precious time, or do we not think anyone as physically disabled as Kathy would have much to say?

Kathy, along with many of her friends with disabilities, has found a place where the people want to take the time to "listen" to her, where they want to help her grow in her relationship with the Lord and where they are committed to her care and enjoyment. That place, that "special gathering," is Handi*Camp, a camping program for individuals with disabilities. The week Kathy comes to camp, the adult guests have a physical disability, with most requiring one-on-one care but having no—or a very slight—mental disability. There are other weeks for adults with mental disabilities of varying degrees, and weeks for teens and children with either primarily a mental or physical disability.

For most, Handi*Camp is their vacation that they look forward to from the moment they leave until the moment they return the following year. Handi*Camp is a place where, regardless of the disability, the campers are the participants. Everyone has the opportunity to play baseball, go swimming, roast marshmallows, go on a hayride, make a craft, and so on. The activity is adapted so that all may participate in their own way.

Handi*Camp is also a great place to make new friends and continue former friendships. Many of the campers come back year after year and develop strong relationships with other campers and staff. Communication throughout the year is encouraged.

Although Handi*Camp is fun, it is also a safe place to ask questions about God and learn spiritual truths. At Handi*Camp many have their first encounter with Christ. Through evening chapel, morning Bible class, and evening and morning devotions with their counselor as well as during those "teachable moments" throughout the day, the campers are repeatedly exposed to the truths in God's Word. The salvation message is presented many times through the week in many different ways. Brian had been coming to camp for many years. He had heard the gospel many times during those years. Ryan's first year of camp, the first morning he had devotions with his counselor, he was ready to ask Jesus to be his best Friend.

The Handi*Camp follow-up team offers pen pals (often via e-mail), phone pals, prayer partners, correspondence Bible studies and, when several campers live in the same area, group Bible studies, as means of continuing the learning throughout the year. Efforts are made to find churches near the campers where they will be welcomed and can continue in their walk with the Lord.

A camping program for individuals with disabilities can be offered in your area. All that is needed is an accessible camping facility and many willing, teachable, serving hearts to minister to the physical, emotional, social and spiritual needs of the campers. Remember to make provision for the parents and caregivers! Their task is stressful and draining, both emotionally and physically. Encourage parents to find a support group by contacting other parents who are in the same situation as they are in. Find out what works for them. They need to share their triumphs, failures, hopes and dreams with others who understand.

GOAL SETTING

You will get the most out of the activities you choose for and with your child by setting goals. Goal setting can be done before and after selecting appropriate activities. Prior to selecting activities, you and your child may want to consider the following goals:

- Make new friends
- Develop specific motor skills
- Learn independence
- Participate on a team
- Interact with peers who may or may not have a disability

Goals provide purpose and guide you in choosing an activity for your child and evaluating its benefits. After selecting an activity that best meets your needs and interests, you and your child need to choose specific outcomes and goals that you want to achieve as a result of participating in that activity. Example goals include the following:

- Increased fitness
- Having fun
- Learning a new skill

Remember to keep all goals measurable and achievable. They should be written down and placed where your child will see them often—a bedroom or bathroom mirror, on her most used notebook, and so on. Once a goal is achieved, celebrate it and set another one.

Simple, fun activities are some of the most valuable experiences you can share with children, because such are useful as a communication tool between child and caregiver. Whether it is an hour spent horseback riding or expressing one's feelings through an art form such as moving to music, enrichment and recreational activities can be a wonderful break in routine for children. Along with providing fun, regular use of activities also helps children discover their strengths, develop self-esteem, feel acceptance and belonging, and improve their quality of life. Each activity provides its own unique benefit that will stay in a child's memory and world for a long time.

NOTES

The epigraph to part IV is from Polly Berrien Berends, *Gently Lead: How to Teach Your Children about God While Finding Out for Yourself*, rev. ed. (New York: Crossroad, 1998), 60.

1. Avery Rogers, "Wheelchair Dancing," ExploreDance.com, November 12, 2001, http://exploredance.com/article.htm?id=23&s=author&sid=1764.

2. Bruce O. Boston, "Rhythm and Music in Childhood Education" (paper presented at the Early Childhood Music Summit, Washington, DC, June 14–16, 2000).

3. Michelle Lazar, "Benefits of Music for Children with Special Needs: Tips for Parents and Educators," United Cerebral Palsy, http://affnet.ucp.org/ucp_channeldoc.cfm/1/16/98/98-98/5093.

4. Barbara Martin, "'I Know I Can Do It': Sports Are for Disabled Children, Too," The Cure Our Children Foundation, http://www.cureourchildren.org/sports.htm.

5. Ibid.

6. Ibid.

7. SpringHill Camps, "Welcome," http://springhillcamps.com.

8. Joni and Friends, "Family Retreats," http://www.joniandfriends.org/family-retreats.

CHAPTER THIRTEEN

DEVELOPING PROJECTS THAT

BRING HEALING AND HOPE

* * *

Debbie Childs

CHILDREN with disabilities in the Asian region do not have much hope for a future, especially those who are poor and live in the slums and villages. Labeled "hidden children," most of them exist within only the four walls of their home. The professional community considers these children hidden because in the villages, due to beliefs and superstition, the parents and community feel that children with special needs bring shame and disgrace to the family. Because these children are mostly hidden, accurate statistics are scarce.

The people of North India lack the understanding that these children are created in the image of God and that all these children will respond and can improve with prayer, training, cognitive and physical intervention, medication, proper nourishment and love.

In 2003 I arrived to North India with three goals:

1. to train people in the villages how to work with children who are developmentally disadvantaged,

2. to learn the culture and the language of India, and

3. to manifest the vision that God had put on my heart many years before—to start a children's home for street children and orphans.

I spent three years reaching my initial goals, and during that time, God showed me that children who are developmentally disadvantaged are as neglected as street children and orphans and that I should provide some type of residential care for them as well.

Figure 13.1 A Child at the intervention center. Photo taken by field staff.

But I am getting ahead of myself. The projects I am involved with got their start in one small village on behalf of one child. This chapter chronicles the project development journey that I have taken with other professionals—a journey that we are still on. Currently, we are looking forward to the not-so-distant future when we will open a child development program.

RESEARCHING THE NEED

In March 1999 a child, Anugrah ("grace" in Hindi), was born with cerebral palsy. His parents knew nothing about this diagnosis and began searching for information. Anugrah's doctors gave them medical advice but were unable to help his parents assess and plan for their son's cognitive and physical needs. His parents searched for resources within the 20-kilometer area surrounding their small village, but they found nothing. They would need to go to the city for help.

In the city they met a developmental pediatrician who assessed Anugrah and provided his parents with the information they needed to understand their child's special needs. The father, grateful that he now had some knowledge, began to wonder about other children and families in the surrounding villages where he was a community development worker. Were there other children who were developmentally disadvantaged like Anugrah living in the villages? In all the years that he had been working in the villages, he had not noticed. He recalled a few children who had physical problems or who behaved differently, but he had certainly never seen a large number.

The father, Robert, decided to research and conduct surveys in the villages. He discovered many children who had both physical and mental delays. In fact, the need was greater than he had ever imagined. Robert was a director at a Christian nongovernmental organization (NGO) that did community-based development work. With the help of the developmental pediatrician, he decided to hire a few people who had previously worked in community development and launch a pilot project in the villages. Robert and the pediatrician submitted a proposal and were granted funding for the pilot project. They hoped to help the parents and assist these children—one child at a time.

When informal community services became available in the villages, the parents of these "hidden" children realized that someone cared, and they requested even more help. They asked for a place where the children could go—a place where they could learn like their siblings who attended public schools.

COORDINATING A PILOT PROJECT

As a first step, Robert trained someone to provide basic social services: visit families in the villages, work with their children one-on-one, and give the mothers a few hours of refreshment.

The parents again requested that the children meet together somewhere to receive help and education. After a year's pilot program in the villages (July 2002 to June 2003), Robert located a small, empty space on a hospital campus, funding was granted, and people, mostly from the village, were hired.

Pilot Project Highlights
- Worked with 27 children in the villages.
- Of the 27 families who participated, 16 responded positively.
- Inspired to develop the project to the next level.

While God worked out all the details of the newly formed pilot project, He simultaneously worked in the heart of a teacher in the United States to answer His call of working with at-risk children in Northern India. The two paths crossed, and in 2003 both an intervention center and a community-based rehabilitation (CBR) program were established to serve children who are marginalized, poor and developmentally disadvantaged.

ROLLING OUT THE INTERVENTION CENTER AND CBR PROGRAM

The intervention center, located on a hospital campus, ran simultaneously with the CBR program, which was taking place in the villages. Initially, 24 children attended the intervention center in two groups, with each group attending twice a week. We picked up the children and brought them to the center, where the staff worked with them in a school-like setting. The center quickly grew to accommodate all 24 children five days a week.

To increase the number of children we could serve, we hired more CBR program staff (women from the village) to work one-on-one with children in their village homes.

Intervention Center Curriculum

In the beginning, we aspired to reach three goals at the intervention center.

One goal was to first teach the children life skills, the objective being to help the children be less of a burden on their parents. Most mothers, whose time and energy were depleted from the lack of modern conveniences, were further exhausted tending to other siblings, preparing meals, providing basic care to farm animals, washing clothes by hand, and a hundred other responsibilities that burdened these mothers from before the sun rose to late in the night. If we could teach the children independence skills, it would encourage the entire family.

Providing physical therapy was another early goal. Half the children desperately needed physical therapy in both large-motor and fine-motor skills. A physiotherapist from the hospital nearby trained the staff to give therapy to the children; the American teacher trained them in fine-motor skills.

Our final goal was to provide basic education (see table 13.1) so that, over time, as many children as possible could advance to vocational training. Inclusion in the government-run schools was unheard of in the villages. Teachers in public schools alone had from forty to sixty children in a room and therefore had no time or energy to give extra help to a child who was developmentally disadvantaged.

Initially, the center's teaching staff consisted mostly of people from the villages. Some, like Anugrah's father, had been involved in previous community development work and had an interest in working with these children. Others, who had a family member who worked at the hospital (nearby), joined the staff because they lived on the hospital campus, which was shared with the intervention center.

Table 13.1 Intervention Center Classroom Schedule

Time Period	Activity
8:50–9:20	Songs, Attendance, Short Story
9:20–9:45	Games
9:20–9:45	Stimulation Group
9:45–10:10	Special Activity: • Monday—Story • Tuesday—Art • Wednesday—Music • Thursday—Story • Friday—Art
10:10–10:35	Lunch
10:40–11:00	Manipulatives
10:45–1:00	Prevocational Training
11:00–11:25	Math Activities
11:00–11:25	Communication Group
11:00–1:00	Literacy
11:35–11:55	Musical Movement
12:00–12:15	Free Choice Board
12:15–1:00	Free Choice
12:15–1:00	Computer Group
Note: Life skills and Bible stories are taught in each group throughout the day. Therapy is provided for 45 minutes to an hour to those children who need it.	

On-site and visiting professional staff, from both India and abroad, trained the teachers, who, for the most part, had never worked with children with special needs. The professional staff included one on-site teacher from the United States. The remaining staff, all from India, included an occupational therapist, a physiotherapist and a psychologist. A pediatrician from a nearby hospital was in charge of medical services. Visiting students and professionals from around the world have continued to filter in and out since the center opened. Some have come for a few weeks, others for several months. All have had a huge impact on the children, staff, parents and community.

At the same time the center was running, the CBR program was evolving in a fifteen-kilometer radius around the center.

CBR Program Services

The CBR program initially helped approximately one hundred and ten children with disabilities. Ages ranged from infant to eighteen, and a small number of older people up to age thirty also received services. We trained village women to work with the children and their parents in the home on a one-to-one basis. The hired staff saw children once or twice a week, depending on their needs. The children in the CBR program were also taught life skills, academics, and so on, at a slower rate so that they could then possibly go to a public school or learn a skill through vocational training to help provide income for their family.

The family aspect proved to be a time-consuming challenge for both programs.

IMPACT OF FAMILY ON CHILDREN AND PROGRAMS

As much as the children were progressing, we were also interacting with each child's family system, many of which were dealing with a host of problems. The children faced myriad issues: poverty, family crisis, superstition, malnutrition and other major medical concerns.

Some villagers tried to convince the parents that the people who were trying to help were wasting their time and effort on these children. They believed the children were worthless and would never make a significant difference in the family's status. When we launched awareness programs in the communities, we learned that many villagers were superstitious and considered these children a curse from God or believed that the children were being punished for sins in their previous lives.

Another superstition had to do with medical care. The local village doctors had no experience working with children with special needs, yet the villagers argued that their doctors were sufficient and that the care the center's hospital provided at a discounted rate was not necessary. Many parents of the children who were prescribed long-term medication to manage seizures believed that they should medicate their children only for a short period of time. This false belief resulted in children having all-night seizures and caused more damage to them. Several children went into comas, and one child died from not receiving seizure medicine.

Over the last several years, we have seen substantial improvement in the children. The local staff has a higher skill level, and community awareness has increased significantly.

Parents of children who attend the intervention center have also formed a parents association and have already advocated for additional services for their children. Many agencies in the city are beginning to network with others to lobby local officials and even higher government for assistance in providing additional family services that will make a difference in the lives of these children and their families.

Ongoing Challenges

Over the years, several recurring issues have challenged us, both at the intervention center and in the field (CBR program).

Available Services Cannot Meet the Need

As more people learn about the intervention center and the CBR program, more children are becoming "unhidden" in the villages. But the resulting need far outweighs the services available. Special schools are available in the city, but in the villages they are nonexistent. Families often come to the intervention center from hours away, some at a day's travel, because they have heard about our work and about the improvements the children have shown.

Many families love their children. They have traveled to various places and spent money without receiving solutions for their child's problems. They come to us looking for help, but with limited space and staff, especially professional staff, we can only do so much if we are to maintain the high-quality standards of our work. Unfortunately, the best we can offer is to assess their child, give them some insight into how to help him in their own home and suggest activities to do with him.

Lack of Professional Staff

Lack of professional staff is an issue not only for us in the villages but also for the centers in the cities. The problem is not a lack of professional colleges but rather a lack of qualified graduates. Often they either have no hands-on experience with children with special needs or they have decided to go abroad to earn higher salaries. The professionals that we can afford to hire usually have only bachelor's degrees, and after a couple of years they leave to pursue their master's degrees.

The same is true of the staff member whom we train to be paraeducators. Many have families to raise, and others want to further their education. Our unmarried male staff members want to get married but would be unable to support their wives and family on a meager salary. Our programs are funded by outside agencies, and the funds for salaries and hourly wages are low.

Lack of Parental Involvement in Child's Education

Because we started with an intervention center (school-based concept) and provide transportation for the children, several of the parents have not taken full ownership of their child's education. We hold parent meetings and workshops to educate them, but they do not feel the same effort should be given to these children as to their children who attend regular public schools.

Initially the CBR staff visited children in their homes on a one-on-one basis. In villages where three to five children were being seen individually, we decided to rent a small building out in the village area, and we invited the parents to bring their children to meet as a group for a few hours. The children met a couple of times a week in social groups to interact with other children like themselves. The parents could support each other and, in general, learn how to work with the children. The responses to these social gatherings were mixed.

We found in the small-group setting that after the parents attended a few sessions, they would send a sibling to attend with their child. After a few more sessions, they might drop their child off alone or the child would not attend at all. The groups would end up consisting of only one or two children. The mindset of the parents was that they would rather have their children attend the intervention center than be in the village in the CBR program. The parents preferred the bigger intervention center (which had a five-day program) to the small social groups that met only a couple of times a week.

Many of our families in the CBR program also want their children to attend the intervention center because they have less responsibility for their children if we are caring for them four hours each day.

Transportation Expenses

Providing transportation to and from the intervention center is problematic because maintaining vehicles and supplying gasoline eats up hundreds of dollars.

Residential Care Is Unavailable

Virtually no long-term residential care exists for children who are developmentally disadvantaged. Several of our children have needed a "home" to go to. In some cases, the parents did not want their child. Some families are so poor that, no matter how much we try to help or educate the parents, they are unable to care for their child's needs. Several of our children in this situation have died. Other children remain in difficult living situations because there is no place for them to go.

A BROADER VISION: A CHILD DEVELOPMENT PROGRAM

To face the challenges confronting us, we knew we had to develop a much broader vision. We crafted a new vision statement and a statement of our core belief, which will drive us to complete that vision.

Our Vision for the Future

Empowered communities that are healthy, learning, prospering, caring stewards of their natural resources, living in harmonious relationships, worshipping the true and living God, and reaching out to others in need.

A few of the children in our center who died could neither walk nor talk. All they could do was lie on a cot. But were they not also created in the image of God? My vision is to have a place in the home (not institution) where all children will be rocked, hugged, fed, read to, sung to, and shown the love of Christ.

Our Core Belief

We believe that children with developmental disadvantages are created in God's image and are messengers from God in our midst.

To fulfill our vision of reaching out and helping more children, we as a professional staff met several times and brainstormed how we could best serve the children and their families. The result is the following in-progress plan for a child development program.

- We will use the existing intervention center only for training staff and implementing specialized programs (see table 13.2).

- Once the staff-training curriculum is in place, we will apply for accreditation so that we can award certificates to those who complete the course. This will provide a great opportunity to village women who have little chance of furthering their education above high school.

- Except for specialized classes, children will now meet in the villages. Small groups of 10–12 children will meet daily in designated locales called "learning centers."

- One fully trained paraeducator will work alongside one or two newer paraeducators in teaching the children and working with the parents at the learning centers.

- The specialized programs held at the intervention center will cover a variety of areas (see table 13.2).

Table 13.2 Specialized Programs the Intervention Center Will Offer

Program	Description
Group classes	Serving autistic children.
Preschool	Providing advanced academics for children whose cognitively delays could be due to malnutrition or never having had the opportunity to learn. After a child's cognitive level increased, we would enroll the child at a public school.
Prevocational and vocational training	Geared for older children whose physical or mental delays keep them from participating in an academic setting. Learning a skill will increase self-esteem and independence, and, ideally, give them an opportunity to provide income for themselves and their families.
Respite care	Services would include going to the child's home to look after the child while the parents take a break, or taking the child out for a day so the parents can remain in the home.
Short-term crisis recovery	Designed for children in crisis who need to be temporarily removed from their home until the family situation is under control. This service might also apply to a child who undergoes major surgery and needs ongoing care while recovering.
Long-term care	No matter how much we work with some parents, their children remain uncared for and unwanted. Some have died from parental neglect. The children in long-term care would be treated as the caregiver's own child. Children would live in a home-like setting and have their living, health, and spiritual needs met. They would attend school or vocational training. Children with complex, multiple needs, such as those mentioned previously who could not walk or talk, would be eligible for long-term care and would receive the same love and attention.

Our Theme Verse

For You formed my inward parts;

You covered me in my mother's womb.

I will praise You, for I am fearfully and wonderfully made;

Marvelous are Your works,

And that my soul knows very well.

My frame was not hidden from You,

When I was made in secret,

And skillfully wrought in the lowest parts of the earth.

Your eyes saw my substance, being yet unformed.

And in Your book they all were written,

The days fashioned for me,

When as yet there were none of them. (Ps. 139:13–16, NKJV)

STARTING YOUR OWN PROJECT DEVELOPMENT JOURNEY

The following list contains important points, or principles, to remember when you start your journey to launch a project for children with special needs. These principles are gleaned from our own experience. Although certainly not exhaustive, this list provides guidance to those seeking to walk this path of project development.

Start out small, building gradually as your staff grows in number and skill level.

> If you start a project in a new area and people find out you are there, it will mushroom into something huge unless you control it from the beginning. Our motto is "one child at a time." To provide each child with the best care and learning opportunities, we need to keep the project small until we have adequate staff.

1. Have brainstorming sessions when you begin planning your project. Identify what is realistic.

2. Have an established curriculum in place before you begin.

3. Develop a partnership with the parents.

   - Walk with them!

   - Encourage parents to take ownership of their child's education from the beginning.

   - Help them form a parents association.

4. Set realistic expectations with the parents regarding their child's improvement.

   Many parents underestimate the amount of time required for their child to show noticeable improvement.

5. Be open to learning from your students.

   As professionals, we think we are going to change the children and the people, when in reality it is they who change us.

6. Get to know the families you are working with.

   If you work with a family that lives in a village, stay with them for a couple of days. Get to know what the real needs of the parents are and their preferred way to be helped. Do not rely on what you think they need or how you think they could be best helped.

7. Educate not only the parents, but also the community and its local leaders.

8. Partner with churches to get them involved with the children and their families.

   - Suggest that members of the church sponsor one of the children to meet basic needs such as clothes, medicine and school supplies.

   - Encourage the church to serve the mothers of these children. Offer counseling services and access to people with whom they can share.

- Recommend that the church provide Christmas gifts for the children.

9. Have a well-established relationship with a hospital and/or doctors, dentist, ophthalmologist and so on.

   There will be many medical issues. Negotiate with the hospital or doctors to provide services and medicines to poor families at reduced cost.

10. Network, network, network.

    Build as many relationships as you can with others who are doing the same work. Stand-alone projects will not work.

11. Nothing is impossible!

    All children will improve in some way if you keep praying and working with them. Never give up!

FACES OF HOPE

We have faced many challenges, and the child development program is still under development, yet we have also rejoiced over each child's progress. The children we serve represent faces of hope. We share a few of their stories with you to give you a snapshot of our work. All names have been changed to protect each family's privacy.

Asha

Asha was five years old when she came to the intervention center. Malnourished and developmentally disadvantaged, Asha was autistic and suffered from seizures. For the first two years, we worked closely with her family to teach them how to give Asha better nutrition and keep her hydrated with more water. During the hot summers, temperatures can reach up to 45 degrees Celsius.

We also encouraged her family to supervise Asha at all times. Because Asha was autistic, she would wander away from her family's living area and into the streets. No one would notice. Several times, one of our staff members happened to be on the main road and saw Asha wandering. On each occasion, the staff member scooped her up and took her home. A couple of times, Asha was close to busy traffic and was nearly hit by a car or a tractor. In fact, she was hit by a car near her house. She had crawled under the car and, unknowingly, the owner backed the car over her. Miraculously, she suffered only a bruised head and body.

The other problem was with her seizures. Because her family was so poor, we provided Asha's medical care. We gave her parents medication for Asha's seizures and explained how to give it to her. Still, Asha was having seizures several times a week. Then we would find out that her parents had run out of medicine or their neighbors had told them that Asha needed the medicine only temporarily. Asha even ended up in the hospital emergency room in a coma after having seizures all night.

We supplemented Asha's diet at the intervention center, because she only weighed about 12 kilograms at the time. Yet her parents had no understanding of the seriousness of her health issues, and her body was rapidly declining. After much prayer, I asked Asha's family if I could have custody of her to raise her and give her the care that she needed. Initially they agreed, but within a few days reconsidered. Asha stopped attending the intervention center.

When Asha returned to the center a year later, at age eight, she weighed only 15 kilograms. She now had chronic infections in addition to her seizures. We knew that her body could not take much more. When Asha was hospitalized, I asked the family again for custody. I told them that if her situation did not change soon, she would die. After a family meeting, they decided it was best that I take care of her, and Asha moved in with me.

We had one scare in December 2008 when she had an allergic reaction to a seizure medicine. She developed Stephens-Johnson Syndrome, a life-threatening condition, and she was in intensive care from December 8 to December 26. Fortunately, by April, she fully recovered.

Now 11, Asha is healthy, happy and slowly gaining weight. We celebrated her birthday last month! I have gotten to know Asha's family over the last three years that she has lived with me. They truly love their daughter, but they are too poor and lack the skills or time to take care of her. They are now happy she is with me.

I have also learned what it is like to raise a child who is developmentally disadvantaged. Even with the more modern conveniences (that you can get in a developing country), it has been difficult, especially when she was recovering from the syndrome. Seeing through the eyes of a poor family in the village has given me a new perspective. I am grateful to God for her returned health and the relationship I have with her parents.

Rajeev and Priya

Rajeev is developmentally disadvantaged and has been attending our intervention center for seven years. He is approximately thirteen years old. In the
beginning, he would show improvement, but then his family would take
him out of the center for several weeks. This went on for a couple of years.
We did have him at a point, though, where he participated in activities and
he began speaking.

When his parents and two siblings left the state to visit relatives, they
did not return for six months. When Rajeev came back, he was different; he
no longer spoke and would sit and stare with no expression on his face. He
developed all kinds of infections and his face swelled. The doctors could not
figure out why he was having so much difficulty. It was hard to find out what
was wrong, because his mother is illiterate and his father, who is mentally ill,
had suffered a breakdown.

Since the beginning, his grandparents did not want Rajeev and asked
me several times a month if I would find some place to send him. But even
the bigger city hostels would not board children who are developmentally
disadvantaged.

We did not know how we could help Rajeev or his sister, Priya. They
were not getting the nutrition that they needed; when we sent food home,
we suspected that they were not getting even that. Rajeev's younger brother,
who does not have developmental delays, received much better treatment.
Unlike Rajeev, he wore nice clothes and had a nice round stomach. Priya
is also cognitively fine but had never attended a public school. She, too,
changed after the six-month absence.

Both Rajeev and Priya needed to leave their home. With the parents in
their condition and the grandparents not wanting them, it did not leave a lot
of hope for their future. Priya contracted tuberculosis (TB), and Rajeev had
been exposed. Without our involvement with the family, they would not get
the proper medicine and nutrition that they need to live.

Children like Rajeev and Priya are why we decided on a two-phase program: short-term crisis recovery and long-term care. Many children in similar situations need help. Rajeev and his little brother now live in our home.
Priya, who recovered from TB, still lives at home under difficult conditions.

*

CHAPTER FOURTEEN

MAKING CHRIST ACCESSIBLE

* * *

Julie Bohn

Affirmation

> *As God's creations, we are fashioned uniquely,*
> *Each endowed with individuality of body, mind and spirit*
> *To worship freely the One who has given us life.*
> *Each of us has abilities; each seeks fulfillment and wholeness.*
> *Each of us has disabilities; each knows isolation and incompleteness.*
> *Seeking shelter from the vulnerability we all share,*
> *Claiming our promised place in God's Household of Faith,*
> *We are transformed by invitation, affirmation and love.*
> *In grateful response, we . . .*
> *Worship and serve God, the source of hope and joy;*
> *Celebrate and serve one another, rejoicing in our diversity;*
> *Transform and serve the world, until we become a Community*
> *Which reflects God's Oneness and Peace.*
> *Let the House of God be open to all who would enter and worship.*[1]

* * *

IS THERE a place for children and adults with disabilities in the church? I believe the answer is a resounding "Yes!" The church is incomplete without them. I have attended "Expressions of Love and Praise" worship services, which are special worship services that bring glory to God and must bring Him great pleasure.[2] There the greeters, ushers, song leaders, candle lighters, prayer leaders and most of the congregation have a mental

267

disability. Their worship is the purest worship I have had the privilege of experiencing, for their single-minded focus is on God alone. They are free in their expressions of worship: clapping, raising their hands, doing hand motions or creative movement. They rejoice in the opportunity to praise the Lord for what He is doing in their lives and are faithful in lifting each other up in prayer. They are cheerful givers, proudly putting their coins and bills in the offering plate. This group of worshippers supports a boy with disabilities from Africa and a girl with disabilities from Honduras with their love, their prayers and their sacrificial giving.

There is much that individuals with disabilities can gain from and give back to the church. They need to be told—in a way they will understand—about Jesus, our Lord and Savior, who wants to be their best friend. Those who are believers need to experience worship with other believers. They long to be taught what the Bible says about God and how to please Him in the way they live their lives. They often have compassionate hearts that desire to help others using the spiritual gifts the Lord has given them.

Unfortunately, our churches are often not accessible to individuals with disabilities. Due to lack of ramps or elevators or paths that are smooth enough and wide enough, individuals in wheelchairs cannot get into some churches. They may not be able to use a restroom because there is none big enough for them to get into with their wheelchair. Many times it is our attitudes that prevent families from bringing their family member who has a disability. Often we communicate that they are not wanted, that they are a shame or embarrassment, that their behavior is not acceptable for a church setting because it might interrupt the service, that we do not know what to do with them or say to them (nor do we want to learn), or that their sin or lack of faith is what is allowing this disability and thus they should not be a part of our church. As a result, their despair and guilt are heightened.

Let us look at what the church's response should be to children with disabilities in light of God's love for them. How should the church, as the Lord's representative on earth, care for these special children?

GOD VALUES CHILDREN WITH DISABILITIES

To effectively minister to and with children with disabilities we must understand God's heart for all people. In Genesis 1:27 we are told, "So God created mankind in his own image, in the image of God he created them; male and female he created them." We are all created in the image of God regardless of our size, color, ability levels, culture, heritage, strength, wisdom and so on. Because of this we all have a mind with the ability to think, emotions to give life meaning, and a will to choose to follow after the Lord.

Not only did God create us in His own image, He also fearfully and wonderfully made each of us and has a plan for each of our lives. In Psalm 139:13–16a David gives praise to the Lord:

> For you created my inmost being;
> you knit me together in my mother's womb.
> I praise you because I am fearfully and wonderfully made;
> your works are wonderful,
> I know that full well.
> My frame was not hidden from you
> when I was made in the secret place,
> when I was woven together in the depths of the earth.
> Your eyes saw my unformed body;

Like David, each of us was formed by God in our mother's womb. Because He is our Creator we were each fearfully and wonderfully made. Nothing about us is a surprise to God or a mistake. He knew Michael would be born with cerebral palsy. He knew Anna Marie would be blind. He knew Nada would be deaf. He knew Mitchell would have Down syndrome. In the Old Testament, God knew Moses would have a speech impediment. Exodus 4:10–12 tells us that Moses tried to use his slow tongue as an excuse for not fulfilling his calling of leading the people out of Egypt. The Lord responded to him: "Who gave human beings their mouths? Who makes them deaf or mute? Who gives them sight or makes them blind? Is it not I, the LORD? Now go; I will help you speak and will teach you what to say." God would be glorified by working through Moses' weakness to accomplish His purposes. He does the same with each of us regardless of whether we can see, hear, speak, use our arms or legs, or read and reason well. Paul shares what the Lord told him in 2 Corinthians 12:9: "My grace is sufficient for you, for my power is made perfect in weakness." Therefore, Paul says, "I will boast all the more gladly about my weaknesses, so that Christ's power may rest on me." The Lord works through our weaknesses so that, through dependence on His grace, we can fulfill His purposes for His glory in this fallen world.

The Lord also works through those who acquire a disability after birth due to illness or injury. Psalm 139:16b says, "All the days ordained for me were written in your book before one of them came to be." It was not a surprise to the Lord when Daniel had an auto accident and now must use a wheelchair for the rest of his life. The Lord is using Daniel with his disability—he is the director of a disability ministry in Canada that includes a summer camping program for children with disabilities. God was not caught unaware when Bert had a diving accident that left him a quadriplegic. The Lord helped Bert to develop his artistic gifts within the limits of his disability and was glorified through Bert's beautiful watercolors and professional graphic art. The Lord uses the accidents and illnesses that change our lives to shape us into the people He wants us to be. We may not always be able to see God's whole purpose for all people with disabilities, but we know He intends to receive glory from all of His creation.

Once we accept these truths ourselves, it is up to us to communicate them and teach them to others, especially those with disabilities. It is the church's responsibility to present Christ so that individuals may come to a saving knowledge of Christ. We are to help those who trust Christ to find their God-given gifts and their God-given purpose. Those gifts can then be developed to help them fulfill their purpose. These are also our responsibilities to children with disabilities.

As ones created in the image of God, people with disabilities have the same needs as any of us and are of equal value to God. Thinking back to my friends at Expressions of Love and Praise, I realize that there is much we can learn from them. Their love and concern for each other is a good model for any church. Their purity of worship is something we should all strive for in our own personal worship of the Lord. Their willingness to talk freely about Jesus, their best friend, is the kind of boldness we all should have in telling others about our Savior.

WHERE DOES THE CHURCH BEGIN?

Ministry to children with disabilities within a specific church often begins when the parents of a child with a disability seek suitable spiritual education for their child. Occasionally someone not related to a child with a disability will be burdened for this type of ministry. Either way, the starting point must be in prayer. Only the Lord can work in people's hearts to make them "accessible" to children with disabilities. Reading this book shows that you have some interest in working with these special children. Begin by praying for the church's pastors, Christian education personnel and then the entire congregation. Pray that their eyes would be open to see those with disabilities, their families and their needs, and that their fears (and yours) would be dispelled by education and involvement. Pray that the ministry will be driven by God's love, guided by the Holy Spirit, and result in the Lord being glorified and lives being changed by Christ. Most importantly, pray for opportunities to develop relationships with children with disabilities and their families. Pray for the Lord to be working in people's hearts to grow the support for ministry. Pray for a team of people to minister and a clear vision of what the ministry could look like.

Determine to Whom You Will Minister

As you and others are praying, a team of people who are interested in starting a disability ministry should find out which families in the church and local community have a family member with a disability. Visit the families and begin to develop a relationship with them. Discover their needs. Locate and visit any group homes, care facilities, institutions or orphanages that have children with disabilities. Begin to establish relationships with the children there within the guidelines of the various institutions. You may find other churches or organizations in your area that are already ministering to various groups of this population. If so, consider partnering with them rather than starting your own ministry for those groups. You may find that a specific group is not being ministered to and may want to start there. For example, when I first started attending my former church, there was another church in the area that had Sunday school classes for children and adults with mild mental disabilities. Yet there was no church ministering to adults with severe and profound mental retardation. We started a Sunday school class for this group rather than duplicating the ministries of another church.

Raise Church Awareness

As with any ministry, the church leadership, as well as the rest of the congregation, needs to be made aware of the need for the ministry to people with disabilities so that they can be supporting the ministry, especially through prayer. As people become aware of the need, they can pray about their role in meeting the need.

There may be some objections to beginning this type of ministry. Some common responses include: "People with disabilities are not our target audience" or "We do not have any individuals with disabilities in our church" or "We do not feel our church is called to this ministry." Others may be so bold as to admit that they are uncomfortable around individuals with disabilities or think they will be too disruptive for the atmosphere the church is trying to promote. The church leadership may need to be reminded that Jesus, in Matthew 22:39, commands us to love our neighbor as ourselves, and in Mark 16:15 commissions us to "go into all the world and preach the gospel to all creation." Neither of these commands have exception clauses. Our neighbors include individuals with disabilities. Most mission statements for churches include some phrase referring to reaching the lost in their community. Part of that community includes individuals with disabilities.

One good way to educate the congregation, thus dispelling fears and quenching objections, is to have a Disability Awareness Sunday. The entire day—from Sunday school classes to the worship service—is focused on disability issues. The pastor's message may be on suffering, acceptance of others, God's view of disabilities or a variety of other topics related to disability. Individuals with disabilities and/or their family members can share testimonies during the service or during Sunday school. Members of the disability ministry team can share how the Lord has been working in their lives as they begin to develop relationships with children with disabilities and their families. Sunday school classes, from children to adults, can do awareness activities or a Bible study on disabilities. See Appendix A for some passages that can be used, along with other ideas for Disability Awareness Sunday.

The focus of a Disability Awareness Sunday is to heighten the awareness of the joys and needs of individuals with disabilities and their families. You can develop many additional creative and effective ways to raise awareness in conjunction with the children and the families themselves.

Evaluate Church Accessibility

An important step in defining the focus of a ministry to children with disabilities is to evaluate the church's physical accessibility. It may be found that children in wheelchairs cannot get into the church, which would greatly impact the type of ministry the church would initially be able to provide. The people in your church who are responsible for the building (for example, building committee, elders or trustees) should conduct an assessment of the church's accessibility. The Accessibility Checklist found in Appendix B can be a helpful tool in this task.

We must ask whether there are things the church can do right away to make the building and grounds more accessible. If the church is planning a building project, someone who uses a wheelchair should be invited to share insights and add perspective for the building committee. For example, proposed construction may meet the architectural standards of the Americans with Disabilities Act (or other relevant authority), but it still may not be entirely suitable for someone in a wheelchair. Such discrepancy is often seen in bathroom stalls. The wheelchair may fit in the stall, but the door cannot be closed while the helper is transferring the individual to the commode. This leaves the individual who is being transferred fully exposed until he is on the commode and his wheelchair is removed. Having someone who actually uses a wheelchair involved in the planning can prevent this kind of indignity.

Define the Vision

As the disability ministry team is praying for God's guidance and direction, discovering the needs of the people to whom they will be ministering, creating awareness within the church body of those needs, and evaluating building accessibility, it also needs to be developing the vision and purpose of the ministry. Having a clear purpose builds morale as it unites people, reduces frustration as it defines what will and will not be done, allows concentration and focused effort, attracts cooperation as people learn where the ministry is headed, and assists in evaluation by stating a standard from which to measure growth.[3] Discuss and pray with the team about what type of ministry the Lord seems to be envisioning. Some questions to consider include: What resources are available? Is the Lord moving people to minister, to provide resources, to give of their time? Where will the focus be? On the children? On their families? On evangelism? On providing spiritual education at the church? On taking spiritual education to their place of residence?

One church I have worked with, the Reformed Presbyterian Church of Ephrata, took their church mission statement (which already encompassed individuals with disabilities with the phrase "people from all walks of life") and added a "Special Needs Ministry" vision statement to outline the "why and how to" of including the children of their congregation and others in their community who also had disabilities. This vision statement, which is based foremost on Scripture, stems from their core beliefs that human life has value because we are created by and in the image of God and that ministry should be carried out in mercy and with gratitude to God, not with condescension or pity, or out of duty. The vision statement states: "By holding fast to the biblical principle that all human beings have value and dignity because we are created in the image of God, we aim to become a church that ministers to and alongside people with differing abilities out of our deep understanding of our common need for grace."[4]

Their Special Needs Ministry has five objectives: Facilitating the integration of people with disabilities into the body life of the church; educating the congregation on issues of disability in the context of ministry; guiding small groups in providing appropriate support to adults with a disability and families with a family member who is disabled; initiating "Family-Specific Support Groups" for families in extreme disability-related circumstances; and promoting outreach to people with disabilities. With this purpose and plan, their ministry is growing, and Christ is changing their own lives as well as the lives of individuals with disabilities in the process.

THE CHURCH AND THE CHILD

> *If you are paralyzed, you can still "walk" with God.*
> *If you are blind, you are nevertheless able to "see" the light.*
> *If you are deaf, you are still able to "hear" the Word of God.*
> *And even if you are mentally handicapped, you can have the mind of Christ.*

—Joni Eareckson Tada[5]

Sharing the Gospel

The greatest need any of us has is to have a personal relationship with the Lord Jesus Christ. Regardless of what other services or ministry the church offers, the opportunity should be available for children with disabilities to hear the gospel. "Faith comes from hearing the message, and the message is heard through the word about Christ" (Romans 10:17). The message of the gospel is the same for all people, regardless of disability: "Jesus loves us. We are sinners deserving of and headed for death. Jesus died for our sins and rose again. Jesus wants to be our best friend. He wants us to be a part of His family. We need to turn from our sin and trust in Him." Yet the presentation of this message may need to be different depending on the disability of the listener.

We must ensure the gospel is a part of any ministry to children with disabilities, both by sharing it with them and living it before them. Any gospel presentation should be preceded by some type of relationship building and should be given in love demonstrated by touch, tone of voice and eye contact, just as Jesus himself "saw" people with disabilities (John 5:6; 9:1) and touched them (Luke 5:13; John 9:6). In addition, we can make the gospel more accessible to children with different types of disabilities. For example, the gospel should be communicated through sign language and visuals to children who are deaf.

Children with mental disabilities need a simple presentation of the gospel. Most of them know what a friend is and what it means to be part of a family. It is best to talk about trusting Christ in terms of one of those relationships—either making Jesus their best friend or becoming a part of God's family. In this way they can understand the relationship aspect that is so central to the gospel. Phrases like "trusting Christ" or "accepting Christ" or "asking Jesus into your heart" or "praying to receive Christ" are too abstract for children with mental disabilities. (Jesus would not fit in your heart, and the other terms are difficult for even most adults to explain.)

Difficult concepts need to be explained clearly to such children. For instance, sin can be explained as the bad things we do and the things that God does not like (for example, calling names or not helping or disobeying parents). Repentance can be described as feeling sad or sorry that we disobeyed our parents and Jesus and not wanting to disobey again. Forgiveness can be understood as when our parents and Jesus do not stay mad about what we did.

The concept that "all have sinned" is sometimes difficult for children with mental disabilities to comprehend. They may think that they do not sin because they have not done anything really bad like killing someone. They may also not be able to imagine that you would ever sin because you are always nice to them and love them. It is important to spend time talking with them and figuring out ways to demonstrate how they have sinned, such as disobeying their parents, calling someone a name, hitting or pushing someone or lying. It is also helpful for you to confess some of your sins so they know that you sin too. Finally, it is best to use pictures along with the Bible and simple explanations. Handi*Vangelism has several simple tools that are useful in sharing the gospel with children who have disabilities. See appendix E for contact information.

Another communication issue to consider is that children with mental disabilities may become upset when a picture of Jesus on the cross is shown. They seem to have a greater sense of what Jesus went through for us and are often greatly disturbed. Appreciate their sensitivity and seek such sensitivity for yourself. When giving a visual presentation of the crucifixion, quickly move Jesus off the cross, into the grave and out of the grave.

In my experience, individuals with mental disabilities often have much a greater spiritual IQ than their mental IQ. For instance, Mark, who has Down syndrome, can share insights from the Bible that are appropriate for a chapel service of his peers. Billy, who also has Down syndrome, can lead a discussion on spiritual issues for his Sunday school class. Of all the people who have mental disabilities, only about five percent are so severely intellectually disabled that they are unable to understand the gospel well enough to make Jesus their best friend. What happens to the five percent who cannot believe? I agree with Robert Lightner:

> *Because Christ was so concerned with those who could not believe and because He did so much for them during His life, we have reason to believe that He loves them and grants them eternal life when they die . . . the price has been paid in full, the debt is canceled until it is rejected. Therefore, God can receive*

into His presence all those who did not receive His Son by faith
because they could not do so.[6]

Sunday School or Bible Class

The gospel can and should be shared one-on-one, but it can also be incorporated into a Sunday school class or Bible class. This can look many different ways. Children with disabilities can be a part of their same-age peers' regular Sunday school class with a personal shepherd or buddy to assist them. When they can no longer benefit from the regular Sunday school class because they cannot understand the concepts being taught or because their behavior is too distracting to the other students and hinders their learning, then starting a special class may be appropriate. Some children may not be able to get to church because of their living situations. In such cases, starting a Bible class at the group home, care facility, institution or orphanage may be the best approach.

When bringing in a child with a disability, it is helpful to learn basic background information about her. A form such as the Sunday School Registration Form (Appendix C) can assist in this process. Going through the form with her family member or caregiver will help assure them that the children's workers are interested in their child and want to make her Sunday school experience the best it can be. It will also give the workers an opportunity to ask questions to help them prepare to meet her needs the best way possible.

Using Personal Shepherds or Buddies

Some children with disabilities can learn quite well in a regular Sunday school class. This is especially true of those who only have a physical disability, are deaf or blind, are on the higher-functioning end of the autism spectrum with little if any mental retardation, have only mild learning disabilities, or have mild mental retardation. They may only need some personal assistance to be able to participate fully in the class. Having a trained personal shepherd or buddy assigned to each child with a disability will ensure the child is getting the most out of the class. Peers can be shepherds if minimal assistance is needed. Teens make great shepherds for younger children. Adults will be needed if there are behavioral issues to consider in addition to personal assistance.

It is best to have more than one shepherd trained for each child, and the shepherds should be rotated on a regular basis. Shepherds should be given general training in a number of areas; for example, how to explain concepts in a variety of ways and how to give "hand-over-hand" vs. "do it for them" assistance ("hand-over-hand assistance" means that the shepherd guides the student's hand while the student holds the scissors, writing instrument or other tool, with the resulting craft project looking like the student did it with just some basic assistance, rather than looking like it was done by the shepherd). Shepherds will also need training in the basics of discipline consistent with the classroom and church guidelines. Discipline should not be expected of nor tolerated by a peer shepherd.

Shepherds should also receive specific training from the child's caregiver about the child's particular situation: physical needs, positioning, phrases used in discipline or things to watch for (for example, seizures). Shepherds should also be familiar with the child's Sunday School Registration Form. The best way for specific training to occur is to have the shepherds spend some time with the family while getting to know the child.

Special Classes/Adaptations

Children with disabilities can often be integrated into Sunday school or Bible class with few adaptations to the curriculum, especially when a "hands-on" curriculum (where the children are interacting with each other and with objects throughout the lesson) is already being used. Instructional activities involving visuals and objects, fine- and gross-motor activities, role-playing skits, music, and activities that engage all the senses are helpful for all children but are especially beneficial for those with disabilities. The use of stamps, stickers and similar precut materials are helpful for children with physical disabilities. Giving children who are blind objects that they can feel while listening to a Bible story can make the story come alive for them. For a child who is blind and can read Braille, providing the lesson in Braille and having a Braille Bible available will also help. A sign-language interpreter is a must for children who are deaf and know sign language.

Because the purpose of Sunday school or Bible class is to get to know Jesus and the Bible better, the time may come when a special class needs to be started for children with disabilities who are not benefiting spiritually from the regular Sunday school class. That time usually comes in the upper elementary grades or junior high. When it becomes difficult for the shepherds to make Sunday school meaningful for children with disabilities, then the children need classes of their own taught at their levels. They may be able to join with their peers for the worship portion of the class and then go to a separate room or rooms for the Bible lesson. The Bible story should be told visually as well as verbally, using visuals, video, puppets, flannel graph and so on to communicate the main parts of the story. Details are not as important to this class as repeating the main biblical principle in multiple ways. Having the children act out the Bible story is a great way to have them review it. When doing so, it is essential that the part given to the child with a disability communicates the main point of the lesson so the right message is reinforced. I learned this lesson the hard way. One week the class was acting out Daniel 6. I gave Sheri the part of the officials who said, "Do not pray!" That is what Sheri learned from that lesson and it took a while to undo that mistake in judgment on my part.

Children with mental disabilities can and should learn Bible words. Take the verse you want them to memorize (for example, Mark 16:15: "Go into all the world and preach the gospel to all creation"). Decide what the verse is saying and have them memorize those Bible "words" rather than the whole verse (for example, "Tell others about Jesus"). Bible applications should be practical, either something they can actually do in class or something they can role-play to practice in their home, school or other setting. (Again, when role-playing make sure they are playing the part they are to learn.)

If children cannot come to the church for Sunday school (perhaps due to lack of staffing where they live, church not being a priority where they live, the severity of their disability or other reasons), then consider how the church can take Sunday school to them. Contact the appropriate personnel at the group home, residential care facility, institution or orphanage where the children live and discuss what your disability ministry team would like to do. Be clear and specific but brief. Let the facility personnel ask the questions. You will need to find out how to obtain approval, when is the best time to come and where the class can be held. A consent form will probably be needed for the caregiver to sign, giving permission for each child to attend the class. It is important when working with secular organizations to commit to following their guidelines for interacting with the children. In these situations the ministry is not only to the children but also to the facility staff who will be watching the interaction with the children as well as the interaction with the staff. Submitting to their guidelines, routines and schedules will be a testimony to them.

The same type of lessons that are used when Sunday school is at the church can also be used at the facility where the children live. Be sure to include a time of worship along with the Bible lesson and application—find out in advance what equipment is available (for example, CD player, piano, DVD player). Make the Bible applications applicable to life where the children are living. Develop relationships with the staff to encourage them and to find out ways the lessons can be applied in the children's daily lives. For example, the staff will know that Debra has a problem with taking things from other children or that Lee and David have a hard time getting along. Build that information into the applications of the Bible lessons. It will be a testimony to all as the Lord works in those situations, changing the children to be more like Himself. In fact, non-Christian staff members have even come to a relationship with Christ through observing Bible classes that they either had to attend with the children or that were held in the facility where they work.

Worship Service

In many churches, children's worship and Sunday school are going on at the same time that the adults are in the main worship service. If that is the case, then the special class can be held during that time.

If children with disabilities are expected to attend the worship service with their parents, it may be wise to provide "worship buddies." This allows the children to remain with their caregivers throughout the singing time. During the sermon, the worship buddy can take the children out to do some meaningful Bible activities with them at their own level. This might be a good time to work on memorizing Bible words or more deeply understanding the meaning of the worship songs. It is also a perfect time for the one-on-one sharing of the gospel.

If the children have already had Sunday school prior to this worship time, then the worship buddy should vary the activities from what was done in Sunday school. They can use this time to play a Bible review game, watch a Bible story on DVD or review a Bible story by acting it out. This time should be less mentally intense and more physically involved than the Sunday school hour in order to keep their attention and interest level high. It is good to provide children who use a wheelchair with an alternative place to sit during this time (for example, a bean bag chair or someone's lap) to help prevent the sores that develop from sitting in the same position for too long.

Service to Others

God has given children with disabilities at least one spiritual gift, just as He has anyone else who makes Jesus their best friend. One of our responsibilities as a church is to help these children learn how to serve the Lord by serving others. Look for ways they can minister in the body.

For example, Cindy is a greeter. Her mother places the bulletins on the tray of her wheelchair. Her communication device is programmed with a greeting message. When someone comes in, Cindy gives them a huge, welcoming smile and hits the button to play the greeting while the person is picking up a bulletin. It would be difficult not to feel welcomed by Cindy's warm smile. Sarah is great at making cards for those in the church who are ill. Mark loves to pray for people. David loves to give hugs or a handshake.

Our church bodies are not complete unless everyone who has made Jesus their best friend, including children with disabilities, is serving in some way.

THE CHURCH AND THE FAMILY

In Ghana where I have ministered, as well as in many other cultures, having a child with a disability is considered a shame and an embarrassment or a curse of the devil. These children are kept hidden, locked away in a back room, or are kicked out of their homes and forced to fend for themselves. At best this usually means a life of crime and hardship including stealing, begging, prostitution or child slave labor. Often though, the disability is so severe or the streets are so harsh that these children do not last long on their own and die quickly or are killed. In the Ukraine, as in many other cultures, the father often leaves, not being able to handle having a child with a disability. This places an extreme hardship on the mother and other family members, not to mention the pain of abandonment that the child feels. This is true in America as well. Four out of five couples will divorce when they have a child with a disability.

In these cultures, the church has a major responsibility in teaching the parents and other family members about how much God loves their child and has a purpose for them. These families need to know from God's Word that it is their responsibility and privilege to care for and raise these children who are so precious to God. Paul tells us in several places that individuals have a responsibility to see that their family members are cared for. In a passage on the care of widows in 1 Timothy 5:7–8, Paul makes a strong statement about caring for family members: "Give the people these instructions, so that no one may be open to blame. Anyone who does not provide for their relatives, and especially for their own household, has denied the faith and is worse than an unbeliever." In Ephesians 6:4 Paul speaks directly to fathers saying: "Fathers, do not exasperate your children; instead, bring them up in the training and instruction of the Lord." These and many other passages make it clear that the family, specifically the fathers, have a responsibility not to discard their children, but to bring them up in and with the love of Christ. This needs to be taught anywhere the Bible is taught. Parents must understand and accept the awesome responsibility the Lord has given them to raise a child with a disability.

As parents begin to understand and accept their responsibility, they will need support and encouragement from the church body. Galatians 6:2–5 shows us the two sides of what this looks like. First, verse 2 tells us to "carry each other's burdens, and in this way you will fulfill the law of Christ." When a family first finds out their child has a disability, they will be in shock and will go through a grief process. Their dream of having a perfect child will have died, and they will be experiencing grief in the death of that dream child. The family will be in crisis and will need listening ears, shoulders to cry on, and people to help with day-to-day life while they deal with this "death" and a whole new lifestyle. They will have to learn a new language, possibly two: the medical language associated with the disability (for example, ataxia, dysmetria, paresthesias) and the language and acronyms of the disability world (for example, IFPs, IEPs, PT, OT, IST); people who do not have children with disabilities do not have to learn these languages. They may need to learn and perform new medical procedures and other challenging tasks required in caring for a child with a disability. They need someone to bear these burdens with them. We can clean their house, take care of the lawn, bring meals, and go to doctor appointments with them. It is better to say, "I am going grocery shopping today. What can I pick up for you?" than "Call if you need anything." We can tell them, "I am cooking supper for you tonight. Would you like me to bring it to your house or would you like to come over here?" Be specific in offering help. Accept "No, thank you" graciously if they refuse, but continue to offer. Be there to listen without judging. Let them be angry without feeding the anger. Remember that being with them at this time is more important than saying anything.

Later, as the family comes to grips with their new life, Galatians 6:5 comes into play: "For each one should carry their own load." Eventually the initial crisis time will pass and the family will need to establish a "new normal" for themselves. The effect of the disability on their lives is not going to go away, so they will need to learn to "carry their own load." This does not mean that the church abandons them—far from it. But the crisis relief and the day-to-day life responsibilities of meals, shopping, cleaning and so on need to gradually be given back to them. This does not mean that they have to do all of it alone, but it does mean that it is their responsibility to see that it gets done.

The church must continue to support them. Each family member should have a prayer partner whom they can share their hearts with and be held accountable to. It will be important for them to be a part of a small group that either consists entirely of families who have children with disabilities or that is mixed with families that do not. Both types of groups have a place and meet different needs. It is important to make sure that accommodations are made for the various church functions for these families to be able to participate. If the church is having a family fun night, for example, make sure that it is at a place where children with disabilities can get to, and includes activities they can participate in. Invite the whole family over for dinner, making sure any special diets or other accommodations for the child with a disability are taken into consideration. It may be easier for a church family to bring dinner to the home of the child with a disability instead of asking the child's family to pack up all that is necessary for them to go to another's house. The main point is to keep the families of children with disabilities in fellowship and in prayer.

Another extremely helpful way that the church can minister to such families is to provide respite care. Theirs is a difficult load to carry, especially if there is a lot of physical care involved or if the child is a challenge behaviorally. Seek several people from the church to volunteer as respite providers. These respite providers should spend time with the family learning the child's routines, becoming familiar with caring for the child and letting the child and family become familiar with them. When the provider and the family are both comfortable with the care the provider can give the child, the provider should offer to watch the child. Offer an afternoon so the mother can go shopping or relax for a few hours alone. Offer an evening so the parents can go on a date. Offer a weekend so that the rest of the family can get some quality time with the parents. Provide a game night for several children with disabilities so that their families can do something together. The ways in which respite care can be offered are endless once the provider and the child are familiar with each other and the family is comfortable with the provider, allowing them to relax while they are away and not be thinking all the time about how their child is doing.

THE INTERNATIONAL CHURCH

Most of practical ideas that have been covered in this chapter apply to the American or Western style of church. In the cities and larger towns in most countries, these ideas can be adapted easily. Church accessibility, however, can look different outside of these Western-style churches. In rural areas it may mean making sure that the walking path to the church is smooth, clear and wide enough for someone in a wheelchair or who uses crutches or crawls to get to the church. In such villages the main accessibility barrier is the attitude toward children with disabilities and their families. Communicating God's welcoming love through an invitation delivered in person at the home of such families will go a long way in paving the way to the church. Showing these families love, respect and honor will soften hearts to prepare them to hear the gospel.

As mentioned previously, children with disabilities are often considered a shame and embarrassment and are kicked out of the home. It is up to the church to come alongside these children (and adults) who are on their own. It may initially mean providing whatever support is available while sharing Christ's love. Several times I have attended a storefront church in Ghana where people with disabilities who live on the street come every Sunday afternoon to worship and hear Bible teaching. Most of the worshippers get there on their own by crawling, walking or wheeling themselves or by hiring someone, usually a street child, to push them. Others are picked up by the group leading the service. After the service they may be provided with food or even a meal, or soap or other supplies. The worshippers know that this group of believers will help them obtain medical services or try to meet other practical needs. In this way the church provides as much as they can in the way of Christ's love and His Word and material support, even though they lack funds to establish a residential or vocational center.

Residential facilities are needed for children with disabilities and the children of people with disabilities who live on the street. Both groups of children are vulnerable and defenseless. This makes them easy prey for all sorts of evil including child slavery, child prostitution and child sacrifice. Getting them off the street must be addressed quickly once the church becomes aware of their existence. One children's home I visited in Ghana provides three meals a day, clean clothes, school fees, healthcare, glasses, braces and other practical needs, as well as a loving Christian environment. The older children take turns leading morning devotions, and an adult caregiver leads the evening devotions. All of the children at the home had a greater understanding of their eternal salvation because they were aware of their earthly salvation in getting off the streets.

Vocational centers are also needed to provide vocational training to people with disabilities. But learning a trade is not enough when no one will buy from them or use their services because of the stigma of their disability. The church can play a major role in being the model leaders in their community by making a point to buy from or hire individuals with disabilities.

Another practical way that the church can help is by making sure that children with disabilities are registered with the social welfare office of the country. This makes their families aware of and eligible for the services and benefits that are offered, which may include free medical care or transportation. Some countries also waive school fees. Just the act of making sure that families are registered can open many doors of service.

Churches can also inform families about clinics for pre- and post-natal care and proper immunizations, or even sponsor a clinic of their own. One of the most common physical disabilities in countries outside of the West is polio, which can be prevented if families get their babies immunized. That simple act can prevent all the difficulties associated with having and raising a child with polio. In many major cities various organizations provide free vaccinations. But often families in outlying areas will not know about these clinics. Church members can take the initiative to find out when and where the clinics are and let the families know. The church can even provide transportation to the city for the vaccinations. Any of these acts of service will make a huge difference in the lives of children with disabilities and their families, as well as be a powerful witness for the church.

CONCLUSION

The church can minister to children with disabilities and their families in many ways. Only a few have been highlighted in this chapter. As the church prays and seeks God's guidance, He will show what the needs are and how He wants them met. All that the Lord requires are open, teachable servant's hearts that desire to love all people as He loves them. His love shining through us to children with disabilities can change not only their lives for Christ, but can also be a testimony to the greater community of the Lord's love and acceptance of each of us and of our love for Him. Like Jesus said, "Truly I tell you, whatever you did for one of the least of these brothers and sisters of mine, you did for me" (Matthew 25:40). When I think of individuals with disabilities and the church's ultimate responsibility to them, I think of Isaiah 35:3–6a:

> Strengthen the feeble hands, steady the knees that give way; say to those with fearful hearts, "Be strong, do not fear; your God will come, he will come with vengeance; with divine retribution he will come to save you." Then will the eyes of the blind be opened and the ears of the deaf unstopped. Then will the lame leap like a deer, and the mute tongue shout for joy.

This passage is referring to what will happen when Christ returns and ushers in the millennial kingdom, but the same is true of heaven. When I think of this passage, I think of the child who is born blind. If someone takes the time to share the gospel with him and he receives it, the first person he will ever see is Jesus. If someone takes the time to share the gospel with a child who is deaf and she receives it, the first sound she will ever hear is Jesus' voice welcoming her home. If we take the time to share the gospel with children who use wheelchairs and they receive it, the first person they will be able to leap in the arms of will be Jesus. Heaven will look much different than earth. Our young friends with disabilities will be there if we have taken the gospel to them here on earth, but we may not immediately recognize them because they will be whole and they will be dancing and singing with Jesus. I cannot wait to join in the dance!

NOTES

1. Ginny Thornburgh, ed., *That All May Worship: An Interfaith Welcome to People with Disabilities* (Washington, DC: National Organization on Disability, 1992), 4.

2. Expressions of Love and Praise is a monthly worship service for individuals with developmental disabilities sponsored by Worship Opportunities Reaching the Developmentally Disabled (W.O.R.D.D.) in Lancaster County, PA.

3. Rick Warren, *The Purpose Driven Church: Growth without Compromising Your Message and Mission* (Grand Rapids, MI: Zondervan, 1995), 86–94.

4. Taken from Steph Hubach, "Special Needs Ministry: Locally" (Ephrata, PA: Reformed Presbyterian Church of Ephrata, 2001).

5. Used by Kathy Sheetz in a Handi*Vangelism Newsletter, original reference unknown.

6. Robert P. Lightner, *Safe in the Arms of Jesus* (Grand Rapids, MI: Kregel, 2000), 22–25.

PART V

Compassionate Responses

God's Love in Action

Love is everything
Love is all around
Love is not hopeless
Love is passion
Love will not stop
Love is an ocean

—Melissa Riggio
(as told to Rachel Buchholz)

*

Chapter Fifteen

Holistic Caregiving:

Strengthening the Church's Response

* * *

Wendy Middaugh Bovard

THE STORY is told of a man who lay by the roadside beaten by robbers. Soon people began passing and saw the injured man. The first person walked past him, rushing on with his planned activities for the day. "Maybe the next one will stop and help me," the injured man must have thought. But lo and behold, the next traveler also walked past him, looking the other way lest his own conviction force him to stop. Finally came the one who has been called the Good Samaritan. "And when he saw him, he had pity on him" (Luke 10:33b). Did this Good Samaritan have more time than the others did? Did he have more resources? What drove the man to stop and be a blessing to another human being with whom he had no relationship and perhaps nothing in common?

Jesus tells this story to a young lawyer in order to demonstrate what makes a good neighbor. After telling the story, Jesus instructed the young lawyer to "go and do likewise" (Luke 10:37). Why has the Church been called to show compassion to the hurting neighbor? Why has the Church been entrusted with the noble responsibility of being a healing balm to so many hurting people in the world today? World Vision president Richard Stearns notes that one of the reasons why the Church is called to respond is because we are exhorted by God Himself to respond (Isaiah 58:6–7; James 1:27).[1] Yet even within the Church today are found the Levites and priests of Jesus' day. Many of us will not stop because our thoughts are clouded by our own judgmental attitudes or misplaced priorities. We may feel sorry for people that seem "different" in our society, but they need more than our pity, they need our voices to be heard for them—a voice for the voiceless. Judgmental attitudes become obvious when children with disabilities are involved. We are quick to label them as "slow," simply because they learn differently. We call them names just because they look "different." Yet the Church is the body that God has commissioned to show them compassion.

The Christian church in Africa is beginning to realize her incredible strength. Although many churches are in poverty-driven areas and still feel helpless, wondering what they can really do to make a difference in the lives of their children, they are realizing that even if they cannot do everything, they can at least do "something." It is with this resolve that faith-based, para-church organizations are partnering with local churches all over Africa and seeing tremendous things accomplished.

Numerous initiatives and networks have specifically targeted churches for such interventions as HIV/AIDS care and education, water and sanitation messaging, and gender violence and trauma counseling in crisis areas. In fact, church-based efforts in the fight against HIV/AIDS have been so effective in Uganda and Rwanda that they are being held up as models of great promise for the entire continent. The local church seems to be in every corner of every country and is positioned perfectly to play a major role in the social reforms that will give children the support they need to grow and develop. This is all a result of the tremendous growth of the church in Africa in the past two decades. Yet if the church is to continue to provide such leadership, there are a few things still needed. In order to be optimally effective, we must know, we must share and we must care.

WE MUST KNOW

We begin by knowing. Jesus challenged His audience by reminding them of the commandment to love their neighbor and by teaching them who a good neighbor is. Jesus spent a lot of His time teaching His own disciples and followers. It is out of His teachings that the New Testament church was born. Today's church must teach its members to be intentional about intervention for, and empowerment of, children with special needs. In Africa this teaching needs to start with educating people that the disabilities of children are not some punishment of God. Once people have learned this truth, they will begin to change their attitudes and reach out to such children in love and support. This is truly a difficult task in a context with so many different tribes, languages and customs. It is not unusual for even pastors to be so influenced by the stories and misinformation surrounding children with disabilities in their communities that they are uncomfortable and unable to lead the congregation into truly Christian care and support of such children. This is why we must help local churches to know the truth of God's love and purpose for these children and to be set free to model that truth to members of their churches and communities. When we know these children personally and choose to become involved in their lives, it opens our hearts to the love that God wants to share through us. This is where knowing actually becomes caring.

We must also know what interventions to provide for children with special needs. What can we do to help these children reach their full potential and discover the purpose for which they were born? In Africa some of the most effective initiatives that have sought to promote holistic models of Christian care and support have included the following elements:

- *Identification* of children with special needs in the communities, including physical and mental disabilities as well as learning disabilities. (This can be done using referrals from church and community leaders.)

- *Assessment* of those identified using a variety of basic assessment tools, starting with a needs assessment that identifies the actual needs of the child and the family in order for holistic care to be undertaken. (There are numerous assessment tools available on the Internet for physical, emotional, educational, social and spiritual care. See appendix D for a sample assessment tool.)

- *Intervention* for the immediate needs of the child and family, which will include debriefing, information sharing, counseling and linking the child to available resources.

- *Development* of a long-term plan for the child and family that may include medical care, nutritional support, educational support, psychosocial support and spiritual support as needed.

- *Follow-up* for the monitoring and evaluation of the long-term plan to ensure that the child's needs are being met and that the family is well supported in the process.

The following case study is an excellent example of intentional intervention for children with special needs in Kenya and Uganda. I personally witnessed this tremendous, professionally run Christian ministry that is meeting the needs of children and their families when my own son David's special need became acute.

Case Study: AIC-CURE International Children's Hospital in Kijabe, Kenya

AIC-CURE International Children's Hospital in Kijabe, Kenya, has been helping children with disabilities for many years through a church-based community initiative. They have partnered with a number of local churches around the country and use these churches to bring information, education and communication to the communities about the needs and potential of children with disabilities, as well as awareness about available assistance for surgical operations and rehabilitation. The hospital is most famous for the wonderful surgical operations they do for children that give them the ability to walk again or to walk for the first time. These operations make children with certain physical disabilities more mobile and independent. In most cases the surgical operations are absolutely life changing for both the child and the family.

The spiritual support team of the hospital works with the families and children to encourage them through various operations and recovery periods in the hospital. They also try to help the parents reject traditional myths that their children with disabilities are a curse, and instead learn that God loves everyone. Many parents and children accept Christ and witness His love through the dedicated staff and doctors.

In order to help the greatest number of children with disabilities, the hospital utilizes local churches to identify the children in the communities who are in need of assistance. The church partners do a home assessment in each case to determine the actual needs of the child and the family, and if the church or community partner is not able to help the child, they connect the family to an organization that can. This is where networking and partnering with a number of special-needs organizations is helpful. AIC-CURE and the church partners make whatever intervention is possible and follow up with a long-term plan for the child and his or her parents that includes ongoing counseling, training, and vocational and educational support.

Local church pastors are trained in counseling and on topics related to the needs of children with various types of physical disability. This training is then taken to the community through programs that offer information and education to community workers and families of children with disabilities. Through this ongoing community involvement they are able to reach many children before certain disabilities become permanent. This is especially helpful in cases where children are severely burned; communities become aware that rehabilitation is possible, and disability can be minimized if the child is helped quickly. The relationship that the church builds with the community also gives them the opportunity to make the proper follow-up and evaluation of the child and the family's progress after the operations.

The AIC-CURE Children's Hospital has been successful in reaching children, especially in rural areas where children with disabilities are usually neglected or kept away from social events. They do this through mobile clinics and evangelism efforts that are hosted by church partners. As well, the hospital has helped to raise awareness of issues related to children with disabilities through the testimonies of the thousands of families that have received Christian love and care from the hospital and its trained church partners.

The faith-based hospital, in partnership with the church-based community effort, has certainly made a tremendous contribution to children with disabilities all over Kenya, as well as created greater awareness and understanding in rural communities of the needs and potential of these "special children." This has created the opportunity for advocacy at national and even international levels.

WE MUST SHARE

Pastor and author Rick Warren speaks on the topic of stewardship by the Church, particularly stewardship of its influence. He notes that "God does not give you influence for your own ego, popularity or fame. The purpose of influence is to speak up for people who have no influence."[2] King David's son Solomon prayed that God would give the king His judgments and his son His righteousness, so that "He will bring justice to the poor . . . He will save the children of the needy . . ." (Psalm 72:4 NKJV). In the same vein, a modern-day King Solomon would use his influence to be a voice for the children with disabilities who have unique needs and secret pain, and would recognize those who have emotional needs that are just as great as their physical needs. We are called to speak out on their behalf and to share in their suffering. We must be the voice for the voiceless. We must share about the needs of children who are disabled or challenged in some way.

In both Rwanda and northern Uganda I have had the difficult privilege of serving children who have been broken and even mutilated by war and genocide. Many of these children were abducted from their homes, forced into battle as child soldiers and regarded as psychological misfits in their communities after their return. These children were exposed to heinous crimes that have scarred them for life. They suffered in silence, and much of the world turned its back on them until some incredible voices began to raise the banner for these voiceless children. Rwandan ambassador to Sweden, Jacqueline Mukangira, has used her influence and her voice since she survived three months of near starvation hiding in bushes outside the capital, Kigali, during the 1994 genocide in Rwanda. With the Anglican archbishop of Rwanda Emmanuel Kolini, she led programs for these children in Rwanda following the genocide, was elected to parliament, and eventually commissioned as an ambassador because of her voice for the voiceless women and children. Together we traveled all over Rwanda and appeared on numerous TV broadcasts, sharing with churches and communities about how to respond to these children in crisis.

Sharing with Children Who Suffer

Why do children suffer? Good question! I must have asked myself this question a thousand times during the four years I cared for our adopted Kenyan baby, Joy Namaritohi, who was living and dying with AIDS. I know I was not the first to ask. The human part of us cries to understand how a God of love could allow children to suffer. In fact, the truly human side of us tries to deny that such suffering even exists. Yet the truth is that children do suffer from physical disability and disease, the emotional pain of rejection, and feelings of loneliness. The question becomes: "What can we do when children suffer such pain?"

Acknowledge the Suffering of Children

Within a biblical context, I believe that the first step that we as Christians are called to take is to acknowledge the suffering of children—to take our heads out of the proverbial sand of busyness and daily routine, and to acknowledge the worldwide suffering of children. How long will their cries go unheard? Or worse yet, will they stop crying for lack of help and hope? Jesus acknowledged children everywhere He went and made several references to them. He knew their problems and on many occasions simply touched them and healed them, even raising them from the dead. He valued their presence and acknowledged their needs, as seen in Mark 10:16 when Jesus picked the children up into His arms, put His hands upon them and blessed them.

Seek to Understand or at Least Accept the Purpose of Suffering

Once we have stopped turning our heads from the pain of suffering children and shielding our faces from their cries, we must seek to understand the pain that they feel and to accept whatever purpose it may have in their life. This is a call for Christians to not only hear the cries of such children, but also to listen to their thoughts and feelings. The only thing worse than suffering is to suffer alone. Mark 10 tells us that parents brought their children to Jesus to have Him touch them. Just as Jesus took those children into His arms, He wants to bring children today close enough to hear their heartbeats and to know their dreams and hopes. The needs of suffering children are just the same as other children; they need to be loved and accepted unconditionally. They need and deserve respect and compassion. Whether their pain comes from years of living misunderstood with a physical disability or from losing a mother to AIDS or from sexual abuse and exploitation, they need to be listened to. They deserve to participate in education, in church activities and in the decisions that affect their lives. And, if we bring them close enough, they can help us to bring the help and healing that they and so many others like them so desperately need. Jesus not only acknowledged their pain, He also held them close, listened to them and encouraged their acceptance. "For the kingdom of God belongs to such as these," He declared (Mark 10:14b).

Make a Commitment and Take Action

After we have acknowledged the suffering of children and made an effort to accept the purpose of that suffering, we must make a commitment to play our God-given role, whatever that may be. "Do not merely listen to the word, and so deceive yourselves. Do what it says" (James 1:22). Christ, the model caregiver, influenced His brother James to write, "Religion that God our Father accepts as pure and faultless is this: to look after orphans and widows in their distress" (James 1:27a). Our action may come in the form of prayer, which seeks God's guidance on how to help these young people, or it may come in actual service to these suffering children—but regardless of the action taken, the caregiver will never be the same. Touching a suffering child is touching the heart of God Himself, and you will never be the same again. It can make you a very bitter person who seeks to blame God for the suffering, or it can make you a better servant who seeks to come alongside more suffering children.

Develop Our Caregiving Skills

The Bible shows us a perfect example of the best Christian caregiver of all time: Jesus Christ Himself. Jesus reached out and touched people in unique ways that brought healing, not only to the body but also to the spirit and mind. He was the true father of "holistic" care, as He showed us how to build relationships that come alongside another, especially battered and broken children. He reflected various qualities of a good caregiver in His own relationships. We see in Matthew 5:1–12 that Jesus *encouraged* others when He blessed people and helped them to put their pain and disappointment in perspective. In John 3:1–20, He *listened* with His ears and with His heart. He heard what Nicodemus was saying, as well as what he was not saying. He knew what each word and action meant and was keen to notice clues that would help him understand. In Mark 4, Jesus *taught* some of life's most important lessons on faith and later went on to *challenge* the disciples with questions that were meant to help them think, develop and remember the lesson for life. For instance, when the terrible storm arose and they all feared for their lives, Jesus asked them why they were afraid and how it was that they had no faith. He even *confronted* wrong thinking in Matthew 15:1–9 when He spoke emphatically to the scribes and Pharisees.

In John 4, Jesus not only listened and confronted, but He also *gave hope* to a desperate woman who needed to be forgiven. A woman hopelessly lost in sin was able to see her opportunity for new life. It gave her hope and changed her life. Philippians 2 tells us that Christ was totally *committed* to His work of reconciliation. He was *humble*. He was a perfect example of a Christian caregiver.

Continue Learning from Experience and from Others

Caregivers must be dedicated to a lifetime of learning. We must make the effort to understand the needs of children with disabilities and to develop skills that will help us provide the holistic care that can bring hope and healing. God created children as complete individuals, full of hope and destined to reach their highest potential. One of the least understood needs of children is the psychological impact from the devastating experiences of trauma and disability. When a child feels hungry, we can give him food; if he has a headache, we may give him a pain reliever; but what do we do when a child is depressed, suffering from anxiety or having suicidal thoughts? Perhaps we can learn the answer from listening to children and young people themselves.

Suffering is not new to the African continent, but it has taken a clearly gruesome turn in the recent conflicts and wars, particularly in the Great Lakes region. Spending time with the young people of Africa has been most educational. How these children and young people survived and are actually functional has earned them respect worldwide. A recent international magazine cover read, "Africa: The Hopeless Continent," and even though the real focus of the article was the deplorable economic situation, it stirred the hearts and minds of African young people. There are young people from every nation on the continent who do *not* believe that Africa is hopeless and are out to prove as much. We know that in order to give hope to the nations we must listen to our young people; even the most vulnerable and desperate ones have their stories as well. We must value their thoughts and give them every opportunity to express themselves. Just being heard is indeed therapeutic in this hostile environment where children have been sidelined. We need interventions that are participatory in nature. This is the source of strength of some recent efforts in psychosocial support for African children and youth.

We must share in the suffering of these children and do everything in our power to help them. All children have a right to the best possible standard of care, and that includes children with disabilities. It should be noted that, in most African countries, the policies that relate to child rights must be aggressively pursued and implemented because the priorities for child care have been misplaced in many previous governments and social structures. We must continue to speak for those who do not have a voice, and continue to advocate for the rights of children living with disabilities. We must share in their suffering and do what we can to make things better for them.

WE MUST CARE

What is involved in Christian caregiving? Christian caregiving is unique because it requires us to have a Christ-like attitude toward children. As well, it is to be based on Christian principles guided by the Word of God. It promotes the spiritual development of the child and recognizes the fact that children need to know God and be confident in His care. Christian caregiving is Christ-centered, in that our focus of hope and healing is in Christ. According to Scripture, Jesus is the model caregiver and has given us a wonderful example.

Christian caregiving must follow the example of Jesus Christ himself and the things He did while He was here on earth some 2,000 years ago. Earlier we looked at the story of the Good Samaritan in Luke 10 to remind us that God expects us to show our Christianity by our love and care for one another. The story of the Good Samaritan also provides us with a model for Christian caregiving.

The caregiver in that story was a Samaritan, from a tribe not particularly accepted by the Jewish community. Yet he was willing to provide emergency relief of drinking water and first aid to one of those who looked down on him. We see that he initiated the caregiving process because of the compassion that he felt in his spirit. That compassion is a gift from God that is essential for every caregiver. Compassion gave the Samaritan the ability to be effective as a caregiver by showing acceptance and love to the injured man.

Once the Good Samaritan had assessed the situation and offered the needed first aid, he came up with an action plan for the complete healing of the injured man. The caregiver knew that the man's injuries would need time to heal and that he would need proper food and rest. He was not satisfied to give only emergency care but insisted on a long-term plan that could bring total healing to the man. This is the real duty of the Christian caregiver. We must look beyond the crisis need for more long-term solutions that will give the person a hope for the future.

Christian caregiving should seek ways of truly curing the person, which means seeing the person through the crisis by means of a plan that will lead to complete healing spiritually, physically and emotionally. Not only did the Good Samaritan offer the man an opportunity for physical healing, but the care and love he showed convinced the man that he was valuable in the sight of man and God. Many people do not know their value to God or to society. They grope in depression and despair with nothing to hold on to. One act of kindness can change a life for all eternity, and the wonderful thing is that what the caregiver did was seen by many and was a testimony that gave courage to others to be caregivers as well.

The Good Samaritan's love and care for the injured man was able to be seen even by the religious leaders who had passed the helpless man earlier in the day. Christian caregiving causes others to want to follow the example and provide care to the needy—we say it is contagious. The care that was given was also correct: the proper treatment based on the need of the injured man. The caregiver did not provide what was not needed but assisted the man based on his actual need. He gave individual care that matched the man's actual need. The Good Samaritan was creative in his approach. When he saw that the man could not walk, he utilized his donkey to carry the man. He used his available resources.

Finally, we notice that the care of the Good Samaritan was consistent and reliable. Not only did he give the initial treatment, but he also followed up on the man's need for healing and recovery. He returned to check on the man's progress and inquire what his further needs may be. He faithfully carried out his duty as he had promised. Many times in our complicated and busy lives it is difficult to have effective follow-up for people with special needs, but it is essential. To begin well is good, but to finish well is even better. We must see that our caregiving follows an organized process and that we monitor it long enough to assure its success. The people we help will need encouragement all along the way and hope for every tomorrow.

Holistic Child Care

Christian caregiving should also be "holistic," seeing the child as a whole, three-part being with a body, mind and spirit. We have seen that Christ Himself was very holistic in His caregiving. Holistic programs not only include counseling with psychological support but also concrete help with social, spiritual and physical needs as well.

For years a number of organizations have been making great efforts and using millions of dollars to help children worldwide, and yet more children than ever (particularly in Africa) are dying of preventable diseases, are engaged in hazardous employment, and are exposed to war and violence, not to mention the millions infected and affected by HIV/AIDS. The most relevant child-based organizations in this day and age are taking a much more holistic approach that is also participatory in nature. Feeding children is simply not enough and eventually only adds to the vicious cycle of poverty. Therefore, community-based programs that develop significant relationships with family units and contribute to the physical, spiritual, emotional and educational well-being of the child are proving to be the most effective models.

As local churches and communities learn how to invest in their children, they are able to realize the fruit of that effort as the children invest back into their communities through participation in educational and development programs. This is not a new discovery, but has been resisted for years because holistic development of children has been seen as an overwhelming job for any one organization. As networking and partnership are being made by organizations ministering to children, the possibilities increase that we may be able to work together to make a much greater and more sustainable contribution by empowering the children of these communities.

It is for this reason that all aspects of a child's development be understood (not only the physical needs but the spiritual, social, emotional and educational needs as well) and that the needs of children be met in ways that empower them to help others.

How Can We Provide Care?

There are several models of care that Christians in Africa are using to provide compassionate, holistic care to children, including church-based community day care, church-based and school-based residential care, family-based foster care, adoption, and home-based care. It is important to note that the choice of caregiving model is influenced by such factors as the child's age, family support (for example, parents, older siblings, grandparents, and so on), the child's unique needs, and available resources. These models of care must also take into consideration the needs of children with disabilities, because in any ministry to children in Africa the caregiver is certain to find lonely and vulnerable children with disabilities. It is not uncommon to come across such children as the church reaches out to children in general within any given community.

Church-Based Community Day Care

Church-based community day care reaches children in poverty-driven areas. The children may be living with parents, relatives or guardians who may not able to provide them with their basic needs. Community day care programs provide children with such basic needs as food, informal education and medical care, and may provide work or income-generating opportunities for the parents/caregivers of the children. Such programs may also support income-generating activities to help the community take care of its children, including shared, sustainable income-generating projects. I have seen this model used most effectively in the war-torn areas of northern Uganda where thousands of children attend school under mango trees and receive a breakfast and late lunch before they return to their IDP (internally displaced persons) camps, villages or population centers.

Church-Based Residential Care

The best option is for children to be able to access all the services they require while living in their own families in their own communities. But some areas of Africa are so remote that this becomes very difficult for children with special needs who may not be able to even begin the process of education and vocational training until they are young adults.

Church-based residential care, as the name suggests, is care for children in a residential setting operated by the church, where their basic needs such as food, shelter, clothing and education, as well as spiritual, social and medical care are provided. In some cases the children attend school in nearby local schools, depending on the location, while in others a school/educational program is part of the residential care program.

The children are looked after by one or more primary caregivers, with some staff residing in the house with them. In many cases in Africa the caregivers may be widows or women who lost their families in conflict. It is recommended that church-based residential care programs maintain a maximum of 12 children per caregiver in order to provide more direct contact with the children. This is in contrast to institutional care, where there are many more children and fewer caregivers. Church-based residential care should be child-focused and family-oriented so the focus is on the needs of the child rather than the adult, and so that the child can benefit from the family support. Ideally, children should have both male and female caregivers in order to provide a mother figure and a father figure and to encourage a more complete family setting.

While the government may control the standards of care, the church usually decides the program, employs the needed staff and oversees the project. In many cases the church provides the land, helps with the construction work for the needed facilities, and offers its services in other child-care-related work. For example, church members may cook for the children, clean their residence, bathe the younger children, work in the vegetable gardens, teach Bible lessons, take the children to health facilities as needed, read with them, transport them to church, sing with them, pray with them and help them visit their families if possible. In some cases, residential child care may take a more traditional approach, where traditional homes are built into what is called a children's village. This entails high church participation whereby church members donate land, plant gardens, establish income-generating projects and volunteer to teach in the school program. The church congregation takes responsibility for orphaned children, and church members mentor the children.

My daughter Reah is the director of a church-based residential and community program for children with and without disabilities called Morning Star Children's Ministries. Reah understands the children with disabilities well because she was born with severe learning disabilities. She was reared in Kenya and was able to learn several languages, but to this day is unable to spell in any of them. Reah's home education was a family affair, and most of our school days were spent using sidewalk chalk to draw and write in big letters and pictures all over the concrete floors of our village home. I used sand, chalk, tall trees and lots of hugs to help Reah learn to read and write and eventually be able to function on grade level when she entered high school. Reah graduated from the famous Rift Valley Academy with honors and the respect of every teacher and student there, as well as overcame incredible obstacles to attend Liberty University. As the director of Morning Star Children's Ministries, she helps vulnerable orphans and children with special needs to know God's love firsthand.

Case Study: Morning Star Children's Ministries, Kiambu, Kenya

By Reah Marie Githaiga, Director, Morning Star Children's Ministries

Reverend Philip Githaiga founded Morning Star Children's Ministries, a church-based residential and community program for orphans and vulnerable children in 2007, a year before we married. Philip was a man of great faith, and served children in crisis with all of his strength until his untimely death in 2009.

I grew up as the daughter of American missionaries who served children for almost 30 years in Kenya, Uganda, Rwanda and Haiti. When my husband died, I was able to put to use my years of experience caring for African children in crisis to organize and train a team of young Kenyan caregivers for the ministry's community and residential child care programs. Running this ministry is an incredible task and not something that any one person can accomplish, so I started building a team of well-trained Kenyans to support and guide the ministry. Our board of directors is a group of mature Christians who have helped shape the direction of the ministry through the difficult time of Philip's passing.

Our mission is to empower and equip the most vulnerable children, including those with physical disabilities, through the strengthening of their spiritual, social, educational, economic and emotional development. We currently we have 48 children. Children who are between the ages of 2 and 16 are considered for the program based on a full study of their familial background in cooperation with the local children's department. Priority is given to children who have lost both parents, street children, and those living with HIV.

Morning Star Children's Ministries is a mission to children that exists specifically to promote healthy, integrated children who are fully developed to their highest potential. Our objectives for the children incorporate the core facets of development (physical, psychological, spiritual, social and cognitive):

- Promote physical growth with nutritional food, proper health care, clean clothing, warm shelter and a loving environment.

- Promote emotional wholeness and good attitudes in individual children through regular counseling.

- Promote spiritual growth through a Christ-centered daily program and practice.

- Encourage good interpersonal relationships by creating a conducive social environment.

- Offer individual education that is flexible, practical and effective.

- Motivate all children in learning the necessary life skills that equip them for a vocation.

At Morning Star we use a holistic resilience model that allows us to build on the strengths of the children in each of these core areas while reducing their vulnerability to the trauma of the difficult life that they find themselves in. While providing for their physical needs we also have exciting Sunday schools, Bible clubs, discipleship and daily devotions to help strengthen their spiritual development and rebuild their confidence in God. They also attend school and learn other educational and social skills as part of the community. The children live in a family atmosphere and help with the daily chores of caring for their goats, rabbits and chickens, which contributes to their emotional development. The children help grow their own vegetables and even share all the extras with other children's homes and the needy in the community. A fish pond that is in the works will also help to provide much needed nutrition for the children and provide yet another source of economic sustainability through the sale of extra fish.

Counseling helps some of the children, especially in cases where the entire family is affected by the death of parents and where hostile relatives have chased them from their rightful homes. We do our best to keep these children together and reintegrate them into their communities and help them fight for their rights to their homes and property. In cases where children can be kept in their communities, we open livelihood and savings opportunities for them in order to help them have the care that they need.

As the director, I work with my managers and other caregivers to work hand in hand with the local Children's Department and the Ministry of Gender and Children Affairs and to promote the development goals of the Kiambu district and the African Charter on the Rights and Welfare of the Child. All children at Morning Star have been informed of their rights and responsibilities, and we encourage them to participate in all decisions that will affect their lives.

The incredible accomplishments of God's special children are the most powerful commentary on what really *can* be done when we work together as churches and communities for the glory of God and the good of the children He loves.

School-Based Residential Care

School-based residential care has similar characteristics to church-based residential care, except that care is provided within a school setting. School-based residential care is becoming increasingly popular in some places. In Kenya, for example, there has been an increase over this past decade in the number of "special schools" that are able to assist children with special needs.

These "special schools" are boarding schools that are developed specifically for children with disabilities. Children live at the school while school is in session and return to their communities to visit their families or other caregivers during school holidays. These schools provide residential care for children of various disabilities, including the physically disabled, mentally disabled, blind and deaf. Such schools have been very helpful in meeting the educational needs of children with disabilities, and many of the schools are operated by faith-based organizations so that the spiritual needs of the children are also met.

Case Study: The Salvation Army Thika School for the Blind

For years, faith-based organizations have been leading the way in providing care and education for children with disabilities in Africa and in giving children the opportunity to grow and develop their God-given talents to the best of their abilities. The Salvation Army is a faith-based organization that has done a tremendous job of helping children with disabilities become productive citizens, equipped with important life skills and vocational skills. The Salvation Army has several schools for children with disabilities in Kenya, including the Thika School for the Blind, which provides school-based residential care. The Thika School was opened in 1946 and has more than 200 students who are totally blind.

The Thika School offers early childhood development for children with disabilities and provides a solid foundation for further learning skills throughout primary education. For students with multiple disabilities, they teach basic living skills, literacy and outdoor activities such as raising chickens and rabbits. The students participate in games and sports activities as well as Scouts and Girl Guides. These activities encourage integration of the students and further develop their discipline and confidence. The Christian Union is the strongest of the school clubs, and encourages the students' faith in Jesus Christ to be strengthened and shared among the students and throughout the community.

Since there is no specific curriculum for special education in Kenya, the school produces its own special books for their students and even revises national examinations, such as the examination for the Kenya Certificate of Primary Education, so their students can participate. In fact, in recent exams the Thika School outscored 15 "normal" schools in their municipality. According to the head teacher, Steven K. Gitau, "This is why blind children don't need our sympathy; they simply need opportunity."

Over half of the school's full-time teaching staff is totally blind. The school has a number of teachers who are pursuing diplomas and bachelor degrees in special education at Kenyatta University and the Kenya Institute of Special Education. In addition to the work on the campus with children who are blind, the Thika School facilitates training for preschool teachers on methods of working with children who are visually impaired. Training takes place in such rural areas as Samburu, Kitui, Isiolo, Narok and Kajiado. This outreach enables the school to create community awareness of the opportunities available for children with visual impairment and other children with disabilities.

Teacher training is an important need for school-based residential care, as well as other special-needs educational contexts. There is now a global push to integrate special students into "regular" schools where possible, but there is still an extreme lack of special-needs teachers trained to accommodate these students and their special educational needs. Schools such as the Kenya Institute of Special Education and other private colleges have trained hundreds of special-needs teachers who are working with children all over the country. These are tremendous teachers with compassion and care for special children who are in need of education, understanding, the unconditional acceptance of a significant adult, and a friendly environment to allow them to develop and grow to reach their potential.

Case Study: A Special-Needs Teacher in Kenya

By Patricia Ndururi, Karundas, Kenya

When I was six years old, we got a baby boy in our family. Having the first boy in the family was a change for us girls, but we were excited. But as baby Peter grew, we began to notice some differences. When it was time for Peter to crawl, he used his knees and the back of his wrists. He eventually learned how to feed and bathe himself, but he continued to walk on his knees and use the back of his wrists to balance himself.

Time went by until I had to go to high school. I knew that my brother was disabled, but I had absolutely no idea what to do for him. I heard other people say that it was a curse, and this worried me because this meant that our family would be outcast. Many people pointed fingers at us, and very few showed any compassion. At school, everyone knew that I had a brother with a disability, and this was also disturbing to me, but all I could do was pray. One day a missionary family came to our village and began helping vulnerable youth. It was then that I began to understand that God had a purpose for my brother. He was able to join the informal classes at the missionary school located in another city, and he roomed with the missionary's son Jonathan so he wouldn't have to make the long journey every day. The missionaries loved and accepted Peter, and he learned to read and write in Swahili and English. Such acceptance of Peter and his disability made a huge impression on our community.

I later joined the Mt. Kenya Home where I helped to teach the children. It was there that I found children with not only physical disabilities but other types of disabilities as well. During this time I began to desire for God to use me in the lives of these special children. He answered my prayer and gave me the opportunity to attend the Special Education and Professional Studies College in Nairobi. I learned so much about working with children with special learning difficulties, including the mentally disabled, visually disabled, hearing disabled, physically and neurologically disabled, learning disabled, and the behaviorally and emotionally disturbed. These studies were followed by student teaching in a school for the mentally disabled in Nakuru town where my eyes and heart were opened and I developed a positive outlook toward children with special needs.

Being a special-needs teacher is very important to me because of how much it means to the children. When I saw how much my own brother could learn, I decided to try to help other children like him get help early enough so that they could accomplish much in their lives. Although special education is somewhat new in Kenya, I have learned a lot. As a special education teacher I help identify the problem areas and teach the children. I also coordinate the referral of their needs to various professionals and specialists. I help campaign for their rights and advocate for the disabled because they need to be helped, cared for and spoken for. I also learned how to deal with behavioral issues since the children may become aggressive in the classroom.

In my special-needs class, most of the children have some learning difficulties due to their backgrounds or illnesses. As a teacher I love to help them communicate what they would like to become when they grow up so that the training we provide is geared towards helping them reach their dreams. One student, Paul, is a good example of the progress the children can make with proper help and support. He is now learning to talk and has gained a lot of confidence by telling stories to the class. He only has one eye and is disfigured, but his confidence and self-esteem are growing daily. He is also improving on memory work in class. Another student, Pingas, needs continuous follow-up so that he can perform well; he wants to be a pilot when he grows up!

I have found that my students with special needs are very sensitive to the needs of other children in the class and seem to grow spiritually with every challenge. The children love to hear stories from the Bible and love to hear about Jesus. I enjoy counseling parents and regular teachers on how to love, educate and accept these children with disabilities and how to have a positive attitude toward them.

Family-Based Care

Family-based care, also known as foster care, consists of temporary care of children in a family setting by nonbiological parents. The child's name is not changed to the foster family's name. In the Western context, the government pays for the child care, the caregivers are trained in foster care, and care is provided by different "foster parents" until the child is 18. In many cases Christian families are able to extend care and nurture to children who would otherwise be in very desperate situations.

In the African context, **family-based** care means that relatives or close family friends bring a child into their family and provide care. Such care often follows the death of the parent(s) or their inability to provide the basic needs for the child's proper development, especially education. There is little or no training or money for these parents/caregivers. Many times the care becomes long-term because the child has nowhere else to go, which is why the child came to the family in the first place. Family-based care is widely used by Christian missions to promote the child's development within a family environment, but it should always be well supervised and monitored to prevent abuse of the child (including requiring the child to do more household duties than other children in the family).

Family-based care has been more successful in some parts of Africa than others. In Rwanda, for example, family-based care has been the most successful. There, adults have taken in children who have lost parents due to the genocide or HIV/AIDS and do their best to provide for their basic needs. Some of the caregivers are related to the children but many are not. The Rwandan government has encouraged people to take care of orphaned children within family settings in order to reduce the need for institutional care, which was otherwise becoming the norm in Rwanda. In Kenya, however, the system of family-based care for nonrelated children has so far not been very successful, mainly due to cultural issues such as land inheritance. It is even more difficult for a family to take on a child with special needs; therefore, most children with special needs end up in institutional care unless relatives are willing to care for the child. In many instances, family-based care consists of very old grandparents caring for grandchildren whose parents have succumbed to AIDS.

Adoption

Adoption is lifetime parental care for a child. The child is legally adopted as a member of the family and even acquires the family name. The child has equal rights as any other child in the family, and the adoptive parents are responsible for meeting the basic needs of the child until he or she reaches 18 years of age.

Adoption can be domestic or international. International adoption is becoming more and more popular globally as young Christian couples who want to make a difference in the life of an orphan travel to host countries to adopt needy children. However, international adoption is not recommended for everyone, and in fact it is very time consuming, difficult and expensive in most cases.

In Africa, developmentally challenged children are often abandoned. One such child was abandoned on a bus traveling from the town of Thika in Kenya. Named for his origin, "Thika" was taken to a hospital, and the hospital called me to see if I could help. When my daughter Rebecca and I reached the hospital, we found little Thika in a wire basket with the look of a two-year-old child but the body of a newborn. We also found two other abandoned children in that same hospital nursery that day: "Naro Moru" (who was named after the nearby town he came from) and another child who had been given the name "Central Hotel" for the place he had been abandoned. With the help of Christian adoption organizations such as Little Angels, all three of these children were adopted by loving Christian families and are doing beautifully with their new families and their new names. Little "Thika" is the pride and joy of his family, his school and his church.

Home-Based Care

Home-based care is the provision of care for people in their homes within the community, mainly in the form of medical and nutritional care and support. In the African context, home-based care is most valuable for people living with HIV/AIDS. Home-based care programs are mostly implemented by churches and community-based organizations. Such programs help to provide for the basic needs of children who are infected and affected. Some of the needs include medical kits and drugs, money, transportation and community volunteers who will give their time to visit the sick.

Home-based care can help families care for children within the community and complement and strengthen the family's ability to care for its children. The holistic care needed by the family may even include income-generating projects that enable the family to contribute substantially to the education and care of their child. For instance, in rural areas schools are few and are often far from where the children live. The transportation expense can be difficult for families of children with disabilities to afford. Educational support can prove invaluable, such as that provided by Christian organizations like Food for the Hungry who sponsor educational and other basic needs, enabling the children to remain in their biological families.

CONCLUSION

It is truly exciting to see how the hearts and minds of Christians across Africa have become open to children with special needs as they recognize them as the special people that God has created. Clearly, we cannot do everything, but we can all do something as we begin to know, to share and to care. It begins with a societal attitude of acceptance and love of special children and their families, and the making of every effort to connect them to the medical, spiritual, educational and vocational services available. These special children have dreams too, and we can help make their dreams come true, one smile at a time.

NOTES

The epigraph to part V appears in Jack Canfield, Mark Victor Hansen, Heather McNamara, and Karen Simmons, *Chicken Soup for the Soul: Children with Special Needs* (Deerfield Beach, FL: HCI, 2007), xvii. Poet Melissa Riggio was born with Down syndrome. She died on April 7, 2008, at the age of 20.

1. Richard Stearns, "Why the Church Is Called to Respond" (speech, "American Evangelicals Respond to the Global AIDS Crisis" conference, Washington, DC, June 11, 2003).

2. Rick Warren, "Prophetic Call: The Role of the Church" (speech, "American Evangelicals Respond to the Global AIDS Crisis" conference, Washington, DC, June 11, 2003).

CHAPTER SIXTEEN

ADVOCACY:

Give the Child a Mighty Voice

* * *

Marjorie McDermid

A MOTHER in Lesotho, southern Africa, visited the local school. The friendly teachers welcomed her until she mentioned that her child had disabilities. They said, "Do you think we will teach a child with disabilities? If the head teacher hears you, he will chase you away."

Disappointed, the mother returned to her home. What could she do? She sought out a teacher in the community and asked her to talk with the school about integration, to which the teacher agreed. The school rejected the teacher and sent her away also.

The determined mother tried a third strategy. This time she went to the chief and told him that, of the three schools in the area, one school was refusing to accept children with disabilities. The chief went to see the head teacher and threatened to report him to the Minister of Education. The head teacher was not dismayed. He did not care. "I don't want my school to teach stupid children," he said.

A few months later the chief contacted the mother and advised her to return to the school. A new head teacher had been appointed. She went to the school, and when she arrived she was overjoyed to find that four children with special needs were already included as students.

This simple but dramatic story vividly points up the importance of advocacy. In simplest terms advocacy means speaking up for a cause or a person. Being an advocate, however, may mean more than verbally speaking on behalf of someone. It may also require taking some positive action, especially in the case of a functionally or developmentally challenged child.

Advocacy for children with disabilities is necessary because society as a whole retains prejudices against those who have a mental or physical difference or handicap. The level of advocacy in more affluent and developed countries may differ from that of other areas of the world. But be assured, the child with a disability and his or her family need caring advocates regardless of their station in life, their financial advantages/disadvantages or religious orientation.

Scriptural Basis for Advocacy

Although the word *advocacy* rarely appears in most popular versions of the English Bible, the significance of its definition is evident.

The NIV translates Job 16:19 this way: "Even now my witness is in heaven; my advocate is on high." We know the advocate of whom Job spoke is Jesus Christ, for Job continues, "My intercessor is my friend as my eyes pour out tears to God; on behalf of a man he pleads with God as one pleads for a friend" (16:20–21).

Jesus speaks up for us to the Father. His right to be an advocate centers on the sacrifice of His own life as an efficacious offering to the Father for our sin. 1 John 2:1 records this fact, giving Christians one of our most prized promises. Here John says, "But if anybody does sin, we have an advocate with the Father—Jesus Christ, the Righteous One."

Foretelling Jesus' ministry, the prophet Isaiah said, "A bruised reed he will not break, and a smoldering wick he will not snuff out. In faithfulness he will bring forth justice; he will not falter or be discouraged till he establishes justice on earth" (Isaiah 42:3–4a).

Jesus' ministry included speaking up and establishing justice for broken people. He backed His words with action. He announced Himself as an advocate who proclaimed not only the gospel but also deliverance for prisoners and sight for the blind (Luke 4:18–19). He had the power not only to proclaim these benefits but also to produce them, which He did. Comparing His love for children as stressed in the Gospels and the record of His ministry to children who were ill or even proclaimed dead, Jesus can clearly be seen as an advocate for the child dealing with disablement.

Advocacy and the Value of a Child

Changing the attitudes of individuals, church bodies, communities and governments will require the advocate to have a clear understanding of the value of the child who is challenged by a handicap.

The way we value other humans has a lot—perhaps everything— to do with how we treat them. If we value something or someone, we will commit to that thing or that person. To the extent that we value persons, we will push their cause and speak up for them. An important part of advocacy, then, is teaching people to value the special-needs child, because attitudes change when values change.

Attitudes Change When Values Change

To effect change in attitudes, values and norms, advocacy must have an educational component. Attitudinal change requires information and understanding. Firsthand knowledge produces the most dramatic change. Getting people into action and introducing them personally to the target group or individual will bring about, in most cases, a change of attitude.

Serving as a church deaconess some years ago, I was asked to assist in a Bible Club at a local home for children with Down syndrome. I remember well the fear I felt. How could I communicate with them? What if I did not understand what they said? How should I address them? (Was there a way out of this assignment?)

On my first encounter I found that, besides lively music and a suitable Bible story, I needed to have lots of hugs ready for these friendly, loving kids who listened, sang and clapped in joyous participation. I learned the truth of Proverbs 11:17a: "Those who are kind benefit themselves." Also, I lost what might have been a lifelong fear of "different" children.

I learned another valuable lesson too: when their wills are crossed, these children can also be angry and ungrateful. They are not so different after all.

An additional important area of advocacy for the child with special needs involves training other children to have patience, treat with respect and show kindness to the child with an impairment. A functionally challenged child feels keenly the rejection and ridicule often meted out by other children. Frequently, getting to know this child is all it takes for another child to become a friend and, in turn, an advocate. Rejection turns to respect and unconcern to compassion when these children are seen as human instead of disabled, different or even ugly.

Educators tell us that teaching someone to have an attitude change is the most difficult of all changes to achieve. Unlike training for knowledge, understanding or to gain a skill, attitudinal training takes more patience and expertise. The old adage is true: "A man convinced against his will is of the same opinion still." The mind-set and will of the attitudinal learner(s) must be touched. Sometimes a change in the person's moral compass is required.

Advocates striving for attitude change have a difficult but not impossible work to do. "This is probably the area most lacking in all societies I have encountered," says Mary Gibson, who has lived and worked many years in a number of cultures and is the mother of a child with a disability, now a young adult.

Attitude toward Justice

"Speak up for those who cannot speak for themselves, for the rights of all who are destitute. Speak up and judge fairly; defend the rights of the poor and needy" (Proverbs 31:8–9).

Justice does not necessarily call for *Christian* love and compassion or kindness. Justice is the child's entitlement to the same rights as any other child. But often people must change their attitudes toward those with disabilities for justice to be achieved. As long as parents, educators, police officers, governments and society itself see these children as not worthy of justice, they will not provide justice. Advocates must convince those who would harm or deprive these children that they are humans worthy to be judged fairly and to receive justice.

Children who live with some physical or mental challenge, as all other children, should be afforded the right to:

- survive
- be respected and accepted
- be loved
- be cared for
- be protected from harmful influences, abuse and exploitation
- participate fully in family, cultural and social life insofar as their capabilities allow
- be educated
- live a productive life
- reach their full potential

> Where these children are being denied any of these things, advocates need to speak up to defend those who cannot defend themselves.

Attitude toward Protection

Children who have disabilities are not immune to abuse and neglect. Indeed, they are sometimes subject to violence and cruel abandonment. In these pages you will read of many ways in which children who are born mentally or physically challenged are mistreated. These children are vulnerable to abuse from those who would take advantage of their handicap and use them for monetary gain—from unprincipled parents to would-be teachers to outright crime figures. Advocacy plays a big role in providing protection for these weak, helpless ones.

A further concern is for the unborn child. With today's modern technology, deformities can be detected in unborn children. These children are highly subject to killing by abortion or to not being allowed to live at birth. If the unborn are fully human, as we believe they are, then to promote the abortion or death of the handicapped from the womb is no different morally than murdering the already-born child. Advocates in this arena must be armed with strong convictions of the God-given rights of every unborn child, regardless of his or her potential abilities or disabilities.

WHO CAN BE AN ADVOCATE?

A worker's business card introduced her as a "child advocate." Someone looking at it asked, "Oh, are you a lawyer?" Far from being a lawyer, she simply cares about children and works for their welfare, protection and care in any way she can. Advocacy can be on a professional level or an informal, personal level. Advocates may be individuals who have compassion for the child as their main weapon. Agencies, governments and churches may also be effective and powerful instruments of advocacy.

Clergy and the Church

If any organization or group of people should bear responsibility for the child who suffers a disability, the organized church and the clergy should take first place. We need to hear the word and obey the word, as James admonishes (James 1:22). Mostly we need to obey, for how often have we heard Jesus say, "Whoever welcomes this little child in my name welcomes me; and whoever welcomes me welcomes the one who sent me. For it is the one who is least among you all who is the greatest" (Luke 9:48)? Even if we think of the child who is blind or deaf or has autism, cerebral palsy or . . . as having the least potential in life, Jesus' word to us is strong: "he is the greatest" among you. This child deserves the best spiritual nurture, health care and education. When we advocate to give him these services, we welcome and serve Jesus and our heavenly Father.

As an advocate, the church, at the least, can:

- Make sure the child gets the necessary and appropriate spiritual nurture.

1. Arrange for one-on-one help for the child during Sunday school and church.
2. If the child is unable to get to church, arrange for someone to take "church" to the child/family in some appropriate way.

- Be an advocate in tough situations at school, with social services or with legal authorities who are not caring.

- Use your influence in getting needed financial aid.

- Encourage congregants to help in getting the child to doctor appointments and so on, when help is needed.

- A marital support group for parents, phone calls and personal visits are some ways of offering hope and encouragement to the parents/caregivers on a regular basis—an important way of speaking up for the benefit of the child.

- Sponsor special events for these children, perhaps in consortium with other churches.

Government and Private Agencies

Many nations have departments or agencies in their governments that, at least ostensibly, deal with the rights of persons who are disabled, including children. As long as government agencies function with integrity and compassion, they are helpful. Sometimes, however, only when some outside organization or individual advocate implements legal force will governments provide what the law allows.

Private agencies, and those run by or affiliated with a church or mission, are formed to help parents/caregivers in their quest for the best of care and provision for the children with handicaps. Finding the appropriate venue of help for your particular need may take some research or prior knowledge.

Today the Internet is a mighty tool for finding and contacting agencies, but parents/caregivers may not have the knowledge or equipment for, or be skilled in, surfing the Web. Advocates can provide valuable information, recommend the child/family needing help and perhaps do some of the leg work to help the usually overloaded caregivers get assistance.

Individuals

All of us who would be advocates must be willing to get involved and stay involved, probably at personal cost. But for our encouragement, the God of the universe promises to guide us, strengthen us and satisfy our own needs.

If you do away with the yoke of oppression, with the pointing finger and malicious talk, and if you . . . satisfy the needs of the oppressed, then your light will rise in the darkness, and your night will become like the noonday. The LORD will guide you always; he will satisfy your needs in a sun-scorched land and will strengthen your frame. You will be like a well-watered garden, like a spring whose waters never fail . . . You will be called Repairer of Broken Walls . . . (Isaiah 58:9b–12)

Parents and Family Members

Probably none are better equipped to be advocates for special-needs children than the parents and family members who have learned how to care for and, when necessary, fight for their disadvantaged loved ones. Having overcome any sense of shame or stigma they felt in bearing these children, often especially hard for fathers, they have coped with the acceptance factor. They have learned, likely through painful experience, the importance of knowing the rights of their physically/mentally challenged children and how to receive and use existing services. They understand the importance of saying no when something is being proposed that will be detrimental. These experiences prepared them to advise and empower other parents to pursue justice for their children in like circumstances.

Sometimes parents find it easier to receive advocacy from another parent than from a professional. With that in mind, advocate parents and family members may become the stepping-stones for other parents/caregivers to accept help from professional advocates.

Family support groups make excellent vehicles for training parents and family members as advocates for their own as well as other children. These "trained" advocates are empowered to liaison between their "special" children and the professionals whose services are needed (for example, teachers, medical caregivers and social servants). A parents association may be set up for the purpose of lobbying for the rightful treatment of their children.

The Children Themselves

Children should also be empowered to speak for themselves. Often they have no voice in decisions made about them. Whenever possible, their input should be sought, and decisions should be made with their desires in view. Obviously the age and mental capability of the child will help determine how efficacious his or her opinion will be, but the child's viewpoint should never be ignored.

Medical Caregivers

Blessed are the parents whose child's medical attendants do not view the child with a disability as nonhuman, whether born or unborn. Medical caregivers who adopt the attitude and belief that a child with a disability is fully human can have a huge influence on the life and well-being of the child through advocacy. These professionals take the responsibility, even though it may not be required of them, to make sure this child's physical and mental health needs are fully met.

Some of the suggestions below will seem obvious and required of medical workers in developed countries, but workers elsewhere may need to be made aware of the opportunities.

- For the unborn child: Because amniocentesis and other tests now make it possible to detect physical and mental abnormalities in the unborn child, parents may be advised, not only by the medical profession but also by well-meaning family and friends, to abort the child. How important to have the advice and encouragement of one such as Dr. C. Everett Koop, renowned pediatrician and former U.S. surgeon general. In his book *The Right to Live, the Right to Die* he says:

    > *Our obligation in such circumstances is to find alternatives for the problems our patients face. I don't consider death an acceptable alternative. With our technology and creativity, we are merely at the beginning of what we can do educationally and in the field of leisure activities for such youngsters.*[1]

- Securing the right kinds of treatment may take advocacy on the part of a primary medical caregiver, making sure that every child who is coping with a disability has a medical "home."

- Assistance in obtaining financial aid may come through referrals (or in some countries, personal requests) from medical personnel to social services organizations or others in a position to help.

- Medical advocates can have a big voice in the development and coordination of efforts of various resources such as state agencies, educators, social workers, therapists, financial agents and caregivers.

- A child with a severe disability or one lacking adequate personal caregivers may need residential care, in which case the medical professional's referral may not only be necessary for placement but also influential in guaranteeing proper and adequate ongoing care.

- The medical caregiver has responsibility in determining the presence and extent of any physical, sexual and/or mental abuse and is influential in arranging for proper treatment and future safety of the child.

Educators

Educators can use their strong and persuasive voices in many ways to influence the parents, the community and the legal/social systems of the country on behalf of the child having special needs. We cite a few possibilities:

- Make sure the educational needs of the child are being met to the extent that his or her potential for learning can be challenged.

- Lobby for the inclusion of the child in school where this procedure is not a normal practice.

- Make the family aware of what the local school may be able to offer the child (for example, reading/speech therapy, and psychological and physical testing).

- Explore the learning needs of the child. (How can he learn best?)

- Point parents to social organizations and special events for the child (for example, Special Olympics, summer camp and churches that provide special classes and/or special events for these children).

- Be the liaison to connect families in the community who have special-needs children.

- Prepare parents for "after graduation" by recommending work options, workshops and further educational opportunities. Recommend the child for a suitable job.

Legal Advisors

The advocacy services of lawyers have influence, authority and leverage beyond what most of us can employ. Their voices are valuable in:

- Protecting the rights of a child as an individual in addition to the right to be protected from abuse and neglect.

- Focusing advocacy to empower the child to speak for himself/herself or directing an advocate to do so.

- Enhancing and supporting the child's relationship with others.

- Making the system work. (Most countries have some laws regarding how the disabled should be treated, but many times someone needs to be aware of the child's rights and enforce them.)

- Securing rights for the child who is disabled where no "system" exists.

- Formulating a mechanism to challenge negative decision making that could affect the child adversely.

Writers

We must never underestimate the capability of the computer in the hands of an advocate. Writing has many outlets today. From letters to the editor and local newspaper editorials to the Web, from radio and TV news to magazine articles, all forms of writing can be effective in bringing awareness and change of attitudes toward the child who has a disability.

You and I

If we are not among the people such as those cited above who have special opportunities and clout as advocates, we are not excluded from being effective advocates. Anyone can speak up for the child who is being disadvantaged and needs a voice. The process is as simple as seeing the need, researching the avenues where help can be obtained, using wisdom and having the courage to speak out. Then take the necessary steps to contact those people who have the authority and ability to give or get help and make them aware of the need.

A worker in France shows us one way to go about advocacy in high places. In her words:

> It was an interesting time, waiting for four hours in a room decorated with nude women, devils' heads and suggestive art shapes—this in the town hall. When we finally saw Mr. S—, I "buttered him up," saying how competent he was and that I was sure he was doing what he could. Then as I described the severe suffering the little boy has been through I wept and pleaded with him, as himself a father and grandfather, to do something. He read the letters we had brought [showing the abuse and need in the child's life] . . . When we left he promised me [he would] put the case on urgent.[2]

THE ADVOCATE'S TOOLS

For efficient and effective accomplishment, every task needs some tools, and advocacy is no exception.

Persistent Research

Seeking help for disadvantaged children may require prior research into such things as existing laws. What government programs are in place to assist families or individuals? Identifying these programs can prove difficult as the mother of a youth disadvantaged from birth has experienced:

> *We need ongoing work and perseverance. Our son is turning 22 this month, and he gets no assistance, nor can we claim him as a dependent. This week he needs to make a list of places where he has tried to get a job. If he can't find a job, the government might kick in something towards his room and board. Plenty of helps are available, but we struggle to find where those helps are.*

Getting a child into the school system is another occasion for persistent research. Obviously the level of ability in these children will vary, but they always take much more time and effort to train and often require one-on-one attention. Few school systems have funding to absorb that kind of need. Finding the school where adequate help is available obviously will be important and will take research.

A Sensitive Heart

The child's family may need a change of attitude toward what help is needed and toward receiving it. The tendency in families is often to treat the child who has a disability differently from the rest of the children. Often parents are forced to spend more time and give more attention to the child suffering a handicap, and different rules of discipline may also come into play. Even though the sibling(s), especially younger ones, have the need for such different treatment explained to them, they may be envious or jealous and/or become angry. Keeping a balance is difficult for the parents but important. The advocate will have an objective view and, with utmost sensitivity, find ways to encourage the parents to neither care obsessively for the "needy" child to the exclusion of the siblings nor banish the "different" one to the sidelines in favor of the "normal" children.

Receiving help is sometimes difficult for the family. They may feel a certain sense of shame and defensiveness, looking on a worker's attempts to be an advocate as an intrusion into their privacy. Or they may misunderstand the advocate's role. In such cases the advocate will need to earn his or her right to intervene for the child. (Advocacy and intervention are close buddies.) Providing advocacy to underprivileged families may require greater understanding of their cultural, social and religious needs.

Permit me a personal memory from many years ago when I was twelve years old. My brother (eight), my sister (four) and I were in the care of our father. Our mother was in a sanitarium for patients with tuberculosis. We lived in an isolated rural district in Canada. Concerned neighbors looked on and observed that, from their perspective, our little sister was being ne-glected. I find it hard to recollect how right or wrong they were. We were neither abused nor hungry, but perhaps sometimes unkempt and probably appeared neglected.

As a result of the neighborly and well-meant concern, something unusu-al for our community happened. A social worker from somewhere appeared at the door of our farmhouse to investigate the conditions. Though many of the details are now blurry to my memory, I shall never forget the look of anguish on my father's face nor the sense of panic I felt. I do not know what was going on in Dad's mind, but I was full of fear and resentment toward this intrusion. I remember lashing out angrily at this kind lady who doubt-less had only our well-being at heart. She left and never returned.

Advocates must cultivate dogged, caring perseverance in the face of re-jection, whether from family members or organizations. In the latter case, be prepared to have your telephone on hold for long intervals and your inquiry passed from one desk to another.

Successful advocates will be well informed, inspired by compassion and connected with the child/children. Compassion, patience and persistence will become their key characteristics, and their benchmark may be summed up in the words of Winston Churchill's famous speech: "Never, never, never give up."

Constant Awareness of the Value of the Child

The most important resource, however, will be the constant awareness of the value of that child. No matter how severe the child's disability, how hope-less the outlook of a despairing family or the cruelty of prejudices faced, the importance of that child to his or her heavenly Father and to you will be the driving force toward ultimate achievement of the advocate's goal: justice for the child with a disability.

NOTES

1. C. Everett Koop, *The Right to Live, the Right to Die* (Wheaton: Tyndale House, 1976), 51–52.

2. Janey DeMeo, Orphans First prayer letter, date unknown.

Chapter Seventeen

Costs and Blessings of Advocacy:

Tabi's Journey

* * *

Tami Snowden

I T WAS my first year of service working with my mission group in Kyrgyzstan. I had left a seventeen-year health-care sales career to follow God's calling of bringing the love of Jesus to orphaned children in Central Asia. As is true for most missionaries, my full-time job during the first year in Kyrgyzstan was to learn the Russian language. My volunteer work at an orphanage, where no one spoke English, allowed me to immerse myself in Russian. I volunteered ten hours a week working with two groups of children: Group 1 consisted of babies, newborn to one year. Group 2 consisted of toddlers, those who were crawling to about two years old. Because I could minister to both the staff and the children and practice my Russian, it was a perfect situation.

Each day I saw countless little faces of those whose mothers did not want them or could not afford to keep them. In Kyrgyz culture, parents who cannot afford to care for their babies give them to orphanages to raise. Sometimes, depending upon their circumstances, they later retrieve their children.

It did not take me long to notice that the orphanage workers had their favorites. They took more time to feed and cuddle the "beautiful" children. They fed the less attractive children quickly and returned them to their cribs immediately. These children were picked up only when they needed a change of clothing or a feeding. Arranged in rows, the children's small wooden cribs had hard surfaces covered only by a thin layer of material. Babies often exhibited the characteristic of holding their tiny hands in tight fists clutched close to their chests and under their chins, a symptom of inadequate attention and suppressed emotion. After a few months, I was no different from the other caregivers; I tended to hold the responsive children more, and I had my favorites, too.

What I did not know then was that I was about to embark on a three-year journey on behalf of a tiny baby, which would change the course of both of our lives. What follows is my personal account of the tenacity, strength and personal cost that advocacy requires.

"POOR, POOR GIRL"

April 2002

A member of my home office is visiting from the U.S. and asked for a tour of the orphanage. We visited the different groups of children, snapping pictures along the way. We were ready to leave when I remembered the building in the back, the facility's quarantine corridor. I rarely visit this area, but I took my colleague for a tour anyway.

Peering down at the tiny baby girl lying in the orphanage crib, camera at hand, we could not bear to take her picture. Guliam, the orphanage director, entered the room as we stood staring at this little life. "Poor, poor girl," she said, shaking her head. The powerful and somber moment made me not want to ask what had happened to this infant named Tabihat. Her facial deformities (multiple facial clefts and a dislodged eye that lies on her left check) are more horrific than anything I have ever seen. I do not even know how old she is.

May 2002

Baby Tabihat, whom I have nicknamed Tabi, recently moved from the quarantine corridor to Group 1. I have observed, sadly, that Tabi's facial deformities frighten most caregivers. Orphanage workers feed Tabi and then immediately put her down. Because Tabi's facial clefts make feeding a challenge, workers usually feed her last.

Shortly after Tabi arrived in our group, I sensed God telling me that I needed to love this girl. I have consciously determined to feed her before the other children, hold her longer and offer her more affection. She is definitely responding to my attention. Unlike most orphaned children, Tabi is affectionate. Whenever I hold her, she lays her head on my right shoulder and clasps her arms tightly around my neck. The more time I spend with her, the more I see her as a very special girl.

January 2003

Because of Tabi's physical deformities, the doctors and workers at the orphanage have assumed that she will exhibit other physical as well as mental problems. Yet, one day recently, I arrived to see Tabi, now one year old, crawling freely around the large play area grabbing toys. No other child had even begun to show signs of crawling, but there she was, developmentally months beyond the other children. This little girl is smart and knows how to fend for herself—there is nothing mentally wrong with this child.

February 2003

As soon as Tabi began crawling, Guliam moved her into Group 2 for toddlers. I notice that Tabi cries more in this group than she did while in Group 1. When she cries, she covers her left, exposed eye. Several workers believe that Tabi covers her eye out of shame. Although this seems inexplicable, the culture in Kyrgyzstan is shame-based as are most of the Soviet-based cultures. Of course, being American, I disagree. I feel strongly that the sunlight and air cause pain to an eye that she cannot shut.

February 24, 2003

I am concerned about Tabi's eye. I e-mailed the prayer team in America and sent them a photograph of her.

Attached you will find a picture of baby Tabihat. She is about thirteen months old and was born with a disfigured face and eye. She is a precious little girl. Smart and independent, she definitely screams when she does not get her way. To date, the orphanage staff has not considered an operation for her. I am sure this surgery is beyond the expertise of a general surgeon. If any of you know of a specialist who might be able to come and operate, let me know! In the meantime, please pray for Tabihat. Pray that she will know Jesus' love for her, and that the orphanage directors will pour their love upon her.

SURGERY DENIED

March 25, 2003—A group of women from the International Women's Club visited the orphanage. They informed me that a plastic surgeon from Germany was in town to perform free facial surgeries for children with cleft lips and palates. I thought this might be the answer to my prayers! Feeling hopeful, I grabbed Tabi and then searched for Guliam. I asked her if I could take Tabi to the hospital to meet the German doctor for evaluation.

Guliam responded abruptly, "No." She told me that Tabi was evaluated last year, and she is not a candidate for any sort of surgery. Apparently, her blood is not good, she does not swallow well, and she is underweight. Guliam says Tabi would never survive surgery.

With a sinking heart, I left Guliam's office in shock and disbelief. Her words devastated me. Does she believe that Tabi's situation is hopeless? Worse, what if Guliam does not care what happens to Tabi?

Cuddling Tabi in my arms as we returned to the group, I came to the devastating conclusion that Tabi has no future in Kyrgyzstan without drastic medical help. I know that her deformities make it unlikely that she will be adopted. Most likely, she faces permanent institutionalization. Even within the institution, I picture her as an outcast for the rest of her life. At that moment, holding Tabi tightly, God spoke to my heart: "Tami, do whatever it takes to get this girl help. Do not give up." I know two things with certainty: I love Tabi, and I love my God. I purpose in my heart that I will fight for Tabi, and I will fight with the greatest force in the world—prayer!

PRAYERS FOR TABI

March 25, 2003—I am praying and asking for prayer. I e-mailed supporters to ask them to partner with me in praying for Tabi's physical health. I also asked for prayers to strengthen her little body for surgery in the near future.

April 26, 2003—One of my hometown prayer supporters, Phil Brothers, e-mailed the Colorado-based ministry Face the Challenge (FTC) on Tabi's behalf. FTC president Mrs. Ginger H. Robinson, BSN, RN, wrote back:

> *Thank you for your e-mail contact about the little girl living in Kyrgyzstan. Face the Challenge is designed to perform several free facial surgeries by sending a surgical team to a specific site rather than bringing single cases to us. Perhaps we can consider her needs or offer you additional options.[1]*

Perfect! Ginger's husband, Dr. Randolph C. Robinson, MD, DDS, FACS, is FTC's cranio-maxillo-facial surgeon. With the hope that they can travel to Kyrgyzstan, I am contacting them myself to request their help.

May 2003—Over the last month, Ginger and I have corresponded frequently. Although FTC is currently overcommitted and reluctant to take another case, they have agreed to treat Tabi!

ANOTHER CHANCE FOR SURGERY

June 1, 2003—I hurried to the orphanage to tell Guliam the great news about FTC coming to Kyrgyzstan. Because of her previous negative response, I prayed desperately for her heart to be open. To my delight, Guliam was ecstatic and wants to do what she can to help Tabi. It was God who softened the heart of Guliam. She has given me permission to take Tabi to the hospital for testing to ensure that she is a candidate for surgery. I am leaving immediately. My dear Kyrgyz friend Gulzata is accompanying me as my translator.

June 2, 2003—Doctors at the Zdal Hospital in Bishkek rarely see an American walk their halls with a Kyrgyz child. I explained to them that a team of surgeons might come from America to operate on Tabi and that she needed to be evaluated before they arrived. We discussed the possibility of the surgery being performed at their hospital. The prospect of this cross-cultural experience thrills the Kyrgyz doctors. They hope that the American doctors might bring desperately needed surgical equipment and provide instruction on surgical procedures. Consequently, Tabi and I received the red-carpet treatment. After a battery of blood tests, an EKG and X-rays, the doctors determined that Tabi is in perfect health. If something was wrong with Tabi's blood in the past, nothing is wrong now. Tabi can have surgery.

June 7, 2003—Tabi still faces many difficulties. The chief facial surgeon in Kyrgyzstan is concerned about Tabi's exposed left eye. The medical intervention that Tabi needs for her eye is beyond his expertise, so he referred us to the Republican Hospital where we met with an eye specialist. The specialist reported that Tabi's left eye should have been removed earlier in life. As her left eye grows, it creates increasing pressure on her right eye. She fears that Tabi is developing glaucoma. She recommends immediate surgery to remove Tabi's left eye. I already contacted the Robinsons for a second opinion. Fortunately, they agree with the Kyrgyz specialist.

June 9, 2003—Guliam is concerned for Tabi: the surgery to remove her eye seems too risky, and she fears that Tabi is too underweight. The orphanage doctors and Guliam are leaning toward declining the surgery for fear that Tabi will not survive.

June 15, 2003—This week I have emphasized that without the surgery, Tabi's left eye will continue to grow and increase pressure on her right eye. I have tried to help the orphanage staff weigh the risks of the surgery against Tabi's future without it—a future that will involve both horrific deformity and possible blindness. Finally, they have agreed to the surgery, and if Tabi survives, we may pursue additional surgeries. The doctors have scheduled Tabi's first surgery for July 8.

SURGERY DAY, PART 1

July 8, 2003—We arrived at the Republican Hospital early this morning. The orderly was a young Kyrgyz woman who escorted me, Tabi, and one of the orphanage nannies to the hospital floor for eye-surgery patients. Tabi is sharing a room with six other patients, all *babushkas* (Russian for "grandmothers"), who immediately complained to the staff that a crying, restless toddler would prevent sleep. Before the staff could resolve the issue, they took Tabi to surgery; we waited more than five hours for her return. During the surgery, I prayed that God would protect her little body and keep her safe. Having convinced the orphanage doctors and Guliam that Tabi needed this surgery, I did not want anything to go wrong. Although my primary concern is for Tabi, I want to preserve the trust Guliam has placed in me.

I was relieved when I saw a nurse carrying little Tabi down the hall toward her room. Tabi wore a little pink shirt and was wrapped in a white blanket. Both eyes were bandaged, and she was asleep due to the effects of the anesthesia. The surgeon not only removed her left eye, but also operated on her right eye to relieve pressure. Unable to wait, I peeked under the bandage where her left eye had been and could not believe the difference. Already, her appearance is improved.

Unfortunately, the hospital does not provide pain medication (probably due to the expense, availability or Tabi's age) so we face this first long night with Tabi crying and keeping the babushkas awake.

July 19, 2003—The babushkas could see Tabi's pain last night, and they came to her side to offer what comfort they could. Tabi's pain has diminished gradually today, and her countenance is better. The eye that caused her so much pain for the first year and a half of her life no longer exists. Tabi is beginning to smile.

July 25, 2003—Tabi stayed in the hospital for a week and blessed everyone. With her babushka roommates looking after her, Tabi took her first steps.

The women helped her walk from bed to bed, visiting each patient. With the surgery a success, one chapter is closed. Now we face the preparation for future surgeries.

August 1, 2003—I received an e-mail from Face the Challenge requesting that Tabi's surgeries be performed in America. My heart sank, and I fear Guliam's possible rejection. I am going to the orphanage to break the news.

APPROVAL FOR TABI TO GO TO AMERICA

August 2, 2003—What little faith I had. I told Guliam that the surgeons would not be traveling to Kyrgyzstan. When I explained that Tabi would need to go to America to have surgery by this particular group of surgeons, she became excited. She was thrilled that Tabi might have an opportunity to be in the best hospitals with the best care. Once again, I feel God's hand preparing the way.

August 5, 2003—As director of the orphanage, Guliam is Tabi's legal guardian, but she is not the final decision maker. We need approval for Tabi's travel from the directors of the Ministry of Health and Ministry of Education. No precedent exists for an orphaned, Kyrgyz minor to leave the country. If the Kyrgyz government allows her to leave, we also need a visa from the U.S. government. I am gathering the necessary forms and signatures from both governments. Let the political red tape begin.

I am well aware of the need for diplomacy, because national pride is paramount in Kyrgyzstan. I pray that God will show me when to push and when to be patient. I want to respect the Kyrgyz government and establish a trustworthy relationship.

Although Guliam is in favor of Tabi's going to America, some of the orphanage doctors are not. They realize that Tabi will get better medical care, but they fear for Tabi's future beyond her surgeries. Some feel that it is unfair to remove Tabi from the orphanage, send her to live with an American family for her recovery, and then return her to orphanage life. They have expressed great concern for what the dramatic changes might do to Tabi's emotional health.

Truthfully, I share their concerns. But I see this as a great opportunity to share my faith. I spoke with the doctors and told them that I believe that God has asked me to help Tabi. I described how God so dearly loves Tabi and all the orphaned children that He moves mountains to help them. I explained that I believe that this opportunity for Tabi to receive excellent medical help could only be from God. If I hesitate to help Tabi because I fear the unknown, then I am not really trusting God with her future. I explained that I have to trust God's heart for Tabi. If God wants Tabi in America for surgery, then He will protect her heart and her emotional health, too. I added that when I returned from America, I hoped to find a Kyrgyz family for Tabi. After listening to me attentively, the doctors are now overjoyed at this opportunity for Tabi.

August 10, 2003—I contacted a Kyrgyz attorney named Asel to help me with some of the necessary legal paperwork. Asel is a generous, intelligent, young lawyer trained by Western attorneys. She specializes in human-rights issues for both the local and expatriate communities. When I told her what I wanted to do, she was willing to help but warned me not to get my hopes up. Although other Kyrgyz citizens have received visas to leave the country for medical treatment, Tabi is a ward of the state, an orphaned minor. Asel believes that the government might be concerned that Tabi will not be returned.

August 15, 2003—I met with Guliam's boss, Evgenia, in the Ministry of Health. Evgenia is the head pediatrician for the baby orphanages of Kyrgyzstan. A kind woman, Evgenia cares greatly for the health and well-being of the children in the orphanages. Like Asel, she is eager to help but doubts that the Ministry of Education will allow an orphaned child to leave the country with a foreigner. Her job is to get her boss, the minister of health, to sign prerequisite documents, which are necessary before the minister of education's approval.

September 2003—I send e-mail updates almost daily to my prayer team with detailed descriptions of the approval process and requests for prayers for every step.

September 15, 2003—My scheduled furlough begins on November 21. Because I am Tabi's escort to America, I feel under pressure to hasten the approval process so that Tabi can leave with me when my furlough begins. Although I am tired and in much need of rest, I know I will gladly delay my furlough if we do not get approval in time.

October 6, 2003—The minister of health has approved our request to take Tabi to America. The paperwork is now being forwarded to the Ministry of Education for approval and final signature. Asel and Evgenia told me about two women in the Ministry of Education who could make this process difficult. These women suspect Americans of wanting orphaned children in order to sell their body parts. The American medical practice of organ transplantation no doubt contributes to the myth and misunderstanding. I need another mountain moved, so I am returning to my prayer team to request prayers for these women, prayers for God to increase my faith, and prayers to persevere in the fight for Tabi.

October 8, 2003—I received a call from a tearful Asel. One of the women in the Ministry of Education has denied our request for Tabi to leave the country. I hurried to Asel's office and called Guliam, who advised me to meet personally with the assistant minister of education. She hopes that this woman will see my heart and change her mind. I pray for favor with this woman and leave it in God's hands.

October 9, 2003—When I walked into the assistant minister's office unannounced today, I found her talking on the phone. Without waiting for her to complete her call, I placed Tabi's picture on her desk and said, "I want to help her." When she ended her call, she told me she is leaving tomorrow for a three-week trip. Because she is so busy, she has passed my paperwork on to her assistant and told him to handle it. She said that he would prepare the documents and that the minister of education will make a final decision tomorrow.

October 16, 2003—Asel called and asked me to hurry to her office. When I arrived, she showed me the signed document from the minister of education. Tabi can go to America! I silently thanked God for orchestrating the timing of the assistant minister's three-week trip so that she would not have time for this case. In her hurriedness, she had signed everything quickly and passed it off to her assistant who completed the process.

October 17, 2003—Asel is working on getting a Kyrgyz passport for Tabi. I am praying about this! The Kyrgyz government does not normally issue passports to children under age 16.

October 18, 2003—To secure a medical visa into the United States, the Kyrgyz doctor who originally evaluated Tabi needs to write a letter explaining that due to the complexity of Tabi's deformities, it would be best for the operation to be performed in America. My experience in health-care sales involved working with American doctors, and if Kyrgyz doctors are like many American doctors, I am worried that this letter will be humbling for him to write. I respect Tabi's doctor, and I do not want to insinuate that he is not capable of performing the surgery. I have prayed through this whole process that God would show me when to push and when to be patient; I know this is a moment not to push, but to be patient.

October 19, 2003—In my apartment before I left for the Zdal Hospital to meet with Tabi's doctor, I opened my hands to God and prayed, "Lord, your will be done for Tabi." My concerns were unwarranted because the doctor expressed great joy that Tabi has the opportunity to go to America for surgery and receive the best medical care. He wrote the letter immediately.

October 30, 2003—Guliam, Tabi and I met with a consular officer at the U.S. Embassy in Bishkek. With all our documents in order, we received Tabi's medical visa to enter the United States. With the U.S. consular officer as witness, Guliam signed a document giving me guardianship of Tabi while we are in America. In God's efficiency, we are fully prepared almost two weeks ahead of my scheduled furlough. We are on our way to America!

LEAVING FOR AMERICA

November 8, 2003—I arrived at the orphanage Saturday evening to pick up Tabi. What a joyous time! I bought a special outfit for Tabi's travel. One of her favorite workers, Nina, bought her some new clothing as well. All the workers gathered around as we dressed Tabi for the trip. Everyone smiled, laughed and talked excitedly. The orphanage staff walked us to the waiting taxi and waved as we headed for the airport and America.

The airport staff and Kyrgyz customs officials at Manas Airport in Bishkek were incredibly helpful during our check-in at the airport. They were proud that their citizen was granted permission to go to America and receive medical treatment. We were checked in quickly and ushered through customs. British Airways upgraded our seats to first class. As we boarded the plane, Tabi experienced sensory overload. Although she has known me for almost two years, she looked at me as though I were a stranger. She ran from me, backed up toward the door of the airplane and screamed. Tabi has only known life in the orphanage, and now everything is unfamiliar to her. The other first-class passengers stared at Tabi and at me. *Oh boy*, I thought, *this is going to be a long flight*. The gracious passengers assured me that Tabi's screaming did not bother them, putting me at ease. As I relaxed somewhat, so did Tabi. I picked her up and put her in my lap. Finally, Tabi and I settled into our seats and the plane departed, headed first to Azerbaijan, then London, and finally Denver. Tabi fell asleep on my shoulder, and as my body relaxed for the first time in months, tears of relief poured from me. I cried and cried during the flight. I felt a mixture of both overwhelming joy and tremendous release from the weeks and months of stress and worry advocating for this precious child.

November 10, 2003—Upon arriving in America, we were greeted by my mother, other family members, and friends who had prayed for almost a year for Tabi. Tabi has an instant family—my family embraced her immediately.

Meeting Dr. Robinson

November 25, 2003—Tabi had her preoperative appointment with Dr. Robinson. His office staff greeted us with arms full of presents and hearts full of love for Tabi. They also had waited for this day to arrive to meet the Tabi for whom they had prayed many months. Tabi received stuffed animals, clothes and a blanket. The staff's warmth, smiles and embraces made us feel that they had known us all their lives. The moment we met Dr. Robinson, I knew that God had handpicked our surgeon. Dr. Robinson had completed his one-year craniofacial surgery fellowship under Paul L. Tessier, MD, the world's father of craniofacial surgery.

Dr. Robinson explained that this initial surgery would be involved. He will close Tabi's right craniofacial cleft, close her cleft lip, and reconstruct her left eye with grafts and globe implant. The surgery will take approximately 6–8 hours.

Surgery Day, Part 2

December 4, 2003—Today was Tabi's big surgery day. A local news team from NBC-affiliate 9NEWS arrived to interview me and to film a portion of the surgery for a story on Tabi's remarkable journey. When reporter Cheryl Preheim asked how I was feeling about today, I responded, "It is a big day. I feel really at peace because I know that this surgery will be so good for her life. Tabi will have a great life ahead of her with a beautiful new face."[2]

Six and a half hours of surgery later, the head nurse came to get me in the waiting room. I felt my heart pounding as I walked anxiously back toward the recovery room. What would Tabi look like? I walked to her bed and peered down at her. I could not take my eyes off her. She looks beautiful—even perfect.

Tabi's Life in America

January 4, 2004—Tabi has blossomed quickly because of the love she is receiving from so many. Although transformed by love and a family, Tabi still grieves the only life she knows—sharing a room with twenty other children. Since leaving the orphanage in November, Tabi cries throughout the night. I rock her to sleep every night and keep her in a crib next to my bed. One evening as I rocked her, tears of grief rolled down my face for the orphaned children who will never be rocked to sleep. Babies in the orphanage are wrapped tightly in a blanket and put into their cribs. Toddlers are told to crawl into their beds, a blanket is placed on them, and then the lights go out. God has given me a deeper sense of His heart for orphaned children. I believe that His heart is that children be raised in families, not in institutions. As good as it may be, an institution cannot replace a family.

January 10, 2004—As thoughts of returning Tabi to Kyrgyzstan surface, I grieve. Not satisfied to enjoy the moment, I worry about what will happen when we return to Kyrgyzstan in July—six months into the future. *Lord, please prepare a family for Tabi so that she will not have to return to the orphanage.* When I play with Tabi, brushing the hair from her face, holding and comforting her and reveling in her little smile, I entertain the desire to adopt her myself. Despite watching God move mountains to bring Tabi this far, I am resolved to the fact that the Kyrgyz government does not permit foreigners to adopt their children.

A MOTHER'S EVER-GROWING LOVE

February 2004—Every day that I care for Tabi, the more we love each other. I am Tabi's momma. No one except Jesus knows the pain I feel each day, believing that I will lose Tabi. I wonder if this is how Abraham felt, believing that he would lose Isaac. I asked God to give me grace to handle the time when I will have to hand Tabi to another family. I know that Tabi trusts me to be there, and I fear that she will *never* understand when I return her to the Bishkek orphanage. In light of this unique, complex and stressful situation, I am seeking the services of a Christian counselor.

March 2004—During my counseling session last week, I asked, "How do I protect my heart in all this?" My counselor answered, "You do not protect your heart, Tami. Tabi needs everything you are and needs unconditional love from you. You have to trust that God will be there to heal your heart when the time comes." After that meeting, it occurred to me: *This is the time I lay down my life for a friend. I must love unselfishly at whatever personal cost.*

March 15, 2004—Throughout the months, my desire to adopt Tabi has grown stronger, but I know that the Kyrgyz government will not permit it. I have been cautious about allowing my heart to believe it might be possible; I pray that God will guide me in what to do with my desire.

March 27, 2004—I sense a green light from God, and I have decided to do whatever I can to adopt Tabi. It will take a miracle, but God has already performed a miracle on behalf of Tabi in getting her to America; He can perform more. "You are the God who performs miracles; you display your power among the peoples" (Ps. 77:14). I do not want to leave one stone unturned. I have already contacted an adoption agency in Denver to begin the adoption process. An international adoption requires paperwork for both countries: the United States and the child's country of origin. I am gathering the necessary documents to receive USCIS (United States Citizenship and Immigration Services) approval. After I adopt Tabi in Kyrgyzstan, she will need this approval to receive an immigrant visa to return to the United States. I am in the dark as to what Kyrgyzstan's requirements are for an adoptive parent, but I am following the adoption-process guidelines of a neighboring country, Kazakhstan. So far, I need a home study, FBI clearance, psychological testing, medical testing and . . . the list goes on.

April 1, 2004—I e-mailed Asel to see if she would be willing to help me pursue Tabi's adoption after I arrive back in Kyrgyzstan.

April 5, 2004—Asel has agreed to help me pursue Tabi's adoption when I go back!

Surgery Again

May 2004—Tabi had another surgery to reconstruct her left eye socket. Throughout the ordeal, she has been a trooper. I marvel at her courage. I can see that she loves "her Dr. Robinson." Tabi's confidence grows and she blossoms every day. She arrived in America speaking a handful of words and, in a few short months, at the age of two, she is now speaking English with the vocabulary of a three-year-old. Tabi blesses everyone she meets. Ginger Robinson said, "Tabi has worked her way deep into our hearts. Although we cannot predict what will happen to her, we are convinced she is handpicked to be used mightily by God."[3] I agree heartily.

June 30, 2004—I received my home study and USCIS approval in time for our July departure back to Kyrgyzstan. I will return to Kyrgyzstan paper-ready to adopt Tabi.

July 2, 2004—As I prepare for the return trip and the potential loss of Tabi, many people have challenged me to keep her in America and never return. As tempting as it sounds, I care about the trust I have established with the Kyrgyz. If other children are ever to be adopted by Americans, I need to return Tabi and dispel the myths concerning body-part sales. I need to return Tabi as I promised.

BACK TO BISHKEK

July 29, 2004—We will step off this plane in a matter of hours. I have no idea what lies ahead of us beyond the doors of baggage claim. In America, I am her guardian—her mother—in Kyrgyzstan, the state becomes her guardian again. Will the police be waiting to take Tabi out of my arms? Will Guliam demand her return to the orphanage? Only God knows. I trust that He has Tabi's best interest at heart and am reminded that He loves Tabi more than I do.

July 30, 2004—No one was at the airport despite my fears! I plan to spend the weekend getting over jetlag; I will call Guliam on Sunday.

August 1, 2004—I called Guliam to tell her we were back. She responded by informing me sternly that I needed to return Tabi to the orphanage by 2:00 p.m. Monday. Guliam's harshness scares me even though I know that the Soviet style of leadership training—harsh, direct-line authority—that pervades much of Central Asia does not always reveal the true meaning. Guliam might be under tremendous threat if I do not return Tabi. That might be why she reverted to this style of leadership. Still, her words took my breath away. One of my consistent prayers is that Tabi will never spend another night in an orphanage. I stood in the kitchen and cried out to God. I do not understand what is happening, but I have to trust Him.

I called America to solicit prayers. I pray that the love between Tabi and me is so strong that it breaks down walls of pride and crumbles hearts of stone.

August 2, 2004—A taxi arrived at 1:30 p.m. to take Tabi and me to the orphanage. I looked over at sweet Tabi, who was excited to ride in a car with no car seat or seat belt and oblivious to what might happen when we arrived at the orphanage. I knew one thing for sure. If Tabi has to stay at the orphanage, then I will stay with her. I will not leave her there alone.

When we arrived at the orphanage and walked into Guliam's office, Tabi ran up to her and gave her a hug. Guliam melted. I told Guliam about my desire to adopt Tabi. I asked her if Tabi could live with me and not stay in the orphanage. She agreed, but informed me that I need formal approval from the Ministry of Health. She scheduled an appointment with the minister of health for tomorrow. Tabi went home with me.

August 3, 2004—The minister of health granted approval for Tabi to live with me. He said documents must be drafted and signed to make it official, but she can remain in my home. God answered the prayer I have prayed for months. Tabi will not have to spend one more night in the orphanage. He is a loving Father!

PERSEVERANCE PAYS OFF

August 15, 2004—I have spent a couple of weeks filling out the paperwork to permit Tabi to stay with me. My roommate, Gulya, says that if the adoption is not complete before the February elections, it will never happen. She said that when election time comes, government officials will be busy trying to win an election, and Tabi's adoption will not be their priority. I trust Gulya's advice. I will call Asel tomorrow and ask if we can begin to submit the adoption paperwork to the government.

September 15, 2004—Fall is nearing, and Tabi's paperwork has yet to be submitted to the government. I wonder if Asel might be fearful to pursue this unchartered territory. She is an established, reputable attorney, and since some Kyrgyz oppose foreign adoption, her work with me could hinder her reputation. I understand her position.

September 20, 2004—I am getting restless. Gulya offered to help me with the adoption. I will call Asel and tell her I will work this adoption on my own with Gulya's help.

September 25, 2004—Gulya and I are working diligently on completing Tabi's adoption paperwork for submission to the Kyrgyz government. My prayer team and I pray fervently for three things: that I will be Tabi's "forever mother," that the process will be easy and quick, and that we will be home for Christmas.

October 15, 2004—I officially submitted the adoption papers. Kyrgyz policy currently forbids foreign adoptions, and many expatriates doubt that Tabi's adoption will succeed. I remain fixed on God's faithfulness to Tabi. Of the many Scriptures I meditate on, two in particular have come to mean a great deal to me. Psalm 2:2–4 inspired me to write this in my prayer journal:

> *God you are greater than all governments. You can do anything.*
> *You scoff at those who stand against you. Lord, please knock*
> *down any pillar that stands in the way of this adoption and give*
> *me and Gulya the favor of Queen Esther.*

I also receive great strength from Romans 4:17–22. Abraham's dedication and belief in God despite all odds offers me comfort and focus. He, too, gave the glory to God.

November 1, 2004—Because Kyrgyzstan does not allow foreign adoption, no established process is in place within the justice system. We need to obtain signatures from the county mayor, minister of education, minister of justice, minister of foreign affairs, minister of the interior, the Cabinet members of the White House, and the prime minister of Kyrgyzstan. Gulya and I work throughout the day, debrief at night, plan our next day, and pray. We have experienced many emotional ups and downs. When Gulya feels discouraged or tired, I am strong, and when I am tired, she is strong. We are a good team. On difficult days, Gulya always reminds me, "Tami, what God started He will finish. God started this whole process for Tabi; He won't leave her or forsake her now."

November 10, 2004—The timing of the adoption process is coinciding with *Ramadan*. I believe God is using this Muslim holiday to move the process forward quickly. All the people who need to sign Tabi's papers want to do what is right and good in the eyes of Allah. Signatures are coming quickly.

December 1, 2004—We await the final signature from the prime minister. With the Christmas season upon us, I am anxious about whether we will be home for Christmas. I am taking my mind off the wait by decorating our apartment and hosting a Christmas party.

December 8, 2004—Tabi and I were making Christmas cookies when Gulya phoned to tell me that the prime minister had signed the final document. I got off the phone and said, "Tabi, God answered our prayers! I am your momma and you are my daughter, and we are going to be together forever." We were listening to a Christmas CD, and as *The Hallelujah Chorus* played, we danced around the kitchen. We *will* be home for Christmas.

STEADFAST TO THE FINISH LINE

December 13, 2004—Unfortunately, the excitement and joy of Tabi's adoption was short-lived. Corrupt members of the Kyrgyz police called Gulya's cell phone requesting money on behalf of Tabi's birth mother. Gulya informed them that Tabi is now adopted and no money will be paid. Then they began to call every two minutes and demanded a meeting to see documents proving that Tabi is legally adopted. Gulya scoffed and said no to such a meeting. I am stunned. How did the police get Gulya's cell phone number? Only the orphanage has Gulya's number. Who told Tabi's birth mother that Tabi was being adopted? Someone from the orphanage, Tabi's birth mother, and corrupt police are in this together, trying to extort money. Who in the world betrayed me? Tabi's birth mother even appeared at my apartment searching for money.

Gulya and I have decided that I should take Tabi out of the country immediately. Because the adoption is legal, we will leave Bishkek and head for Kazakhstan, where we will wait for our appointment for Tabi's immigrant visa.

December 20, 2004—We have been in Kazakhstan for a week waiting for an appointment with the U.S. Embassy for Tabi's immigrant visa. We are staying in the apartment of a missionary family on furlough. I am thankful that in my rush to leave Kyrgyzstan I remembered to grab a string of Christmas lights and a candle. These are our only reminders that Christmas is fast approaching. I found a Mickey Mouse Christmas video in the apartment, which has been playing nonstop.

December 21, 2004—Tabi's immigrant visa was issued! America here we come!

HOME FOR CHRISTMAS

December 22, 2004—God's timing is perfect; we are home for Christmas. The minute Tabi stepped foot onto U.S. soil, she became a citizen. Holiday traffic caused long lines through customs and immigration—and considerable anxiety for my waiting family. Looking at the stamp in Tabi's passport still makes me smile. When we walked through the doors of the main terminal, we were greeted by my mother, sisters, nephews, friends, and a camera-man from 9NEWS. We are celebrating and giving thanks for what will be a truly blessed Christmas.

TIME TO HEAL

January 2005—The stress that I have lived under for close to two years, advocating for and adopting Tabi, has taken a serious emotional and physical toll on me. I am exhausted and sleep many hours. My thoughts are irrational and I am paranoid that someone from Kyrgyzstan will call telling me that Tabi's adoption wasn't complete and that I must now return her. If my phone rings and displays "unavailable number," my heart races and I get short of breath. I'm considering seeking professional help.

January 2005—My doctor's diagnosis is post-traumatic stress disorder (PTSD). In denial, my first flippant thought was, *everything is labeled a disorder these days*. But now, after several counseling sessions, I realize that I have been through difficult and draining circumstances and I have lived under extreme stress for an extended period of time. PTSD should come as no surprise. After all, a missionary normally spends the first couple of years simply learning the language and getting to know and understand the people. Experienced missionaries tell me that cross-cultural living, even when things go well, is stressful. The doctor recommended that I take a leave of absence from ministry to rest and heal. My mission agency has agreed, and my nine-month leave of absence goes into effect immediately.

March 2005—I am still exhausted and have no energy for anything or anyone except to care for my daughter. I continue to feel paranoid that Tabi's birth mother will reappear; I fear that Tabi will be taken away. I cannot relax because I am afraid that something might happen if I let my guard down. My anger and confusion have triggered so many unsettling questions: Who betrayed the confidentiality of my adoption? Who gave Tabi's birth mother my address and phone number? I worry that this situation could mean never returning to Kyrgyzstan. I feel even more pain and heartbreak because I left Kyrgyzstan so quickly. We left behind many friends, my team, my "stuff," and even our dog, Marley.

April 2005—I have concluded that returning to Kyrgyzstan would not be wise for us. This realization is devastating. I had dreams of raising Tabi in her home country, ministering to other orphaned children, and investing in the lives of the Kyrgyz people I have come to love. However, for the love of one child named Tabi, the costs are worth it.

GOD'S GREAT PLAN FOR TABI

May 1, 2005—I continue to recover my emotional and physical health. Tabi and I received an invitation to attend a partnership meeting in Dallas, where individuals and churches with hearts for the Kyrgyz come together. Other missionaries on furlough are also attending. The meeting will be a time to share what is happening regarding the Christian movement in Kyrgyzstan and to network with others.

May 23, 2005—During the meeting in Dallas, we watched the news story by Denver news station 9NEWS, which covered our journey. I was sitting next to a missionary couple, Sue and John, who had worked in Tabi's birth town. After the story ended, they whispered in my ear, "Great story." When I told them Tabi was born in the town where they had worked, they realized they had a connection to her.

John said he met Tabi within 24 hours of her birth at the local hospital. Because John and Sue worked with children with disabilities, the head doctor had called him to report that he had delivered a newborn with serious deformities. The birth mother had already left the hospital, and the doctor did not know what to do with the baby. After John visited Tabi in the hospital, he returned home and told Sue the story. Sue felt a tremendous burden for Tabi and began praying fervently for her. Although they considered taking her themselves, they felt the Lord say, "No." John made phone calls and received the advice that Tabi should be taken to the capital city of Bishkek to receive the best care. John and Sue took money to the hospital and paid for Tabi's transportation to Bishkek.

Meeting Tabi in Dallas three years later, we all witnessed fully God's plan for Tabi. John and Sue knew that they had played a part in the journey to unite Tabi and me.

July 15, 2005—I found my prayer journal from 2002 and opened up to January 13, the day Tabi was born. On that day, January 13, 2002, I was commissioned by my church for my mission work in Kyrgyzstan. A few days later, I left America for Kyrgyzstan. God brought Tabi's story full circle. God's hand was on Tabi from the beginning of her life.

September 30, 2005—The story of Tabi's birth and subsequent adoption is complete. I am grateful and in awe of God's power and guidance throughout the journey. I know firsthand that He is a defender of the weak and upholds their cause. "Do not take advantage of the widow or the fatherless. If you do and they cry out to me, I will certainly hear their cry" (Exodus 22:22–23).

EPILOGUE

Tabi is now nine and will enter fourth grade in fall 2011. Tabi loves to swim, ski, ride her bike and play with Legos. She still needs surgery to build an eye socket for an artificial left eye, but the lack of an eye does not hold her back one bit!

Tabi wants to visit Kyrgyzstan to meet her birth mother. I want that for her, too, but not until she is 18 years old. I still feel emotional pain about not living in Kyrgyzstan. I love Kyrgyzstan! We lived such a simple life. A life that was not hurried, where we spent time with our neighbors drinking tea each night. Mostly, I miss my work in the orphanages and the opportunity to minister to the multitudes of children who live in them. But it would not be wise for us to live there.

I have had the opportunity to return to Central Asia over the past few years to visit orphanages for children with disabilities. They live in a society in which a medical or physical condition such as diabetes, epilepsy or partial blindness labels a child an outcast and condemns the child to life in an institution. During these visits, I am reminded that this would have been Tabi's fate. Instead, she is flourishing. Tabi is an intelligent, confident, happy girl who loves God deeply and desires to serve Him. I give thanks to God for rescuing her and giving her so many opportunities: to be raised in a family, to have an education, to celebrate important milestones. Children raised in an institution do not have these opportunities.

In the United States, I work as an advocate for at-risk and orphaned children, especially those born with facial deformities similar to Tabi's. My desire is that orphaned children find forever families just as God promises them. "A father to the fatherless, a defender of widows, is God in his holy dwelling. God sets the lonely in families . . ." (Psalm 68:5–6).

NOTES

1.   Ginger Robinson, e-mail message to Phil Brothers, April 21, 2003.

2.   "For the Love of a Child: Tabi's Journey," television newscast, 9NEWS (Denver, CO: KUSA-TV, December 4, 2003).

3.   Tami Snowden, "From Kyrgyzstan with Love," ed. Scott DeNicola, *Physician*, May/June 2004, 11.

PART VI

Caregiver Issues

Challenges and Support for Those Who Care

Heaven's Very Special Child

A meeting was held quite far from Earth;
"It's time again for another birth."
Said the angels to the Lord above,
"This special child will need much love.
Her progress may seem very slow.
Accomplishments she may not show,
And she'll require extra care
From the folks she meets way down there.
She may not run or laugh or play,
Her thoughts may seem quite far away.
In many ways she wwon't adapt,
And she'll be known as handicapped.
So let's be careful where she's sent,
We want her life to be content.
Please, Lord, find the parents who
Will do a special job for you.
They will not realize right away
The leading role they're asked to play,
But with this child sent from above
Come stronger faith and richer love.
And soon they'll know the privilege given
In caring for this gift from heaven.
Their precious charge, so meek and mild,
Is heaven's very special child."

—John and Edna Massimilla

CHAPTER EIGHTEEN

IMPACT OF DISABILITIES
ON FAMILY LIFE

* * *

H. Marie Murtha

L IVING with a child who has a disability can have profound effects on the entire family—parents, siblings and extended family members. It is a unique shared experience for families and can affect all aspects of family functioning. On the positive side, it can broaden horizons, increase family members' awareness of their inner strength, enhance family unity and encourage connections to community groups including faith-based organizations. On the negative side, the time and financial costs, physical and emotional demands and logistical complexities associated with raising a child with special needs can have far-reaching effects. The impact on a family will likely depend on the type of condition and severity of the child's disability, as well as the physical, emotional and financial situation of the family and the resources that are available.

In this chapter five families share with me their experiences and feelings about what raising a child with disabilities has meant to them. Although each situation was different and each family was at a different stage in its journey, all were painfully aware that raising a child with disabilities placed stress on the family system.

UNDERSTANDING AND ACCEPTING A DISABILITY

All families have pressure points stemming from the unique challenges of caring for a child with special needs. It is not the child's disability, however, that tears families apart; it is the way a family reacts to it and to each other. Parents' attitudes are key not only to handling pressure points but also to giving all the children the benefit of a stable, loving home to grow and develop in. Positive attitudes flow only from acceptance of a situation. Accepting your new lifestyle as your "new normal" will allow you to learn empowering coping skills.

The mother of a daughter with Dravet syndrome, a severe form of epilepsy also known as severe myoclonic epilepsy of infancy (SMEI), undertook the role of main caregiver, but found that maintaining the right attitude is an ongoing struggle.

> *My initial thoughts and feelings were that God is bigger than this. She is a lovely baby and things are going to get better. I refused to believe that my child would go down the progressive path of Dravet syndrome. We were already 10 and a half years into the journey, so the diagnosis didn't change anything in my heart; it only gave the medical community information on what drugs not to use on her and how to better treat her. As for my spouse, well, he lets me handle anything related to Dravet syndrome. His job is being an engineer; mine is everything else.*

Ephesians 4 describes negative attitudes we need to lay aside if we are to come to the place of acceptance and live a life worthy of the calling God has given us to raise a child with special needs. These attitudes include getting rid of bitterness, rage and anger (4:31). People not faced with the responsibility of caring for a child with disabilities may not understand your expressing these negative emotions. For example, others might feel put out when you make special requests or arrangements on behalf of your child, or they may not know what to do or say if they witness your child in the midst of an angry outburst or a seizure. Perhaps you have had to schedule, at the last minute, a teacher meeting or visit to the doctor, yet your spouse does not seem to understand why you are late for dinner. You can view these situations as opportunities to extend grace to others as well as to teach inexperienced people that there are healthy ways to handle uncomfortable situations. Extend forgiveness and then truly move on. Do not give the enemy a foothold in your life (4:27).

The families I interviewed told me that accepting that their child is special, different or chronically ill is often the result of working through a tangle of confusing emotions rather than an immediate conclusion. The parents of a son with a hearing impairment learned through trial and error what was best for their son.

Since it was a gradual process of suspecting and then confirming his deafness over a two year period, we had no sudden surprise or feelings of despair or grief. But there were some feelings of guilt. Did we do something wrong during the pregnancy? Did something go wrong during his infancy? All sorts of things ran through our minds. It was definitely a disappointment that his hearing loss was not repairable. But on the other hand, we now knew what was wrong and had a basis from which we begin to educate ourselves about raising a deaf child. The foremost question in our mind was, "How can we make him like other children, or as close as possible?" We soon found out this was not possible nor in the best interests of the child.

We also had to learn a new language. Up to that point, we had become extremely frustrated with no ability to communicate with our son other than pointing and guessing. But signing changed all that. We began gaining the ability to communicate. What we learned was: don't try and make your child live a life outside of his disability. Concentrate on the abilities that he does have and work to advance those skills. Don't worry about appearance. Concentrate on what works best for the child!

Those who fully accept the situation, challenging though it may be, have one less hurdle to jump on their journey toward understanding and living out this "new normal" in a healthy way for the entire family. A mother whose daughter, now forty-four, was diagnosed Educable Mentally Retarded (EMR) told me that the situation was heartbreaking. With five other children, she and her husband struggled with redefining their future.

As my daughter developed, I sensed all was not right. She appeared "normal" but did not develop according to the usual child standards. After a series of events that led to a psychological evaluation, we were given the news that she was mentally retarded—the term used then. It was heartbreaking, and rethinking our hopes, dreams and aspirations has been an ongoing process as new challenges arise.

Life was fairly simple in the early years; much more difficult as high school, job placement and independent living all became issues. Many parents became activists, as we did, trying to come up with solutions for our daughter. Some decisions that looked like a good idea at the time turned out to be disasters. And so it goes; looking for a life situation for her in which she could grow and mature to her fullest extent. We wanted her to be happy and not live in an atmosphere of conflict.

Regardless of when or whether parents reach the point of acceptance, raising a child who is "different" creates a marriage and a family that are "different." I am particularly well acquainted with one of the families I interviewed: my brother-in-law and sister-in-law, Martin and Kathryn, raised their son Isaac (Ike) until his death in 2006 at the age of eighteen. Given the challenges of raising and homeschooling ten children, including a son with severe autism, this family is an example of how to do more than merely survive. What is their secret? What did they do right? As you will note in their story, they did not always do everything right. As the other families I interviewed expressed, parenting is a journey that involves trial and error.

CASE STUDY: ISAAC

Martin and Kathryn had a daughter and two sons when Isaac was born. None had medical issues. Isaac was conceived on the mission field in Thailand and was home-birthed like the first two. The parents seemed to walk down the normal paths that unsuspecting parents travel concerning a child needing special medical care. They were not immediately aware that their son had special needs.

Looking back, we can see there were some indications when we considered many little things together, but each little thing taken by itself was not a big deal. It was a gradual realization as he was behind in many developmental milestones and then began to miss them altogether. We had a niece his age and knew other babies around his age, so this became quite apparent by the time he was 18 months old. He went through extensive testing. No one was ever able to give us a reason or a name for why he was the way he was, or a cure. One doctor narrowed it down for us by saying, "Your son experienced trauma to the brain at some point before, during or since birth." (I cannot believe he got paid for that brilliant diagnosis.) Isaac was a mystery. As for his symptoms, those had labels: non-verbal, autistic, mentally retarded, developmentally disabled, mild cerebral palsy, visually impaired, epileptic. In his teens, Isaac developed severe scoliosis and renal failure. In his last years, he needed to use a wheelchair and was tube fed.

But none of that describes what Isaac was like. Kathryn describes her son as a child who "crawled like lightning but did not start to walk until age three."

> *He did not like anything touching his head or face. He had a strong gag reflex. He did not know how to be gentle. When younger, and still able, he liked to climb and jump. He liked to throw things and seemed to enjoy the sound of things hitting the floor. He liked the lights on, all cabinets closed and all surfaces cleared. He did not know the meaning of danger. He liked to push and pull or open and close things. He liked saucepans with little metal rings on the end of the handle. He liked guitars and pianos. He liked to stack things. He loved sliding boards, the higher the better. He liked to run in patterns; eights were one of his favorites; also in and out of garages. He was fascinated by sewer grates. He liked the feel of rice and liked to pull grass. He liked to pull hair and jewelry, especially watches. He liked to pull his pants down. He hated the sound of crying babies. He loved music. He would wave his hands in praise or swing his leg, make deep-sounding sighs and smile in enjoyment of music. He seemed to be a very astute judge of character. He had big brown eyes; a big Bugs-Bunny grin; curly, curly hair; and a loving, sweet, sweet spirit.*

Martin and Kathryn came to the realization that this child, like any child, is a gift from God *just the way he is*. In addition, it was Isaac who helped them grasp the biblical doctrine of the sovereignty of God—He sees, He knows and He is in control. Kathryn feels that Isaac taught his family more about God and biblical theology than some seminaries teach. Not to mention that their ability to use humor went a long way in helping them to leverage this challenging situation.

Teaching His Family to Lean in to God

It is one thing to know biblical principles in your head; it is quite another to have to walk them out. We may be tempted to question fundamental principles of our faith: Is God good? If so, how could He allow children like this to be born? How could He allow this to happen to us—what did we do wrong to deserve this? How can Romans 8:28 ("in all things God works for the good of those who love him, who have been called according to his purpose") possibly be the truth in this situation? Martin and Kathryn were committed Christians with a deep desire to serve the Lord. They had been to Bible school and even served as missionaries, yet Kathryn says their theological views were sometimes misguided.

> We call our son "our wordless theologian" because even though he was not able to speak, he pushed us to the Lord and to the Word of God. He taught us depths about theology and allowed us to experience the grace of God daily.
>
> Initially, I think we were in denial. "God was good. We were blessed. We were serving Him. This could not happen to us." Then when we couldn't deny that things were not right with our son, we sought God for healing. We decided that God was going to demonstrate His glory (and our great faith) by miraculously healing Ike. We got a lot of well-intentioned advice: "You must not have enough faith." "You must have sin in your life."
>
> Not very helpful.
>
> My husband's answer to the faith comment was, "If you've got the faith, we've got the boy, go ahead and pray." And to the sin comment, he replied, "Yes, we do, but do we have that much more than other people? If God gave us what we deserved for the sin in our lives, we would all be blind and maimed." Or else he would say, tongue in cheek, "Well, I know I don't have any sin, but I'm not sure about her," pointing at me. But seriously, these comments tormented me. I would lie awake nights going over and over these questions, searching my heart for sins of which I needed to repent, wondering what I did wrong. Did I not eat a healthy enough diet when I was pregnant? Should I have avoided air travel when I was expecting? Maybe I didn't push him out quickly enough during his birth and his oxygen supply was cut off. Maybe I didn't keep him warm enough . . . the list of tormenting thoughts was endless.
>
> Freedom finally came when we began to grasp the doctrine of the sovereignty of God. What a burden lifted! God is in control. He is greater than anything I did or didn't do. He not only allowed but created Ike to be the way he is. He loves Ike more than we do. His plans and purposes for Isaac are good and beyond anything we could imagine. He is a trustworthy and faithful God and He

is in this. Sweet rest and peace came with this acceptance. Still, life was challenging, and I had occasional pity parties, wondering why God was having us walk through this, comparing my life with the easier, less complicated lives of other people.

True life change happened when our attitudes shifted from "Why us, God?" to "Thank you, Lord, for choosing us!" I love the phrase, "To this you have been called." It gave us great joy to realize that we were called and chosen by God and that what He called us to He would also give us the grace to do. This carried over into everything that God called us to or brought into our lives. I have a friend who has a daughter with disabilities. When she was born and they found out that, if she lived, her life was going to be filled with challenges, she told her three older children, "Your new sister is very, very special. God looked all over the world for a family that would love her and help her and care for her and pray for her, and He chose us." Her children adore their sister and have never had any resentment towards her. They consider it an honor to have her in their family.

It was an honor and a privilege for me to parent a special child. "To this you have been called." Even now, it encourages me because things I would like to do are put on hold while I care for my elderly mother who is suffering with Alzheimer's.

When we understand these timeless principles of God, raising a child with special needs takes on a completely new, refreshing dimension. In fact, Martin and Kathryn's beliefs and attitudes overflowed into the attitudes of Isaac's siblings and their extended family and provided their marriage with stability.

A Marriage Must Be Nurtured

Shattered dreams for your child can be difficult to cope with. When a man is looking forward to playing baseball with his son, maybe coaching Little League or boasting to his friends of his son's good grades or other achievements, but has to accept that it will never happen, it can be a bitter pill to swallow. Kathryn's point of view is that a couple must continue to uphold love, honor and loyalty as priorities in a marriage despite challenges, disappointments and uncertainty.

Who wants to be married to a haggard, grouchy, complaining,
miserable woman? What happened to the bright, happy, adoring
and adorable bride that he married? A woman needs to make
sure that she does not neglect her husband and that she continues
to love and honor him. A loving, cheerful attitude toward him
is much more effective in getting him to care about her needs
than a whining, nagging attitude. As for the husband, he needs
to cherish his wife and make sure that she gets a break now and
then.

Bitterness and depression may be inevitable emotions for parents who
are struggling to accept their child's diagnosis, but unchecked, these feelings
naturally lead to marriage problems. Kathryn says she realized early on that
"we had several things going for us."

We were already Christians. We had received good teaching on
marriage and family. We prayed together. We believed that chil-
dren were a gift as well as a responsibility entrusted to us by the
Lord, and we were aware that there would be work and sacrifice
involved in parenting. We believed that marriage is a covenant
before God and we were in it for the long haul, for better or
worse, not just as long as it made us happy. We never got into the
blame game of thinking that our son's disability was the fault of
the other one of us.

But what do you do when you marry "for better or for worse" and it ends
up "worse"—at least by the world's standards? Psalm 127:3 (THE MES-
SAGE) says, "Don't you see that children are GOD'S best gift?" Notice it
does not say *healthy* children are God's best gift. Although Marty and Kathryn both realized this biblical principle early on (as did several of the families
I interviewed), they each had to learn to embrace the fact (not just accept it)
that God had called them to a different path. Resentments had to be dealt
with, and truly loving and cherishing each other had to take place. Kathryn
is open and honest about a crucial struggle that finally led to peace between
them.

A huge hurdle for me was resentment. My husband could be
tired at night and just sit down and relax and then get up and
go to bed whenever he felt like it. He could hop in the car and
go to the store or wherever he wanted to go, whenever he wanted

to. I couldn't. One day he came home from work and was disap-pointed that dinner wasn't ready yet. I told him that I had to make special arrangements just to go to the bathroom that day. He never complained about dinner being late again; in fact, he often helped make dinner and found cooking therapeutic. He is a much better cook than I am.

Bedtime could be particularly trying when we were both tired at the end of the day. Besides the other children needing baths, pajamas, teeth brushing, stories and prayers, and often a baby to be diapered and fed, there was our son's bedtime routine, which was considerably more involved. I'd been taking care of the kids all day. He'd been working all day. We both thought we deserved to relax. There were times when I got our son ready for bed while seething with resentment toward my husband, or that he got him ready for bed thinking that he was very noble and sacrificial and I should be very appreciative.

A turning point happened for my husband one year at a Joni and Friends Family Retreat. The retreat pastor told a story about a man in a POW camp who was treated with extra cruelty because of his Christian testimony. He was given the vilest and most disgusting job of shoveling raw sewage. Because of the stench, no one else went anywhere near where he was working and so he was very much alone. This made it possible for him to sing and worship the Lord without anyone knowing or stopping him. What was meant to break him became a wonderfully sweet time of fellowship with the Lord as he worked. He made a deep valley into a time of praise. My husband was deeply moved by this story and from that time on, whenever he was home and able to, he would not only get our son ready for bed, he would sing to the Lord the whole time, which our son loved. It became the favorite part of my husband's day and is now one of his sweetest memories.

For me, grasping the truth of Jesus' words, "Truly I tell you, whatever you did for one of the least of these brothers and sisters of mine, you did for me" (Matthew 25:40), made a huge differ-ence in overcoming resentment and seeing my work of serving my husband and children (and now my mom) as an honor. The old missionary motto came back to me, "If Jesus Christ be God and died for me, then no sacrifice can be too great for me to make for Him." Even if I'm not a great missionary hero, I can serve the Lord by serving with love as unto Him wherever He calls me. I also love this quote from Frederick William Faber's All for Jesus: *"The colored sunsets and starry heavens, the beautiful mountains and the shining seas, the fragrant woods and painted flowers are not as beautiful as a soul that is serving Jesus out of love in the wear and tear of common unpoetic life."*

My husband and I both felt that our love and esteem for one another grew by leaps and bounds as we observed the way the other loved and cared for our son. Shoot, we still love anybody who loved our son; they are the dearest people on earth to us.

Sibling Relationships

In any family, each sibling, and each relationship that siblings have, is unique, important and special. These sibling relationships can be powerfully affected by a sibling's disability. Brothers and sisters influence each other and play important roles in each other's lives. In fact, sibling relationships make up a child's first social network and are the basis for his interactions with people outside the family. Brothers and sisters are playmates first; as they mature, they take on new roles with each other.

The impact of having a sibling with a disability varies considerably from person to person. For many, the experience is positive and enriching, and it teaches them to accept other people as they are. Some become deeply involved in helping parents care for the child with a disability. It is not uncommon for siblings to become passionate protectors of their brother or sister with special needs, and siblings often experience feelings of great joy when their sibling achieves even the smallest gain in learning or development. But many siblings also experience feelings of bitterness and resentment toward their parents or the brother or sister with a disability. They may feel jealous, neglected or rejected as they watch their parents focus most of their energy and attention on the child with special needs. Many siblings swing back and forth between positive and negative emotions.

Not many people would consider a child with special needs to be a blessing from God, much less a blessing to their siblings. But it is possible. Isaac influenced several of his siblings' career paths. He also enabled them to demonstrate character traits not usually developed in young children. How many children volunteer anywhere for anything, much less for special needs projects?

Isaac was the fourth of ten children, the youngest being born just seven months before Ike went to be with the Lord. The firstborn is twenty-five years older than the youngest child. The first nine children were born about two and a half years apart, with a five-year gap before number ten. Looking back, Kathryn says she feels very grateful that they did not stop having children after having one with a disability.

> *The next child after Isaac, our Mary, was born just two years after Isaac. Of all the children, they were the closest in age. I might have been hesitant to have another child had I known that Isaac was disabled, but I was already expecting her by the time we realized the extent of his problems.*

> *Prior to having Isaac, I was laid back about children reaching developmental milestones, thinking that each child develops at his own pace and not really paying much attention to when he did what. That changed dramatically after Isaac. I watched every little bit of progress in Mary's development and was relieved when she did everything ahead of schedule. She quickly passed Isaac in development and pulled him along with her. She was so good for him and such a joy to us, bringing smiles and laughter in the midst of the anguish we were going through with him. I felt that having many siblings did not necessarily mean that Ike got less attention from us; instead it meant that there were more people to love him.*

Kathryn told me she is also grateful for the influence Isaac had on his siblings. She describes her children as having very compassionate hearts.

> *They all understand what is truly important in life. They are not self-absorbed. One is going into occupational therapy after having worked as an aide in a special-needs classroom for several years. Another is going into nursing. The older children have all volunteered at Joni and Friends Family Retreats, serving families affected by disability, and Mary was able to go on a Wheels for the World outreach distributing wheelchairs in Thailand. Our kids joke that other parents are proud when their children graduate from college or have successful careers or amazing talents, whereas we are filled with pride and joy when we hear about them performing very unpleasant "clean up" jobs as they serve the disabled.*

When our son Liam was about two years old, he spoke his first complete sentence. He yelled, "Mom! Iya, seejoo!" This meant, "Mom! Isaac's having a seizure!" Not many two-year-olds are able to identify seizures.

When our son Jed was learning to talk, he shared a room with Ike. We kept a monitor on in the room so that I would know if Ike was having a seizure. We would hear Jed in his crib, talking away to Ike each morning, pointing to everything and telling him what he saw: "Ike, bear. Ike, bed. Ike, blanket. Ike, tree. Ike, book . . ." On and on. We would peek in to see Isaac listening with a big smile. As Jed got older, he would sometimes notice Isaac having a seizure before we heard it on the monitor. Jed would already be out of bed sitting next to Ike and holding his hand while we were dashing into the room.

When Isaac was frustrated or not feeling well, he was soothed by music. We have more than one musician in the family. At a talent show one year at the Joni and Friends Family Retreat, we finally thought of a talent for Isaac to demonstrate. We put him on stage in his wheelchair and then, while his three sisters played "Silent Night" (his favorite song) on the violin, piano and harp, he waved his arms in the air, smiled broadly, nodded his head and kicked his crossed leg. We called his talent "encouraging his siblings in their instrumental endeavors by his evident enjoyment and enthusiasm."

To encourage language development, we were taught to repeat back to him sounds that he made and then create meaningful words out of those sounds. One of the sounds he would make sounded like, "baa baa mmm." At the dinner table one of the kids would often say, "Let's play baa baa mmm. This meant we would all repeat whatever sounds Ike made. He would say, "baa baa mmm," and we would repeat it together; then he would say, "baa baa baa mmm," and we would repeat it. He would go on to vary the number of "baas" before the "mmm" to see if he could trick us. Sometimes he would be laughing so hard that he could not even get another "baa" out.

Recently one of our daughters was remembering something about Ike while our now four-year-old, Maggie (who was just a baby when Ike went to be with the Lord), was sitting next to her. She said to Maggie, "Aw, you don't remember Ike, do you? You were just a baby." Maggie found this offensive and said decidedly, "Yes I do!"

"Oh, really? What do you remember? Did he ever say anything to you?"

Without a pause, Maggie declared, "Yes. He told me, 'You're my favorite sister!'"

When parents verbalize positive attitudes and model encouraging behavior by example, healthy siblings are more likely to respond positively to a sibling with special needs.

A Lesson in Loving

In contrast to how some siblings felt in other families I interviewed, Isaac's eldest sister, Rachel, felt it was "special" to be his sister. Some families may treat the child with special needs as fragile or even too "different," but Isaac's family treated him "normal," with teasing, arguing and so on. Rachel remembers that during her childhood:

My parents never made any of us feel guilty, forced or pressured when it came to helping with or loving Ike. They set an example of loving him; they told us how special he was and how special our family was that we got him. I think a lot of us siblings felt more protective and caring for him because of that. We also just felt special ourselves because of Isaac. I think at times we felt a little conspicuous (during the preteen and early-teen, identity-intense years), but we liked it, too.

My parents also never made any of us feel less important than Ike. He got a lot of attention but so did all of us in different ways. I think the only kids that got slightly ignored were the ones that were in the middle and were well-behaved or loners (two in particular). So I think if my parents changed anything it would have been to bring those two into the fold a bit more by realizing that they were always good or always isolating themselves.

Being the sibling of an MRDD (Mental Retardation and Developmental Disabilities) kid, I was a lot older than Ike, but he made a big impact on my life. I think I was more protective of all my siblings because my parents were often busy with him. It made me protective of my parents and their hurts and pains, probably because I was more aware of those things being the oldest. It made me question many things about God and Christianity as I grew up, and I often struggled with trying to figure out why. I think the good things that came out of that is that now I have a high sensitivity toward people and where they might be coming from. I know the agonies that a family can experience behind closed doors, and I know that a lot of people don't or can't understand it, so it is like a secret. People carry stuff like that around all the time, and I guess I am more aware of it. One would think that I would be more comfortable in the MRDD/special-needs culture (which a lot of my siblings are), but I find it overwhelming and emotional. I still haven't figured that one out. I am probably more comfortable than most people, but I don't choose it.

The power of treating the "special" kid as normal is huge. We would tease Ike, fight with him, play with him and so on, as normal as was possible based on his interactions. It created a camaraderie between us and him; a closeness. It also made him feel loved, and for as long as he was able, he would interact. There were little things that made Ike happy, and I think they made us happy too. Little achievements were such a huge success to us. What would normally be resentment was quickly checked when we realized we were doing it for Isaac and he was our "special" brother, so nothing was really a sacrifice for him (Mom and Dad modeled this, too).

Seeing my parents sacrifice over and over and over, for him and for all of us, made me realize what unconditional love is. It made me see God's love. Isaac's rewarding kick of the crossed legs and his big, crooked-tooth smile was enough reward for everything we did for him, from saying hello to giving him a toy to playing a song on the piano. He taught us how to really love.

Lasting Vacation Memories

What became an annual vacation for the entire family is not available to just any family. It was only through Isaac that he and his family were able to attend Joni and Friends Family Retreats. Founded by international advocate for people with disabilities Joni Eareckson Tada, this family camp program is designed for families who live with disability. Isaac and his family returned each summer, and Kathryn says:

> I wish that every family living with the challenge of a disability could experience a week like this. It was so good to be with other families who were "walking the same walk" and to share each other's joys and struggles. I cannot begin to describe how blessed we were by those four and a half days each summer.

> Even with all the supportive people in our lives, there were times when I felt very alone and as though no one else could really relate to the "abnormality" of life with a disabled child. Joni and Friends Family Retreats were such a blessing to us. When our son was 10 years old, a family from church sent us to a Joni and Friends Family Retreat, or "Jonicamp" as our children called it. Words cannot begin to describe the blessing this was for our family. It was truly a foretaste of heaven for us. We arrived weary and heavy laden, and left refreshed and filled with joy. There are many camps for special-needs kids, but this was for the whole family.

> Going out in public with a child with special needs is often awkward. You never know what kind of odd behavior your child is going to demonstrate, and you get a lot of stares. Not at Jonicamp. It is a place where people with special needs not only fit in and feel normal but also feel genuinely welcomed and loved. A volunteer is assigned to assist each of the families throughout the week. The family is not looked at as an oddity but received like royalty. All meals are provided, and not having to plan, shop for, prepare or clean up for meals for a large family for five days was truly a vacation to me. Your volunteer helps you find seats in the dining room, helps you juggle all your plates in the food line and even feeds your child if you requested. The retreat offers special activities for everyone.

> In the morning, the children attend a VBS (vacation Bible school), and a volunteer accompanies your special child one-on-one throughout the activities. While the children are enjoying that, the adults enjoy a wonderful time of singing and encour-

agement, a life-changing teaching. Afterward, adults have the opportunity to talk and share in a small group and pray with other parents who can actually understand and relate to their lives, to laugh and weep and pray together. It is unbelievable how quickly solid and lasting friendships can be formed when sharing this common bond.

Afternoons hold opportunities for fun activities for families to enjoy together: boat rides, tubing, horseback rides, swimming, sports, and a climbing wall or zip line. The beauty shop is open for a manicure, massage, facial, or to have your hair done. You can hang out in the coffee shop and play games or do karaoke, and there was even a hot-air balloon one year. If you prefer, your volunteer will hang out with your children while you take a nap.

Each evening, a different event is scheduled: an ice cream social; a hoedown complete with wheelchair-accessible hayrides, a petting farm and square dancing (you have never seen square dancing unless you have seen it done with wheelchairs!); a romantic date night for couples while the children enjoy a fair and the teens go out for a special time together; and on the last night, a talent show, which is always touching.

Going once would have been life-changing and a tremendous gift to us, but we got to keep going back each year. That week each summer was always a highlight of the year for our family. One of my sweetest memories is our annual drive home. We would discuss the fun we had over the week, the things we learned, the people we met and so on, and then one of the children would look at Isaac and say, "Thanks, Ike, for taking us to Jonicamp!" One by one, the rest of the family would chime in with their thanks, ending in unison with, "One-two-three, thank you, Isaac!" to which he would respond with his big smile and nod. Such a happy memory!

Other vacations, even the simplest and least expensive, were not possible for this family. Kathryn says, "For almost 10 years, before Jonicamp became one of our annual activities, it was easier for us to just stay home." She and Marty coped with their frustration and took an occasional family day trip instead.

Other than day trips to an amusement park once or twice a year, we never went on a family vacation. The amusement park was not so bad when our son was a baby and still in a stroller, but once he started running it made for a very exhausting day. There were a few years, though, when he loved the rides and so we would take him and go. It was a challenge because one person had to be with him at all times, we usually also had a nursing baby (or pregnant mom) and other small children to look after. Looking back, I'm not quite sure how we managed. Our son did get away once, which was very frightening, but, fortunately, we located him fairly quickly. I think our enjoyment came from watching the children's enjoyment. As our son's health deteriorated, I would stay home with him and the younger children while my husband took the older children to the amusement park.

Kathryn and Marty were eventually able to maintain an annual family camping trip, but not without some sacrifice on Kathryn's part.

Because of our large family size coupled with our income, the only affordable vacation for our family would have been camping. But the prospect of camping with our son sounded miserable. He wouldn't know to shoo mosquitoes, so they would feast on him. He adored zipping and unzipping zippers, and the tent opening would have quite a workout and the bugs given ample opportunity to get in. He was fascinated by fire and it would require an ongoing effort to keep him away from the campfire. Same with the lake. He loved to run and, without a contained area, we would be chasing him all over the park. And there are a host of other reasons why, in our case, camping with our son would have been the opposite of a vacation.

Eventually, my husband began to take the kids camping for one weekend each year, along with one or more of his brothers and their children. I stayed home with our son and whoever was the baby at the time. I enjoyed camping as a child and would have loved to have been part of making camping memories for my children, so this was a hard sacrifice for me. (Still is, as this tradition continues, and now I am home caring for my mother who has Alzheimer's and lives with us.)

Isaac and his family also benefited from Kathryn's parents, who understood the situation and ensured that their home was specially prepared for Ike.

> *Even the years that we did not take a vacation, we did have a little haven that we often resorted to. We were blessed with unusually supportive parents whom we regarded as some of our best friends. My parents lived in a condo, 30 to 40 minutes from us. My dad enjoyed carpentry, and he built removable barricades that he would set up when we were coming over. They would remove anything breakable and then barricade the stairs, block access to their living room, and leave their family room and a large area for Isaac to roam freely. He called it "Iking the house." It was the only place we could go and relax. We would go there occasionally for the weekend for a family sleepover. We would watch movies (for many years we did not have a TV at our house, which made this a real treat), and the kids could play ping-pong or video games. My mom would cook for us and put out nice snacks. It was such a blessing. Every family should have such parents!*

Developing a Strong Support Network

Early on, Marty and Kathy realized that they could not do this alone and recognized the importance of their support system. They also proactively reached out to their community to increase and enhance the level of support they received.

> *We were unusually blessed to be surrounded and supported by the best grandparents, extended family, friends, church family, and all of the dear people at Isaac's school. I know that most people do not have that kind of support and feel lonely. That is why ministries such as Joni and Friends, special-needs outreaches at churches, and support groups are so vital.*
>
> *As for extended family and friends, from the time Isaac was three until he was five years old, we did an extensive home therapy program with him. The key words in the program were "intensity, frequency and duration." It was more than we could do by ourselves, so we recruited volunteers from church, friends and family to help. We trained them in what to do and they would*

come in for an hour a week to work with him. This helped peo-
ple get to know him better and become comfortable with him.

Rather than feeling frustrated or angry when people did not understand, they used this situation with Isaac as an opportunity to teach others concerning the usually uninformed, awkward issues when dealing with children with special needs.

When Isaac was older, maybe eight or nine, I invited his teacher to come to our house to lead a workshop for a group of children about Isaac and his differences and what they could do to help him and how to interact with him. We did it twice—once for a group of cousins (he had 17 in the area whom he frequently saw at family gatherings), and once for a group of children of friends that we often visited. I think it was very helpful.

I knew parents who printed up pamphlets or brochures about their child to give to people who were meeting him for the first time. They would include information such as the child's name and age and what the child's disability was, things he/she liked and disliked, activities the child could and couldn't do, and suggestions on how to best interact with the child. I thought this was a good idea.

Aunt Sheryl and Uncle Jim

Not all families have the luxury of having loving aunts and uncles nearby to be part of their support team. If they are available and willing, not only will they bless the family but also they will have an unusual opportunity to be blessed themselves. Jim and Sheryl played a major supporting role in caring for Isaac and being part of his therapy support team. They said, "Isaac was considered 'special needs', but we considered him 'very special'—God's special gift to our family. He was named perfectly. Isaac means laughter and that is what Isaac was about."

Communicating with him was not hard, even though he could not talk. His eyes, the noises he made, his actions were beautiful, and you just wanted to be around him. When Isaac walked into the room with our family, he lit up with a big smile and laughter. It was like he knew his purpose in life and he lived it. The gifts God gave him were laughter, smiles, sharing his love,

the love of Christ, compassion. When we talked to Isaac in a loving way, he would lay his head on our shoulder and he would
just give the biggest smile. It would melt your heart. His smile
was contagious. He loved being part of his family. It seemed to
us God had placed him in this family not for him but for us.
His grandfather called him "Iscicle." He lit up when Grandpa
called him that. He knew that was endearing. When we called
out, "Isaac John!" real loud, he would just burst into laughter.

Once, Jim and I were caring for him while his family attended a
family funeral in Kentucky. We picked him up from school on a
Friday and he threw his book bag in the back seat. He somehow
knew it was Friday and no school for the weekend. A big smile
came on his face and was his way of communicating, "School is
out for the weekend! Yay!"

Another time, we went on a family outing over the weekend and
it was Grandpa's annual gas-company picnic at an amusement
park. He rode all the rides he was able to and enjoyed himself
immensely, laughing all day long. Life was lived to the fullest
by Isaac, and each day was a gift to him and us. It was how he
taught us to live; live it to the fullest because each day was a gift
from God.

Isaac also loved music, and a big part of his life was surrounded by family who played piano, violin and harp. We did some
therapy with him while the children were practicing. While we
laughed and talked together with family, Isaac smiled those big
smiles, mostly when he would hear his siblings in the background
playing their instruments. The music brought great joy to him,
and the smile and sighs he would make were heart wrenching.
We believe Isaac worshipped God with his smile and his sighs
while hearing precious music. We believe Isaac loved God with
his whole heart, soul and mind; he knew God and it showed by
his actions. The love of Christ surely showed through him. Some
of his favorite songs were "Silent Night" and "Happy Birthday,"
although any music lit him up, but those were two he was no-
ticeably moved by.

Isaac had special communication with each family member; for
some, he would butt their heads as a greeting; for others, he

would squeal when he saw them; for some, he would make such amazing laughter sounds; and for others, when he saw them, he would stand up and start running. He seemed to realize he was loved, accepted and respected as a gift from God. Isaac John Murtha changed our lives. Isaac brought joy and laughter to us. Isaac was a gift from God to our family.

Include Extended Family in Your Support Network

Many resources deal with the nuclear family and, as a result, the grandparents may be forgotten in terms of how deeply the birth of their son's or daughter's child with special needs affects them as well. Aunts and uncles are also impacted and, if available, all can be an integral part of the support team.

Grandparents, aunts, uncles, cousins are all part of the family dynamics. For example, Chuck Colson and R. C. Sproul are two public figures who have grandchildren with special needs. They, too, have shared in the process of grieving: lost dreams, anger, "Why us?" They, too, have had to come to terms with being catapulted into this life of "new normal." Just because a person is "religious" does not mean she is therefore guaranteed or has earned the right to a typical child.

Chuck Colson was made infamous through his participation in the Watergate scandal of the Nixon era, then famous through his Prison Fellowship ministry after his conversion experience. He was initially heartsick at the diagnosis of his grandson, Max, with severe autism. A good friend told him God must love him very much because he will now learn about sacrificial love.

R. C. Sproul is a well-respected Bible scholar, preacher, teacher, prolific writer and founder of several ministries. Through his granddaughter, Shannon, who has severe autism, he has learned that she is made in the image of God *as she is.* He now understands that the biblical principle of the sovereignty of God is not just a lofty academic principle he teaches, but he lives it and participates in it through the lives of this granddaughter and her family. He views the concept of human dignity and worth as delusional apart from God.[1]

Parenting Teenagers and Grown Children

Once a parent, always a parent. Whether a child is twelve or forty-two, Mom is still Mom, and Dad is still Dad. The joy of watching our young children grow and change is unmatched, and it is always encouraging when we see them develop into mature adults, strike out on their own and begin their own families. But for some parents this is a long-forgotten, impossible dream that will never be realized. A child with special needs may forever be age twelve. Those who have played a significant role in the lives of children when they were younger will continue to play an important role in their lives as they grow older, even as caregiving arrangements and lifestyles change. Many parents feel uncertain about whether their child is ready for a more independent lifestyle—let alone when and how to make this transition—and letting go often becomes an emotionally charged issue.

The parents of adopted twins, a boy and a girl from Bulgaria, talked to me about their concerns for their now teenaged children. The mother describes the process of understanding the true extent of their children's needs as "quite a journey." Post Traumatic Stress Syndrome (PTSS) from living in an orphanage, developmental delays and autism are just a few of their diagnoses.

> *We are concerned about our twins' futures. As they get older and become adults, life will get harder for them. Our goal is for them to maintain their independence as much as possible and find appropriate jobs. Also, concerning their future, we need to make a will. But who will take care of them if anything happens to us with no extended family available? We are looking into a future-planning course held by the local board of developmental disabilities in our area. Hopefully they will be able to help us identify a team of people to be our children's caregivers when the need arises.*

Even though it may be hard to imagine your adult child living without you, you can take comfort in knowing that God is still there, loving and caring for your child even more than you do. (See Psalm 139:13; Matthew 10:30–31; and James 1:5.)

Adult children with special needs, who may have adjusted to a certain level of "normalcy," have parents who will always carry with them a high level of concern and involvement. These parents may feel that they must be available on demand, in a way that other parents of adult children do not experience. The mother whose daughter was diagnosed EMR expressed her continual concern for, and involvement in, her daughter's daily life.

She was clearly unprepared for supported living with roommates who had different backgrounds. After nine years and some adjustments, she is in a living situation in which she is happy and staff is able to handle conflict resolution. There is a very big but here. Over the years, she has developed stress-related physical conditions. My challenge with her now is working with physicians to help her through colitis and depression. We usually have one specialist appointment every two months that I feel compelled to attend. Her agency manages all other appointments.

My life still revolves around this daughter's needs. I usually do not see her but once a week, but we have short phone conversations a few times a day. I encourage activities through her staffing agency and Special Olympics. Of course, that leads to more involvement on my part, typically for fundraising for the activities. I am 72 years old and still the primary advocate for my daughter. I am certain challenges will continue. I am trying to wean her away from so much dependency on me. I feel like I am walking a tightrope, because I want to be supportive, but I also want to help her learn to live independently.

The father whose son has a hearing impairment is now the grandfather of two boys and told me about his son's accomplishments.

Our hearing-impaired son now lives in Rochester, New York, which has the largest deaf community in the United States. He is married to a hearing wife, who is a sign-language interpreter, and they have two hearing boys, two years old and nine months old. He has his own business designing and maintaining websites, and he also works part-time at Rochester Institute of Technology teaching sign language and interpreting for the deaf and blind. I am truly happy for him. So where did he end up? Mostly in the deaf world. God didn't make us to be isolated.

This father wisely concluded that finding emotional support is crucial, not just to survive—but to thrive—as a family with special needs.

BUILDING AN EMOTIONAL SUPPORT SYSTEM

Author Emily Perl Kingsley uses an excellent analogy to describe the experience of living with disability. She writes that it is like arriving unexpectedly in a foreign country that, over time, you come to know and appreciate.

Kingsley explains that to adjust to this new place, you will need a guidebook, you will need to learn the language, "and you will meet a whole new group of people you would never have met."[2] A theme in the Book of Proverbs is the value of good counsel. Proverbs 1:5 and 12:15 speak of the wisdom of listening to counselors; Proverbs 11:14 and 15:22 of the security provided by multiple counselors. "Oil and perfume rejoice the heart; so does the sweetness of a friend's counsel that comes from the heart" (Proverbs 27:9, Amplified Bible). Families that have a child with special needs must build an emotional support system, full of friendly and reliable counselors, to function in a healthy way.

The mother whose daughter was diagnosed EMR built her support system by interacting with families that also had a child with disabilities. She says, "This daughter is and has been a blessing to all of us. I have made many friends who are in the same situation. We are a support and a joy to each other."

Whether it is a group of friends, a blog, books, camps or hotels, knowing that someone else out there has "walked a mile in your moccasins" can be very refreshing and can help lighten the load. The father whose son has a hearing impairment described the support of his neighbors, many of whom learned sign language on behalf of his son.

> We had amazing support from family, friends, church and school systems while continually educating ourselves about deafness and the deaf world. We joined the Deaf Club on West Sixth Street in the downtown area, where we went on Friday evenings to learn more about the deaf culture. We had a very close neighborhood and the people took time to learn basic signs so they were able to communicate with our son. His best friend lived next door and learned to sign as fluidly as our son.
>
> Although I regret that church was not a greater influence in our lives during that time, I can't say enough about a community of neighbors, about 20 families that continually gave us encouragement, support and love. It definitely would have been harder without them!

Your potential "counselors" may sometimes come from unexpected sources. As the parents of adopted twins with special needs found, you may need to actively seek out support and be open to educating people who have no prior experience with children with disabilities.

We do not have extended family to count on. They either live out of town or are deceased. The church is our support. We have had to build our own support and hire competent babysitters for a date night once a month.

We have made an effort to break down barriers between "normal" friends and our children by inviting people into our family. Often, lack of knowledge is what keeps people from interacting with a family like ours. We even like to invite people on our boat, named Special Needs.

Thanks to today's technology and level of awareness, an emotional support system is not far away. Online support is available through reading blogs or writing your own; the plethora of internet resources makes research easier than ever. Other avenues of support include your extended family, friends who have children with special needs, church support groups and parachurch organizations. All these crucial lifelines can be grasped by weary, worn-out families. Like other families I interviewed, the mother of a daughter with Dravet syndrome found it helpful to extend her support system to include those who had no experience with children with disabilities.

True friends "get it" from just being around and seeing how life goes here. Other so-called friends who did not want to be a part of "normal" life in our home are long gone. Even several family members chose not to be a part of it because they are self-centered, and others are just afraid. For our friends, the best education in how a family with children with special needs functions is just being with us in our daily life.

My entire life revolves around special needs. My friends either have children of their own who have special needs or have taught children with special needs. My faith and church family were/ are my strength: prayer and more prayer from the body of Christ. Getting out despite bad days to make a difference in someone else's life keeps me going. Work or watching sports on television are my husband's coping mechanisms.

CONCLUSION

The families interviewed in this chapter, with their various circumstances, do exhibit quite a few similarities: suspecting that something was not right;

journeying through a range of emotions that include disbelief, shock, grief, anger and frustration; adapting to constant change; and dealing with the pros and cons of each decision they make. Most of the parents would agree that after accepting a child's diagnosis, they needed to work together to plan and provide care for their child, and they relied on the cooperation of all family members. Depending on whom you read, 80–90 percent of marriages crumble under the weight of this load. Communication and cooperation are key factors in a positively functioning family—between husband and wife, as well as siblings. Appropriate humor can lighten the load, and enjoying simple pleasures is a skill worth honing. Yet these families desperately need respite. They need community: people to love, understand and help them without judging them. Their kids need friends.

The challenges of raising a child with special needs can either weaken or strengthen a family's faith. In the end, the impact of a disability on a family comes down to attitude. Is your glass half-empty or half-full? Attitude is the only thing we are in charge of and can change. Disabilities can become possibilities.

Notes

The epigraph to part VI appears in Jack Canfield, Mark Victor Hansen, and Heather McNamara, *Chicken Soup for the Unsinkable Soul: Stories of Triumph and Overcoming Life's Obstacles* (Deerfield Beach, FL: HCI, 1999), 116. This poem, written in 1952, honors the Massimillas' daughter Ruth, who was born with Down syndrome.

1. "When Disability Hits Home: Chuck Colson and R. C. Sproul," *Joni and Friends Television Series*, episode no. 28, season 2, http://joniandfriends.org/television/when-disability-hits-home.

2. Emily Perl Kingsley, "Welcome to Holland" (essay, 1987).

CHAPTER NINETEEN

SUPPORTING THE CAREGIVER

* * *

Judy Raymo

A LL parents have dreams for their children. Those of us who are parents of children with special needs are no exception. Our dreams may not include college or medical school. We may be all too aware that we are not bringing up the next Albert Einstein or Michael Jordan. But we can realistically dream that our children will become kind, gentle, loving, giving people, and our world could certainly use more of these!

The give-and-take of parental interaction can be difficult for us. We may become oddly quiet when parents mention their son who scores all the goals at soccer, or their daughter who brings home perfect report cards. One father of a "special" child defined love this way: "You give everything and expect nothing in return." But hearing about the accomplishments of other people's children may still cause a twinge of pain.

We may be more comfortable discussing medical procedures or Individualized Education Plan issues or some other special-needs topic. In a way, we live in two worlds: that of "normal" children and families, and that of children who are different. Often we return home zombie-like from nights spent at the hospital with a sick or postsurgical child. (Try sleeping on a plastic fold-out chair with bright lights snapping on every half hour as nurses scurry in and out, while the kid in the next bed wants to watch TV all night!) Once home, we immediately pick up the whirling activity schedule of our other children, not to mention several days' worth of chores we did not get done.

We participate in all ordinary experiences of life, plus more. When we go shopping with our children, people may stare or ask rude questions. We carry the same responsibilities as everyone else, but we also spend hours waiting, waiting, waiting for medical appointments, procedures, prescriptions, evaluations, phone calls to be returned, and so on. Then there are the emergency rushes to the hospital and the times we get discouraging reports. Sometimes we are worn out—physically and emotionally.

How Can Friends Help?

Some simple words and actions can give a caregiver a heartening boost and will be deeply appreciated. Often parents who have children with special needs find that their friends become distant because they no longer share the same experiences or they feel that giving has become one-sided. We parents need to keep in touch with life beyond the world of special needs and keep reaching out to our friends. We need our friends to include us and our children in normal activities whenever possible. We need friends who will treat our children as children, who have the same needs, interests and hopes as any children.

We need friends who look for the best in our children, acknowledge what is appealing about them or notice their progress, no matter how small. As with any parent, what is better than seeing another person truly enjoy and appreciate your child? What warms a parent's heart more than a comment like the one I heard from our eight-year-old's teacher: "Shawn is the kindest little boy. He has such a kind heart."

We need friends who continually love and care in practical ways. When someone has a crisis, friends, church members and colleagues at work all seem to rally around to help in various ways until the crisis is over. Parents of children with special needs live constantly in a degree of crisis. An encouraging e-mail or card anytime reminds us we are not forgotten. The gift of a meal is wonderful after a long day of meetings or evaluations. Babysitting for other children when one must be taken to medical appointments or treatments could make a tough day easier. When a child is hospitalized, other children might need a ride to a sports or church activity. Making arrangements to take a parent out for dessert or a movie or to the gym may give them a break they enjoy. For me, it does not help much to say, "Let me know if there is anything I can do," because I probably will not. But I greatly appreciate thoughtful gestures like the bookstore gift card I received from friends who know I love to read.

Professionals Can Help, Too

We parents need medical and other professionals who listen to us and respect our knowledge of our children. We need to be treated like real people; I have a name, and it is not "Mom!" We need to have professionals who do not make us feel like just another hurried appointment or an interesting disease. I have appreciated doctors and others who have taken the time to call us at home to see how we or our child are doing. I have also been grateful for nurses, therapists and even custodial staff who will "hang out" or initiate a friendly chat with me or my child in the hospital.

We need professionals to be honest, to keep us informed and to get to know us and how we communicate. We do not want to hear only the negative, but also what can be done and what the possibilities are for our children. We appreciate professionals who point out resources to help our children including articles and books, play or support groups, and introductions to other parents who are willing to talk. For instance, the adoption agency we have worked with gave our name to a couple who were considering adopting an infant with sickle cell, and we were able to tell them about our experience with Shawn.

Professionals can help us because of their ability to recognize small changes and progress in our children. Sometimes we wonder if anything is improving. When Joey came to us at age seven months, his development was at newborn level and his prognosis was questionable. For months we questioned whether he would ever smile, roll over, sit up or anything. When we took him to his first evaluation at our Regional Child Development Center at age eleven months, the therapists delighted us by pointing out how Joey recognized and preferred his family. This encouraged us to interact with him even more enthusiastically.

Professionals should not underestimate the encouragement it is to parents to be told when we are doing a good job. We want to work together with whoever is helping our child, so we appreciate people who make us part of the team and take the time to explain treatments, therapies and so on. We also appreciate professionals who try to see the whole picture of our family's life and who know that parents are often experiencing lots of stress. When one of our children is in the hospital, I can begin to feel guilty if I am not able to be there twenty-four hours a day. When the nurses understand that I have other young children at home who also have needs, and that I am not a "bad" mother or deserting my sick child if I am not with him constantly, it is a relief.

EMPATHY AND ENCOURAGEMENT

Even though we parents often present a strong and cheerful outlook, we feel our children's pain. At times we need a bit of encouragement from someone who understands that it is hard, even if we seem to "have it all together."

In our family's case, sickle cell anemia has become a regular part of life, and we tend to minimize the disease and emphasize what is normal for Shawn (whose sickle cell is quite severe). At age eight, he views his medical difficulties as a minor annoyance in a busy round of school, AWANA, sports and playing with his friends. When he has to go to the hospital, he is most worried about whether it is bingo day in the playroom. Yet this little boy has been through three surgeries (one to remove his spleen), lost the hearing in his left ear due to a "minor" stroke, spent many days and nights hospitalized for sickle cell pain and fevers, had more blood draws than I can count, goes to the hospital every three weeks for apheresis—a procedure involving a huge needle inserted into each arm and sitting still for several hours while connected to a machine that removes his red (sickled) blood cells and replaces them with healthy donor cells—and is at risk for stroke and organ damage and other complications of sickle cell. At certain moments, as his mom, the thought of all he has faced, and will face the rest of his life, can be overwhelming.

As a parent, I am not looking for sympathy for me or for my children. But I sometimes wish other people could appreciate the quiet, matter-of-fact courage we see in our "special" children every day.

GOD LOOKS ON THE HEART

Our eleven-year-old Joey was born severely premature and was a patient in the Children's Hospital of Philadelphia for his first seven months. He has bilateral VP shunts, vision impairment, and mild cerebral palsy because of a grade four brain hemorrhage at birth. Joey struggles with fifth grade math. He trips over the two steps between our hallway and dining room every time he goes up them. He cannot process the sight of a baseball flying towards him fast enough to catch it—or even to avoid being hit by it. He runs with a slow, lopsided gait. This year it was becoming obvious that his peers were advancing far beyond him in soccer skills, yet he badly wanted to play on a team. I took the plunge and signed him up for "special soccer."

Suddenly Joey was a star. He went after the ball, he dribbled, he passed, he scored goals! Seeing him with an opportunity to be one of the best players in the game made me happy. What warmed my heart more was to watch as Joey noticed that some of the other kids were not able to run to the ball to kick it away from him. Joey began to carefully place the ball where one of the others could reach it, and then he would step back out of the way so that child could make a kick. Joey may not have the academic abilities, or the athletic skills, or the social savvy of the typical eleven-year-old, but his thoughtfulness and care for children more disabled than him reminded me that what matters in a person is not limited by disability. (For an update on Joey, see chapter 20.)

A friend of ours, Peter Teague, is president of Lancaster Bible College and the parent of a child with special needs. He writes:

> *Being created in the image of God means more than having certain abilities and attributes. It means that ALL humans are the image of God, regardless of what they can or cannot do. We are all image-bearers of the living God. He has lovingly, tenderly, and sovereignly put His fingerprint on each soul.*
>
> *As the father of a daughter, Jessica, who is severely disabled, I have learned much about the value of human life. The world's standards of value would classify Jessica's life as of less value. She has many "deficiencies"—she cannot talk, she cannot care for herself, she cannot read, she cannot work, and at times she cannot control her behavior. Jessica needs care 24 hours a day, seven days a week. But does she have value to God? The answer is an emphatic, "Yes!" Jessica is an image bearer of the living God, and He created her for a purpose.*
>
> *God's Word reminds us that God makes no mistakes by creating those with disabilities. Jeremiah 1:5 reminds us, "Before I formed you in the womb I knew you."*
>
> *For these past 22 years while raising Jessica, my wife and I asked God to show us how He could be glorified through Jessica's life. He has used her life to make us and our other three children who we are today. He has taught us lessons about compassion, unconditional love, patience, grace, prayer, perseverance, to name a few. He has used her life to help us minister to countless others who are facing similar challenges in raising a child with a disability.[1]*

What helps us parents and caregivers for children with special needs? Not to be called "saints" and told how wonderful we are to care for these children! Yes, bringing up children with special needs is often physically exhausting and emotionally stressful. But what helps us most is people seeing our children as uniquely created individuals whose lives are worthwhile and who can teach us "normal" folks many things. Our disappointments, frustrations, tears, sleepless nights and hours of practical care giving are blessed when we catch a hint that we are contributing to the development of people who matter and who belong to the Savior who loves them.

NOTE

1. Peter Teague, Jessica & Friends Community Newsletter, 2003, 1.

PART VII

Concluding Reflection

The Beatitudes for Friends of Someone with a Disability

Blessed are you who take time to listen to difficult speech,
for you help us know that if we persevere, we can be understood.
Blessed are you who walk with us in public places and ignore the stares of strangers,
for in your companionship we find havens of relaxation.
Blessed are you who never bid us to "hurry up," and more blessed, you
who do not snatch our tasks from our hands to do them for us,
for often we need time rather than help.
Blessed are you who stand beside us as we enter new and untried ventures,
for our failures will be outweighed by times when we surprise ourselves and you.
Blessed are you who ask for our help,
for our greatest need is to be needed.
Blessed are you who help us with the graciousness of Christ,
for oftentimes we need the help we cannot ask for.
Blessed are you when, by all these things you assure us
that the thing that makes us individuals is not in our peculiar muscles,
nor in our wounded nervous systems, nor in our difficulties in learning,
but in the God-given self which no infirmity can confine.
Rejoice and be exceedingly glad,
and know that you give us reassurances that could never be spoken in words,
for you deal with us as Christ dealt with all His children.

—Author unknown

CHAPTER TWENTY

BE A FRIEND

* * *

Joey Raymo

A FEW months ago Joey was one of the speakers for "Youth Sunday" at our church. The theme for the service was "What's Your Excuse?" Twice, in front of audiences of four hundred to five hundred, he talked about his life and faith, the disabilities he's struggled with, and how God put him into our family. Joey was calm and collected, but plenty of tears flowed in the congregation. I couldn't help wishing that the people who told us we should "send him back" when we first adopted him could have been there to see what God has done in the life of one child who started out with "four strikes" against him. Joey, whose birth weight, prematurity, and severe brain hemorrhage made him a candidate for "pulling the plug" (except that God sent him to the Children's Hospital of Philadelphia, where Dr. Everett Koop's Christian ethics reigned), is graduating from high school next week.

To the amazement of his teachers and case managers, Joey has met all the academic requirements for graduation. Even better, God has made him a light in the dark world of public high school. The police officer assigned to the school these last three years told us, "The one bright spot in working here has been getting to know Joey."

None of us should limit or doubt what God can do in the lives of His children!

—Judy Raymo

MY TESTIMONY

My name is Joey Raymo, and I'm a senior at Burnsville High School.

How many of you know someone in your school or neighborhood who has a physical or mental disability? How many of you avoid them or don't talk to them or think they're weird? How many of you try to make friends with them?

I was born three and a half months prematurely and weighed 800 grams (one pound, twelve ounces). I had lots of medical problems. I had a grade 4 brain hemorrhage, the most severe level. I was fed by tube and stayed in the hospital till I was seven months old.

I still have shunts that drain extra brain fluid from my head to my stomach so pressure won't build up. It takes longer than normal for my brain to process what I see, so if you throw a ball at me fast, it will probably hit me before I can catch it. I have short-term memory problems and mild cerebral palsy. I had to have eye surgery because my eyes weren't aligned, and I have nystagmus—rapid eye shaking—sometimes.

My parents adopted me straight from CHOP (the Children's Hospital). They thought it might be too hard, but God led them to adopt me. The doctors said probably I wouldn't sit up, walk or talk, and that I might be blind. I didn't walk or talk until I was over two years old. I've had lots of therapy and surgeries and special education.

When I was little and first started trying to run, I loped along lopsided and slow. Now I run cross country and track at school. One of my favorite experiences was finally running a mile in under six minutes, after working on it for five years, and having all my teammates and coaches cheering and encouraging me. It's also great when I beat my dad in 5k races!

Even though I have disabilities, God can still use me. Here is a verse I like: "Religion that God our Father accepts as pure and faultless is this: to look after orphans and widows in their distress and to keep oneself from being polluted by the world" (James 1:27). God put me in my family—thanks, Mom and Dad, for adopting me.

I would like to challenge you to try to make friends with someone who has a disability. It would make me happy, and I think it would make God happy, for you to do this.

APPENDIX A

Disability Awareness Sunday Ideas

1. Include people with disabilities in the service as speakers, musicians, greeters, ushers and so on.

2. Include music that has a disability message (for example, "Sometimes Miracles Hide" by Bruce Carroll).

3. Include a volunteer card in the church bulletin that lists volunteer needs for your ministry (for example, buddies for children in Sunday school, worship buddies for adults with disabilities, teachers for a special class, people to pray for the families and the ministry, respite providers for the families).

4. Include an invitation in the prior week's bulletin for members to invite friends, neighbors and family members who might have a special interest in disability issues.

5. Provide a week of devotional guides for members to do as a family in preparation for the Sunday.

6. Complete an accessibility audit of your church (see appendix B).

7. Invite family members of individuals with disabilities to give a testimony.

8. Invite people from a nearby group home to visit the church and provide a refreshment time to welcome them.

9. Survey the congregation to identify special needs within the congregation.

10. Have the service, or at least the songs, signed. Invite a deaf choir to "sing."

11. Take up a special offering for the ministry (for example, accessibility ramp, large-print or Braille Bibles, special sound system for hearing impaired, designated handicapped parking spaces).

12. Include disability-awareness activities in Sunday school. For example, create a wheelchair obstacle course, do activities while blindfolded, or practice buttoning a big shirt or tying shoes while wearing heavy gloves.

13. Study Bible passages related to disability issues. Some Bible study options include:
    - 2 Samuel 9, David and Mephibosheth
    - Exodus 4:10–12, Moses
    - Mark 2:1–12, the friends of a man who was paralyzed lowered him through the roof
    - John 9, healing of a man born blind
    - Psalm 139, God's design for us
    - 2 Corinthians 12:7–10, God's power revealed in weakness

Appendix B

Architectural Accessibility Checklist

The following guidelines will help you to determine the accessibility of your church and the areas in which you need to make adaptations. The cost-reducing adaptations that are included in this checklist will help you to see that these adaptations are possible.

These accessibility specifications are based on the widest possible mobility aid used by the person with a disability, the lowest physical strength, and the most general level of manual dexterity available.

	YES	NO
A. PARKING		
1. Marked spaces, 12 feet wide so the door can be opened	____	____
2. No loose grave	____	____
3. Surface slope of the parking spaces does not exceed 1/4 inch per foot	____	____
4. Spaces should be near an entrance witth either curb cuts to the sidewalks or a ramped curb 3 feet wide with a rise no greater than 1 foot for each 12 feet	____	____
B. WALKS AND RAMPS	YES	NO
1. Graded or ramped entrances look as normal and aesthetic as possible to avoid the stigma of "speciall"	____	____
2. 4 feet wide (minimum of 32 inches)	____	____
3. Nonslip surface, if possible	____	____
4. Ramp rise not greater than 1 foot for each 12 feet	____	____

5. Handrails 32–38 inches apart and 30–32 inches high   _____ _____

6. 6-foot-wide level platform at the top and
   bottom of the ramp   _____ _____

7. Cleared of ice and snow in the winter   _____ _____

Adaptations:
   •   Portable ramps (Handi-Ramp); cost varies according to the size of the ramp

C. ENTRANCES   YES   NO
   1. At least one entrance to the church that is ramped
      and wheelchair accessible   _____ _____

   2. Doors that open out since they need less than 8 pounds of
      pull to open   _____ _____

   3, Double egress doors in the vestibule, one opening in and the other out   _____ _____

   4. Doors with vertical handles—lever or paddle-type handles, not round knobs _____ _____

   5. Blunt door sills   _____ _____

   6. For newer buildings and new additions: sliding doors with
      recessed lower channels   _____ _____

   7. Kick plates the full width of the door and 1 foot high on the push side
      for the wheelchairs to push the door with the foot pedal   s   _____ _____

   8. Doorways that are a minimum width of 32 inches   _____ _____

Adaptations:
   •   To widen doorways, remove the door, frame and buck, then install sliding doors
   •   Install swing-clear hinges to the door causing it to open out, thus adding 2 inches to the
        doorway
   •   To retrofit a round door knob, add a Handi-Lever to the knob, making it a lever type
        handle

D. STAIRS   YES   NO
   1. Risers not greater than 7 inches high   _____ _____

   2. No nosing on the risers   _____ _____

   3. Rubber treads or nonslip strips on the risers   _____ _____

4. A painted strip at each stair edge, with a slightly raised, abrasive strip
on the top step to indicate where the stairs begin, for the visually impaired   ____ ____

5. Handrails on both sides, 32 inches from the stairs, extending 18 inches
beyond the top and bottom stairs   ____ ____

E. BATHROOMS   YES   NO
1. At least one wheelchair-accessible restroom on each floor (may be unisex)   ____ ____

2. Wheelchair turning space, 5 x 5 feet   ____ ____

3. Door openings with a clearance of 60 inches in the restroom, opening out with a clearance
of 42 inches   ____ ____

4. A stall doorway 32 inches wide   ____ ____

5. Stall dimensions 3 feet wide and 5 feet deep   ____ ____

6. Handrail or grab bar 32 inches from the floor and 1 1/2 inches
from the wall, on each side (available from Sears)   ____ ____

7. Toilet 1 foot 5 inches from the floor   ____ ____

8. Urinal 1 foot 5 inches from the floor   ____ ____

9. Toilet fixtures designed to be operated with one hand;
no foot operated flushing devices   ____ ____

10. Space beneath the sink for a wheelchair to fit   ____ ____

11. Sink height a minimum of 29 inches and a maximum of 34 inches   ____ ____

12. Levers on the sink, not knob faucets; or a one-lever faucet   ____ ____

13. Paper towel dispensers no higher than 40 inches from the floor   _____

14. Wastebasket within reach   ____ ____

15. Mirror at a height reasonable for a person in a wheelchair, 3 feet 4 inches ____ ____

16. Nonslip floor   ____ ____

17. Wheelchair-accessible drinking fountain with a push bar within easy reach   ____ ____

Adaptations:

- To widen a stall, move the side wall of the stall component out, remove the door, and replace the door with an extend-rod and curtain
- Supply the handicapped-accessible stall with a raised toilet seat
- Use a child's plastic potty seat insert for the seat
- Install handrails or grab bars, or purchase toilet bars which attach to the toilet and the floor
- Install a kitchen paper-towel dispenser on the side of the counter or on the wall
- Use a floor wastebasket
- Mount a full-length mirror on an accessible wall
- Have a cup dispenser available in the bathroom if the water fountain is too high
- Ribbed tile, rubber-studded tile, or nonslip paint on the floor; no wax (alternative: strip the wax)

F. ELEVATORS   YES   NO
1. Wide doors   ____ ____

2. Controls 54 inches or less from the elevator floor   ____ ____

3. Raised, recessed or Braille numbers on the buttons for the blind ____ ____

4. Handrail on at least one side, 32 inches from the elevator floor ____ ____

G. SANCTUARY   YES   NO
1. Level with the entrance, or a ramped area up to it   ____ ____

2. Scattered "pew cuts" for wheelchairs, 32–36 inches wide; not in the front or back of the sanctuary ____ ____

3. Seating spaces with extra leg room for people using crutches, walkers, braces or casts ____ ____

4. Railing along stairs leading to the platform or choir loft ____ ____

5. Ramping up to the platform, or an area with a lectern and microphone accessible to those with mobility impairments ____ ____

6. Choir area accessible to those with mobility impairments, with space for wheelchair users ____ ____

7. Bookstands or lapboards available for those unable to hold hymnals, Bibles or prayerbooks _____ _____

8. Large-print Bibles, hymnals and prayerbooks _____ _____

Adaptations:

- Use portable ramps, with trained personnel
- Shorten pews by 36 inches or remove 2 or 3 pews

H. AMPLIFICATION   YES   NO

1. Amplification for the hearing impaired _____ _____

2. Induction loop around the sanctuary _____ _____

I. LIGHTING   YES   NO
1. Lighting comes from below the speaker's face to illuminate his face for those who read lips _____ _____

2. No flickering lights, which can cause fatigue to the visually impaired _____ _____

J. SAFETY   YES   NO
1. Vocal exit signs available for the visually impaired _____ _____

Appendix C

Sunday School Registration Form

Student's name _____

Address _____

Telephone _____ Date of birth _____ Sex _____

Parent/guardian's name _____

Address _____

Telephone _____

Person to contact if parent/guardian cannot be reached _____

Address _____

Telephone _____

Student's diagnosis _____

Assistive devices: ___ wheelchair ___ braces ____ crutches ____ walker ____ other ____

(Please specify "other" _____)

School placement/level _____

Please check those phrases that most accurately describe the student:

Writing Skills	Reading Skills
___ does not write/type	___ likes to be read to
___ does write/type	___ likes to read
___ writes words	___ out loud
___ writes sentences	___ to himself/herself

Spelling level? _____   Reading level? _____

School teacher's name _____ Telephone _____

Is the student's behavior age-appropriate? _____

MEDICATION:

List all medication the student uses:

_____

_____

Are there any side effects our staff should know about?

_____

_____

Should any medication be taken by the student, either regularly or in an emergency, while he/she is with us?

_____

_____

PLEASE ACCOMPANY THE MEDICATION WITH THE DOCTOR'S PERMISSION AND INSTRUCTIONS FOR OUR ADMINISTRATION.

Is the student allergic to any medication? _____

Is the student allergic to bee stings? _____

Is the student subject to seizures? _____

 How often? _____

 How long does it last? _____

 Describe a usual seizure: _____

 _____

 How do you handle the student during a seizure? _____

 _____

 What do you do for the student after a seizure? _____

 _____

Does the student need transportation?

 _____ yes   _____ no

PERMISSION:

I hereby give _____ my permission to attend Sunday school class and/or church as indicated by me. He/she may ride on the church bus or van, or in private cars designated by the church, to church, special class parties, and/or special class trips.

_____

Signature

_____

Relationship to student

_____

Date

MEDICAL RELEASE:

In case of a medical problem while _____ is with
the Sunday school class or church, I understand every reasonable effort will be made to contact me in case of an emergency. In the event that I cannot be reached, I give my permission
to the staff to secure appropriate medical treatment for him/her. I also give permission for
release of information for insurance purposes.

Doctor's name _____ Telephone _____

Hospital of choice _____

I release the church personnel of any responsibility except as agreed upon in this statement.
I have had the opportunity to discuss this agreement with a Sunday school class or church
staff member.

_____   _____   _____

Signature   Relationship to student   Date

_____   _____

Signature of staff member   Date of interview

CONSENT FOR PHOTOGRAPHS:

We give out consent to _____ to photograph
_____ while attending the Sunday school class, church
activities or class-related activities. I also give my permission for any photographs or slides
of him/her to be reproduced as publicity for the program or for training purposes.

_____   _____   _____

Signature   Relationship to student   Date

Ability Skills Form

Ability Skills, Part 1

Student's Name:

Dressing Skills

___ can dress self completely

___ needs help w/ buttons, zippers, snaps

___ needs help w/ underpants, slacks

___ needs help w/ shoes, socks

___ can put brace on without assistance

___ can take brace off without assistance

___ needs total assistance

Comments:

Eating Skills

___ can feed self

___ can serve self food

___ needs help to prepare food

___ needs to be fed

___ uses special equipment, please specify:

_____

_____

___ needs straw for beverages

Foods that cannot be eaten:

_____

_____

_____

Comments:

Sitting Skills

___ can sit without support

___ needs to use a chair with back support

___ cannot maintain sitting position without complete support

Comments:

Ability Skills, Part 2

Student's Name:

Toileting Skills

___ can care for own needs

___ must be reminded to go

___ needs help getting on/off toilet

___ needs help with clothing

___ needs special help, please describe:

Hearing Skills

___ can hear well:

___ right ear

___ left ear

___ hearing loss, but can hear well with a hearing aid:

___ right ear

___ left ear

___ has difficulty hearing when using hearing aids:

Speech/Communication

___ speech usually understood by a stranger

___ speech is often hard for a stranger to understand

___ often only the family understands

___ uses only a few words, please specify:

_____

_____

_____

___ no speech; uses gestures

___ no speech:

How does he/she say "yes"?

How does he/she say "no"?

___ uses a language board

___ understands written words

___ understands spoken words

Comments:

Ability Skills, Part 3

Student's Name:

Vision

__ no problems with vision

__ problem:

__ right

__ left

__ both

__ aids:

__ no aids

__ glasses

__ used for close-up vision

__ used for distance vision

__ other, please specify:

_____

__ vision with aid:

__ normal

__ low vision

__ almost blind

__ totally blind

Comments:

Walking

__ can walk without problems

__ has difficulty walking:

__ on rough terrain

__ with balance

__ cannot bear weight on legs:

__ right

__ left

__ both

__ does not use aids

__ uses aids:

__ braces

__ crutches

__ walker

__ wheelchair

__ transfer board

Comments:

Arm/Hand Use

__ has no limitations

__ has limitations:

__ right

__ left

__ both

__ degree of control:

__ total

__ moderate

__ minimal

__ hand skills:

__ can use scissors

__ can use pencil

__ can point

Comments:

Appendix D

Rapid Developmental Assessment

The following assessment can be carried out to determine the level of the child's physical, social, emotional and vocational skills, depending on the child's age. It can be used as a prescreening and a postscreening tool to monitor the child's progress.

The term *appropriate* refers to age-appropriate. The checklist helps the caregiver identify possible gaps and work with the child on specific life skills. The following informal rating scale is used for each assessment area:

- Always (A)
- Sometimes (S)
- Not Yet (NY)

PHYSICAL SKILLS ASSESSMENT

1.	Able to put on proper clothing and footwear	A	S	NY
2.	Hygiene skills:			
	• Bathes properly daily	A	S	NY
	• Brushes hair in morning and after bathing	A	S	NY
	• Brushes teeth two times a day	A	S	NY
3.	Care for personal belongings:			
	• Puts dirty laundry in basket	A	S	NY
	• Puts clean clothes in correct dresser or shelf	A	S	NY
	• Keeps school items in book bag	A	S	NY
	• Able to clean up after self in bathroom	A	S	NY
	• Able to make bed	A	S	NY
	• Able to wash, dry and fold laundry (older children)	A	S	NY
4.	Eats mannerly and properly	A	S	NY

5.   Participates in physical activity   A S NY

6.   Demonstrates safe behavior:

   •   Takes caution in dangerous situations (crosses street safely)   A S NY

   •   Understands consequences to wrong behavior   A S NY

7.   Uses hygiene products appropriately (including lotion, shampoo,

     personal products)   A S NY

8.   Medical care:

   •   Comes to an adult when hurt (younger children)   A S NY

   •   Washes cuts with soap and water, use of band-aid   A S NY

   •   Applies ice to bruises   A S NY

   •   Takes medication properly   A S NY

9.   Cooking skills:

   •   Can wash dishes   A S NY

   •   Can make simple meal, following instructions   A S NY

   •   Can work stove and oven safely (older children)   A S NY

10. Understands how their body works   A S NY

SOCIAL SKILLS ASSESSMENT

1.   Contributes to the household:

   •   Does chores when asked   A S NY

   •   Able to take initiative in cleaning   A S NY

2.   Treats others with respect:

   •   Says please and thank you   A S NY

   •   Says I'm sorry when needed   A S NY

   •   Uses utensils and stays seated during meals   A S NY

   •   Is respectful about entering others' rooms   A S NY

   •   Asks permission to touch the belongings of others   A S NY

   •   Asks for hugs appropriately   A S NY

   •   Is helpful toward others   A S NY

3.   Builds healthy relationships:

   •   Can introduce self and greet others properly   A S NY

   •   Offers visitors a seat or a snack   A S NY

   •   Can participate in healthy conversations   A S NY

   •   Can acknowledge the departure of others   A S NY

- Is able to gain the attention of others appropriately   A S NY
- Can interrupt conversations politely   A S NY
- Is able to share belongings with others and return others' belongings properly   A S NY
- Avoids negative behavior (says no when a peer asks them to do something wrong, can ignore teasing)   A S NY
- Is able to say no when they are uncomfortable   A S NY
- Shows good sportsmanship   A S NY

4. Is able to express love appropriately   A S NY

5. Is developing communication skills:
- Can communicate their needs to others   A S NY
- Can communicate their opinions   A S NY
- Is able to comprehend what others say to them   A S NY
- Is able to listen without interrupting others   A S NY

6. Is developing decision-making abilities:
- Is able to think through the positive and negative consequences before acting   A S NY
- Is able to think of alternative solutions to problems   A S NY

7. Resolves conflicts peacefully:
- Is nonviolent when angry or frustrated   A S NY
- Is able to accept constructive criticism   A S NY
- Is able to give constructive criticism respectfully   A S NY
- Is able to compromise and resolve conflicts   A S NY

8. Is able to empathize with others   A S NY

EMOTIONAL SKILLS ASSESSMENT

1. Can identify their emotions and express them appropriately:
- Is able to name the emotion they are feeling   A S NY
- Is able to name the source (incident) of the emotion   A S NY
- Is able to manage their anger, being assertive but nonviolent   A S NY

- Is able to cope with failure and loss by expressing themselves verbally versus acting out aggressively   A S NY

2. Can give and receive appropriate expressions of love:

   - Is willing to receives hugs and safe touch from people they trust   A S NY

   - Is able to ask for hugs when they want them   A S NY

   - Does not cling to people excessively   A S NY

   - Does not ask for physical affection from strangers   A S NY

3. Can understand their behavior in relation to their emotions   A S NY

4. Can discern between safe and unsafe situations   A S NY

EDUCATIONAL SKILLS ASSESSMENT

1. Educational participation:

   - Attends school   A S NY

   - Can follow homework directions   A S NY

   - Can complete homework independently   A S NY

2. Willing to try new problems and challenge self   A S NY

3. Basic skill development:

Reading:

   - Can recognize letters and connect to sounds   A S NY

   - Able to read beginning-level book   A S NY

   - Shows understanding of what they read   A S NY

   - Knows parts of speech (noun, verb)   A S NY

Writing:

   - Can write letters correctly   A S NY

   - Can spell names and other small words   A S NY

   - Can write in complete sentences   A S NY

Math:

   - Can add (single, double, triple digits; fractions)   A S NY

   - Can subtract (single, double, triple digits; fractions)   A S NY

- Can tell time   A   S NY

- Can multiply (single, double digits; fractions)   A   S NY

- Can divide (single, double, triple digits; fractions; remainders)   A   S NY

- Can decide which math skill to use for a problem   A   S NY

4. Can recheck work and correct mistakes   A   S NY

5. Can utilize resources:

- Can find word in dictionary   A   S NY

- Asks for information when needed   A   S NY

- Ages 13 and up:

6. Has thought of career options and next step to take   A   S NY

7. Independent living skills:

- Can find and purchase items at store   A   S NY

- Can utilize public transportation   A   S NY

- Can sew (mend clothing)   A   S NY

- Can meet responsibilities without reminders   A   S NY

- Able to be where they need to at correct time   A   S NY

Appendix E

Disability Ministry Resources

GENERAL RESOURCES

The Amputee Network. *The Amputee Network Blog* (http://amputee-network. blogspot.com) assists with prosthetic rehabilitation and facilitates the confidential exchange of useful information among amputees and professionals with special skills, with the common goal of improving the amputee's quality of life.

Angelotti, Maren. *Of Different Minds: Seeing Your AD/HD Child through the Eyes of God*. Ventura, CA: Regal Books, 2009. Readers will learn why their child is wired a little differently and how to cope with and educate this incredible person. The book also addresses parental denial, the mystery and fear surrounding learning differences, the toll on marriage, and how to parent these children.

Bethesda Lutheran Homes and Services, *Building a Developmental Disability Ministry: A Manual for Congregations*. Watertown, WI: Bethesda Lutheran Communities, 2007. Guides leadership teams through all the various ministry-building stages: from planning to implementation, evaluation and ongoing ministry development.

Breeding, MaLesa, Dana Hood, and Jerry Whitworth. *Let All the Children Come to Me: A Practical Guide to Including Children with Disabilities in Your Church Ministries*. Colorado Springs, CO: Cook Communications Ministries (NexGen), 2006. By combining philosophy and strategies, this book will equip the typical church volunteer teacher to meet the needs of all the children in her classroom.

Carter, Erik W. *Including People with Disabilities in Faith Communities*. Baltimore, MD: Brookes Publishing Company, 2007. This how-to book gives readers workable strategies and photocopiable forms for identifying indicators of welcome, encouraging community outreach, and gathering important information about the support needs of people with disabilities and their families.

Children's Disabilities Information (http://www.childrensdisabilities.info) provides essential articles and resources for parents of children with disabilities and special needs.

Colson, Emily. "Blue Sports Car," *Dancing with Max* (blog), February 7, 2011, http://emilycolson.com/2011/02/289/. This blog post tells the story of how she first started using "picture talks" and how she realized that her autistic son had an amazing memory. Follow Emily and see examples of her picture talks.

Disabled World. "Famous People with Disabilities," 2006, http://www.disabled-world.com/artman/publish/article_0060.shtml. A list of some well-known people with various disabilities and conditions; including actors, politicians and writers who contributed to society.

Finnegan, Joanne. *Shattered Dreams, Lonely Choices: Birthparents of Babies with Disabilities Talk about Adoption*. Westport, CT: Bergin & Garvey, 1993. The author and several families interviewed express with candor the overwhelming pain they felt when receiving "the news," the frustration when searching for options, the "no-win" feeling of decision making, the resolve with a final decision, and finally, life after the decision.

Fuller, Cheri, and Louise Tucker Jones. *Extraordinary Kids*. Colorado Springs, CO: Focus on the Family, 1997. Written by an educator and a mother of a child with a disability, this book provides hope, inspiration and insights a parent needs to capture the unique joy of parenting their children with special needs and help them reach their full potential.

Group Publishing. *Children's Ministry Pocket Guide to Special Needs: Quick Tips to Reach Every Child*. Loveland, CO: Group Publishing, 2008. Equip your children's ministry to identify and confidently reach out to kids with special needs. This handy pocket guide contains relevant teaching techniques, age-appropriate ways to inspire positive peer relationships, tips for partnering with parents, and more!

Hubach, Stephanie O. *Same Lake, Different Boat: Coming Alongside People Touched by Disability*. Phillipsburg, NJ: P & R Publishing, 2006. Designed to renew our minds to think biblically about disability in order that our lives, our relationships and our congregations might wholly reflect Christ.

Joni and Friends. *Special Needs, Smart Pages: Advice, Answers, and Articles About Ministering to Children with Special Needs*. Ventura, CA: Gospel Light, 2009. Provides churches of all sizes a comprehensive resource to help them reach out to individuals with different kinds of special needs, including autism, cognitive brain disorders and physical disabilities.

Lerner, Marc. *The Life Skills Approach* (blog), http://www.lifeskillsapproach.com. A blog about having a high quality of life while dealing with your challenge. Marc Lerner has also published an e-book, *A Healthy Way to Be Sick*.

Linder, Beverly. *A Never-Give-Up Heart: Raising Kids Who Face Harder-Than-Average Challenges*. Raleigh, NC: Lulu Publishing, 2010. Offers biblical encouragement to parents of children with disabilities, reminding them that God does not give a "stone" in place of "bread" to his beloved.

Marsh, Jayne D. B., ed. *From the Heart: On Being the Mother of a Child with Special Needs*. Bethesda, MD: Woodbine House, 1995. Several mothers from a parent support group explore the intense, sometimes painful, emotional environment of raising a child with special needs. The successes, setbacks, struggles and joys shared cover important aspects of daily life.

Maxwell, Jane, Julia Watts Belser, and Darlena David. *A Health Handbook for Women with Disabilities*. Berkeley, CA: Hesperian Foundation, 2007, http://www.hesperian.org. Free download written to help women with disabilities overcome the barriers of the social stigma of disability and inadequate care and improve their general health, self-esteem and abilities to care for themselves and participate in their communities.

Meyer, Donald J., ed. *Uncommon Fathers: Reflections on Raising a Child with a Disability*. Bethesda, MD: Woodbine House, 1995. This book written for fathers by fathers is a compelling collection of 19 essays about the life-altering experience of having a child with a disability.

Mitra, Sophie, Aleksandra Posarac, and Brandon Vick. *Disability and Poverty in Developing Countries: A Snapshot from the World Health Survey. SP Discussion Paper No. 1109. n.p.: World Bank Social Protection and Labor Unit*, 2011, http://siteresources.worldbank.org/SOCIALPROTECTION/Resources/SP-Discussion-papers/Disability-DP/1109.pdf. This study aims to contribute to the empirical research on social and economic conditions of people with disabilities, presenting a snapshot of the poverty situations of working-age persons with disabilities and their households in 15 developing countries.

Mullins, Aimee. "Aimee Mullins and Her 12 Pairs of Legs" (video), TED, 2009, http://www.ted.com/talks/lang/eng/aimee_mullins_prosthetic_aesthetics.html. Aimee Mullins is an activist for women, sports and the next generation of prosthetics. TED is a website for "Ideas Worth Spreading" that publishes a variety of topics, many of which you will find interesting and worthwhile.

Naseef, Robert A. *Special Children, Challenged Parents: The Struggles and Rewards of Raising a Child with a Disability*, rev. ed. (Baltimore: Brookes, 2001). A valuable aid to parents dealing with fear, guilt, shame, sibling rivalry, marital strain, and the needs of fathers.

Newman, Barb. *Autism and Your Church*. Grand Rapids, MI: Faith Alive Christian Resources, 2006. This unique resource will help your church welcome people with autism into the full life of your congregation.

————. *Helping Kids Include Kids with Disabilities*. Grand Rapids, MI: Faith Alive Christian Resources, 2001. Equips teachers, church activity leaders, and kids with the information they need to practice inclusive education in community.

Niemann, Sandy, Devorah Greenstein, and Darlena David. *Helping Children Who Are Deaf.* Berkeley, CA: Hesperian Foundation, 2004, http://www.hesperian.org. Free download written for family and community support for children who do not hear well.

Niemann, Sandy, and Namita Jacob. *Helping Children Who Are Blind.* Berkeley, CA: Hesperian Foundation, 2000, http://www.hesperian.org. Free download written for family and community support for children with vision problems.

Pierson, Jim. *Exceptional Teaching: A Comprehensive Guide for Including Students with Disabilities.* Cincinnati, OH: Standard Publishing, 2002. A guidebook covering most disabilities and how the church can reach out to individuals who have those disabilities and their families.

Pierson, Jim, Louise Tucker Jones, and Pat Verbal. *Special Needs, Special Ministry.* Loveland, CO: Group Publishing, 2004. A practical, real-world guide to help you learn from the successes and failures of churches with special-needs programs, launch or further develop a special-needs ministry, and gain insight from experts in the field.

Pinsky, Mark I. *Amazing Gifts: Stories of Faith, Disability, and Inclusion.* Herndon, VA.: Alban Institute, 2011. Pinsky has gathered "stories of people with disabilities and the congregations where they have found welcome." He has taken special care to include the widest range of disabilities, including nonapparent disabilities like lupus, chronic pain, traumatic brain injury, depression and mental illness.

Rapada, Amy. *The Special Needs Ministry Handbook: A Church's Guide to Reaching Children with Disabilities and Their Families.* Charleston, SC: Booksurge, 2007. Educationally, spiritually and experience based; a practical instructional guide and inspirational resource written for church leaders, Sunday school teachers and families with disabilities.

Sullivan, Tom. *Special Parent, Special Child: Parents of Children with Disabilities Share Their Trials, Triumphs, and Hard-Won Wisdom.* New York: Putnam, 1995. Six families caring for children with disabilities (including blindness, cerebral palsy and Down syndrome) are given in-depth interviews that reveal their special struggles, their methods for overcoming problems and their advice to others.

Talk, Trust and Feel Therapeutics. "Thought Stoppage Halts My Beat Myself Up Thinking," http://www.angriesout.com/bully30.htm. Provides links and book suggestions for helping with "thought stoppage," anger and bullying.

Thornburgh, Ginny, ed. *From Barriers to Bridges: A Community Action Guide for Congregations and People with Disabilities.* Washington, D C: National Organization on Disability, 1996. Guidebook designed to foster dialogue between people with disabilities, their family members, religious leadership and the larger community.

————, ed. *That All May Worship: An Interfaith Welcome to People with Disabilities.* Washington, D C: National Organization on Disability, 1992. A handbook to assist congregations to welcome people with disabilities into all aspects of worship and religious life.

United Nations Children's Fund (UNICEF). *The State of the World's Children; Special Edition: Celebrating 20 Years of the Convention on the Rights of the Child.* New York: United Nations Children's Fund, 2009, http://www.unicef.org/rightsite/sowc/pdfs/SOWC_Spec%20Ed_CRC_Main%20Report_EN_090409.pdf. The report addresses the progress that has been made in the last 20 years and the role the Convention will play in moving us forward into the future.

————. *The State of the World's Children 2011; Adolescence: An Age of Opportunity.* New York: United Nations Children's Fund, 2011, http://www.unicef.org/sowc2011/pdfs/SOWC-2011-Main-Report_EN_02092011.pdf. Millions of adolescents worldwide are denied their basic rights to quality education, health care and protection, and are exposed to abuse and exploitation. UNICEF recognizes the need to turn this vulnerable age into an age of opportunity.

Vredeveld, Ronald C. *Caring Relationships: Helping People with Mental Impairments Understand God's Gift of Sexuality.* Grand Rapids, MI: CRC Publications, 2001. Provides Christian guidance in the area of sexuality for persons with cognitive impairments.

————. *Expressing Faith in Jesus: Church Membership for People with Intellectual Disabilities*, rev. ed. Grand Rapids, MI: Faith Alive Christian Resources, 2005. This book and the companion Resource Kit guide church leaders and friends with intellectual disabilities through baptism, confirmation, or profession of faith.

Weinhouse, Don, and Marilyn Weinhouse. *Little Children, Big Needs: Parents Discuss Raising Children with Exceptional Needs.* Niwot, CO: University Press of Colorado, 1994. Geared primarily for parents, presents stories and quotations drawn from interviews that the authors (both educators) conducted with the parents of 50 children representing a wide range of disabilities.

Werner, David. *Disabled Village Children,* 2nd ed. Berkeley, CA: Hesperian Foundation, 2009, http://www.hesperian.org. Free download reference book to help meet the needs of children with disabilities.

World Health Organization and the World Bank, World Report on Disability. Malta: World Health Organization, 2011, http://whqlibdoc.who.int/publications/2011/9789240685215_eng.pdf. Estimating that more than one billion people are living with some sort of disability, the report urges governments and their development allies to invest more leadership and financing in services and programs that could unlock the potential of people with disabilities.

MEDICAL RESOURCES

Allen, Patricia Jackson, Judith A. Vessey, and Naomi Schapiro. *Primary Care of the Child with a Chronic Condition*, 5th ed. St. Louis: Mosby, 2010.

American Academy of Pediatrics (http://www.aap.org) provides information on many pediatric health conditions and concerns.

Auerbach, Paul S., Howard J. Donner, and Eric A. Weiss. *Field Guide to Wilderness Medicine*. St. Louis: Mosby, 1999.

Batshaw, Mark L., ed. *Children with Disabilities*, 6th ed. Baltimore: Brookes, 2007.

Burg, Fredric D., Richard A. Polin, Julie Ingelfinger, and Anne A. Gershon. *Current Pediatric Therapy*, 18th ed. Philadelphia: Saunders, 2006.

Conant, Jeff, and Pam Fadem. *A Community Guide to Environmental Health*. Berkeley, CA: Hesperian Foundation, 2008. Free download at http://www.hesperian.org.

Gorske, Arnold. *Health Education Program for Developing Countries: Handbook*. N.p.: Health Education Program for Developing Countries, 2009. Free download at http://www.hepfdc.org.

Graef, John W., Joseph I. Wolfsdorf, and David S. Greenes. *Manual of Pediatric Therapeutics*, 7th ed. Philadelphia: Lippincott Williams & Wilkins, 2008.

Mahmoud, Adel A. F. Tropical and Geographical Medicine Companion Handbook. New York: McGraw-Hill, 1993.

Mayo Clinic (http://www.mayoclinic.com) provides information on health topics.

Menkes, John H. *Textbook of Child Neurology*, 7th ed. Baltimore: Lippincott Williams & Wilkins, 2005.

Mutel, Cornelia F., and Kelly J. Donham. *Medical Practice in Rural Communities*. New York: Springer-Verlag, 1983.

Palmer, Dennis, and Catherine E. Wolf. *Handbook of Medicine in Developing Countries*, 3rd ed. Bristol, TN: Christian Medical & Dental Associations, 2008.

Provence, Sally, and Audrey Naylor. Working with Disadvantaged Parents and Their Children: Scientific and Practice Issues. New Haven, CT: Yale University Press, 1983.

Swaiman, Kenneth F., Stephen Ashwal, and Donna M. Ferriero. *Pediatric Neurology: Principles and Practice*. 2 vols., 4th ed. St. Louis: Mosby, 2006.

Vanderkooi, Mary. Village Medical Manual: A Layman's Guide to Health Care in Developing Countries. 2 vols., rev. ed. Pasadena, CA: William Carey Library, 2009.

WebMD (http://www.webmd.com) provides information on health topics.

Werner, David. *Where There Is No Doctor: A Village Health Care Handbook.* With Carol Thuman and Jane Maxwell, 2nd rev. ed. Berkeley, CA: Hesperian Foundation, 2010. Free download at http://www.hesperian.org and http://www.healthwrights.org.

Zinkin, Pam, and Helen McConachie. *Disabled Children and Developing Countries.* London: MacKeith, 1995.

PERIODICALS

Breakthrough is a full-color quarterly magazine providing inspiration and ideas for congregations and teachers serving people with intellectual disabilities. Included are reviews of curricula, helpful hints, success stories and resource information. Bethesda Lutheran Communities (http://www.bethesdalutherancommunities.org), 600 Hoffman Drive, Watertown, WI 53094, Phone: (920) 261-3050.

Lift Magazine is a composite of inspirational articles and tidbits of information written by real people for real people impacted by disability. These writings show how the spiritual or faith life intersects with a practical, fresh approach to overcoming the disability life experience. Lift Disability Network (http://www.liftdisability.net), PO Box 770607, Winter Garden, FL 34777, Phone: (407) 228-8343.

EDUCATIONAL THERAPY

National Institute for Learning Development (NILD) (http://www.nild.org) was established in 1982 to assist schools, organizations and individuals in the development of programs for students with specific learning disabilities. NILD has therapists in mission schools in many countries besides the United States. 801 Greenbrier Parkway, Chesapeake, VA 23320, Phone: (877) 661-6453.

DISABILITY MINISTRY ORGANIZATIONS

Bethesda Lutheran Communities (http://www.bethesdalutherancommunities.org) strives to share the love of Christ with children and adults who have intellectual and developmental disabilities. Provides resources to educate friends, families, congregations and other service providers about developmental disabilities. 600 Hoffman Drive, Watertown, WI 53094, Phone: (800) 369-4636.

Christian Church Foundation for the Handicapped (http://www.ccfh.org) ministers to the disability community through direct service, by enabling others through training and resources to effectively minister to persons with disabilities, and through partnerships with churches and organizations to better meet the needs of people with disabilities across the country. CCFH currently manages an independent living program, as well as two residential living programs for those with disabilities. PO Box 9869, Knoxville, TN 37940, Phone: (865) 546-5921.

Friendship Ministries (http://www.friendship.org) is a not-for-profit organization that exists to help churches and organizations around the world share God's love with people who have intellectual disabilities. 2215 29th Street SE #B6, Grand Rapids, MI 49508, Phone: (888) 866-8966.

Handi*Vangelism Ministries International (http://www.hvmi.org) is a faith-based mission that exists to share the love of the Lord Jesus Christ and to equip the Church to share His love with people around the world who have disabilities, medical or mental health challenges or broken hearts, so that they may become growing and serving members of the body of Christ. PO Box 122, Akron, PA 17501, Phone: (717) 859-4777.

Hesperian Foundation (http://www.hesperian.org) provides many fantastic resources on health care in developing countries at the village level, including the free downloads listed in the "General Resources" and "Medical Resources" sections. 1919 Addison Street, Suite 304, Berkeley, CA 94704, Phone: (510) 845-1447.

Joni and Friends (http://www.joniandfriends.org) presents the gospel of Jesus Christ to all people affected by disability and their families who are served through its programs around the world. Trains, disciples and mentors people affected by disability to exercise their gifts of leadership and service in their churches and communities. PO Box 3333, Agoura Hills, CA 91376, Phone: (818) 707-5664.

LifeWay Special Needs Ministries (http://www.lifeway.com/n/Ministries/Special-Needs) provides resources to help you minister to kids, adults, and families with special needs. Resources include leadership training events, free downloads, adaptation tips and personal consultations. 1 LifeWay Plaza, Nashville, TN 37234, Phone: (800) 622-8610.

Lift Disability Network (http://www.liftdisability.net) is a community where the disability family is embraced, encouraged and empowered. An intersection where helplessness meets hopefulness, a place of healing for wounded souls, a connection to faith for a better life. PO Box 770607, Winter Garden, FL 34777, Phone: (407) 228-8343.

Love In the Name of Christ (http://www.loveinc.org) is movement of Christian churches working together, across denominations, to show God's love to neighbors in need. PO Box 270305, Saint Paul, MN 55127, Phone: (800) 777-5277.

Mark 2 Ministries (http://www.mark2ministries.org) exists to encourage and equip the local church to evangelize, disciple and integrate individuals with disabilities into their congregation. The ministry teaches the church how to develop Sunday school classes and Bible studies to reach out to the disabled community. PO Box 3842, Carmel, IN 46082, Phone: (317) 777-8070

CHARITABLE ORGANIZATIONS PROVIDING MEDICAL SUPPORT AND ASSISTANCE

Blessings International (http://www.blessing.org) demonstrates God's love by providing medicines at a discount to medical missions teams and by supporting projects around the world to facilitate medical care for the underserved. 1650 North Indianwood Avenue, Broken Arrow, OK 74012, Phone: (918) 250-8101.

Christian Medical & Dental Associations (http://www.cmda.org) maintains a list of mission organizations that provide health care to developing countries and upcoming short-term medical/dental mission trips that give medical professionals the opportunity to participate in programs that deliver health care in developing countries. PO Box 7500, Bristol, TN 37621, Phone: (423) 844-1000.

Doctors Without Borders / Médecins Sans Frontières (MSF) (http://www.doctorswithoutborders.com) is an international medical humanitarian organization that works to deliver health care in over 60 countries. 333 7th Avenue, 2nd Floor, New York, NY 10001, Phone: (212) 679-6800.

Health Wrights (http://www.healthwrights.org) is a nonprofit organization developed by David Werner (author of *Where There Is No Doctor*), committed to advancing the health, basic rights, social equality and self-determination of disadvantaged persons and groups. Website includes an extensive list of other organizations that help people with disabilities. PO Box 1344, Palo Alto, CA 94302, Phone: (650) 325-7500.

International Rescue Committee (http://www.rescue.org) responds to the world's worst humanitarian crises and helps refugees to rebuild their lives. 122 East 42nd Street, New York, NY 10168, Phone: (212) 551-3000.

A Leg to Stand On (http://www.altso.org) provides free prosthetic limbs, corrective surgeries, and rehabilitation for children with limb disabilities in the developing world. 267 Fifth Avenue, Suite 800, New York, NY 10016, Phone: (212) 683-8805.

The Little Light House (http://www.littlelighthouse.org) is a Christian developmental center in Tulsa, OK, providing specialized education and therapy tuition-free to children with disabilities, birth through age six. Their Global Outreach provides training through an internship program and also sends teams internationally to train teachers, therapists and caregivers how to provide educational and therapeutic support services to children with disabilities. 5120 East 36th Street, Tulsa OK 74135, Phone: (918) 664-6746.

Mercy Ships (http://www.mercyships.org) operates hospital ships to deliver excellent medical care, hope and healing to the poor worldwide as a demonstration of the love and mercy of God. As appropriate doctors are available, corrective surgery services may be offered to children with disabilities. PO Box 2020, Garden Valley, TX 75771, Phone: (903) 939-7000.

Operation Blessing (http://www.ob.org) is an international Christian relief agency that delivers hunger relief, medical and surgical care, orphan care and other humanitarian services with the love of Jesus Christ to a hurting world. PO Box 2636, Virginia Beach, VA 23450, Phone: (800) 730-2537.

Operation Smile (http://www.operationsmile.org) is a charity organization providing corrective surgery to children born with a cleft lip, cleft palate, or other facial deformity in various places worldwide. 6435 Tidewater Drive, Norfolk, VA 23509, Phone: (757) 321-7645.

Rehabilitation International (http://www.riglobal.org) is an international organization that seeks to advance the rights and inclusion of individuals with disabilities worldwide. They promote the strategy of Community-Based Rehabilitation (CBR). 25 East 21st Street, 4th Floor, New York, NY 10010, Phone: (212) 420-1500.

Samaritan's Purse (http://www.samaritanspurse.org) is an international Christian relief agency that provides disaster relief and medical care to children in need worldwide. Their Children's Heart Project arranges corrective surgery for children with congenital heart disease and other heart problems when surgery is not available to them in their home country. PO Box 3000, Boone, NC 28607, Phone: (828) 262-1980.

Save the Children (http://www.savethechildren.org) is an independent humanitarian relief organization that provides food, medical care, and education to children in times of crisis and networks with other relief organizations to meet the needs of suffering children worldwide. 54 Wilton Road, Westport, CT 06880, Phone: (800) 728-3843.

Smile Train (http://www.smiletrain.org) is a children's charity that provides free corrective surgery for cleft lip and palate to children worldwide. They also provide speech therapy, rehabilitation, dentistry, and orthodontics and train medical doctors and professionals in 75 countries. They provide free training resources and educational information about cleft surgery to medical professionals. 41 Madison Ave., 28th Floor, New York, NY 10010, Phone: (800) 932-9541.

UNICEF (http://www.unicef.org) provides humanitarian relief, including nutrition, medical care, education and protection to improve the state of children worldwide. UNICEF also does research on conditions that affect children and put them "at risk" worldwide, including disabling disease and disabling conditions. 3 United Nations Plaza, New York, NY 10017, Phone: (212) 326-7000.

USAID (http://www.usaid.gov) is an independent federal government agency that advances the foreign policy objectives of the United States by promoting economic growth, global health care, agriculture, trade, democracy, conflict prevention and humanitarian assistance. USAID has helped children throughout the world grow into healthy, productive adults. Priorities have been in child survival and disease control. Ronald Reagan Building, Washington, DC 20523, Phone: (202) 712-4810.

Wheels of Hope (http://www.wheelsofhope.org) works with Joni and Friends (http://www.joniandfriends.org/wheels-for-the-world) and Hope Haven International Ministries (http://www.hopehaveninternational.org). These organizations demonstrate the love of Christ to disabled individuals by providing donated wheelchairs and durable medical equipment to those in need worldwide. 9800 Morges Drive SE, Waynesburg, OH 44688.

World Health Organization (http://www.who.int) provides leadership on global health issues, research and policy affecting global health concerns, including children with disabilities. The WHO website includes an extensive listing of health topics. Avenue Appia 20, 1211 Geneva 27, Switzerland, Phone: +41 22-791-21-11.

World Vision (http://www.worldvision.org) is a Christian humanitarian organization dedicated to serving the poor through a demonstration of the love of Christ with food, medical care, disaster relief and other multifaceted ministries, including medical equipment and care for children with disabilities and help for children in crisis. PO Box 9716, Federal Way, WA 98063, Phone: (888) 511-6443.

Appendix F

Rights of Persons with Disabilities

"The Convention on the Rights of Persons with Disabilities is an international treaty that identifies the rights of persons with disabilities as well as the obligations on States parties to the Convention to promote, protect and ensure those rights. The Convention also establishes two implementation mechanisms: the Committee on the Rights of Persons with Disabilities, established to monitor implementation, and the Conference of States Parties, established to consider matters regarding implementation.

"States negotiated the Convention with the participation of civil society organizations, national human rights institutions and inter-governmental organizations. The United Nations General Assembly adopted the Convention on 13 December 2006 and it was opened for signature on 30 March 2007. States that ratify the Convention are legally bound to respect the standards in the Convention. For other States, the Convention represents an international standard that they should endeavour to respect."[1]

PREAMBLE

The States Parties to the present Convention,

a. Recalling the principles proclaimed in the Charter of the United Nations which recognize the inherent dignity and worth and the equal and inalienable rights of all members of the human family as the foundation of freedom, justice and peace in the world,

b. Recognizing that the United Nations, in the Universal Declaration of Human Rights and in the International Covenants on Human Rights, has proclaimed and agreed that everyone is entitled to all the rights and freedoms set forth therein, without distinction of any kind,

c. Reaffirming the universality, indivisibility, interdependence and inter-relatedness of all human rights and fundamental freedoms and the need for persons with disabilities to be guaranteed their full enjoyment without discrimination,

d.   Recalling the International Covenant on Economic, Social and Cultural Rights, the International Covenant on Civil and Political Rights, the International Convention on the Elimination of All Forms of Racial Discrimination, the Convention on the Elimination of All Forms of Discrimination against Women, the Convention against Torture and Other Cruel, Inhuman or Degrading Treatment or Punishment, the Convention on the Rights of the Child, and the International Convention on the Protection of the Rights of All Migrant Workers and Members of Their Families,

e.   Recognizing that disability is an evolving concept and that disability results from the interaction between persons with impairments and attitudinal and environmental barriers that hinders their full and effective participation in society on an equal basis with others,

f.   Recognizing the importance of the principles and policy guidelines contained in the World Programme of Action concerning Disabled Persons and in the Standard Rules on the Equalization of Opportunities for Persons with Disabilities in influencing the promotion, formulation and evaluation of the policies, plans, programmes and actions at the national, regional and international levels to further equalize opportunities for persons with disabilities,

g.   Emphasizing the importance of mainstreaming disability issues as an integral part of relevant strategies of sustainable development,

h.   Recognizing also that discrimination against any person on the basis of disability is a violation of the inherent dignity and worth of the human person,

i.   Recognizing further the diversity of persons with disabilities,

j.   Recognizing the need to promote and protect the human rights of all persons with disabilities, including those who require more intensive support,

k.   Concerned that, despite these various instruments and undertakings, persons with disabilities continue to face barriers in their participation as equal members of society and violations of their human rights in all parts of the world,

l. Recognizing the importance of international cooperation for improving the living conditions of persons with disabilities in every country, particularly in developing countries,

m. Recognizing the valued existing and potential contributions made by persons with disabilities to the overall well-being and diversity of their communities, and that the promotion of the full enjoyment by persons with disabilities of their human rights and fundamental freedoms and of full participation by persons with disabilities will result in their enhanced sense of belonging and in significant advances in the human, social and economic development of society and the eradication of poverty,

n. Recognizing the importance for persons with disabilities of their individual autonomy and independence, including the freedom to make their own choices,

o. Considering that persons with disabilities should have the opportunity to be actively involved in decision-making processes about policies and programmes, including those directly concerning them,

p. Concerned about the difficult conditions faced by persons with disabilities who are subject to multiple or aggravated forms of discrimination on the basis of race, colour, sex, language, religion, political or other opinion, national, ethnic, indigenous or social origin, property, birth, age or other status,

q. Recognizing that women and girls with disabilities are often at greater risk, both within and outside the home of violence, injury or abuse, neglect or negligent treatment, maltreatment or exploitation,

r. Recognizing that children with disabilities should have full enjoyment of all human rights and fundamental freedoms on an equal basis with other children, and recalling obligations to that end undertaken by States Parties to the Convention on the Rights of the Child,

s. Emphasizing the need to incorporate a gender perspective in all efforts to promote the full enjoyment of human rights and fundamental freedoms by persons with disabilities,

t. Highlighting the fact that the majority of persons with disabilities live in conditions of poverty, and in this regard recognizing the critical need to address the negative impact of poverty on persons with disabilities,

u.   Bearing in mind that conditions of peace and security based on full respect for the purposes and principles contained in the Charter of the United Nations and observance of applicable human rights instruments are indispensable for the full protection of persons with disabilities, in particular during armed conflicts and foreign occupation,

v.   Recognizing the importance of accessibility to the physical, social, economic and cultural environment, to health and education and to information and communication, in enabling persons with disabilities to fully enjoy all human rights and fundamental freedoms,

w.   Realizing that the individual, having duties to other individuals and to the community to which he or she belongs, is under a responsibility to strive for the promotion and observance of the rights recognized in the International Bill of Human Rights,

x.   Convinced that the family is the natural and fundamental group unit of society and is entitled to protection by society and the State, and that persons with disabilities and their family members should receive the necessary protection and assistance to enable families to contribute towards the full and equal enjoyment of the rights of persons with disabilities,

y.   Convinced that a comprehensive and integral international convention to promote and protect the rights and dignity of persons with disabilities will make a significant contribution to redressing the profound social disadvantage of persons with disabilities and promote their participation in the civil, political, economic, social and cultural spheres with equal opportunities, in both developing and developed countries,

HAVE AGREED AS FOLLOWS: . . .[2]

NOTES

1.   United Nations Enable, "Frequently Asked Questions regarding the Convention on the Rights of Persons with Disabilities," http://www.un.org/disabilities/default. asp?navid=24&pid=151.

2.   Read the complete text of the Convention on the Rights of Persons with Disabilities: http://www.un.org/disabilities/convention/conventionfull.shtml.